Contemporary Special Education Research

Syntheses of the Knowledge Base on Critical Instructional Issues

Edited by

Russell Gersten
University of Oregon/Eugene Research Institute

Ellen P. Schiller
Abt Associates Inc.

and

Sharon Vaughn
University of Texas at Austin

LAWRENCE ERLBAUM ASSOCIATES, PUBLISHERS
2000   Mahwah, New Jersey   London

Lawrence Erlbaum Associates, Inc., Publishers
10 Industrial Avenue
Mahwah, NJ 07430

Cover design by Kathryn Houghtaling Lacey

Library of Congress Cataloging-in-Publication Data

Contemporary special education research : syntheses of the
    knowledge base on critical instructional issues / edited by
    Russell Gersten, Ellen P. Schiller, and Sharon Vaughn.
p.   cm. (The LEA series on special education and disability)
    Includes bibliographical references and index.
ISBN 0-8058-2879-6 (cloth : alk. paper) —
    ISBN 0-8058-2880-X (pbk. : alk. paper)
1. Handicapped—Education—Research—United
    States—Methodology. 2. Special education—
    Research—United States—Methodology.
    3. Meta-analysis. I. Gersten, Russell Monroe, 1947–
    II. Schiller, Ellen P. III. Vaughn, Sharon, 1952–
    IV. Series
LC4019.C575 2000
371.9'07'2—dc21   99-055039
                                                         CIP

Books published by Lawrence Erlbaum Associates are printed
on acid-free paper, and their bindings are chosen for strength
and durability.

Printed in the United States of America
10 9 8 7 6 5 4 3 2 1

Contents

Foreword

Joanna P. Williams
Teachers College, Columbia University

The 1975 Education for All Handicapped Children Act (Public Law 94-142) and the 1991 Individuals with Disabilities Education Act (IDEA) and its 1997 Amendments reflect our nation's strong commitment to bringing all individuals to full participation in all aspects of life. Research in special education has grown tremendously as a result of this legislation and commitment. In fact, the number of research studies has increased so voluminously that it has become difficult to sift through all the findings to determine what in fact the current state of our knowledge really is.

Meta-analysis provides a methodology for synthesizing a set of research findings so that we can identify those that hold up across studies and determine to what extent a finding can be generalized across populations and across settings. Such syntheses also reveal gaps in our knowledge and suggest questions for further empirical investigation.

In addition, meta-analysis also helps make findings visible and accessible, so that they become easier to interpret and to consider in policy formulation. In education, where public policy is determined in large part by social needs, values, and political concerns, it is especially important to have a clear understanding of what the research evidence shows, so that it will be given the weight it deserves in making policy.

One of the main themes of research in special education—perhaps its main theme—is intervention. How can we design and develop instructional interventions that will yield the most effective outcomes? The "special" in education implies that special populations require special kinds of instruction. We know that in many situations special education students need a distinctive approach to instruction, involving a slower pace, a more elaborated sequence of steps, extensive practice, and clear feedback. What other characteristics of instruction are especially suitable for these students? In special education we look for matches between students and intervention.

Meta-analysis helps us focus on the interaction of student characteristics such as age, gender, and disability status with factors like variation in materials, such as type of text used in reading instruction; methodological variables, such as amount of instruction; and teacher characteristics, such as years of classroom experience. Do those or other intervention factors affect educational outcomes? If so, are the differences in outcomes substantial enough to be taken into account in the development of large-scale instructional interventions?

Of course, methodology is no substitute for deep understanding of the topic under investigation. Probably the best meta-analysts are those who, in addition to knowing how to conduct a meta-analysis, have done primary research in the area. They are the ones who have a feel for the important variables and who will make insightful choices about what comparisons to make.

The contributors to this volume all have contributed substantially to the primary literature, and they bring this expertise as well as their methodological expertise to their task. They offer here comprehensive and thoughtful syntheses of important bodies of research, which are supplemented by useful discussion of policy implications. These chapters provide up-to-date, informative summaries of our current knowledge and a base from which we can venture further into the critical area of instructional intervention in special education. They will without doubt provide valuable assistance to researchers, teachers, administrators, and policymakers.

Preface

Only since the late 1980s has there been sufficient special education research published that meta-analyses and syntheses can be conducted. In this volume, seven sets of authors grapple with synthesizing the knowledge base on an array of critical topics in the field of special education. Anyone who has attempted a meta-analysis or a comprehensive research synthesis is aware of how formidable a task it is. Issues that seem relatively easy or straightforward when described in a textbook are usually extraordinarily intricate and perplexing when put into practice. Every decision, from defining the target population to exclusion criteria for studies, invariably opens up a can of worms. Where one expects many studies, often there are few. And where relatively few are expected, there are often far too many to be able to synthesize properly.

The textbooks oversimplify the meta-analysis process. Meta-analysis and research synthesis involve objective techniques, but the ultimate goal is illumination of the topic at hand. As writers, each of us has faced the problems of discerning—with validity—the underlying patterns in the data, of struggling to articulate what they really mean, and of finding ways to communicate this to others.

The great American poet, Charles Olson, was an admirer of science and technology in an era when it was unfashionable. He wrote eloquently of the gifts we gain from scientific inquiry. But he cautioned:"And the too strong grasping of it, when it is pressed together and condensed, loses it ... " (Charles Olson, 1966).

Hasn't anyone who has done a meta-analysis or a research synthesis at some point asked herself or himself: "Is that all there is?" Clearly there must be more here, than a series of weighted and unweighted mean effect sizes. The continual struggle is to discern trends that are valid.

Each of these chapters represents years of work and, often, struggle. We believe the effort and the occasional agonies are reflected in the depth of insight provided in each of the chapters.

Four of the research teams use meta-analysis as their major analytic tool. Three of the meta-analyses deal with learning disabilities. Batya Elbaum, Sharon Vaughn, Marie Hughes, Sally Watson Moody, and Jeanne Shay Schumm synthesize what we now know about effective instructional grouping practices for reading. Doug Fuchs, Lynn S. Fuchs, Patricia G. Mathes, and Mark W. Lipsey examine differences between students classified as learning disabled and other low-achieving students on a range of academic performance measures. They also discuss policy implications. H. Lee Swanson reviews the entire corpus of instructional research on learning disabilities in order to discern underlying principles of effective teaching and instructional design.

Janet G. Marquis, Robert H. Horner, Edward G. Carr, Ann P. Turnbull, and colleagues examine the research on behavioral supports for low-incidence special education populations. These researchers experiment with several different analytic methods for performing meta-analysis with single-subject research designs.

Russell Gersten and Scott Baker apply a qualitative research synthesis technique, what Ogawa and Malen (1991) called a *multivocal approach*, to review what they know about effective instruction for English-language learners. The qualitative methodology entailed not only a review of the literature but also interactions with professional educators and researchers around the country.

Cindy M. Okolo, Albert A. Cavalier, Ralph P. Ferretti, and Charles A. MacArthur synthesize the knowledge base on how technology supports literacy development, across the full spectrum of disabilities categories.

Research in education, as well as in other applied fields, defies stakeholders' needs for simple conclusions to big problems. A major reason for conducting a research synthesis is to try to resolve issues of interest in the field.

Perhaps one of the biggest concerns individuals have when releasing the findings from a synthesis or meta-analysis is that the results will be taken either too literally or not seriously enough. The former concern results from the implicit assumption that a research synthesis or meta-analysis provides the final word on a topic. This is virtually never the case.

The danger in providing these conclusions in abbreviated form is that all of the conditions that mediate their interpretation will be lost. In this book, three sets of authors provide guidance on how syntheses and meta-analyses can wisely be used and soundly conducted.

Ellen P. Schiller and David Malouf provide their views on how syntheses might be used as tools to bridge the often referred to gap between research and practice. Harris Cooper, Jeffery Valentine, and Kelly Charlton provide insights for both the use and misuse of the methodology of meta-analysis, and Kenneth Kavale and Steven Forness describe the application of meta-analyses to determine and influence public policy decisions.

The editors of this book would like to acknowledge the contributions of the following reviewers: Scott Baker, Eugene Research Institute; Roland Good, University of Oregon; Kenneth Kavale, University of Iowa; Tom Keating, Eugene Research Institute; Ron Nelson, Arizona State University; and Jeanne Schumm, University of Miami. In addition, the editors would like to thank reviewers of earlier technical reports such as Lynn S. Fuchs, Robert Rueda, Rose Marie Weber, and Bernice Wong. Their commentaries helped us all further distill what we had learned. And virtually all of us received expert mentoring from Harris Cooper of the University of Missouri at Columbia.

We would like to acknowledge the support of the Research-to-Practice Division of the Office of Special Education Programs of the U.S. Department of Education and the Director, Lou Danielson, for the support provided for these syntheses. And finally we would like to express our appreciation to Karie Hume of Portland State University, who did a superb job as an administrative assistant for this project and to our dynamic index team—Katie Tate, Camas Davis, and Francis Keating.

REFERENCES

Ogawa, R. T., & Malen, B. (1991). Towards rigor in reviews of multivocal literatures: Applying the exploratory case study method. *Reveiw of Educational Research, 61*, 265–286.

—Russell Gersten
—Ellen P. Schiller
—Sharon Vaughn

What Instruction Works for Students With Learning Disabilities? Summarizing the Results From a Meta-Analysis of Intervention Studies

H. Lee Swanson
University of California–Riverside

In this chapter, I review some of the empirical evidence collected from a comprehensive educational intervention research synthesis for students with learning disabilities (Swanson, Hoskyn, Lee, & O'Shaughnessy, 1997). The synthesis used meta-analytic techniques to aggregate the research literature on intervention. Meta-analysis is a statistical reviewing technique that provides a quantitative summary of findings across an entire body of research (Cooper & Hedges, 1994; Hedges & Olkin, 1985). The results of individual studies are converted to a standardized metric or effect size. These scores are then aggregated across the sample of studies to yield an overall estimate of effect size. Particular attention is given to the magnitude of the effect size estimate. According to Cohen (1988), .80 is considered a "large" effect size estimate, .50 a moderate estimate, and .20 a small estimate.

One of the major purposes of our (Swanson et al., 1997) meta-analysis was to identify effective instructional models that yield high effect sizes, as well as the components that make up those models. As an extension of an earlier synthesis (Swanson, Carson, & Sachse-Lee, 1996), we tested whether treatments that include components of *strategy instruction* (SI), *direct instruction* (DI), and/or both instructional models yield significant difference in effect size. Our earlier synthesis found that strategy and direct instruction models yielded higher effect size than competing models, but the instructional components that made up those models were not analyzed.

Because the terms strategy instruction and direct instruction are used in various ways by researchers and practitioners alike, further clarification of how studies were analyzed in the current synthesis as a function of treatment approach is necessary. Given the overlap between strategy and direct instruction models, we draw upon the literature to operationalize these approaches in the following manner. Components of direct instruction are reviewed by Engelmann and Carnine (1982); Kameenui, Jitendra, and Darch (1995); and several others. They suggest that direct instruction emphasizes fast-paced, well-sequenced, highly focused lessons. The lessons are delivered usually in small groups to students who are given several opportunities to respond and receive feedback about accuracy and responses. Based on these reviews and others, those activities coded that reflect direct instruction in the present synthesis were as follows: (a) breaking down a task into small steps, (b) administering probes, (c) administering feedback repeatedly, (d) providing a pictorial or diagram presentation, (e) allowing for independent practice and individually paced instruction, (f) breaking the instruction down into simpler phases, (g) instructing in a small group, (h) teacher modeling a skill, (i) providing set materials at a rapid pace, (j) providing individual child instruction, (k) teacher asking questions, and (l) teacher presenting the new (novel) materials. Any study that included a minimum of four of these codes in the treatment phase was labeled a direct instruction.

Components related to effective strategy instructional programs are reviewed elsewhere (for a review see Borkowski & Turner, 1990; Levin, 1986; Pressley & Ghatala, 1990). Some of these components include advance organizers (provide students with a type of mental scaffolding in which to build new understanding, i.e., consist of information already in the students' minds and the new concepts that can organize this information), organization (information questions directed to students to stop from time to time to assess their understanding), elaboration (thinking about the material to be learned in a way that connects the material to information or ideas already in their mind), generative learning (learners must work to make sense out of what they are learning by summarizing the information), and general study strategies (e.g., underlining, note taking, summarizing, having students generate questions, outlining, and working in pairs to summarize sections of materials), think about and control one's thinking process (metacognition), and attributions (evaluating the effectiveness of a strategy). Based on these reviews, we categorized studies as reflecting strategy instruction if they include at least three of the following instructional components:

1. Elaborate explanations (i.e., systematic explanations, elaborations, and/or plans to direct task performance).
2. Modeling from teachers (verbal modeling, questioning, and demonstration from teachers).

3. Reminders to use certain strategies or procedures (i.e., students are cued to use taught strategies, tactics, or procedures).
4. Step-by-step prompts or multiprocess instructions.
5. Dialogue: teacher and student talk back and forth.
6. Teacher asks questions.
7. Teacher provides only necessary assistance.

Based on these criteria, studies to be classified fell into one of four models: strategy+direct instruction (referred to as the combined model), direct instruction (DI)-alone, strategy instruction (SI)-alone, and non-strategy+nondirect instruction. As a validity check on our classifications, we compared our classification of the treatment conditions with that of the primary author's general theoretical model and/or the label attached to the treatment condition. There was substantial overlap (approximately 70% of the studies) between those studies we classified as direct instruction and strategy instruction models with the primary authors' titles or description of the independent variables. For example, frequent terms provided by the author were: *strategy, cognitive intervention, monitoring, metacognition, self-instruction,* and *cognitive-behavior modification* for the strategy model. Those that were classified as direct instruction by our criteria used such labels as: *directed instruction, advanced organizers, adapting materials,* or *corrective feedback* or *direct computation.* Those approaches that were below the component threshold (did not include the minimum number of components for being labeled as either direct instruction or strategy intervention) used, for example, such labels as *reinforcement-only, modeling-only,* or *social skills training.*

Although considerable attention was devoted to coding studies on instructional variables, there were two additional areas of interest related to instruction that we considered in our synthesis. One focused on whether some domains of instruction are more resistant to change as a function of treatment than others. One conceptual model that has some consensus in the field is that learning-disabled (LD) children are of normal intelligence, but suffer information-processing difficulties (e.g., Borkowski, Estrada, Milstead, & Hale, 1989; Deshler & Schumaker, 1988; Fletcher et al., 1994; Stanovich & Siegel, 1994; Swanson & Alexander, 1997). A popular assumption that has emerged in the last few years is that LD children have specific processing deficits that are localized to low-order processes, particularly phonological processing deficits (e.g., Francis, Shaywitz, Stuebing, Shaywitz, & Fletcher, 1996; Siegel, 1992; Stanovich & Siegel, 1994). Phonological processing is "the association between sounds with letters, that is, the understanding of the grapheme-phoneme conversion rules and the exceptions to these rules" (Siegel, 1993, p. 38). This assumption finds some consensus in the field because reading problems are pervasive in LD populations, and there is a plethora of research that suggests phonological coding underlies most of these problems (see Stanovich & Siegel, 1994, for a review). Although this may be true, there has been no synthesis of intervention studies to determine if specific processes or skills related to reading are more resistant to change than other academic domains.

The second area related to instruction we considered was whether variations in aptitude interact with the magnitude of treatment outcomes. More specifically, we assessed whether studies that include samples with intelligence and reading scores at various levels yield different treatment outcomes than those studies in which such levels are not specified. Reading scores at or below the 25th percentile in reading recognition (see Siegel & Ryan, 1989; Stanovich & Siegel, 1994) and standardized intelligence performance at or above 85 have been considered as critical cutoff scores for defining learning disabilities (LD; see Morrison & Siegel, 1991, for discussion of this issue). The rise in the use of cutoff scores in the experimental literature has been in response to the poor discriminant validity of discrepancy scores in defining children with LD from generally poor achieving children (see Stanovich & Siegel, 1994, for a review). The treatment validity of such a cutoff score definition, however, has not been tested as a function of treatment outcomes. That is, we assume that the face validity of a definition is enhanced if one can show that such a definition is significantly related to treatment outcomes.

Key Constructs

Three constructs were important in our synthesis of the research: LD, treatment, and outcome. First, although we took a nonjudgmental stance on the quality of the definition of LD reflected in intervention studies (e.g., operational vs. a school district definition vs. Federal Register definition), we held to a general parameter that such students must have at least normal intelligence (standardized intelligence scores at or above 85) or the study states *explicitly* that participants are in the normal range of intelligence. The study must also state that the participants perform poorly (as indicated by teachers and/or psychometric tests) in at least one academic (e.g., reading) and/or behavioral domain (social skills). We coded the variations of definitions reflected in the database (discrepancy vs. cutoff scores; school identified vs. research identified; specific academic difficulty vs. multiple academic difficulties) to investigate the relationship between the definitional parameters related to learning disabilities and actual treatment outcomes.

Second, the term *treatment* or *intervention* was defined as the direct manipulation by the researcher of psychological (e.g., metacognitive awareness), medical (e.g., drug) and/or educational (e.g., teaching, instruction, materials) variables for the purposes of assessing learning efficiency (e.g., rate, time), learning accuracy (e.g., percent correct), learning understanding (e.g., amount of verbal elaboration on a concept), or a combination of all three. In general, treatment was administered in the context of school as an extension of the regular classroom, special education classroom, and/or clinical services. This extension varied from three instructional sessions to several continuous instructional sessions over months or years. Because of the vastness of the topic, however, additional boundaries were necessary in our analysis. The intervention literature that focuses on administrative decisions and *does not* reflect a manipulation of treatment conditions (e.g., educational placement - resource room) falls outside the boundaries. Educational research based on intervention that occurs as an extension of the educational placement of children, adolescents, and adults with LD within various educational (e.g., classroom or college) placements is included. Moreover, attention is directed to only those instructional interventions that include students with LD. Excluded from the analysis, however, are interventions in which the effects of intervention on students with LD cannot be directly analyzed or partialed out in the analysis. Also, within the area of educational intervention, it was necessary to place parameters on the level or scope of intervention. At one end of a rough continuum, we distinguished between treatment techniques that include separable elements, but that do not, by themselves, reflect a free-standing treatment (e.g., teacher presents advance organizers). At the other end of this continuum are broad approaches that reflect policies and organizational arrangements (e.g., consulting-teacher model that provides help to a LD student in a regular classroom). We excluded those treatments that were at the top of the continuum. Although there are some gray areas in our selection, we have found it possible to identify instructional programs that are added to the typical instructional routine.

Finally, treatment outcomes included six general categories of information. These categories were:

1. Article or technical report identification (funding sources, citations).
2. Methodological characteristics (e.g., sampling procedure, reliability and validity of measures, internal and external validity, treatment integrity).
3. Sampling characteristics (e.g., psychometric information, chronological age, gender, ethnicity, sample size, type of definition, marker variables).
4. Parameters of intervention (e.g., domain, setting, materials, duration and length of session).
5. Components of intervention (e.g., group vs. individual instruction, number and description of steps in intervention, level of student response to instruction, maintenance and transfer).
6. Effect size (e.g., magnitude of treatment effects).

Data Collection

The PsycINFO, MEDline, and ERIC online databases were systematically scanned for studies from 1963 to 1997 that met the inclusion criteria described next. The computer search strategy used the following terms: *learning disabled (disabilities)*, or *reading disabled (disabilities)*, or *dyslexic*, or *educationally handicapped*, or *slow learners*, paired with variations of *intervention* or *treatment* or *training* or *remediation* or *instruction*. This search yielded approximately 3,000 abstracts that included articles, technical reports, chapters, and dissertations. We examined all the abstracts prior to study selection to eliminate those studies that clearly did not meet the inclusion criteria (e.g., articles were reviews or position papers). Because the computer search procedures excluded unpublished studies and the most recent literature, researchers (as identified by journal board affiliations with the *Learning Disability Quarterly, Journal of Learning Disabilities,* and *Learning Disabilities Research and Practice* and/or membership in the International Academy for Research in Learning Disabilities) were sent letters requesting copies of unpublished and/or ongoing intervention studies. We also hand searched the following journals for articles that did not emerge from the computer search: *Journal of Learning Disabilities, Journal of Educational Psychology, Learning Disability Quarterly, Reading and Writing, Learning Disabilities Research and Practice, Exceptional Children,* and the *Journal of Special Education.* In addition, every state department and 200 School District Directors of Educational Research were sent a letter requesting technical reports on intervention studies for children and adolescents with LD.

Data Evaluation

The pool of relevant literature (3,164 reports, abstracts, dissertations, or articles) was narrowed down to studies that utilized an experimental design in which children or adults with LD receive treatment to enhance their academic, social, and/or cognitive performance. This procedure narrowed the search to *913* databased articles (or reports) that appeared potentially acceptable for inclusion in the quantitative review. After a review of these studies, each databased report was evaluated on *five* additional criteria for study inclusion. These criteria include:

1. The study includes at least one between-instruction comparison condition (i.e., control condition) or within-design control condition (e.g., repeated measures design) that includes participants with LD. Thus, studies that included *only* a pretest and posttest *without* an instructional control condition of LD participants were excluded.

2. The study provides sufficient quantitative information to permit the calculation of effect sizes. Effect sizes were calculated from the means (*M*s) and standard deviations (*SD*s) of the performance outcomes for the experimental and control conditions, or from tests of the significance of the differences in performance between instruction conditions (e.g., *t* or *F* tests, χ^2, exact *p* values).

3. The recipients of the intervention were identified as children or adults with average intelligence, but with problems in a particular academic, social, and/or related behavior domain. The mean IQ score reported for the LD participant sample could occur on any standardized verbal, nonverbal, intelligence test, or subtest. The cutoff score for inclusion in the synthesis was a reported mean IQ score of > 84 for group design studies and for individuals in single-subject design studies. Studies that reported no IQ score, but stated that the group IQ or individual IQ scores (as in single-subject studies) were in the average range were included in the analysis. If a study did not report or *state* that IQ was in the average range, the study was not included in the general analysis.

4. The treatment group received instruction, assistance, or therapy that is over and above what they would have received during the course of their typical classroom experience. That is, the study focuses on treatment, rather than merely a description of the child's current placement followed by an evaluation. The fine line between intervention and experimentation was drawn by requiring that the training or remediation had to have been dispensed over a minimum of *3* days.

5. The study has to be written in English.

Although design issues (no control condition) are the most frequent criteria for article exclusion, the inability to calculate effect sizes, lack of clarity about whether students with LD were included (e.g., IQ scores < 84 or average IQ was not stated), the inability to separate the performance of students with LD from other ability groups, no information on sample size, and/or faulty statistical applications (e.g., incorrect degrees of freedom) were also frequent reasons for article exclusion. Ten studies were deleted because effect sizes were clearly outliers (in some cases effect sizes > 10.0). The total number of studies agreed on for the synthesis was 180.

Summary of Analysis

Although several analyses were computed on effect sizes, we have summarized some the most important findings into two tables. Table 1.1 proves information on the magnitude of effect size as a function of the dependent measures, and Table 1.2 contrasts various studies on method-

TABLE 1.1

Weighted Mean Effect Sizes for Group Design Studies as a Function of Dependent Measure Category

| | | | | | LD Treatment Versus LD Control | | | |
| | | | | | 95% Confidence Interval for Weighted Effects | | | |
	N	K	Effect Size d Unweighted	Effect Size d Weighted	Lower	Upper	Standard Error	Homogeneity (Q)
1. Cognitive Processing	41	115	.87 (.64)	.54	.48	.61	.03	311.67**
1a. Metacognitive	9	27	.98	.80	.66	.94	.07	83.91**
1b. Attribution	7	17	.79	.62	.44	.79	.08	31.99*
1c. Other Processes	25	71	.65	.46	.38	.53	.03	176.07**
2. Word Recognition	54	159	.71 (.56)	.57	.52	.62	.02	431.45**
2a. Standardized	23	79	.79	.62	.54	.69	.04	205.61**
2b. Experimental	35	80	.72	.53	.48	.60	.03	223.073**
3. Reading Comprehension	58	176	.82 (.60)	.72	.68	.77	.02	565.95**
3a. Standardized	16	38	.45	.45	.36	.54	.05	33.87
3b. Experimental	44	138	.84	.81	.75	.86	.02	489.54**
4. Spelling	24	54	.54 (.53)	.44	.37	.52	.04	100.44**
4a. Standardized	8	20	.61	.45	.34	.57	.06	34.15
4b. Experimental	18	34	.48	.44	.33	.54	.05	65.94**
5. Memory/Recall	12	33	.81 (.46)	.56	.43	.70	.06	42.72

6.	*Mathematics*	28	71	.58 (.45)	.40	.33	.46	.04	128.28**
6a.	Standardized	9	22	.41	.33	.23	.46	.05	25.72
6b.	Experimental	21	49	.59	.42	.34	.51	.04	101.43**
7.	*Writing*	19	67	.84 (.60)	.63	.54	.72	.05	157.45**
7a.	Standardized	3	7	.37	.36	.14	.58	.11	5.01
7b.	Experimental	16	60	.80	.68	.59	.78	.04	145.27**
8.	*Vocabulary*	11	20	.79 (.44)	.78	.66	.89	.05	38.58**
9.	Attitude/Self-Concept	25	86	.68 (.69)	.39	.33	.45	.03	210.65**
10.	*Intelligence*	9	32	.58 (.59)	.41	.30	.52	.06	54.37**
11.	*General Reading*	15	31	.60 (.50)	.52	.41	.65	.06	55.15*
12.	*Phonics/Orthographic Skills*	29	175	.70 (.36)	.64	.60	.69	.02	453.70**
12a.	Standardized Phonics	8	60	.72	.67	.62	.73	.03	275.87**
12b.	Experimental Phonics	21	78	.76	.60	.52	.67	.04	175.22**
13.	*Global Achievement* (grades, total achievement)	10	21	.91 (.76)	.45	.31	.58	.07	56.64**
14.	*Creativity*	3	11	.84 (.49)	.70	.52	.87	.09	33.61**
15.	*Social Skills*	13	36	.46 (.22)	.41	.30	.51	.05	28.46
16.	*Perceptual Processes*	10	37	.74 (.65)	.26	.17	.35	.04	46.64
17.	*Language*	9	52	.54 (.48)	.36	.28	.44	.04	75.53*

Note. ( ) = standard deviation.
*p < .01. **p < .001.

TABLE 1.2
Effect Size Estimates as a Function of Unit of Analysis, Methodological, Instructional, and Sampling Variables (Outliers Removed)

	Sample Size	K	Mean	SD	Weighed Mean	Ind. Sample	χ^2
All Studies	33,845	1,207	.66	.59	.54	362	—
	4,871	180	.79	.52	.61		
Methodology							
Number of Treatment Sessions							
3 to 10	8,103	353	.66	.57	.51	—	
	1,750	72	.77	.53	.71	138	
11 to 30	7,137	330	.72	.63	.62	—	
	1,462	64	.85	.53	.78	126	
>31	16,885	507	.62	.57	.57	—	15.72**=
	1,411	41	.74	.50	.66	88	3.32[a]
Treatment Integrity (Procedural Validity)							
Reported	18,714	722	.62	.58	.47		
	2,209	67	.81	.51	.74		
Not Reported	12,635	411	.72	.60	.59	132	37.29**
	2,330	103	.82	.55	.69	104	.60
Internal Validity Rating (Includes five variables)[b]							
Low	24,668	927	.67	.60	.56		
	3,629	135	.83	.55	.74	274	
High	6,681	206	.63	.54	.48		8.81**
	913	35	.74	.74	.62	66	2.97
Total Sample Size							
1. <25	8,643	588	.77	.63	.63		
	1,672	166	.88	.55	.78	232	
2. >24 and <50	15,366	508	.55	.55	.48		
	1,624	52	.64	.47	.55	102	

	N	K				Ind.	F
3. >49 and <100	5,167	85	.56	.41	.50		
	409	6	.49	.14	.47	12	
4. >99	4,566	28	.60	.50	.79		94.49**
	1,165	6	.80	.43	1.12	16	49.68**
							(4 > 1 > 2 = 3)
Variation of Teacher (Researcher) in the Admin. of Treatment							
1. Different Teacher-CTRL & Exp	6,254	218	.60	.42	.64		
	1,447	41	.66	.35	.76	80	
2. Same Teacher-CTRL & Exp	12,927	506	.64	.57	.49		
	1,487	70	.77	.47	.62	136	
3. Cannot Determine (No Info)	14,561	483	.71	.67	.55		38.92**
	1,936	69	.90	.63	.75	132	6.03*
							(1 = 3 > 2)[c]
Variation of Setting Between CTRL and TRT							
1. CTRL & TRT Occur in Different Classroom/Setting/School	11,786	413	.69	.63	.58		
	1,505	60	.82	.53	.69	110	
2. CTRL & TRT Occur in Same Classroom	8,849	368	.61	.56	.50		
	775	39	.70	.45	.59	64	
3. No Information	13,107	426	.67	.57	.60		22.08**
	2,509	81	.82	.54	.71	188	(3 = 1; 3 > 2, 2 = 1)
							6.31*
							(3 = 1 > 2)

Note. In Row 1 the unit of analysis was calculated across all studies and dependent measures. In Row 2 the unit of analysis was averaged within each study. K = number of dependent measures. Ind. = number of independent samples. CTRL = control condition. EXP = experimental condition.
[a]Chronologically partialed out. [b]Composite score related to control and experimental comparability on materials, instructional time, administration consistency, subject mortality, random assignment, reliability of measures, and ceiling and floor effects. [c]Read as 1 and 3 ("different teacher" and "cannot determine") are statistically comparable, but both are significantly larger in effect sizes than 2 ("same teacher").

*p = .05. **p = .01.

11

ological and setting variables. We also provide a figure (see Fig. 1.1) that shows how the magnitude of effect size is influenced by variations in intelligence and reading level. We finish this section by describing a two-tier analysis we used to identify the locus of effective instructional treatments. Before we review these two tables and Fig. 1.1, a brief characterization of the studies is necessary (for a more in-depth analysis see Swanson, Hoskyn, & Lee, 1999).

Study Characteristics. The analyses yielded 180 group design studies that included 1,537 effect sizes comparing LD students in the experimental condition with LD students in the control condition. The mean effect size across the 180 studies was .79 (SD = .52). A prototypical intervention study includes 22.47 minutes (SD = 29.71) of daily instruction, 3.58 times a week (SD = 1.58), over 35.72 (SD = 21.72) sessions. The mean sample size for the study is 27.06 (SD = 40.15). The mean treatment age is 11.16 with a standard deviation of 3.22. The most frequent sampling and treatment assignment procedures use (a) participants from an intact sample (a nonrandomly selected sample) with no random assignment to treatment conditions (35%), or (b) an intact sample with random

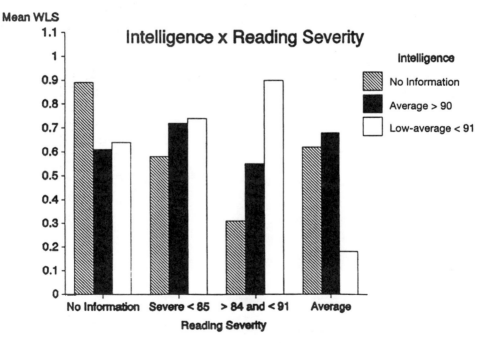

FIG. 1.1. Estimates of effect size.

assignment to treatment and control conditions (42% of studies). The average year of publication for studies was 1987 (*SD* = 5.41), with publication dates ranging from 1972 to 1997. The most frequent year of publication was 1992 (12% of the studies). The most frequent publication outlets were the *Journal of Learning Disabilities* (16%), *Learning Disabilities Research and Practice* (7%), *Learning Disability Quarterly* (13%), and *Exceptional Children* (7%). Thirteen percent of the studies in the synthesis analysis were drawn from dissertations.

Materials for the experimental conditions were commercial (33% of the studies), novel (i.e., materials developed by the researcher, 54% of the studies), or a combination of commercial and novel (9% of the studies), or were not classifiable (four of the studies). The most frequent commercial materials (*N* = 54) were related to direct instruction (e.g., Corrective Reading, Distar, SRA, 8%), Houghton Mifflin series (4%), Orton–Gillingham approach (4%), and Lindamood–Bell (4%). For those studies that primarily utilized commercial materials in the experimental treatment, 25 of the 54 studies (46%) did not report the materials used (or used no commercial materials) in the control condition. In terms of student activities during treatment, 30 of the studies had participants monitor or evaluate (via recording, counting, charting, checking, graphing, and/or verbalizing) their academic behavior.

Although the majority of studies had samples identified as LD, studies varied tremendously on the criteria and detail for participant selection. In terms of reporting group mean scores on psychometric information, only 104 studies (64%) reported group mean scores for intelligence, 84 studies (50%) reported group mean scores on achievement scores in reading, and 22 studies (12%) reported group mean scores in mathematics. Beyond IQ, reading, and mathematic scores, psychometric information on other characteristics of the sample was infrequently reported (< 3% of the studies). In terms of those studies that reported scores, 83.7% of the studies that reported IQ scores used the WISC–R (Wechsler Intelligence Scale for Children–Revised) as the measure of intelligence, and 20% of the studies that reported achievement scores used the Wide Range Achievement Test as the measure of reading achievement. The mean reported treatment IQ for the LD sample was 93.51 (*SD* = 16.51, range of 85 to 115). Of those studies reporting standardized reading scores (42%), the mean reported standard score was 71.44 (*SD* = 25.38).

Table 1.1. Prior to the analysis of effect sizes, it was necessary to separate the effect sizes into 17 categories of dependent measures that reflect a broad array of treatment domains (e.g., reading, writing, etc.). Table 1.1 provides the weighted means and standard deviations of effect sizes (absolute value of *d*) as a function of the dependent measures across studies. If the number of dependent measures *(K)* within a category exceeded 50, we attempted to subgroup the categories by standardized (normed referenced measures) and experimental (researcher developed) measures. This was not possible for all categories, however, because of the infrequent use of standardized measures. For example, the cognitive processing category was divided into metacognitive, attribution, and "other" because few standardized measures were reported in the primary studies.

There are two findings of primary interest in Table 1.1. First, the most frequent dependent measures reflected across the various studies are measures of reading. These studies include measures of word recognition, word skills, reading comprehension, and general reading. Also frequently represented are measures of cognitive processing. Second, the magnitude of the estimates of effect size related to treatment impact vary across categorical domains. Effect sizes to be considered marginal according to Cohen's criteria (effect sizes below .45) occurred in the domains of spelling, mathematics, attitude, intelligence, social skills, perceptual processes, and language processes. Those areas that approached Cohen's (1988) threshold of .80 for a "large effect" are reading comprehension (.72), vocabulary (.78), and creativity (.70). When the categories were divided into subcategories, the high effect sizes related to reading comprehension emerged on experimental ($M = .84$) measures when compared to standardized measures ($M = .45$). The subcategory related to metacognition also yielded an effect size (.80) that met Cohen's criteria.

Table 1.2. Table 1.2 provides a comparison of weighted and unweighted effect sizes as a function of study variations in methodology. The weighted mean effect size estimate (weighted by the reciprocal of the sampling variance) is the primary measure used to compare studies across the various contrasts. To assess the stability of the results, two units of analysis were considered. One unit calculates effect size estimates for each dependent measure as if all the measures were independent of each other. The second averages the effect sizes across dependent variables within each study (i.e., each study contributes only one effect size to the analysis). As shown in Table 1.2, the number of independent samples was also computed. When the number of independent samples exceeded $2 \times K$ (the number of studies), then the studies included more than one experimental treatment. When the number of independent samples is lower than $2 \times K$, then there was reliance on using the same participants in multiple treatments.

As shown in Table 1.2, studies that include from 11 to 30 sessions yield higher effect sizes than those that include between 3 and 10 sessions. No significant differences in effect sizes were found between studies that lasted more than 31 sessions and those that lasted between 3 and 10 sessions.

However, when the unit of analysis includes averaging effect size estimates within studies, no significant differences emerge in effect size as a function of the number of sessions. Those studies that report treatment integrity (i.e., the degree to which independent variable is carried out as designed) yield lower effect sizes than those that do not report treatment integrity, but the differences in effect size were not significant.

We categorized studies into high and low internal validity on the variables of setting, different materials, comparability of teachers across conditions, reporting of reliability, procedural validity, and random assignment (scores ranged from 6 to 18, with a score of 6 reflecting high internal validity). As shown in Table 1.2, studies with high internal (scores < 10) validity yield lower effect sizes than studies of low internal validity. However, when effect sizes are averaged within each study there is no significant difference in estimates of effect size in studies with high and low internal validity. Those studies that included standardized testing as part of the pre- and posttest measures had significantly lower effect sizes when compared to studies that relied on experimental measures (.92 vs. .69).

Those studies that had a high degree of overlap between the control group and the treatment group in terms of the number and types of instructional components yield significantly lower effect sizes than those studies with minimal overlap (.71 vs. .85). The unweighted effect size was analyzed when we considered studies of high and low sample size. This is because the weighted effect sizes is based on the reciprocal of the sample sizes. Those studies that report lower effect sizes include larger samples sizes than those that include small samples. A Scheffé test showed that studies that had a total sample of less than 25 yielded higher effect sizes than those studies with larger sample sizes.

Because several methodological variables were clearly related to the magnitude of effect sizes, it was necessary to create a methodological composite score related to internal validity and methodological sophistication for the subsequent comparisons. Studies that included: (a) instructional sessions greater than 10 (selection of this variable was based on the assumption that the intensity of instruction—as reflected by the number of sessions—yields more reliable and stable outcomes than shorter intervention sessions), (b) random assignment to treatment, (c) measures of treatment (procedural) integrity, (d) utilization of standardized tests, (e) internal validity scores on the abbreviated scale of 11 (discussed later), and (f) high control and treatment condition overlap in terms of steps and procedures (at least three steps and/or procedures overlap), were assigned a score. The amount of psychometric data reported was also included in the methodological composite score (if additional psychometric information beyond an IQ score was reported—e.g., reading scores—the study was weighted positively). For each of the seven variables weighted positively and negatively, a score of 2 or 0 was assigned for each variable, respectively. For each study, the weighted score varied from 14 to 0, with 14 reflecting methodologically superior studies. This methodological composite score was used in the subsequent analysis to qualify the outcomes related to effect size estimates. The mean methodological composite score across studies was 7.25 ($SD = 2.92$). Based on the methodological composite score, studies were divided into three classifications, high (score greater than 10), medium (score between 6 and 11), and low methodological sophistication (score less than 6). As shown in Table 1.2, studies that achieved higher methodological sophistication had significantly lower effect size estimates than those studies weak in methodological sophistication.

The scale for internal validity of each study alluded to earlier included a rating of the following items: (a) subject mortality, (b) Hawthorne effects and selection bias, comparable exposure between treatment and/or controls to (c) materials, (d) instruction time, and (e) teacher, (f) procedural validity checks, (g) practice effects on the dependent measure, (h) floor and ceiling effects, (i) interrater reliability, (j) regression to the mean ruled out as an alternative explanation of findings, and (k) homogeneity of variance between groups. For each of the 11 items, a score of 1 reflects internal validity control, 2 reflects no validity control, and 3 reflects no validity information. The mean rating score (11 is high and 33 is low) was $M = 22.16$ ($SD = 2.64$).

The mean outcomes on effect size as a function of the characteristics of studies in terms of funding and the type of publication were also analyzed. No significant differences emerged in the magnitude of effect size for studies that reported a funding source and those that did not. Those studies that were published in dissertations had significantly lower sizes than those published in journals.

Studies were sorted by those that reported the setting in which treatment occurred and those that did not. Those studies that do not report the setting ($N = 102$) in which the intervention occurred yield lower effect sizes than those that do report the setting. Setting information was further divided into those studies that reported that treatment occurred in a self-contained classroom, resource room, regular classroom, or failed to report the type of classroom setting where the treatment occurred. The number of studies reporting no information ($N = 102$) was reduced ($N = 86$) in the comparisons between the type of classrooms because 16 of these studies failed to report a mean age score (instead age or grade ranges were provided) for the sample. Only four studies, with a total sample size of 151 participants, provided information on effect sizes related to the regular classroom. Significant differences related to setting occurred whether the unit of analysis was averaged within study or each dependent measure was considered as a separate independent event. As shown, larger effect sizes occurred in resource rooms when compared to other settings.

Several effect size differences emerged related to information on sample characteristics. The general pattern was that studies that fail to report psychometric information on participants with LD yield significantly higher effect sizes than those studies that report psychometric information. For example, studies were categorized by the amount of psychometric information reported. Four categories were developed for comparisons (no information, standardized intelligence test scores, standardized intelligence scores + standardized reading test scores, and standardized intelligence test scores + reading scores + mathematics scores). A significant chi-square emerged for both units of analysis. The Scheffé test indicated that those studies that provided no psychometric information on the LD sample produced larger effect sizes than those studies that report intelligence, reading, and/or mathematics scores. No significant differences were found between those studies that reported intelligence scores and those that reported standardized intelligence scores and reading and/or math scores.

Given that psychometric information is related to effect size, the sample characteristics were further categorized by the reported range in intelligence scores and the range of reading scores. Three categories for comparison were created for intelligence: those studies that reported mean standard scores between 85 and 92, those that reported mean standardized intelligence scores greater than 92, and those that did not report standardized information. If studies provide multiple IQ scores (verbal, performance, nonverbal, etc.), these scores were averaged within studies. The highest effect sizes occur when no information is presented.

The next category considered in our sample analysis was reading severity. If multiple standardized reading measures were provided in the study, reading scores were averaged across word recognition and reading comprehension. Four categories were created for comparisons: scores below 85, scores above 84 and less than 91, scores greater than 90, and no standardized scores reported. Significant chi-squares emerged between the four categories of reading for the two types of unit of analysis. When examining the differences using a weighted least squares (WLS) method, high effect sizes emerge when no IQ and reading scores are reported when compared to the other conditions. However, when methodology was partialed out in the analysis, effect sizes for studies that report scores below 85 were comparable to those studies that reported no scores. The lowest effect sizes occurred between studies that reported reading scores between 84 and less than 91 and those studies that reported scores above 90.

Because the discrepancy between intelligence and achievement scores was a frequent way of defining samples, we categorized studies that "stated" the sample has a discrepancy between potential or IQ and achievement (or some specific academic domain) versus those that did not. Although we placed no restrictions on the type of discrepancy reported, the study must use the term *discrepancy* and state that the participants were at least 1 year behind in some achievement domain. The influence of the discrepancy variable is only significant when the unit of analysis was not averaged within studies. Higher effect sizes occurred when no discrepancy information is presented when compared to those studies that report discrepancy information. However, no significant differences were found in effect sizes when averaged within studies. Sample characteristics that fail to emerge as significant when considering the main effects were the age and gender of the participants.

Figure 1.1. Standardized measures of intelligence (primarily a Full Scale Intelligence Quotient [FSIQ] score on the WISC) and reading (primarily word recognition) were the most frequent means of identifying the LD sample. The independent results of intelligence and reading on the magnitude of effect size are provided in Table 1.1. Effect size estimates, averaged within each of the 180 studies, were analyzed to determine whether combinations of intellectual and reading levels influenced treatment outcomes. This preliminary analysis was done because standardized scores at or below the 25th percentile in reading recognition (see Siegel & Ryan, 1989; Stanovich & Siegel, 1994) along with standardized intelligence scores above 84 are considered reasonable cutoff scores toward operationalizing the term LD (see Morrison & Siegel, 1991, for discussion of this issue). Four levels of reading severity (no information, < 85, > 84 and < 91, > 90) and three levels of intellectual performance (no information, low-average [< 91], average [> 90]) were analyzed, via a WLS regression analysis with the methodological composite score partialed from the analysis. Studies that did not report mean ages of the sample (N = 20) were excluded from the analysis.

A 3 (Intelligence: high vs. low vs. no information) × 4 (reported reading severity: < 85, > 84 and < 92, > 91, and no information) WLS (analogue to an analysis of variance [ANOVA] and analysis of covariance [ANCOVA]), which partials the influence of methodology and chronological age, was computed. When methodology and age were partialed from the analysis, significant effects were isolated to the severity of reading × intelligence interaction, $\chi^2(6, N = 160) = 13.95, p < .05$. Figure 1.1 shows the findings that emerged related to this interaction. The important findings are related to those studies that report both IQ and reading level. The results indicate that those studies that produced the highest effect sizes report a minimal discrepancy between intelligence and reading (low-average intelligence scores [< 91] and comparable reading scores [between > 84 and 91]) when compared to other studies that report psychometric scores.

Two-Tier Analysis. To isolate the locus of treatment effects on outcome measures, a two-tier structure was used (also see the Wiesz, Weiss, Han, Granger, & Morton, 1995, discussion of a similar approach). The unit of analysis was the aggregated (averaged) effect size of each study. For the first tier, those studies that overlapped in components between direct and strategy instruction were separated for analysis. Thus, four general interventions models were compared: DI-alone (direct instruction components, but no strategy components), SI-alone (strategy components, but no direct instruction components), direct instruction coupled with strategy instruction (combined model, which includes both strategy and direct instruction components), and those studies that do not meet the threshold of the components of direct instruction or strategy instruction (referred to as the *nonSI & nonDI model*). The four models were compared by partialing out the influence of the methodological composite score. Significant differences in effect size emerged among the four models when the methodological composite score and age were partialed in the analysis. A Scheffé test of weight least square means (WLS M) indicated that the combined model ($N = 55$, WLS $M = .84$) yielded significantly higher effect sizes (all $ps < .05$) than SI-alone ($N = 22$, WLS $M = .72$), DI-alone ($N = 28$, WLS $M = .72$) and the nonDI & nonSI models ($N = 43$, WLS $M = .62$) (combined > DI-alone = SI-alone = nonDI & nonSI).

Component Level. For the second tier of analysis, we attempted to determine the component level at which instructional factors influenced the magnitude of effect size. We focused on 20 instructional components. Based on comprehensive reviews that have identified instructional components that influence student outcomes (e.g., Adams, 1990; Becker & Carnine, 1980; Foorman, Francis, Fletcher, & Lynn, 1996; Foorman et al., 1997; Graham & Harris, 1996; Pressley & Harris, 1994; Rosenshine, 1995), we reclustered (or reconfigured) the instructional activities into approximately 20 clusters of components for later analysis. We coded the occurrence or nonoccurrence of the following instructional components:

1. *Sequencing* (statements in the treatment description about breaking down the task, fading of prompts or cues, matching the difficulty level of the task to the student, sequencing short activities, and/or using step-by-step prompts).

2. *Drill-repetition* and *practice-review* (statements in the treatment description related to mastery criteria, distributed review and practice,

using redundant materials or text, repeated practice, sequenced reviews, daily feedback, and/or weekly reviews).

3. *Anticipatory or preparation responses* (statements in the treatment description related to asking the child to look over material prior to instruction, directing the child to focus on material or concepts prior to instruction, providing information to prepare student for discussion, and/or stating the learning objective for the lesson prior to instruction).

4. *Structured verbal teacher–student interaction* (statements in the treatment description about elaborate or redundant explanations, systematic prompting students to ask questions, teacher and student talking back and forth—dialogue, and/or teacher asks questions that are open-ended or directed).

5. *Individualization + small group* (statements in the treatment description about independent practice, and/or individual pacing, and/or individual instruction, and small-group instruction).

6. *Novelty* (statements in the treatment description about the use of developed diagrams or picture presentations, specialized films or videos, instruction via computers, specification that new curriculum was implemented, and/or emphasis on teacher presenting new material from the previous lesson).

7. *Strategy modeling + attribution training* (statements in the treatment description about processing components or multisteps related to modeling from the teacher; simplified demonstrations modeled by the teacher to solve a problem or complete a task successfully; teacher modeling; teacher providing reminders to use certain strategies, steps, and/or procedures; think-aloud models; and/or the teacher presenting the benefits of taught strategies).

8. *Probing-reinforcement* (statements in the treatment description about intermittent or consistent use of probes, daily feedback, fading of prompts and cues, and/or overt administration of rewards and reinforcers).

9. *Nonteacher instruction* (statements in the treatment description about homework, modeling from peers, parents providing instruction, and/or peers presenting or modeling instruction).

10. *Segmentation* (statements in the treatment description about breaking down the targeted skill into smaller units, breaking into component parts, segmenting and/or synthesizing components parts).

11. *Advanced organizers* (statements in the treatment description about directing children to look over material prior to instruction, children directed to focus on particular information, providing prior information about task, and/or the teacher stating objectives of instruction prior to commencing).

12. *Directed response/questioning* (treatment description related to dialectic or Socratic teaching, the teacher directing students to ask questions, the teacher and student or students engaging in dialogue, and/or the teacher asks questions).

13. *One-to-one instruction* (statements in the treatment description about activities related to independent practice, tutoring, instruction that is individually paced, and/or instruction that is individually tailored).

14. *Control difficulty or processing demands of task* (treatment statements about short activities, level of difficulty controlled, teacher providing necessary assistance, teacher providing simplified demonstration, tasks sequenced from easy to difficult, and/or task analysis).

15. *Technology* (statements in the treatment description about utilizing formal curriculum, newly developed pictorial representations, uses specific material or computers, and/or uses media to facilitate presentation and feedback).

16. *Elaboration* (statements in the treatment description about additional information or explanation provided about concepts, procedures or steps, and/or redundant text or repetition within text).

17. *Modeling by teacher of steps* (statements or activities in the treatment descriptions that involve modeling from teacher in terms of demonstration of processes and/or steps the students are to follow).

18. *Group instruction* (statements in the treatment description about instruction in a small group, and/or verbal interaction occurring in a small group with students and/or teacher).

19. *Supplement to teacher involvement besides peers* (statements in the treatment description about homework, parent helps reinforce instruction).

20. *Strategy cues* (statements in the treatment description about reminders to use strategies or multisteps, the teacher verbalizing of steps or procedures to solve problems, use of think-aloud models, and/or teacher presenting the benefits of strategy use or procedures).

These 20 components capture an array of intervention approaches. For example, the *Segmentation* component would be a characteristic of analytic and synthesis approaches (e.g., phonics instruction), whereas the *Anticipatory or preparation response* component characterizes treatment approaches that activate prior knowledge or provide a precursor to the main instructional activity (e.g., Meichenbaum's cognitive-behavioral model). The component that reflects the *Control of difficulty or processing demands of task* addresses the variations in teacher support (e.g., the teacher provides necessary assistance, tasks sequenced from easy to difficult, i.e., help is provided to the student that covaries with the learner's ability) of the student and are reflective of activities such as mediated scaffolding (e.g., Rosenshine, 1995). Following an explicit set of steps and prompting the use of these steps (Strategy cue) are important activities that underlie strategy instruction.

Two approaches, via a WLS regression analysis, were used to isolate those instructional components that play a significant role in predicting effect size. These approaches were used to control partially for preselection bias (control for order) of the instructional components and our capitalization on chance in the WLS regression analysis. First, we used a stepwise selection procedure in which the order of entry is determined via a mathematical maximization procedure. That is, after the methodological composite score and age are entered, the component with the largest correlation to effect size enters followed with the second component with the largest semipartial coefficient correlation, and so on. The results indicated that methodological composite score and age contributed approximately 6% of the variance in predicting effect size. The first instructional component to enter the regression model was control of task difficulty, increment in $R^2 = .06$, followed by small interactive groups with an increment in $R^2 = .05$, followed by directed response/questioning; increment in $R^2 = .02$. The complete model was $R^2 = .18$. Thus, three components (control of task difficulty, small interactive groups, and directed response/questioning) contributed approximately 12% of the variance in predicting effect size estimates. No other components entered significantly into the model.

Second, we identified those components that when combined yield the highest adjusted R^2 in predicting effect size estimates. The squared multiple correlation, adjusted for the number of explanatory variables, was used to quantify the predictive power of the given model. The adjusted R^2 was .04 when the methodological composite score and age was used to predict effect sizes across studies. The adjusted R^2 was improved to .20 when methodological composite score and age included sequencing, drill-repetition-practice-review, segmentation, directed response/questioning, controls of task difficulty, technology, small interactive groups, mediation other than peers or teachers, and strategy cuing. Thus, nine instructional components contribute to 16% of the variance in predicting effect size estimates.

IMPORTANT FINDINGS AND IMPLICATIONS

Based on a synthesis of intervention research conducted in the last 30 years for students with LD, we identified five important findings. First, a combined direct instruction and strategy instruction model is an effective procedure for remediating LD when compared to other instructional models. The effects size ($M = .84$) of the combined strategy instruction and direct instruction model meets Cohen's (1988) criterion of .80 for a substantial finding. The important instructional components that primarily make up this model are: attention to sequencing, drill-repetition-practice, segmenting information into parts or units for later synthesis, controlling of task difficulty through prompts and cues, making use of technology, the teacher systematically modeling problem-solving steps, and making use of small interactive groups.

Based on our findings related to the combined model, we conclude that effective instruction is neither a bottom-up nor a top-down approach in isolation. Lower order and higher order skills interact in order to influence treatment outcomes. Clearly, performance at complex levels (writing prose, inferring the meaning of text) cannot occur without some critical threshold of skills. Students with LD vary in these skills. What is clear from our synthesis, however, is that varying degrees of success across treatment domains draws from treatments that focus on both high- and low-order instruction (i.e., strategy and direct instruction). Our results clearly show that combinations of these specific components that reflect both of these orientations enhance treatment outcomes. This combined model was contrasted with one approach (direct instruction-only) we considered a bottom-up model and the other (strategy instruction-only) a top-down model. Based on magnitude of their effect sizes for the DI and SI models (.68 for DI-only and .72 for SI-only) in isolation, both approaches appear viable for students with LD. No doubt, there has been some lively debate over the years in the literature as to whether instruction should be top-down, via emphasizing the knowledge base, heuristics, and explicit strategies, or a bottom-up emphasis that entails hierarchical instruction at the skill level. However, these approaches in isolation were smaller in the magnitude of effect sizes than the combined model.

Second, we also found that regardless of the general models of instruction, only a few instructional components increase the predictive power of treatment effectiveness beyond what can be predicted by variations in methodology and age. The important findings from our regression analysis were that only 9 of the 20 components discussed earlier significantly contributed to effect size estimates. Taken together, we think attention to the following components are critical to treatment outcomes:

1. Sequencing (breaking down the task, fading of prompts or cues, sequencing short activities, step-by-step prompts).

2. Drill-repetition and practice-review (daily testing of skills; e.g., statements in the treatment description related to mastery criteria, distributed review and practice, using redundant materials or text, repeated practice, sequenced review, daily feedback, and/or weekly review).

3. Segmentation (breaking down targeted skill into smaller units and then synthesizing the parts into a whole; e.g., statements in the experimental condition included breaking down the task into short activities or step-by-step sequences, breaking down targeted skill into smaller units, breaking the text or problem into component parts, segmenting and then synthesizing components parts).

4. Directed questioning and responses (the teacher verbally asking process-related and/or content-related questions of students; e.g., treatment may include dialectic questioning, students are directed by teacher to ask questions, teacher and student engage in dialogue, the teacher asks questions).

5. Control difficulty or processing demands of a task (task sequenced from easy to difficult and only necessary hints and probes are provided the child; e.g., statements in treatment reflect short activities with the level of difficulty controlled, the teacher provides necessary assistance, the teacher provides simplified demonstration, the task is sequenced from easy to difficult, discussion is given to a task analysis).

6. Technology (e.g., use of a computer, structured text, flow charts to facilitate presentation; utilization of a structured curriculum, emphasis on pictorial representations, uses of specific or structured material, use of media to facilitate presentation and feedback).

7. Modeling of problem-solving steps by teacher (teacher provides demonstration of processes or steps to solve problem or how to do a task; e.g., writing, comprehension, decoding words).

8. Group instruction (instruction occurs in a small group; students interact with other students and/or teacher within the group).

9. A supplement to teacher and peer involvement (may include homework, parent or others to assist in instruction).

10. Strategy cues (reminders to use strategies or multisteps, the teacher verbalizes problem solving or procedures to solve, instruction makes use of think-aloud models, teacher presents the benefits of strategy use or procedures).

Third, only studies in the domains of reading comprehension, vocabulary, and creativity approached a threshold for a large effect when the confounds related to methodology were partialed from the analysis. The magnitude was .81 for reading comprehension, .73 for vocabulary, and .78 for creativity. Studies that produced effect sizes in the moderate range ($> .60$ and $< .70$) were in the domains of cognitive processing (e.g., metacognition, attribution, problem solving), word recognition, memory, writing, intelligence (performance on standardized tests), attitude/self-concept (attitude scales), phonics/orthographic skills (e.g., word skills such as reading pseudowords or recognizing correct spellings), and global achievement (e.g., teacher grades, class ranking). Those categories of dependent measures in which effect sizes were relatively low (.40 to .55) across intervention studies were spelling, mathematics, general reading (word recognition and comprehension are confounded on standardized tests), social skills (e.g., behavior ratings), perceptual processes (e.g., visual-motor, handwriting), and language processes (e.g., listening comprehension).

Given the findings on treatment and domain, we must make some comment on an in-depth analysis from our original report (Swanson et al., 1997). Although not discussed earlier, we did investigate in detail potential domain × treatment interactions. The important findings related to the analysis of main and two-way interactions for domain and treatment were as follows:

1. The combined model is more effective on reading-related (e.g., word recognition and comprehension) measures than nonreading-related (e.g., mathematics, social skills) measures.

2. The effectiveness of the combined model is particularly pronounced on reading comprehension measures when compared to reading recognition measures.

3. Bottom-up instruction (direct instruction alone) yields higher effect sizes than top-down (strategy instruction alone) models on word recognition, but not reading comprehension measures. Taken together, the results support the notion that a certain level of treatment specificity emerges across academic domains. The comparison of outcome measures showed that the effectiveness of the combined model is most pronounced on reading-related domains. Also the results indicate that the advantages of bottom-up instruction when compared to other models emerge primarily on word recognition measures.

Fourth, as shown in Fig. 1.1, LD participants with a high discrepancy between IQ and reading are more resistant to change as a function of treatment (based on the magnitude of effect size) when compared to LD participants whose poor reading and IQ scores are in the *same* low range (i.e., both IQ and reading scores are in the standard score range of 85 to 90). Although our findings are not related to particular type of treatment or domain category, they support the notion that greater changes emerge in studies whose samples *do not* exhibit a discrepancy (i.e., the WLS $M = .90$ when both intelligence and reading scores are in the 84–91 range when compared to studies with a discrepancy when IQ score > 90 and reading level < 85 [WLS $M = .72$] and when IQ score > 90 and reading level < 90 [WLS $M = .55$]). Thus, greater changes emerge in studies that include low average IQ and low reading scores versus those that include discrepancy in intelligence and reading.

Given that we did find the aforementioned two-way interaction (IQ × reading) significant, we performed a number of regression modeling programs to isolate potential definition × treatment interactions. Perhaps the most important finding related to treatment outcomes are that the sorting of studies on the basis of cutoff scores did influence treatment outcomes. The combined model yields higher effect sizes when cutoff scores (i.e., studies report reading scores at or below the 25th percentile in reading recognition and standardized intelligence performance above 84) can be computed when compared to studies in which cutoff scores cannot be computed.

Finally, methodological variations have a profound impact on treatment outcomes. The results clearly show that outcomes are influenced by variations in some methodological variables. Those isolated methodological variables that yield significant effects on the magnitude of effect size estimates are summarized as follows:

1. Studies that use a different teacher between control and experimental groups yield significantly larger effect sizes than those studies that use the same teacher.
2. Those studies in which control and treatments occur in a different setting (i.e., classroom and school) yield significantly higher effect sizes than those in the same classroom setting.
3. Those studies that rely on experimental measures yield significantly higher effect sizes than those studies that rely on standardized measures.
4. Those studies that published in dissertations yield significantly lower effect sizes than those published in journals.
5. Those studies that have a low overlap in terms of the number of instructional components between control and experimental conditions yield significantly higher effect sizes than those studies that have a high overlap in terms of instructional components (sequences, steps, methods, and procedures).
6. Studies that report less psychometric information yield larger effect sizes than studies that report more psychometric information.
7. Those studies that report no information on IQ reveal higher effect sizes than those studies that report information on IQ.
8. Those studies that do not report the setting in which the intervention occurred yield significantly lower effect sizes than those that do report the setting.

One obvious conclusion from our current synthesis is that some methodolgical artifacts significantly influence the magnitude of effect size. Interventions that vary from the control condition in terms of setting, teacher, and number of instructional steps (and the results are published in journals) yield larger effect sizes than studies that fail to control for such variations. Thus, methodological artifacts must be taken into consideration when interpreting treatment effects. We think probably the most serious threat to interpreting treatment effects are situations where intervention studies "stack the treatment condition" with more steps and procedures than the control condition. This artifact alone guarantees that the experiential condition will unequivocally yield higher effect sizes than studies with minimal overlap across all domains. *However, it is important to note that we controlled for many of these artifacts in our analysis of treatments.* We did this by partialing methodological composite score, age, setting, and aptitude variables in our regression analysis. We found that when these variables were controlled (the methodological composite score was used as a covariate in the WLS analysis) approximately 15% of the variance in effect size was related to specific instructional components. Thus, we feel optimistic that we have identified some very important instructional components that lead to successful interventions for students with LD.

Some readers may argue that meta-analysts should not correct for study imperfections because the purpose of meta-analysis is to provide only a description, not an estimate of what would have been found across well-designed studies. But a number of meta-analysts (e.g., Hunter & Schmidt, 1994) argue that most scientific questions are better addressed by results from studies that control for artifacts than studies that yield results distorted by artifacts. We assumed that corrections for methodology (imperfections) across a wide variety of studies are essential to the development of a cumulative knowledge base for the instruction of students with LD.

Some would argue that our conclusions related to methodology are somewhat pessimistic and that our comments and recommendations do not take into consideration the difficulty of doing classroom research. In addition, we have not considered alternative designs or methodological models that do not lend themselves to a quantitative synthesis. These are appropriate criticisms. However, we would argue that because research in the classroom is a multivariate phenomenon, our best chances of identify effective instruction will emerge from those studies of high internal validity. Because the knowledge base on effective intervention for students with LD is still evolving, we see as the most significant problem in intervention research that of enhancing the internal validity (credibility) of studies within the scientific community. We think attending to some of the methodological issues we've raised will steer intervention research in a positive direction.

Summary

Our synthesis has characterized intervention research within the field of LD over the last 30 years. When controlling for variations in methodology across studies, we identified several important instructional components that yield high effect sizes. We suggest that a combined model that includes components of direct instruction and strategy instruction is a viable heuristic for positively influencing academic performance for students with LD. In spite of the limitations in subject descriptions, we were also able to identify some aptitude variables (intellectual range and severity of reading deficiency) that played an important role in predicting treatment outcomes.

ACKNOWLEDGMENTS

This study was supported by a U.S. Department of Education grant (H023E40014), the Chesapeake Institute, and Peloy Endowment Funds awarded to the author. This chapter is a summary of the *group design* section submitted to the U.S. Dept. of Education, entitled "Interventions for Students With Learning Disabilities: A Meta-Analysis of Treatment Outcomes" by Swanson, Hoskyn, Lee, and O'Shaugnessy, October 1997. The group design section of this report is also discussed in detail in Swanson, Hoskyn, and Lee (1999). The views of this report do not necessarily reflect the U.S. Department of Education or the Chesapeake Institute.

REFERENCES

Adams, M. J. (1990). *Beginning to read.* Cambridge, MA: MIT Press.

Becker, W., & Carnine, D. (1980). Direct instruction: An effective approach for educational intervention with the disadvantaged and low performers. In B. Lahey & A. Kazdin (Eds.), *Advances in child clinical psychology.* New York: Plenum.

Borkowski, J. G., Estrada, M. T., Milstead, M., & Hale, C. A. (1989). General problem-solving skills: Relations between metacognition and strategic processing. *Learning Disability Quarterly, 12,* 57–70.

Borkowski, J. G., & Turner, L. A. (1990). Transsituational characteristics of metacognition. In W. Schneider & F. E. Weinert (Eds.), *Interactions among aptitudes, strategies, and knowledge in cognitive performance* (pp. 159–176). New York: Springer-Verlag.

Cohen, J. (1988). *Statistical power analysis for the behavioral sciences* (2nd ed.) New York: Academic Press.

Cooper, H., & Hedges, L. V. (1994). *Handbook of research synthesis.* New York: Russell Sage Foundation.

Deshler, D. D., & Schumaker, J. B. (1988). An instructional model for teaching students how to learn. In J. Graden, J. Zins, & M. Curtis (Eds.), *Alternative educational delivery systems:*

Enhancing instructional options for all students (pp. 391–411). Washington, DC: National Association of School Psychologists.

Engelmann, S., & Carnine, D. W. (1982). *Theory of instruction: Principles and applications.* New York: Irvington.

Fletcher, J., Shaywitz, S. E., Shankweiler, D. P., Katz, L., Liberman, I., Stuebing, K., Francis, D., Fowler, A., & Shaywitz, B. A. (1994). Cognitive profiles of reading disability: Comparisons of discrepancy and low achievement definitions. *Journal of Educational Psychology, 86,* 6–23.

Foorman, B. R., Francis, D. J., Fletcher, J. M., & Lynn, A. (1996). Relation of phonological and orthographic processing to early reading: Comparing two approaches to regression-based, reading-level-match design. *Journal of Educational Psychology, 88,* 639–652.

Foorman, B. R., Francis, D. J., Winikates, D., Mehta, P., Schatschneider, C., & Fletcher, J. M. (1997). Early interventions for children with reading disabilities. *Scientific Studies of Reading, 1*(3), 255–276.

Francis, D. J., Shaywitz, S. E., Stuebing, K. K., Shaywitz, B. A., & Fletcher, J. M. (1996). Developmental lag versus deficit models of reading disability: A longitudinal, individual growth curves analysis. *Journal of Educational Psychology, 88,* 3–17.

Graham, S., & Harris, K. R. (1996). Self-regulation and strategy instruction for students who find writing and learning challenging. In C. M. Levy & S. Ransdell (Eds.), *The science of writing: Theories, methods, individual differences, and applications* (pp. 347–360). Mahwah, NJ: Lawrence Erlbaum Associates.

Hedges, L. V., & Olkin, I. (1985). *Statistical methods for meta-analysis.* San Diego: Academic Press.

Hunter, J. E., & Schmidt, F. I. (1994). Correcting for sources of artifactual variation across studies. In H. Cooper & L. Hedges (Eds.), *The handbook of research synthesis* (pp. 324–335). New York: Russell Sage Foundation.

Kameenui, E. J., Jitendra, A. K., & Darch, C. B. (1995). Direct instruction reading as contronym and eonomine. *Reading & Writing Quarterly: Overcoming Learning Difficulties, 11*(1), 3–17.

Levin, J. R. (1986). Four cognitive principles of learning strategy instruction. *Educational Psychologist, 21,* 3–17.

Morrison, S. R., & Siegel, L. S. (1991). Learning disabilities: A critical review of definitional and assessment issues. In J. E. Obrzut & G. W. Hynd (Eds.), *Neurological foundations of learning disabilities* (pp. 79–97). San Diego: Academic Press.

Pressley, M., & Ghatala, E. S. (1990). Self-regulated learning: Monitoring learning from text. *Educational Psychologist, 25,* 19–34.

Pressley, M., & Harris, K. R. (1994). Increasing the quality of educational intervention research. *Educational Psychology Review, 6,* 191–208.

Rosenshine, B. (1995). Advances in research on instruction. *Journal of Educational Research, 88*(5), 262–268.

Siegel, L. S. (1992). An evaluation of the discrepancy definition of dyslexic. *Journal of Learning Disabilities, 25,* 618–629.

Siegel, L. S. (1993). The cognitive basis of dyslexia. In M. Howe & R. Pasnak (Eds.), *Emerging themes in cognitive development* (pp. 33–52). New York: Springer-Verlag.

Siegel, L. S., & Ryan, E. B. (1989). The development of working memory in normally achieving and subtypes of learning disabled children. *Child Development, 60,* 973–980.

Stanovich, K. E., & Siegel, L. S. (1994). Phenotypic performance profile of children with reading disabilities: A regression based test of the phonological-core difference model. *Journal of Educational Psychology, 86,* 24–53.

Swanson, H. L., & Alexander, J. E. (1997). Cognitive processes as predictors of word recognition and reading comprehension in learning-disabled and skilled readers: Revisiting the specificity hypothesis. *Journal of Educational Psychology, 89*(1), 128–158.

Swanson, H. L., Carson, C., & Sachse-Lee, C. M. (1996). A selective synthesis of intervention research for students with learning disabilities. *School Psychology Review, 25*(3), 370–391.

Swanson, H. L. Hosykn, M., & Lee, C. M. (1999). *Interventions for students with learning disabilities: A meta-analysis of treatment outcomes.* New York: Guilford Press.

Swanson, H. L., Hoskyn, M., Lee, C. M., & O'Shaugnessy, T. (1997) Interventions for students with learning disabilities: A meta-analysis of treatment outcomes (Final Report). Washington, DC: U.S. Department of Education.

Weisz, J. R., Weiss, B., Han, S. S., Granger, D. A., & Morton, T. (1995). Effects of psychotherapy with children and adolescents revisited: A meta-analysis of treatment outcome studies. *Psychological Bulletin, 117*(3), 450–468.

Chapter 2

The Professional Knowledge Base on Instructional Practices That Support Cognitive Growth for English-Language Learners

Russell Gersten
Scott Baker
Eugene Research Institute

In decrying the high levels of passion and low levels of rational discourse on the subject of the education of English-language learners, Yzaguirre (1998) noted that a shift in emphasis toward instructional issues and variables is likely to significantly improve both the level and the quality of discourse on the topic. Scholars such as Goldenberg (personal communication, 1994; 1996) and Moll (1988) have argued convincingly that research needs to go beyond which language is used to teach English-language learners and beyond which model of bilingual education is best, and move toward a delineation of instructional methods for how to teach successfully. Goldenberg (personal communication, October 8, 1994) noted, for example, that "The language of instruction debate has so dominated discussion of how to best serve the needs of language minority children that other issues, which are at *least* equally important, have not been adequately addressed." In 1989, Figueroa, Fradd, and Correa decried the lack of "a substantive body of empirical data on actual, well-controlled interventions . . . that improve the academic abilities of students who are English-language learners" (p. 17). By and large, despite huge interest in the topic, this is still the case.

The recent report by the National Academy of Sciences (NAS) (August & Hakuta, 1997) on the knowledge base of effective education for English-language learners laments that little has been learned from large-scale program evaluation studies, which have focused primarily on issues of the language used for instruction and the optimal time for introducing English. These program evaluation studies are problematic because of significant, and in many cases inherent, methodological limitations such as noncomparable control groups, lack of pretest data, and poor understanding of how specific programs actually get implemented in classrooms. The report also critiques the methodology utilized in the "effective schools" studies (e.g., Lucas, Henze, & Donato, 1990; Tikunoff et al., 1991) and concludes they are seriously flawed as well.

The NAS recommended that more research be conducted that examines the effects of specific instructional practices on the academic learning outcomes of English-language learners. These studies should be linked to more specific research questions that can help guide practice such as: "What methods work best to give English-language learners access to the academic and social opportunities that native English speakers have while they are learning English? [Are] effective teacher practices for students generally sufficient to help English-language learners succeed in school?" (August & Hakuta, 1997, p. 193).

After synthesizing the descriptive research on cognitive operations and processes used by English-language learners, Fitzgerald (1995) concluded that the principles of reading instruction derived from advances in cognitive psychology that are commonly recommended for general classroom use are likely to be effective for English-language learners. She generated several hypotheses concerning the adaptations necessary for English-language learners. They are likely to require particular care in wording of questions, the pace of lessons will vary, and strategies used to activate background knowledge will be different.

The purpose of this synthesis was to examine the current state of the knowledge base on the effectiveness of specific instructional practices for English-language learners. The guiding question was seemingly straightforward: What do we really know about effective teaching practices for English-language learners in the elementary and middle school grades? Although it appears straightforward, the issues raised by the NAS (August & Hakuta, 1997) and Fitzgerald (1995), among others, about investigating instruction for English-language learners, suggests that providing an adequate answer is more difficult than it seems.

In 1994, when we began this project, we were able to locate only four instructional research studies with valid designs. By 1997, that number had doubled to eight. The small number of controlled experimental studies led to our decision to conduct both an exploratory meta-analysis using the methodologies outlined by Cooper and Hedges (1994) on the set of eight instructional intervention studies, and to supplement this with qualitative synthesis techniques.

Developing a methodology to synthesize the extant knowledge base on this topic was difficult because it is a highly fragmented body of knowledge and there are deep-rooted conceptual differences among scholars and researchers who investigate this topic. Consequently, we utilized the framework for research synthesis articulated by Ogawa and Malen (1991) in their seminal article on *multivocal research synthesis.*

What Is a Multivocal Synthesis?

Ogawa and Malen (1991) called for integrative syntheses of a professional knowledge base on topics for which there are scant empirical data, such as site-based management. They introduced multivocal synthesis methodology and urged its use for topics "characterized by a preponderance of diverse writings and a paucity of systematic investigations . . ." (p. 265):

> This strategy enables researchers to conduct . . . [an] open-ended search for relevant information, identify the major patterns associated with the phenomenon of interest, develop or adopt constructs that embrace the patterns, articulate tentative hypotheses about the meanings of the constructs and their relations, and refine questions and/or suggest conceptual perspectives that might serve as fruitful guides for subsequent investigations. (Ogawa & Malen, 1991, p. 271)

Using multivocal synthesis methods, researchers evaluate the methods and results of a given set of studies and use rigorous qualitative procedures to analyze "the words . . . in these diverse writings" (Ogawa & Malen, 1991, p. 265) to determine potential underlying belief systems and biases.

The research literature on effective instructional practices for English-language learners is appropriate to multivocal synthesis techniques because there are a variety of serious perspectives and little data. Each serious perspective needs a "voice" and to have its validity as a source of evidence considered. As Ogawa and Malen (1991) forcefully argued, "the literatures for some of the most prominent topics in education . . . are multivocal. They are characterized by an abundance of diverse documents . . . [that are often] profuse [and] disparate . . ." (p. 266). Failure to attend to issues raised in the full gamut of literature, and in our view, failure to seriously examine patterns that emerge from experimental research through meta-analytic techniques lead to a limited understanding of issues.

Two formal data sources were included as "voices" in our multivocal synthesis: (a) experimental (i.e., intervention) studies and (b) descriptive studies of instructional practices that utilized classroom observation techniques. We did not weigh the findings from highly subjective or interpretative research as heavily as we did research conducted with valid experimental designs and reliable measures or qualitative studies that seemed to provide a more dispassionate analysis of issues raised.

Unique to our multivocal synthesis was the use of professional work groups as a third data source. These work groups, which included practitioners and researchers, helped identify relevant and irrelevant concepts for the integrative synthesis. We consider the input from these end-users a high priority and believe their contribution helped us develop an informed sense of the propositions and practice issues considered important by the most knowledgeable groups in the field. We believe their participation strengthens the validity of the interpretations that emerged and provides an important linkage between practice and research.

Data Sources

The various data sources and how they fit within the context of the integrated, multivocal synthesis are presented in Fig. 2.1. As the figure shows, the first data source consisted of quantitative studies using experimental or quasi-experimental designs that examined the learning outcomes of specific instructional approaches. We analyzed these studies using traditional meta-analysis techniques (Cooper & Hedges, 1994).

The second and third data sources were qualitative in nature. The second source consisted of studies of the learning environments of English-

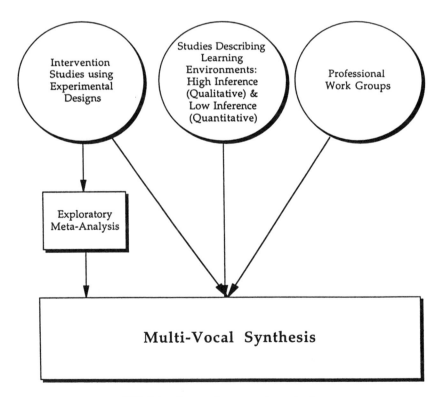

FIG. 2.1.   Integrative research synthesis.

language learners that focused on analyzing and describing instructional practices. Although some of the studies in this category used reliable observation instruments to generate quantitative data, we relied on primarily qualitative methods to integrate our interpretation of these studies within the context of the overall syntheses.

The third data source consisted of information gathered from the professional work groups. The studies we analyzed were important in our work with the professional work groups. Our research team read and coded these studies in preparation for the group discussions. In particular, we used our understanding of the studies to discuss the feasibility of applying specific principles of effective instruction in real classroom settings.

Our goal was to develop valid interpretations (Wolcott, 1994) from these disparate data sources. For the qualitative analyses, we followed Wolcott's dictum, "to open things up rather than seal them up . . . offering a new perspective gained after extended reflection. . . . The process can be stimulated and nurtured, but . . . it cannot be rushed" (p. 260). In fact, we devoted 3 years to this process.

METHOD

Literature Search

Studies were included in the synthesis if they focused on English-language learners in Grades kindergarten through 8, and were conducted between 1985 and 1997.

For the intervention studies, we selected studies that used experimental and quasi-experimental designs that clearly measured the effect instructional variables had on students' academic outcomes. We utilized recognized standards (Wortman, 1994) for determining which studies were eligible for analysis. The intervention studies had to meet the following criteria:

1. Some objective measure of student performance was used to evaluate effectiveness of the intervention.
2. The study included a comparison group.
3. Sufficient data were reported for computation of an effect size (e.g., a study that reported posttest means but no standard deviations would not qualify).
4. If the study did not use random assignment of students to treatment, then pretest data must have been reported. In addition, pretest differences had to be less than one half of a standard deviation unit on relevant academic measures (so appropriates statistical adjustments could be made).

Studies that analyzed classroom learning environments were included in the analysis if they were based on classroom observations that used either reliable measures or a standard interpretive framework in their analysis. We divided studies in this category into those that relied on low-inference instruments for documenting and analyzing classroom practices and those that relied strictly on qualitative interpretations.

The following terms were used in our electronic searches for relevant studies: (a) *English-language learner,* (b) *language-minority,* (c) *bilingual education,* (d) *limited-English proficiency,* and (e) *bilingual special education.* The following electronic databases were searched: ERIC, National Clearinghouse on Bilingual Education (NCBE), Dissertations Abstracts International, and National Information Center for Children and Youth with Disabilities (NICHCY).

In addition, we utilized a range of Internet searches for publications using PLWeb (using the limiters *bilingual, instruction,* and *disability*). The following web sites were searched for relevant studies: Urban Education Center for Research on Education, Diversity, and Excellence; Center for Research on the Education of Students Placed At Risk; and the Office of Bilingual Education and Minority Languages Affairs.

Manual scans of reference lists from selected research studies and other publications were also checked for additional studies. We also conducted a hand search of recent issues of 26 major relevant journals in education. Our final tally included 8 intervention studies[1] and 15 studies that analyzed classroom instruction.

Coding of Intervention and Descriptive Studies.   Our reading and coding of both the intervention and classroom observation and analysis studies proceeded in the following manner. One member of the research team read a study and entered the relevant data into a data display matrix (Miles & Huberman, 1994). This researcher reported key features of the study to other members of the team. Team members then discussed the study's methodology, findings, and interpretations, and unresolved issues and questions were noted. The data display matrix was revised repeatedly during this series of initial interactions among research team members.

These discussions also provided the framework for how we would engage as a research team in the process of posing interpretations of the

---

[1]The fact there were only eight studies in the intervention category was recently confirmed in a report by the National Academy of Sciences (August & Hakuta, 1997). Because of the small number of studies, we consider this an *exploratory meta-analysis.* One single-subject study (Rousseau, Tam, & Ramnarain, 1993) met our overarching purpose for the quantitative analysis (i.e., to find empirical support for beneficial instructional practices), but in not using a between-groups design was not amenable to meta-analysis techniques. Thus, we included this study in our pool of quantitative studies, but analyzed it separately from the exploratory meta-analysis.

data, which in some instances were in sharp contrast with the interpretations posed by the study's author(s). Alternative interpretations and explanations of research findings are an essential aspect of qualitative research, one we felt should be central to our synthesis.

Professional Work Groups

We conducted five professional work groups across the United States. Our major goal was to tap into participants' concepts about effective instructional practices for English-language learners. We reasoned that work group participants could identify what they saw as themes and problems in current practice, or problems with recommendations about best practice.

These professional work groups differed from focus groups in that (a) all participants were professionals (teachers, staff development specialists, administrators, researchers) rather than consumers, and (b) our interactions with them were significantly longer (i.e., a total of 5 to 7 hours per group) than traditional focus groups. These participants and their professional positions are presented in Table 2.1.

Although we initially proposed to conduct separate work groups with teachers and researchers, we decided that integrated heterogeneous groups were preferable. In preparatory meetings, teachers indicated they did not want to be "excluded" from the deliberations of researchers. These somewhat heterogeneous groups seemed to work well, and overall we felt they yielded more diverse discussions among participants. Our work group sessions were conducted in different geographic regions of the country because location was viewed as a variable that might influence how the groups responded.

We invited all researchers who had conducted research involving English-language learners supported by the Office of Special Education Pro-

TABLE 2.1
Educational Roles of Professional Work Groups

Participant Roles	Meeting Location				
	VA	CA	Wash., DC	FL	AZ
Researchers		3	6	1	3
Administrators	1				2
Teachers[a]	1	5	1	3	1
Psychologists	1			2	1
Staff Development	3		1	3	6
Total	6	8	8	9	13

[a]Teacher participants included bilingual, special, and general education teachers.

grams. Several of these researchers had also conducted research supported by the Office of Educational Research and Improvement. School district personnel represented State Education Agency directors, school administrators, program administrators, and teachers.

Some of the work group sessions were audiotaped. In-depth notes by members of the research team were recorded at all sessions. In some cases, participants' written notes were also collected.

We asked each of the groups to respond to three broad topics:

1. *Four propositions* that helped guide the synthesis (see Table 2.2). Each group provided feedback and suggestions for revising the propositions, including making major deletions or additions.
2. *Initial findings* from our literature search and analysis.
3. A request for *real-world examples* illustrating a key principle or dilemma.

Using Propositions to Facilitate Discussions and Guide the Synthesis. Our synthesis of the research began by developing a series of propositions about potentially useful instructional principles with English-language learners. We

TABLE 2.2
Propositions That Helped Guide the Synthesis and Promoted Discussion
in the Professional Work Groups

---

1. Merging English Development (ESL or ESOL) Instruction With Content Instruction
This proposition addressed the practice of merging English as a Second Language (ESL) instruction with content area instruction to develop students' knowledge of the more abstract language used in academic learning as opposed to conversational English. We proposed that some content areas (e.g., math, science) and some techniques are more promising than others.

---

2. Modulation of Cognitive and Language Demands
This proposition was that effective teachers intentionally balance cognitive demands when the goal is to encourage English-language expression (be it written or oral); in contrast, when the cognitive task is inherently demanding (e.g., a new science concept or complex literary content, such as character clues), teachers allow students to use their native language.

---

3. Transfer of Native Language Skills to English
One very important issue for effective instructional practice with English-language learners is the issue of transfer, or applying native-language skills to assist in learning a second language. This proposition was that explicit strategy instruction is required on how to access native-language abilities and skills when learning content in English.

---

4. Structures That Support Cooperative Learning
This proposition was that there are certain *specific techniques* in implementing cooperative learning that lead to superior student outcomes.

---

used these propositions, presented in Table 2.2, to help guide our reading and analysis of the extant literature, and as a discussion catalyst for the professional work groups.

These propositions were derived in large part from the first author's extensive observational research in classroom environments serving English-language learners (Gersten, 1996a, 1996b; Gersten & Jiménez, 1994; Gersten & Woodward, 1994). This type of "grounding" is a cornerstone of qualitative research (Pressley, 1996; Strauss & Corbin, 1994).

The first three propositions most clearly focus on instructional strategies specifically with English-language learners. The fourth, cooperative learning, is a strategy that can be used effectively with all students. However, because of its potential to facilitate student discourse, we felt it warranted a specific investigative focus with English-language learners.

We sent the propositions to the participants prior to meeting with them. During the meeting we asked them to respond to, or comment on, each proposition. We reminded participants that these were *propositions*, and we expected and hoped they would change based on their feedback.

Beginning with the second work group, we added an additional task— the delineation of a list of principles and practices deemed to be productive for English-language learners. We presented the list generated by Group 2 (California) to Group 3 (Miami) as a work-in-progress so that each group could continue to refine it. Figure 2.2 outlines the process.

The specific focus in each work group varied somewhat, primarily due to the unique composition of the members. For example, the San Diego work group, composed mostly of teachers and teacher supervisors, developed a rather practical set of practices. In contrast, the Washington, DC, work group was composed primarily of researchers and was more theoretical.

In facilitating these meetings, we tried to "probe beneath the surface" (Blaunstein, 1995; Vaughn, Schumm, & Sinagub, 1996), to seek areas of discomfort with current practice and current theories advocated by state agencies and national organizations such as the National Association for Bilingual Education (NABE). We wanted the groups to articulate what they saw as problems in current practice, and to provide the details of how teachers worked out solutions to vexing problems. To a large extent, this succeeded.

It is important to note that the professional work groups were conducted concurrently with our analysis of the published literature and issues raised in the literature helped frame questions we posed to the groups. Similarly, perspectives gained from the professional work group discussions guided and shaped our interpretations of issues and themes raised in the published literature.

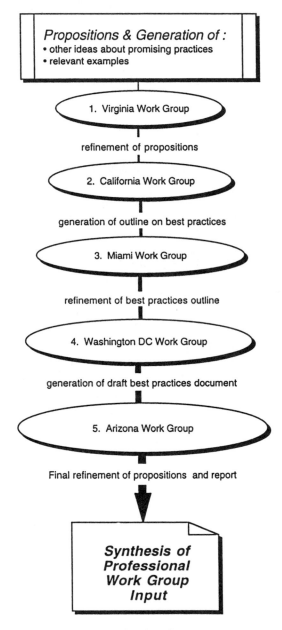

FIG. 2.2.   Professional work group process.

Overview of the Data Analysis Procedures
for the Multivocal Synthesis

A unique feature of the synthesis is the comparisons conducted within a data source (e.g., intervention studies), and across data sources (i.e., intervention studies, descriptive observation studies, and the professional work groups). The major techniques we used to generate and refine themes and issues, and to develop valid interpretations from the data sources are based on standard principles of qualitative research.

For a period of 18 months, we used an iterative process of forming tentative interpretations, rereading and reexamining study features, posing new interpretations, looking for corroboration in other data sources, and often, returning to the original study. In this process, we found the use of memos and minireports on critical articles useful. In the Appendix we present a list of other sources read that helped us understand and contextualize specific findings and data patterns.

We borrowed freely from the suggestions of major qualitative methodologists such as Wolcott (1994) and Miles and Huberman (1994). In particular, we followed guidelines for integrative syntheses using qualitative methods (Noblit & Hare, 1988; Ogawa & Malen, 1991). We also learned from a few qualitative integrative reviews of aspects of the published literature (Fitzgerald, 1995).

Each study's features were entered into a data display matrix that reflected in-depth analysis by the whole group. It included not only the surface features of the study (e.g., subject area, language of instruction, grade level, length of treatment, number of observations), but also our appraisal of the validity of the assertions made by the authors based on the design of the study and measures, and our sense of the major themes, issues or findings that emerged. The data display matrices were electronic and periodically updated based on subsequent review by research team members following procedures suggested by Miles and Huberman (1994).

Studies were clustered and reclustered electronically according to the questions that began to emerge. Occasionally, we added categories as themes emerged and changed. For example, we added the category *Language Used During Instruction by Teacher and by Students* after the first wave of coding. The coding process and use of data display matrices allowed us to examine the features of individual studies in relation to the entire body of data sources.

We intentionally did not stick to one clustering of studies at a time, but rather "roamed" through the data set to explore trends, issues, and hypotheses following practices recommended by Noblit and Hare (1988). As mentioned previously, this helped us juxtapose disparate data sources to test our interpretations.

As a research team, we constantly revisited our set of interpretations and inferences, and did additional reading and rereading to explore alternatives. We used the following set of questions to guide the development and prioritization of our interpretations:

1. Which interpretations and recommendations have the most promise, based on level of evidence and strength of research support?
2. What recurring issues pervade the set of studies and other data sources?
3. What are the most frequent conclusions/findings/interpretations (i.e., areas of convergence)?
4. What are areas for further inquiry/research efforts, as identified by researchers? As identified by experts in the field?

As we began to note patterns within and among the data sources, we started looking for what Miles and Huberman (1994) referred to as the "critical case" (i.e., the case that "proves" or solidifies a finding or interpretation) as well as "potential disconfirming cases." Serious analysis of potentially disconfirming cases can actually "teach us much about the assumptions that guide various studies" (Noblit & Hare, 1988, p. 62).

Another type of integration involved studies with findings that appeared to "refute" one another. Similarly, we noted several studies where the descriptions seemed quite rich and valid, but our interpretations diverged considerably from the authors' (e.g., Perez, 1994; Ruiz, 1995). These conflicts led to in-depth explorations of alternative hypotheses, as recommended by qualitative methodologists (e.g., Miles & Huberman, 1994).

We tried to understand how and why researchers may have viewed things differently. Noblit and Hare (1988) suggested that after examining and noting differences in interpretations, researchers may come to recognize the "descriptive account of the other as reasonable" (p. 54). We found this aspect of analysis and interpretation to be among the most difficult, yet rewarding, tasks of the synthesis.

Through this process, a study's features and characteristics often took on different weight than they did in earlier discussions. Sometimes, a new variable or construct emerged as important. Noblit and Hare (1988) discussed this as a process in which "what was hidden becomes apparent; we better understand what was studied by making clinical inferences from the studies" (p. 75).

For example, after critical examination of the first set of five studies and summarization of the work group findings, the following emerging issues continued to arise in our weekly discussions:

1. General student engagement versus student intellectual engagement.

2. Whether student "talk" (or discourse) was in a student's first or second language, and the value authors placed on each (i.e., some authors clearly favored native language discourse without providing a clear rationale).

3. Problems defining the presence of cross-culturally competent or culturally relevant teaching.

We followed Noblit and Hare's (1988) dictum that each study read and analyzed helps understand and interpret the next study, as well as to reanalyze what was previously read and discussed. They called this process *reciprocal translation.*

Initial analysis of the professional work group data involved writing up each of the sessions and compiling all the work group data into one draft summary. The data were sorted using a software program, Hyperqual, and across the work groups, data chunks were placed into six general categories: Instructional Strategies, Collaboration, Supports, Culture, Other Unresolved Issues, and Ideas for Dissemination and Communication. After this initial "chunking" of the data, key patterns for each of the categories were examined in depth to get a sense of areas of agreement and convergence on effective instructional practices among researchers, teachers, and administrators.

The ultimate goal—and the objective of the current level of analysis—was to use these data to confirm underlying themes from the literature. We used data from the groups to assess what was working and not working for teachers and their students and to specify areas for which curriculum seemed particularly weak. We listened for instances where teachers or researchers talked about past practices that were discontinued due to administrative fiat, but for which there was still the belief that they could be effective. Finally, we listened for areas where the groups seemed conflicted or confused.

Throughout this process, we continued to revise the documents we used to record our interpretations (e.g., the propositions, the data display matrices, the list of instructional approaches). In Table 2.3, we present an example of how a working proposition was refined to lead to a more meaningful and potentially useful one over the 2-year period.

To reiterate, the major principles used in the multivocal data analysis and interpretation were:

1. Significant input from practitioners for generation and refinement of interpretations (Ogawa & Malen, 1991).

2. *Triangulation* across various data sources (Patton, 1990).

TABLE 2.3
Evolution of a Working Proposition

The original proposition was: *It is effective to merge English as a second language instruction with content instruction to develop students' knowledge of the more abstract language used in academic learning as opposed to conversational English.*

This proposition was presented to each of the professional work groups. In no case did participants indicate that they knew more than the research team about which content area worked best. Thus, we feel, with some confidence, that there is neither empirical evidence nor even "craft knowledge" indicating which content area is best for merging ESOL instruction and content instruction.

However, in the conversations that ensued, other issues rapidly surfaced. In particular, the California professional work group engaged in a detailed discussion concerning how content area ESOL almost invariably fails to provide adequate time for language learning. In other words, participants felt that teachers often emphasize content acquisition over building English-language abilities. This point was also emphasized by several researchers doing observational research in California schools (Echevarria & Graves, 1998).

We then revisited and discussed the cycle of English-language development methodologies used in American schools in the past 20 years and assessed their strengths and weaknesses. To summarize briefly: Problems with the traditional approach that stressed syntax and grammar was that generalization and transfer were often limited (Tharp & Gallimore, 1988). Problems with the "natural language" approach used in the 1980s were that conversations between an adult and 32 students were rarely natural, natural language didn't easily fit the conditions and constraints of classrooms, and cognitive demands were too low. The California group concluded that a balance of the three might well be ideal, rather than the current move toward only using content area ESOL as the sole means of second-language acquisition.

This proposition was further refined in subsequent work groups. In one of these groups it was noted that this proposition linked nicely with the working Proposition 2 about intentional modification and modulation of cognitive demands depending on whether a teacher's goals were primarily cognitive in nature or language learning.

3. Use of *propositions* generated from immersion in environment and published research to help guide discussion and analysis.
4. *Constant-comparative* method of traversing data sources to develop and refine interpretations (Strauss & Corbin, 1994). Conscious juxtaposition of disparate studies (Gersten, Morvant, & Brengelman, 1995; Noblit & Hare, 1988).
5. Serious entertaining of rival hypotheses (Noblit & Hare, 1988).
6. Reciprocal translation (Noblit & Hare, 1988).

RESULTS AND DISCUSSION

We present the analysis and findings for each of the data sources in the following sections. In the first two sections, we present the set of studies included in the meta-analysis and then the set of studies describing and analyzing instruction in classrooms. In the third section, we present our findings and interpretations from the professional work groups. Following these separate sections, we present the integration of the findings across the three data sources.

Data Analysis Procedures for Exploratory Meta-Analysis

The basic index of effect size used in this exploratory meta-analysis was Glass' delta, defined as the difference between the treatment and comparison group means divided by the comparison group standard deviation (Glass, McGaw, & Smith, 1981). For studies that reported pre- and posttest scores, we calculated posttest effect sizes adjusting for pretest performance using procedures suggested by Wortman and Bryant (1985). In this adjustment, the effect size is calculated in the following way: The quantity of the pretest experimental mean minus the pretest comparison mean is divided by the comparison pretest standard deviation. This quantity is subtracted from the unadjusted posttest experimental mean minus the unadjusted posttest comparison mean divided by the comparison posttest standard deviation.

For the four studies that reported posttest data only, we subtracted the mean of the comparison group's unadjusted posttest score from the mean of the treatment group's unadjusted posttest score and divided by the comparison group's posttest standard deviation. In the one study that did not report means and standard deviations (i.e., Henderson & Landesman, 1995), effect sizes were estimated from the F ratio following the procedures described in Rosenthal (1994). In Table 2.4, we present each of the eight studies in the exploratory meta-analysis and how they were categorized for the purpose of the meta-analysis.

All the participants in the studies were English-language learners. In two studies, the participants also had learning disabilities. Six studies were conducted in elementary schools, two in middle schools. Five of the eight studies were conducted primarily in English, the students' second language (marked with a single asterisk in the reference section). Three studies were conducted primarily in Spanish, the students' native language (marked with a double asterisk in the references).

Six of the eight studies used a between-subjects group design with one experimental condition and one comparison condition. One study included three intervention conditions with no traditional comparison group (Waxman, de Felix, Martinez, Knight, & Padrón, 1994). One study utilized a counterbalanced, within-subjects design (Echevarria, 1995).

All but one study (i.e., Cardelle-Elawar, 1990) utilized multiple dependent measures. With multiple outcome measures, a single average effect size was computed so that each study included only one effect size per

TABLE 2.4
Features of Intervention Studies

Study	Number of Students	Grade	Duration of Treatment	Assignment of Students to Treatment	Primary Language of Instruction	Content Area	Type of Dependent Measure	Language of Dependent Measure
Cardelle-Elawar (1990)	80	6th	6 hours (over 3 weeks)	Intact groups	English	Math	Experimenter developed	English
Echevarria (1995)	5	2nd–3rd	25 lessons (over 1 year)	Counter-balanced	Spanish	Reading	Experimenter developed	Spanish
Goldenberg et al. (1992)	10	K	1 year	Random	Spanish	Reading	Experimenter developed	Spanish
Henderson & Landesman (1995)	102	7th–8th	2 years	Intact groups	English	Math	Experimenter developed	English
Klingner & Vaughn (1996)	26	7th–8th	27 days	Random	English	Reading	Experimenter developed *and* Standardized	English
Muñiz-Swicegood (1994)	95	3rd	6 weeks	Random	Spanish	Reading	Standardized	English and Spanish
Saunders et al. (1998)	36	5th	1 year	Intact groups	English	Reading, language arts, and math	Standardized	English
Waxman et al. (1994)	219	1st–5th	6 months	Intact groups	English	Reading and language arts	Standardized	English

aggregation. Cooper and Hedges (1994) underscored that this approach retains as much data as possible while minimizing any violations of the assumption that the data points used in the analyses are independent.

Findings of the Exploratory Meta-Analysis

In Table 2.5, we present effect size data for the eight studies for each dependent variable. When possible, the effect sizes in this table are adjusted for pretest differences. In total, 19 effect sizes were calculated, ranging from −.56 to 1.95. The mean effect size was .31, the median, .25. Overall, the median effect size indicated the interventions had a positive, but small impact on student learning.

The effect sizes were aggregated across the eight studies to consider important variables for analysis and interpretation. Because of the small number of effect sizes included in any particular meta-analytic comparison, we decided to base our interpretations on the median effect size in each analysis. The median typically is a more reflective measure of central tendencies in small sets of studies.

In examining the types of dependent measures used, the effect sizes are small for both standardized measures (median effect size = .17) and experimenter-developed measures (median effect size = .29). There is a good deal of variability, however, ranging, among experimenter-developed measures, from −.22 for *Instructional Conversations* (Echevarria, 1995) to 1.95 for tailored feedback in math (Cardelle-Elawar, 1990). Our results did confirm what other meta-analyses (Rosenshine & Meister, 1994; Swanson, in press) have found, namely that experimenter-developed measures typically result in higher effect sizes than standardized tests. The magnitudes of the difference between the two was much less than is typically reported in other meta-analyses, however.

Effect sizes are also relatively low when comparing across content areas. The median effect size for reading studies was .29 whereas the median for language was .62 and math was 1.07. It is important to note that although the test manuals indicate the language subtests are measures of "language," the focus is exclusively on written *conventions* of language (i.e., capitalization, use of commas, tense agreement, sense of what constitutes a paragraph) and they do not assess critical aspects of language learning, such as vocabulary and the correct use of syntax.

Withstanding these caveats, the pattern of findings (i.e., the effect size in math was higher than language, and language was higher than reading) is one that invariably is found in national and local assessments with English-language learners (Gersten & Woodward, 1995; Natriello, McDill, & Pallas, 1990). Latino students, for example, tend to perform very poorly on English-language reading tests, and much higher on mathematics tests.

TABLE 2.5
Individual Effect Sizes Used in the Aggregation of Effect Sizes

Study and Description of Experimental Intervention	Mean Effect Size for All Measures	Effect Size for Individual Measures	
Cardelle-Elawar, M. (1990). *Elementary School Journal, 91*(2), 165–175. Students were pretested on 20 math story problems and responded to eight statements that reflected difficult aspects of the problem. Teachers taught to give feedback to students over 3 weeks that addressed pretest errors and student statements. Errors classified into difficulties in (a) knowledge of English, (b) understanding how to produce math statements from prose, (c) determining procedural sequence for solving problems, and (d) accurate computation.	1.95	Math story problems	1.95
Echevarria, J. (1995). *Exceptional Children, 61*, 536–552. Teachers taught using *Instructional Conversations* format. Focus on themes and expanded discussions, inferential comprehension, and elaborated student dialogue.	–.22	Oral Retell Idea Units Literal Recall	.25 –.36 –.56
Goldenberg, C., Reese, L., & Gallimore, R. (1992). *American Journal of Education, 100*(4), 497–536. Teachers introduced a new *libro* (small book) every 3 weeks, reading story several times over a few days. Books sent home and parents told to enjoy them and not use them to teach decoding or word recognition. However, parents used the *libros* to teach decoding and accurate reading.	.79	Letters & Sounds Other Lit. Measures	.72 .86
Henderson, R. W., & Landesman, E. M. (1995). *Journal of Educational Research, 88*(5), 290–300. Combination of explicit teaching of concepts and thematic applications. Themes included fine arts, the ocean, crime, careers, the environment, world issues, sports, and the future. Students worked in cooperative groups of five, with assigned roles (e.g., manager, engineer, accountant). Each job had duties that required math skills. These aligned with scope and sequence in textbook.	.18	Math Concepts Math Computation	.22 .14
Klingner, J. K., & Vaughn, S. (1996). *Elementary School Journal, 96*(3), 275–294. All students taught Reciprocal Teaching in groups of six or seven; students learned six reading comprehension strategies. Content and discussions primarily in English, but students encouraged to	.12	Standardized Reading Reading Comp. Reading Strategies	–.20 .32 .25

use Spanish to understand concepts. Students in peer tutoring group then tutored Grade 6 students in reading comprehension strategies. Tutees eventually became the "teacher." Students in cooperative learning group worked in groups of three or four. Used Reciprocal Teaching framework, with students serving as facilitators.

Muñiz-Swicegood, M. (1994). *Bilingual Research Journal, 18*(1–2), 83–97.
Students read text (in Spanish) and were taught to generate questions at the end of each paragraph. Students led dialogues in small groups, asking questions of one another. Group size reduced until students worked in pairs. Finally, students generated questions on their own and discussed questions and answers with teacher individually.

English Reading	.39
Spanish Reading	.22

.31

Saunders, W., O'Brien, G., Lennon, D., & McLean, J. (1998). In R. Gersten & R. Jimenez (Eds.), *Effective strategies for teaching language minority students* (pp. 99–132). Belmont, CA: Wadsworth.
Three critical intervention components were included in literacy instruction:
1. Teaching background knowledge through vocabulary, relating concepts to personal experiences, and academic applications.
2. Reading and working with text, with a focus on building vocabulary, developing comprehension strategies, and writing about the content.
3. Developing a piece of writing that expresses story theme provided students with extended opportunities to write. Feedback from teachers and peers used to help students revise and improve written products.

English Reading	.47
English Language	1.03

.75

Waxman, H. C., de Felix, J. W., Martinez, A., Knight, S. L., & Padrón, Y. (1994). *Bilingual Research Journal, 18*(3–4), 1–22.
In *Effective Use of Time* condition (Stallings, 1980) small teacher groups learned to use time effectively and provide more explicit instruction. Instruction broken down into concrete behaviors with observations and coaching provided. Most interactions provided in large-group training sessions.

In *ESL in Content Area* condition (Chamot & O'Malley, 1989), the focus was on problem solving in science, math, and reading in English and Spanish. Some concepts explained in Spanish—this amount reduced over time. Teacher training sessions addressed cognitive strategies.

Reading	.27
Language	−.20

.04

Nature of the Intervention

Our data indicate that when the independent variable(s) in a study was well defined and/or implementation was carefully assessed or monitored, the median effect sizes were higher than they were when the nature of the instructional interventions were more loosely defined (.31 vs. .18). In three of the eight studies, students were randomly assigned to treatment conditions. When random assignment was used, the effect sizes were smaller than when quasi-experimental designs were used (.31 vs. .47). In other words, by and large, studies that employed higher quality comparison groups tended to have somewhat weaker effects. This matches findings from Swanson (in press), who investigated instructional interventions for students with learning disabilities.

A Potential Pattern Related to Instructional Framework

One of the most interesting patterns of findings, although clearly tentative, occurred when comparing instructional approaches that were largely based on extensions and adaptations of effective teaching research of the 1980s (Brophy & Good, 1986) with approaches that attempted to integrate aspects of social constructivism and cognitive psychology. The former focused squarely on the development of reading, writing, and math problem solving, and, to a high degree, relied on teacher-led instruction, with modeling, immediate individualized feedback, and opportunities for extended practice. Approaches focusing on constructivism and cognitive psychology are characterized by active student participation in the development of solutions to academic problems, student dialogue and opportunities for expanded academic discourse, and a focus on the development of metacognitive strategies as a critical component in solving academic problems.

The three intervention studies with the largest overall effect sizes, and the only studies with effect sizes that Cohen (1988) would describe as moderate to large in magnitude (i.e., Cardelle-Elawar, 1990; Goldenberg, Reese, & Gallimore, 1992; Saunders, O'Brien, Lennon, & McLean, 1998) used intervention components that were extensions of instructional approaches described by Brophy and Good (1986), Rosenshine (1986), and others in the 1980s. These studies extended these practices to be responsive to the unique learning needs of English-language learners. Saunders et al., for example, focused heavily on teaching students vocabulary critical to understanding academic content and provided extensive feedback (both teacher and peer) to students on their use of English to communicate their understanding.

In Cardelle-Elawar (1990), the sophisticated use of the recurrent finding from the effective teaching literature, that strategy feedback invariably leads to higher levels of math achievement, was replicated (Good &

Grouws, 1977; Hiebert & Wearne, 1993; Kelly, Gersten, & Carnine, 1990). In Cardelle-Elawar's application of this principle, strategic and extensive feedback was provided to teach students how to attack solving math story problems. These instructional strategies focused on accurate computation and comprehending subtle aspects of language that provided critical information in understanding the problem.

Goldenberg et al. (1992) designed an instructional approach for parents to use at home to help their child learn to read. As designed, the approach had a strong constructivist orientation. Parents were supposed to read small books with their child strictly for enjoyment. In fact, they were explicitly instructed *not* to use the books for teaching decoding or accurate word reading. The observations Goldenberg and his colleagues conducted in the homes, however, indicated that decoding and accurate word reading were precisely the components of instruction that parents focused on most.

The Saunders et al. (1998) instructional approach was actually an artful blending of approaches adapted from advances in cognitive psychology with approaches that extended instructional principles discussed in the effective teaching literature. Consistent and moderate to strong positive effects on standardized measures in both reading and language were found.

In contrast, the studies with the two lowest effect sizes (the *CALLA* approach in Waxman et al., 1994; Echevarria, 1995), which were zero and negative in magnitude, included two of the most frequently recommended approaches for teaching English-language learners, Cognitive Academic Language Learning Approach *(CALLA)* and *Instructional Conversations.*

Both of these instructional approaches devote extensive opportunities for students to engage in what are claimed to be challenging language development activities, which are assumed to lead to superior academic achievement outcomes. Both of the approaches also resulted in patterns of effect sizes that defy simple interpretations. In the Waxman et al. (1994) study, Chamot and O'Malley's complex cognitive strategies, in *CALLA,* led to negative effects in reading (.27), but positive effects in language (.20). In our review of *CALLA* instructional materials, this makes sense. The program has excellent English language development activities, but content covered appears to be less than would typically occur.

The Echevarria (1995) study presents a complex if somewhat puzzling pattern of findings. The *Instructional Conversations* intervention was intended to increase students' language use during reading instruction, and it was hoped it would have a positive impact on comprehension, knowledge of story structure, and the ability to elaborate on stories read and discussed. Ironically, the effect size was small and positive for story structure (.25), but negative both for the richness of the narrative retellings (–.36) and for literal comprehension of the story (–.56). It is interesting that traditional basal reading instruction led to larger and moderately strong effect sizes for literal comprehension and the richness of story retellings.

From our reading of the study, it appears that Echevarria (1995) omitted, or significantly reduced the importance of, the explicit instruction component of *Instructional Conversations*. This is increasingly viewed as an important component of *Instructional Conversations*, as articulated by Saunders and Goldenberg (1996). In Echevarria's study, teachers may have been well trained to engage in the aspects of *Instructional Conversations* that focus on enriching student discussions of narrative text, but in the absence of explicit instruction to help students comprehend critical information, their understanding and deep processing may have been restricted.

Single-Subject Study

To analyze the single-subject study (i.e., Rousseau, Tam, & Ramnarain, 1993), we interpreted the percentage of nonoverlapping data points (Mastropieri, Scruggs, Bakken, & Whedon, 1996) in each condition for two dependent measures: the percentage of words students read correctly, and the percentage of comprehension questions students answered correctly. We summarized the data across the five students who received each of the treatments in the alternating treatments' design.

The unequivocal finding was that the Vocabulary condition was more effective than the Listening Preview condition in improving students' reading. Students performed much higher on both percentage of words read correct (a mean of 95% vs. 50%) and questions answered correctly (97% vs. 68%). In the combined Vocabulary and Listening Preview condition students scored 100% on both dependent measures. At the individual student level, the Listening Preview condition seemed to be extremely ineffective for two of the five students, whereas the Vocabulary intervention was successful for every student. The results of this study support the previous conclusion about extensions of effective teaching showing effects superior to studies using more constructivist techniques.

Brief Overview of Research Describing Instructional Environments

Because our goal, in part, was to "provide a detailed portrait of the phenomenon [being studied] . . . the ways it appears to operate, and the patterns observed in natural settings" (Ogawa & Malen, 1991, p. 274), it was important to include in the synthesis those studies that described and analyzed actual practices observed during instruction.

Fifteen studies were reviewed in this category. These studies focused on observations of students during instruction, and attempted to assess engagement levels, student academic and oral language interactions, and to describe the types of instructional arrangements used to facilitate learning, such as independent seat work, and small- or whole-group instruction. Four studies in this category used low-inference observation systems with reported reliability coefficients to assess aspects of instruction, student language use, and engagement (Arreaga-Mayer & Perdomo-Rivera, 1996; Padrón, 1994; Ramírez, 1992; Tikunoff et al., 1991). The 11 other studies used a wide array of qualitative or interpretive methodologies to better understand dimensions of practice.

Information and analyses gleaned from these 15 studies were used to develop themes for the multivocal synthesis, interpret issues raised by the professional work groups, and provide useful context for understanding aspects of the intervention studies. Table 2.6 references each of these studies.

The predominant picture illustrated by this set of 15 studies was that oral language use by English-language learners in the classroom was consistently low. Students had limited opportunities to respond to challenging, higher order thinking questions, or engage in problem-solving activities that required complex thinking skills. This was equally true when the language of instruction and learning was English, or Spanish, the students' native language in this set of studies. Some of the qualitative studies did note, however, that somewhat more language use occurred when instruction was exclusively in the native language (Lopez-Reyna, 1996; Ruiz, 1995).

Instructional techniques most strongly criticized in descriptive research and observed frequently in these studies include the following practices: (a) asking questions that required one- or two-word answers, (b) the exclusive use of whole-class instruction with no opportunities for students to work in pairs or cooperative learning small groups (e.g., Arreaga-Mayer & Perdomo-Rivera, 1996; Lopez-Reyna, 1996; Padrón, 1994; Tuyay, Jennings, & Dixon, 1995), and (c) a stress on low cognitive tasks such as copying and on the strictly surface features of language learning, such as capitalization and literal comprehension.

Recommendations in these descriptive studies typically related to increasing student engagement levels or increasing opportunities for student learning. For example, Tikunoff et. al.'s (1991) study of exemplary programs identified that programs considered to be effective tended to utilize high percentages of small-group and individual instructional groupings. In fact, Tikunoff et al. did observe high rates of student engagement (96.8%) and task completion behaviors (78.2%).

The set of studies frequently addressed differences in the cultural backgrounds of teachers and students. Terms such as *cultural congruence, cultural mismatch, discourse patterns,* and *participation styles* were used to describe how aspects of culture enhance and/or hinder student learning.

TABLE 2.6
Studies Describing Instructional Environments

Low Inference (N = 4)

Arreaga-Mayer, C., & Perdomo-Rivera, C. (1996). Ecobehavioral analysis of instruction for at-risk language minority students. *Elementary School Journal, 96*(3), 245–258.

Padrón, Y. (1994). Comparing reading instruction in Hispanic/limited-English-proficient schools and other inner-city schools. *Bilingual Research Journal, 18*(1–2), 49–66.

Ramírez, D. J. (1992). Executive summary. *Bilingual Research Journal, 16*(1&2), 1–62.

Tikunoff, W., Ward, B., von Broekhuizen, D., Romero, M., Castaneda, L., Lucas, T., & Katz, A. (1991). *Final report: A descriptive study of significant features of exemplary special alternative instructional programs.* Los Alamitos, CA: The Southwest Regional Educational Laboratory.

High Inference (N = 11)

Echevarria, J., & McDonough, R. (1993). *Instructional Conversations in special education settings: Issues and accommodations.* Washington, DC: National Center for Research on Cultural Diversity and Second Language Learning.

Gersten, R. (1996a). Literacy instruction for language-minority students: The transition years. *Elementary School Journal, 96*(3), 227–244.

Gersten, R., & Jiménez, R. T. (1994). A delicate balance: Enhancing literature instruction for students of English as a second language. *The Reading Teacher, 47*(6), 438–449.

Goldenberg, C., & Patthey-Chavez, G. (1995). Discourse processes in *Instructional Conversations*: Interactions between teacher and transition readers. *Discourse Processes, 19,* 57–73.

Lee, O., & Fradd, S. H. (1996a). Interactional patterns of linguistically diverse students and teachers: Insights for promoting science learning. *Linguistics and Education: An International Research Journal, 8,* 269–297.

Lopez-Reyna, N. A. (1996). The importance of meaningful contexts in bilingual special education: Moving to whole language. *Learning Disabilities Research & Practice, 11*(2), 120–131.

Minicucci, C., Berman, P., McLaughlin, B., McLeod, B., Nelson, B., & Woodworth, K. (1995). School reform and student diversity. *Phi Delta Kappan, 77*(1), 77–80.

Perez, B. (1994). Spanish literacy development: A descriptive study of four bilingual whole-language classrooms. *Journal of Reading Behavior, 26*(1), 75–94.

Reyes, M. (1992). Challenging venerable assumptions: Literacy instruction for linguistically different students. *Harvard Educational Review, 62*(4), 427–446.

Ruiz, N. T. (1995). The social construction of ability and disability: II. Optimal and at-risk lessons in a bilingual special education classroom. *Journal of Learning Disabilities, 28*(8), 491–502.

Tuyay, S., Jennings, L., & Dixon, C. (1995). Classroom discourse and opportunities to learn: An ethnographic study of knowledge construction in a bilingual third-grade classroom. *Discourse Processes, 19,* 75–110.

M. Reyes (1992) and Delpit (1994) are among the most eloquent in their descriptions of how culture may influence the way students respond to and interpret teacher instructions and instructional styles.

The issue of culturally influenced classroom interactions has not been the subject of experimental research. However, much of the literature describing the academic difficulties of English-language learners contends that culturally influenced interactions are a major factor in how English-language learners perform or fail to perform in classrooms. Recently, this line of interpretive research has expanded to include students with disabilities (Lopez-Reyna, 1996; Ruiz, 1995).

Major Findings From the Professional Work Groups

The professional work groups reinforced that the current state of instructional practice with English-language learners was generally quite poor, and that the knowledge base in this area was extremely limited. Although much of the information provided by these groups was more conjectural than we expected, they did prove to be extremely helpful in sorting through a wide array of issues, themes, and paradoxes raised in the intervention and descriptive studies.

For example, the professional work groups helped us better understand the persistent confusion in research studies between English-language development and content acquisition. There was agreement among the groups that Cummins' (1984) distinction between "academic language" (Cummins, 1984), and conversational language in English was a useful way of (a) thinking about instruction, (b) actually teaching in the classroom, and (c) communicating with other teachers. There was some consistency among the professional work groups that limited curriculum materials were available for English-language development, especially in the area of merging English-language development with academic content instruction.

We categorized the content of the professional work group "findings" into a category of overarching themes and guidelines, and a category of specific practices that would enhance learning outcomes for English-language learners.

An overarching theme consistently expressed among the groups was that principles of effective teaching for native English-speaking students were effective for English-language learners. The groups also agreed, however, that these principles have to be *modulated* and shaped to meet the simultaneous goals of English-language development and content acquisition. In other words, effective teaching with English-language learners was more than just "good teaching," but the general research base on reading and math instruction serves as a solid foundation for effective teaching of English-language learners.

A key to this modulation seems to be that English-language learners needed frequent opportunities to use oral language in the classroom. This daily and active use of language should be structured to include both conversational language and academic discourse. Techniques such as classwide peer tutoring seem promising.

The groups consistently expressed support for the principle that English-language learners should be taught through the use of challenging material that does not get "watered down" merely because students are not fluent in the language of instruction. However, they frequently commented on how very difficult it is to implement this principle effectively.

Findings from the professional work groups also included the delineation of specific instructional strategies that can be used successfully with English-language learners. Each group (except the first) refined, clarified, and occasionally rejected statements of the earlier groups, and thus the list that emerged reflects to some extent, "group wisdom" about specific aspects of teaching.

Our research team integrated the strategies across the professional work groups, and identified intervention studies and descriptive studies that seemed to illustrate the principles. These specific instructional strategies and supporting studies are presented in Tables 2.7 and 2.8. The principles in Table 2.7 are grouped together because, in our view, they help elicit aspects of a framework one group referred to as "dynamic, structured teaching."

The principles in Table 2.8 are grouped together because they represent a major topic in the professional work groups, how to effectively merge English-language development with academic instruction. Many

TABLE 2.7
Professional Work Group Suggestions Regarding
the Importance of an Overall Teaching Framework

Quality Indicator

One key indicator of a quality program is that students are talking, speaking, writing, and reading. These academic behaviors should be observable in every subject area. The following specific points mentioned in the professional work groups further illustrate this feature.

Instructional Principles

1. Utilize teaching structures and formats that elicit frequent student responses and extended student responses. (Echevarria, 1995; Waxman et al., 1994)
2. Utilize more extensive modeling and think-alouds than is found in current practice. (Jiménez, 1997; Muñiz-Swicegood, 1994)
3. Include student and teacher talk, specifically "academic talk," rather than just sharing or conversational talk. Academic talk includes discussion of concepts. (Saunders et al., 1998)
4. Share learning strategies with students: for example, why the teacher has chosen to use a particular learning strategy, labeling the strategy, and telling students why the strategy might be helpful. *Instructional Conversations* can be a technique/strategy for this and for having students talk about important concepts in the content area. (Cardelle-Elawar, 1990; Chamot, Dale, Malley, & Spanos, 1993; Echevarria, 1995; Saunders et al., 1998)

TABLE 2.8
Professional Work Group Suggestions on Merging
English Language Development With Content Area Learning

---

1. English-language development programs must include development of oral and written proficiency, development of academic language (Cummins, 1994) and basic conversational English, and systematic proactive teaching of conventions and grammar. (Fashola et al., 1996; Saunders et al., 1998; Waxman et al., 1994)
2. In teaching English during English-language development, avoid oversimplifying instruction with contrived, intellectually insulting material. In subjects such as science, native-language instruction could be confusing to students, because teachers may not have adequate knowledge of technical vocabulary. (Lee & Fradd, 1996b)
3. Use visuals and extensive use of written language to reinforce verbal content when teaching in English. (Rousseau et al., 1993; Saunders et al., 1998)
4. Employ strategic use of synonyms. Teachers' word choice and sentence structure needs to be consistent and concise during second-language learning. Teachers also need to pay attention to their use of metaphors and similes and other highly culture-specific phrases and expressions. (Cardelle-Elawar, 1990; Gersten & Jiménez, 1994)
5. Focus on approximately five to eight core vocabulary words per lesson. Some strategies include: careful selection of words (evocative words to stimulate instruction, key words for understanding a story), linking words or concepts to words known in the native language, showing new words in print, using visuals (e.g., concept maps) to depict concepts or word meanings. (Rousseau et al., 1993; Saunders et al., 1998)
6. Published curriculum materials can serve as effective starting points in promoting English-language learning. However, it is very important to determine if published programs actually provide adequate focus and structure for teaching English. Goldenberg and Sullivan (1995) found counterexamples with published materials that did not promote English-language learning.
7. During the early phases of language learning, it is important that a teacher modulate and be sensitive in providing feedback and correction on language usage; however, during later stages of language learning, it is important that the teacher identify errors and provide specific feedback to students. (Cardelle-Elawar, 1990)
8. Native language use during English-language development must be strategic. At times, it might be useful to use both native language and English during instruction; however, teachers need to be aware of the risk of overreliance on simultaneous translations. (Klingner & Vaughn, 1996)

---

instructional problems have centered on attempts to merge content area learning with English-language development in so-called "sheltered" approaches. Therefore, we asked each group about specific technologies or principles that they found productive in the integration of language and content knowledge development.

We stress the lack of empirical support for any specific practice or approach, in part, because current literature in bilingual education and bilingual special education, suggests that much is known about effective instructional practices and strategies for English-language learners. Many studies claim to describe effective practice, yet virtually none of them provide the type of outcome data necessary to draw firm conclusions.

For example, in studies that describe effective practice, both Tikunoff et al. (1991) and Gersten (1996a, 1996b), focused on classrooms that had been "nominated" as exemplary bilingual classrooms. However, there is no empirical evidence that these classrooms enhance student learning, as August and Hakuta (1997) aptly noted. Yet it is equally true that observations of these classrooms using both reliable, low-inference measures (Tikunoff et al., 1991) and high-inference (qualitative) observations (Gersten, 1996a, 1996b; Gersten & Jiménez, 1994), indicated a very different type of bilingual instruction is possible than the instruction described by many researchers (e.g., Ramírez, 1992; Ruiz, 1995). In these exemplary classrooms, student language use is relatively high, as is student engagement in learning activities.

The point needs to be emphasized, however, that well-designed and executed experimental studies are needed to uncover the causal links between features of instruction and learning outcomes. Yet during the period from 1985 to 1996, we found a mere eight studies that utilized a valid experimental or quasi-experimental design to explore the impact of instructional strategies on student learning for English-language learners in Grades K–8. The fact there were so few studies was corroborated by the recent review by the NAS (August & Hakuta, 1997). Because there are only a handful of studies, and because the foci among the set of studies vary widely in terms of the age of the participants (kindergarten in Goldenberg et al., 1992, to middle school in Henderson & Landesman, 1995), intervention length (30 days in Cardelle-Elawar, 1990, to 1 year plus in Henderson & Landesman, 1995, and Saunders et al., 1998), and content focus (e.g., reading, math, language), we could not make any firm generalizations about specific instructional components that lead to enhanced outcomes.

We did note the failure of two widely recommended approaches for teaching English-language learners—*Instructional Conversations* and *CALLA*—to produce the positive outcomes in literacy that one might have anticipated. Both approaches did produce positive effects: *CALLA* produced a small effect on a standardized language measure, and *Instructional Conversations* resulted in a small effect in the structure of story retellings. However, the average effect size in these studies was zero *(CALLA)* or negative *(Instructional Conversations)*, and the approaches seemed particularly ineffective in the areas of reading and reading comprehension.

In the case of the *CALLA* in the Waxman et al. (1994) study, part of the problem may have been weak levels of implementation. A large number of teachers in several schools were given limited training in a complex, fundamentally different way of teaching. With *Instructional Conversations* (i.e., Echevarria, 1995), implementation was assessed and proven to be of high quality.

Part of the difficulty with *Instructional Conversations* may have been that the explicit instruction component that advocates of *Instructional Conversations* increasingly advocate (see Saunders & Goldenberg, 1996) may have been missing. Saunders and Goldenberg came to this conclusion after participating with a group of elementary school teachers in a study to describe and implement *Instructional Conversations.* Initially the teachers they worked with had extremely negative views of explicit instruction, characterizing it as "rigid and formulaic and in direct contrast to the kinds of teaching they wanted to do" (p. 144). The same teachers held very positive views of contructivist teaching practices such as *Instructional Conversations.*

In working with Saunders and Goldenberg (1996), these teachers were asked to develop curriculum and instruction consistent with the state's language arts framework, read and discuss numerous articles on direct instruction and *Instructional Conversations,* and implement *Instructional Conversations* with their English-language learners. Not only did the teachers develop a generally more positive view of explicit instruction over time, but:

> The relevance of direct teaching emerged consistently as the group worked to identify the elements of *Instructional Conversations* across the year. In fact, direct teaching was written in and detailed as an element of *Instructional Conversations* precisely because the group came to realize that *Instructional Conversations* often require direct teaching. (Saunders & Goldenberg, 1996, p. 152)

For example, one story about a country mouse and city mouse required an understanding of differences between the country and the city, of which many of their students were entirely oblivious. The teachers believed that using *Instructional Conversations* with their English-language learners without first teaching differences between the country and city would result in superficicial discussions and shallow levels of comprehension. As one teacher said "If we don't make sure that they have that deep understanding [of the story], then our later questions could just go over their heads" (Saunders & Goldenberg, 1996, p. 151).

This critical aspect of *Instructional Conversations* may have been deemphasized or completely missing in Echevarria's (1995) study. In any case, we were unable to ascertain that direct teaching was part of the *Instructional Conversations* approach. The outcome, too, is far from conclusive. The extremely small number of students ($N = 5$) and the erratic pattern of results, leading to negative effects in richness of retell and literal comprehension, but positive effects on structure of the retellings, leads us to cautiously observe that the study overall failed to indicate a clear pattern of either positive or negative effects.

THREE POSSIBLE THEMES OF EFFECTIVE INSTRUCTION

Our analysis of the published studies and our work with the professional work groups led to the emergence of three themes of effective instruction for English-language learners. We explore these themes in the remainder of the discussion section.

Approaches That Extend the Knowledge Base on Effective Teaching to English-Language Learners

The first theme is that instructional approaches that extended and modulated practices validated in the instructional research literature of the 1980s and earlier 1990s seemed to produce positive effects. These more traditional approaches ranged from classwide peer tutoring (Delaquadri, Greenwood, Whorton, Carta, & Hall, 1986) to Jane Stallings' (1980) system for increasing academic engagement through the increased use of active teaching behaviors (Waxman et al., 1994), to emphasizing accurate decoding and word recognition during reading (Goldenberg et al., 1992). The approaches tend to increase the amount of active engagement in academic learning and/or the quality and quantity of feedback provided to students during lessons.

In our analysis, then, most of the teaching techniques or structures that seemed to lead to enhanced learning outcomes were extensions of the "effective teaching" and peer-mediated instructional research base. These would also include the "tailoring of feedback" used by Cardelle-Elawar (1990) for mathematical problem solving and the provision of focused, explicit instruction on math concepts in Henderson and Landesman (1995).

Although techniques such as *Instructional Conversations* and *CALLA* did not produce the academic learning outcomes expected, these studies are clearly attempting to address an important problem articulated in the professional work groups and the descriptive studies—lack of student speech during instruction. Yet finding the link between increasing student language use and increasing student content area learning remains elusive, as the intervention studies document. We need to know a good deal more about which components of instruction in the intervention studies really contributed to student growth. This problem is most obviously represented in the complex, multifaceted interventions, such as Saunders et al. (1998).

Therefore, one issue or theme that begins to emerge from the exploratory meta-analysis, and which was reinforced in some of the professional work group discussions, was that the empirical research on instruction for native English speakers provides the beginnings of a foundation for improving instruction for English-language learners. However, we need to know much more about how to "tailor" or modulate techniques to better "fit" English-language learners.

In the area of literacy, the most interesting overall finding was that methods that increase academic engagement, such as the Stallings method of professional development (i.e., effective use of time, used in Waxman et al., 1994), with its focus on specific teaching techniques to increase academic engagement, tend to increase achievement. This finding was true for both first-language literacy (Echevarria, 1995) and second-language literacy (Waxman et al., 1994). The analysis also supports the use of certain specific techniques such as preteaching of critical vocabulary prior to student reading (Rousseau et al., 1993), building background knowledge (Saunders et al., 1998), and providing explicit instruction and guided practice in math problem solving (Cardelle-Elawar, 1990).

In general, abhorrence for more explicit methods of teaching, such as those used in Stallings' effective use of time (i.e., Waxman et al., 1994) or Rousseau et al. (1993) can be found in many of the qualitative observational studies, of Ruiz (1995), Lopez-Reyna (1996), and Perez (1994), all of which are of the interpretivist mode (Ferguson, Ferguson, & Taylor, 1992) of qualitative research. Yet these explicit methods seem to be effective if teachers use strategies based on research.

Insights Gained From Professional Work Groups. The sequential and focused nature of the professional work groups allowed us to explore predominantly semantic conflicts by consistently working to operationalize members' comments about instruction and seek clarification about what a given approach would look like when implemented. For example, an early professional work group advocated *structured dynamic teaching* as an optimal approach. It was unclear to us, and other members of the group, what this really meant. After a lengthy group discussion, there was consensus that it represented a set of instructional activities during which students have an opportunity to participate in fairly lengthy, complex verbal exchanges with their teachers and peers, and where teacher guidance is clear.

With subsequent groups we presented the term structured dynamic teaching and our understanding of its meaning, to that point, and asked the group for their reactions and feedback. In this way we tried to continuously move toward a degree of consensus with the groups about what the important principles and strategies were that constituted effective instruction.

The professional work groups consistently supported a method of instruction we came to label a *hybrid* model that we believe (a) captures the essence of structured dynamic teaching, (b) reflects extensions of validated instructional approaches of the Brophy–Good effective framework, and (c) incorporates principles of teaching emanating from advances in cognitive psychology. One researcher who participated in the discussion succinctly noted the group's tendency to want to synthesize: "Taking the 'best' of both direct instruction and communicatively-based classroom interaction seems to be the most powerful vehicle towards accomplishing effective and optimal instruction." The critical goal of this approach is the simultaneous development of language and academic proficiency.

Principles of Best Practice

We identified five specific instructional variables or principles from our multivocal analysis that, although supported by limited experimental evidence, suggest critical components for instruction: (a) vocabulary as a curricular anchor, (b) visuals to reinforce concepts and vocabulary, (c) cooperative learning and peer tutoring strategies, (d) strategic use of the native language, and (e) modulation of cognitive and language demands. We briefly describe each of these components in this section.

   Building and Using Vocabulary as a Curricular Anchor.   A clear area of consensus among the professional work groups was that vocabulary learning should play a major role in successful programs for English-language learners. The number of new vocabulary terms introduced at any one time should be limited. The standard method of presenting up to 20 or more new vocabulary words that students are expected to learn at a given time is not an effective way to help English-language learners develop vocabulary. Teachers in our professional work groups recommended using lists of seven or fewer words that students would work on over relatively long periods of time. Criteria for selecting words should be considered carefully, so that words are selected that convey key concepts, are of high utility, are relevant to the bulk of the content being learned, and have meaning in the lives of students.

   Restricting the number of words students are expected to learn will help them learn word meanings at a deep level of understanding, an important principle of sustained vocabulary growth. The research of Nagy (1988) and Beck and McKeown (1985) were cited as important resources for helping teachers understand how to teach vocabulary to English-language learners. The professional work groups felt that many teachers needed guidance in selecting vocabulary words for instruction, as districts and conventional texts rarely provide the type of guidance needed.

   One professional work group member provided insights into the methods she used to select and teach vocabulary that were strongly supported by other members of the group. She noted how she chose words for the class to analyze in depth that represented complex ideas—adjectives like *anxious, generous,* and *suspicious,* and nouns like *memory*—words that English-language learners are likely to need help with and words that were linked to the story in meaningful and rich ways. Students had to read the story and look for evidence that certain events or descriptions that were connected to vocabulary instruction pertained to a particular character or incident.

Two of the intervention studies had components that dealt specifically with vocabulary development. Vocabulary learning was the explicit focus of the study by Rousseau et al. (1993). Teachers used a variety of methods to teach word meanings to students including visually presenting the words, defining them, and using gestures and other visual techniques (e.g., pictures). It is interesting that both of the outcome measures (i.e., accurate reading of all the words in the story and comprehension of the story) showed dramatic improvement over a method in which teachers previewed the entire story with students by reading it to them.

In Saunders et al. (1998) as well, critical vocabulary were identified prior to story reading. A range of approaches was used to help students develop a deep understanding of these words. Students were also guided to link critical vocabulary to relevant experiences in their lives.

In both studies, the time-tested practice of introducing new vocabulary prior to reading a new story was used successfully. Echevarria (1998) described how this type of vocabulary instruction can be used with English-language learners:

> One form of vocabulary development includes short, explicit segments of a class time in which the teacher directly teaches key vocabulary. These five minute segments would consist of the teacher saying the vocabulary word, writing it on the board, asking students to say it and write it and defining the term with pictures, demonstrations, and examples familiar to students. (p. 220)

Use of Visuals to Reinforce Concepts and Vocabulary.   Two of the professional work group discussions focused particularly on the importance of using visuals during instruction. These visuals might range from complex semantic visuals (E. Reyes & Bos, 1998), to visuals based on text structures, such as story maps and compare–contrast "think sheets." Visuals are especially successful in supporting English-language development because they are such a good way to help students visualize the abstractions of language.

Two of the intervention studies and several of the observational studies noted that the use of visuals during instruction increased learning. Rousseau et al. (1993) used visuals for teaching vocabulary (i.e., words written on the board and the use of pictures), and Saunders et al. (1998) incorporated the systematic use of visuals for teaching reading and language arts. Visuals also typically play a large role in *CALLA*, although Waxman et al. (1994) did not specifically indicate how visual organizers were used in their study.

The double demands of learning *content* and a *second language* are significant; the difficulty should not be underestimated. Because the spoken word is fleeting, visual aids such as graphic organizers, concept and story maps, and word banks give students a concrete system to process, reflect on, and integrate information.

Implementation of even simple techniques such as writing key words on the board or a flip chart while discussing them verbally can support meaningful English-language development and comprehension. The professional work groups concurred that even the simple integration of visuals is drastically underutilized, and even when used, methods are typically inconsistent or superficial and do not support students' deep processing and thinking.

Further research on how to use visuals to enhance English-language learning is needed. Also, because of the consistent, strong support for the use of visuals expressed in the professional work groups, we believe educators involved in professional and curriculum development, or curriculum selection, should seriously consider this issue, as well.

Use of Cooperative Learning and Peer Tutoring Strategies.   We believe cooperative learning and peer tutoring strategies have the potential to effectively and rapidly increase English-language development, particularly decontextualized language concepts with high degrees of cognitive challenge. One of our original propositions was that certain *specific techniques* in cooperative learning lead to superior student outcomes. In the professional work groups, the need for highly structured cooperative learning groups was often stressed.

Two of the intervention studies used cooperative learning or peer tutoring strategies as critical pieces of their interventions. Klingner and Vaughn (1996) tested whether cooperative learning or peer tutoring was more effective in promoting comprehension with English-language learners with learning disabilities. Although there was some evidence that peer tutoring was the most effective, both of the interventions led to improved learning outcomes. In the intervention used by Muñiz-Swicegood (1994), students worked in successively smaller cooperative groups (until they were finally working in pairs) to learn how to generate and answer questions about what they were reading. Students in this intervention did better on measures of reading comprehension than students who were taught using basal reading approaches.

Strategic Use of the Native Language.   Strategic use of students' native language can help ensure that the development of higher order thinking skills receives adequate curriculum focus. The professional work groups agreed with the general concept that a viable way to achieve this objective is for teachers to use levels of English that students are very fluent with, while simultaneously using more extensive native language to introduce complex concepts and provide students with opportunities to concentrate on understanding challenging context. The professional work groups, however, failed to reach consensus on *how* students' use of their native language could be used strategically for this purpose. This issue was discussed in many of the descriptive studies reviewed (e.g., Gersten, 1996b; Lopez-Reyna, 1996; Ramírez, 1992; Tikunoff et al., 1991).

The strategic use of native language is a controversial issue. Most researchers from the professional work groups cautioned against using dual translations frequently, that is, the extensive use of both the student's native language and second language during instruction. However, one researcher advocated a counterposition, suggesting that written words be provided in both English and Spanish. Many researchers from the observational studies (Gersten & Jiménez, 1994; Lopez-Reyna, 1996; Miniccuci et al., 1995; Tikunoff et al., 1991) proposed using a student's native language as an instructional approach. Yet, the observational findings of Ramírez (1992) indicate that neither more nor less higher order discussion occurred when instruction was in the native language or in English. Thus, our conclusion is that it is beneficial to use students' native language, but it should be done in a strategic fashion, and in general avoid the tendency to provide dual translations.

Two of the intervention studies incorporated the strategic use of native language to help with learning difficulties in the second language. In the Cardelle-Elawar (1990) study, very focused attention was devoted to exploring the meaning of the language used in the math story problems and how students could use a variety of strategies, including their knowledge of Spanish, to help them understand and figure out what the problem in English was asking them to do. This type of intense instruction to determine what specifically is being requested in a problem-solving situation led to very large effects compared to broader instructional approaches. In Klingner and Vaughn (1996), students were encouraged to use their native language strategically to solve specific problems they were encountering in their cooperative learning and peer tutoring groups.

Modulation of Cognitive and Language Demands.   This last instructional strategy carries a different weight of importance, and we view it as the most speculative among those we have proposed. One of the propositions shared with each of the professional work groups was that during English-language content instruction, effective teachers intentionally vary the cognitive and language demands. Typically, there is an inverse relationship between the two. When cognitive demands are high, language expectations are simplified, and teachers, for example, may accept brief or truncated responses in English. In another part of the lesson, cognitive demands are intentionally reduced so that students can more comfortably experiment with extended English-language use.

This proposition was supported in each of the five professional work groups and appears consonant with contemporary theories of second-language acquisition (e.g., August & Hakuta, 1997). Obviously, empirical support for this proposition is needed, although designing a suitable research study around such a subtle principle will be difficult.

Confusion, Tension, and Assumptions About Oral Language Use

The second major theme that emerged from the multivocal synthesis involves concerns and confusions about the role of oral language in academic instruction. All the studies describing classroom learning environments (both low and high inference) noted rare student oral use in the classroom. This issue was stressed both in studies of English-language development and in studies of native-language content instruction.

In the following section, we argue that both extended discourse about academic topics and briefer responses to specific questions about content are cornerstones of academic growth for English-language learners. We believe this is a valid interpretation, based on trends in the research studies and our interactions with the professional work groups.

Our review of the data sources suggests that discussions of potentially effective instructional practices for English-language learners overemphasize natural language use and do not clearly articulate the important distinctions involved when language use is the major goal and when cognitive or academic growth is paramount. To understand this confusion, we review some of the observational research.

Relevant Findings From Research. Ramírez (1992) described typical classrooms as passive learning environments for students. Teachers do the majority of talking and student contributions are in response to teacher questions. Other studies support this pattern (e.g., Arreaga-Mayer & Perdomo-Rivera, 1996; Lopez-Reyna, 1996; Padrón, 1994).

Specifically, Ramírez (1992) reported that student language use and opportunities to engage in cognitively challenging tasks were extremely low. In his observations, the mean proportion of student-initiated language use ranged from .3% to 10.1% of the total time in which students were responding. This low rate of student-initiated responses was corroborated in the high-inference, qualitative observational studies reviewed (Lopez-Reyna, 1996; Perez, 1994; Ruiz, 1995), where student discourse was typically limited to one- or two-word utterances.

Perhaps most astounding is the low level of student oral language use in English-language development classes noted by Arreaga-Mayer and Perdomo-Rivera (1996). They found that only 21% of the time did observed students use written or oral language. In other words, students rarely spoke during classes in which the explicit purpose was English-language development. A tension that emerges from the literature is the implicit assumption of most researchers that increased language use (be it in the students' native language or in English) should be a high-priority goal because it will lead to increased learning. For example, as a rationale for *Instructional Conversations,* Echevarria (1995) wrote that "language is a primary vehicle for intellectual development" (p. 537), and implicit in the philosophy of *Instructional Conversations* is the assumption that increased oral language use by students during reading instruction will improve comprehension.

Yet, *Instructional Conversations* produced negative results on two crucial measures of reading comprehension when contrasted with the type of instruction typical in a more traditional basal reading lesson. In trying to account for the findings, Echevarria (1995) observed that "While it was speculated that the enriched language opportunities that *Instructional Conversations* provide would enhance the students' narrative construction [i.e., elements of story grammar], it is possible that what takes place in the classroom does not contribute to narrative development [i.e., richness of idea units]" (p. 550). She continued by noting that "the discourse rules of the basal treatments tended to elicit more *who, what, where* types of questions . . . while the *Instructional Conversations* discourse attempted to evoke opinion and more complex language . . ." (p. 550). An interpretation of the results is that the basal intervention tended to create more opportunities for analytic discussions.

In other words, increased use of sophisticated language constructions in school may or may not be related to increased academic and cognitive growth. We simply do not have an empirical knowledge base to inform us as to which of the following forms of student engagement provides greater overall benefit for English-language learners: (a) generous opportunities for oral language interactions, (b) reading, (c) writing, (d) listening, (e) content area activities such as those involved in math or science, or (f) the optimal combination of any of the aforementioned.

In the professional work groups, we noted that members often seemed confused by—or vacillated between—two objectives: (a) language learning, in either the native or second language, and (b) content area learning. We do not wish to imply that oral language use in school is an unimportant objective, or that increased use of oral language is inversely related to academic growth in content areas. Rather, we emphasize that these are two distinct goals, and researchers and educators need to be clear about the distinction. Furthermore, findings in some of the descriptive research (Jiménez & Gersten, in press; Lee & Fradd, 1996a; Ruiz, 1995) indicate that increased student dialogue in class can lead to discussions with minimal cognitive challenge and minimal academic content.

Problems in implementation of the intervention approaches that require extensive natural language and authentic dialogue, such as *CALLA* and *Instructional Conversations,* may help explain why they failed to lead to effects in reading. The implementation problems that plagued the large-scale research study by Waxman et al. (1994), for example, were consistently corroborated in the professional work groups. Participants talked about weak, inconsistent, and sometimes incoherent implementation of techniques such as semantic mapping, cooperative learning, and story mapping. One member of the California work group noted that techniques such as semantic mapping and teachers' thinking aloud "all have been used noneffectively in recent years." Extensive discussion in three of the professional work groups addressed weak implementation of cognitively based approaches and limited curricula or manuals available for teacher use.

Likewise, in response to complaints about weak implementation of cooperative learning, one teacher-researcher indicated that by using highly structured groups, she virtually never had the kinds of problems that others discussed as chronic and endemic. In other words, by using established principles of effective instruction such as clear expectations, frequent monitoring, and immediate feedback to students, this teacher was able to overcome seemingly intractable problems in using an innovative practice to increase language use. We believe one reason the highly structured *Classwide Peer Tutoring* [CWPT] method (Klingner & Vaughn, 1996) surpassed the more loosely structured *Cooperative Learning* method was because student roles and task demands were more clearly explained and monitored in the former than in the latter.

Merging English-Language Development With Content Area Learning

The third major theme of the multivocal synthesis that emerged primarily in the professional work groups was encouragement for the increased use of approaches such as *sheltered content area instruction.* We think there were many reasons for this, an important one being that in some districts there are so many language groups that native-language instruction for all or even a majority of English-language learners is not always feasible. A second reason was the trend toward providing students with specific language assistance in Grades 3–6, a time when they leave classes that provide predominantly native-language instruction and move into classrooms that are conducted primarily in English.

We want to clarify that we are not advocating for the exclusive use of instructional approaches that merge English-language development with content area learning (i.e., in opposition to strategic use of native-language instruction). Rather, we advocate for the strategic use of these approaches and hope to uncover some of the current problems, as well as identify specific strategies teachers can use to promote English-language development during academic instruction. Because of the relative novelty of this approach in American schools, discussions in the professional work groups on this topic were often very rich.

We invested a good deal of energy in trying to understand the histories of the various approaches to English-language development (e.g., formal/syntactic, natural language, and sheltered content area), in part because during the first two professional work groups, participants admitted that "definitions of English as a Second Language [ESL] and sheltered instruction are unclear."

The rationale for Content Area English for Students of Other Languages (ESOL) instruction is that students can learn English while learning academic content, and that this type of learning will build academic language (Cummins, 1994, as cited in Echevarria & Graves, 1998) because students will be learning the abstract language of scientific or mathematical or literary discourse. Furthermore, Content Area ESOL is better suited to classrooms than natural language because classrooms are, by and large, places of learning.

However, the professional work groups were consistent in indicating that:

- Content area instruction often leads to sacrifices in learning English.
- Few districts have a curriculum program or approach that promotes students' proper use of the English language.

In discussing concerns about instruction for English-language learners, professional work group members frequently noted how Content Area ESOL almost invariably fails, in the words of one group member, to provide "adequate time for English-language learning." In other words, participants felt that teachers often emphasize content acquisition over building English-language abilities.

In fact "the dilution of ESOL instruction" under the term sheltered content area instruction, and the overall neglect of ESL/ESOL instruction, was a recurrent refrain in the California professional work group. One teacher noted "It's important to use content as a basis for language development . . . [however] there is a risk during content instruction of neglecting language development" (California professional work group, October

1996). Another educator from the district bilingual education office noted that "It's important for teachers to be clear about objectives and goals . . . yet an explicit statement of goals does not exist [in district or state curricula materials]." Some members suggested a set of curriculum goals that include "specific language concepts," noting how so many teachers merely "hope that language occurs" during content area lessons.

One researcher in the group noted how the need for explicit teaching in ESL/English-language development classes "should never be underestimated. . . ." He stressed "the importance of promoting language while promoting thought," voicing the concern that students need experiences in "thinking through" and then verbalizing their ideas in content areas (e.g., science, mathematics, history), in English. Attempts to merge content area instruction with ESOL instruction, though well intended and conceptually sound, are rarely well implemented.

The major problem highlighted in Content Area ESOL was how time for language learning often is truncated or omitted. These concerns are reflected in the data from observational studies by Ramírez (1992) and Arreaga-Mayer and Perdomo-Rivera (1996). Arreaga-Mayer and Perdomo-Rivera noted how the general education and the ESL settings failed to provide instruction to facilitate second-language acquisition. Similarly, Ramírez concluded that in all the varying models of bilingual education, teachers did not promote language development effectively. He stated that "consistently, across grade levels within and between the three instructional programs, students are limited in their opportunities to produce language and in their opportunities to produce more complex language" (p. 9).

This pattern also supports a major finding in our study of issues confronting teachers in the upper elementary grades (Gersten, 1996a, 1996b), and also found in observational research by M. Reyes (1992). We see inadequate time for English-language development as a major problem in current practice.

Several reasons for this problem were identified in the professional work groups. First and foremost was teachers' concern for increased accountability for content learning (as measured by test results), as opposed to the more amorphous goals of English-language acquisition, and a relative de-emphasis in accountability for students' language development needs. Participants in the professional work groups discussed in detail how, based on their observations and experiences in classrooms, the tendency to cover all the content in science or social studies or mathematics almost invariably precluded allowing adequate time for English-language development, especially more formal academic English.

Other comments in the professional work groups focused on failure to systematically impart to students skills in speaking and writing standard English, even in middle school. Whereas many members felt that the policy of never correcting students for grammatical or pronunciation problems during English-language instruction made sense during the early years of English-language development, there was general consensus that students need feedback on their formal English usage as they progress in school, and teachers lack any kind of coherent system for providing it. One professional work group suggested that in the early phases of language learning, teachers should modulate the feedback they provide students, and be sensitive to the problems inherent in correcting every grammar mistake students make; however, during later stages, one member reflected the feeling in the group by noting the "importance of identifying errors and providing specific feedback."

A recent research study by Fashola, Drum, Mayer, and Kang (1996) may provide some direction in this area. Fashola and colleagues noted how errors made by Latino students in English are usually predictable, and how these predictable errors could become the basis of *proactive curricula:* "Rather than simply marking a predicted error as incorrect, the teacher could explicitly point out that the phonological or orthographic rule in English is different from the one in Spanish" (p. 840). After reviewing these issues with professional work groups, and reading about problems with Content Area ESOL in sources as diverse as *The New York Times* and the *Harvard Educational Review* (M. Reyes, 1992), we concluded that an effective English-language development program should include a component devoted to helping students learn how to use the second language according to established conventions of grammar and syntax.

We encourage researchers and educators to consider language learning and content area learning as distinct educational goals, rather than assuming that increased use of oral language in school will automatically lead to an increase in academic learning and the development of higher order thinking skills. Artful and skillful blending of genuine dialogue, about literature or science, and cognitive challenge is an admirable, but perhaps only occasionally realized goal. On the other hand, providing some time each day when English-language learners have opportunities to work on all aspects of English-language development, and providing academically challenging content instruction (be it in native language or English), are likely to be more easily achievable, especially if teachers take time to make goals clear and precise.

In short, instruction for English-language learners should work to blend oral language engagement and intellectual (or cognitive) engagement. These distinctions are also important for those doing instructional research in classroom settings. For example, Saunders and colleagues (1998) described instructional units characterized by high frequency of oral language engagement, but also noted that they "view the intellectual substance of the literature units as the driving force in our program" (p. 29).

SUMMARY AND CONCLUSIONS

1. *We found a total of eight studies* that used valid experimental and quasi-experimental designs to investigate the effects of instructional variables on student learning outcomes with English-language learners. Most of these studies were published in 1994 or later. This lack of an empirical knowledge base should be taken into account when districts or schools are mandated to implement a specific procedure based on "expert knowledge." The knowledge in this area is limited. There are many theories, but very little empirical data.

2. *Within the eight empirical studies,* no clear pattern emerged regarding effective instructional practices with English-language learners. We suggested that there might be a trend supporting instructional approaches that extend effective teaching techniques of the 1980s (i.e., in the more classic view of the findings by Stallings, 1980, and Good & Grouws, 1977).

3. *Studies were often unclear regarding* (a) how interventions were implemented, (b) the level of implementation that was achieved, (c) the language of instruction, and (d) many other "context" variables that would have given a rich picture to intervention research. We remain convinced that the field must better define interventions, and the critical context variables that give them shape and definition.

4. *Distinguishing between language growth and academic growth* is difficult and needs to be more clearly studied and accounted for. There does seem to be an implicit assumption that suggests that increased language use in the classroom leads to increased academic growth. The studies did not support this assumption. If anything, there was a small amount of evidence supporting an inverse relationship between language use and academic growth. The issue is a persistent source of confusion in understanding and interpreting studies, and in instructional programs.

5. *The English-language development* aspect of bilingual education and bilingual special education is cited as a major problem, especially for special education students who may be excluded because they cannot keep up with the pace.

6. *We concluded that a good English-language development program* should include three components. First, one component would focus on the development of proficiency and fluency in English. Both social communication and academic communication of concepts and knowledge that students have previously learned would be addressed. A second component would address the more formal, grammatical aspects of English use. A third component would focus on learning new academic content. In this component, content acquisition would be merged with English acquisition. In contrast to

the first component, the content-learning demands would be high and the language demands lower. It is important to stress that special education students, many of whom have language-related disabilities, need this type of instruction, and should be in programs that include all three aspects. Lack of quality published curricula (as opposed to materials from the military and foreign service) in this area is a major problem.

7. *Regarding future research,* the key is well-designed and valid studies. Federal support has not been strong in this area. Many researchers eschew this population because of the intricacies of measurement. There is no question that there is a limited understanding of the difficulty and complexity of this type of research. The U.S. Department of Education should be made aware of the lack of research and of the difficulties of doing good research in this area.

8. *The work groups with educational professionals* resulted in a set of principles and practices that, we believe, can be very useful in beginning to define best practice. These principles and practices, in particular, highlighted the merger of English-language development instruction with content area learning, which is increasingly used in American schools. For the most part, these principles were consonant with findings from the empirical exploratory meta-analysis. Most assuredly, they should be part of a research agenda.

ACKNOWLEDGMENTS

This chapter was supported by Grant HO23E50013 from the U.S. Department of Education, Office of Special Education Programs. Support was also provided by National Association of State Directors of Special Education. The views expressed, however, represent the authors' and do not necessary reflect the views of the U.S. Department of Education or the National Association of State Directors of Special Education.

We would like to thank the following reviewers who provided insightful and thought-provoking commentary on an earlier version of the manuscript: Robert Rueda, Rose-Marie Weber, Harris Cooper, and Bernice Wong. The authors also would like to thank Ellen Schiller of the U.S. Department of Education for her ongoing support.

We would also like to thank our colleagues Sylvia Smith, Mark Harniss, Janet Otterstedt, and Batya Elbaum, who provided extremely helpful feedback on previous versions of this chapter. Finally, we are extremely grateful to the contributions of Susan Marks, who played a large role in many important facets of this synthesis.

List of Other Sources Read

Citation	Source Type
August, D., & Hakuta, K. (Eds.). (1997). *Improving schooling for language-minority children*. Washington, DC: National Academy Press.	Research synthesis and research agenda.
Collier, V. P. (1989). Age and rate of acquisition of second language for academic purposes. *TESOL Quarterly, 21,* 617–641.	Study of language of instruction.
Chamot, A. U., Dale, M., O'Malley, J. M., & Spanos, G. A. (1992). Learning and problem solving strategies of ESL students. *Bilingual Research Journal, 16*(3–4), 1–34.	Study of problem solving strategies.
Delpit, L. (1994). *Other people's children.* New York: Basic Books.	Book on multiculturalism and cultural issues.
Fashola, O. S., Drum, P. A., Mayer, R. E., & Kang, S. (1996). A cognitive theory of orthographic translations: Predictable errors in how Spanish-speaking children spell English words. *American Educational Research Journal, 33*(4), 825–844.	Study of student learning processes.
Fitzgerald, J. (1995). English-as-a-second-language learners' cognitive reading processes: A review of research in the United States. *Review of Educational Research, 65*(2), 145–190.	Research review.
Garcia, E. (1992). Analysis of literacy enhancement for middle school Hispanic students through curriculum integration. *The Journal of Educational Issues of Language Minority Students, 10,* 131–145.	Case study of students learning through use of integrated curriculum.
Gersten, R., & Woodward, J. (1995). A longitudinal study of transitional and immersion bilingual education programs in one district. *Elementary School Journal, 95*(3), 223–239.	Longitudinal study of transitional programs.
Goldenberg, C., & Sullivan, A. (1995). Making change happen in a language-minority school: A search for coherence. Paper presented at the Annual Meeting of the American Educational Research Association, San Francisco, CA.	Case study of change in one school's primary curriculum.
Gumperz, J. J., & Field, M. (1995). Children's discourse and inferential practices in cooperative learning. *Discourse Processes, 19,* 133–147.	Study of student learning processes.
Jimenez, R. T., Garcia, G. E., & Pearson, P. D. (1995). Three children, two languages, and strategic reading: Case studies in bilingual/monolingual reading. *American Educational Research Journal, 32*(1), 31–61.	Study of student learning processes.
Kayser, H. (1987). A study of three Mexican American children labeled language-disordered. *NABE Journal,* Fall.	Case study of students with language disorders.
Kiernan, B., & Swisher, L. (1990). The initial learning of novel English words: Two single-subject experiments with minority-language children. *Journal of Speech and Hearing Research, 33,* 707–716.	Study examining student learning processes.
Leon, R. E. (1994). The effects of the presence of extraneous information in mathematical word problems on the performance of Hispanic learning disabled students. *New York State Association for Bilingual Education, 9,* 15–26.	Study examining student learning processes.

(Continued)

Citation	Source Type
Medina, M., & de la Garza, J. V. (1989, Winter). Initial language proficiency and bilingual reading achievement in a transitional bilingual educational program. *NABE Journal,* 113–125.	Descriptive study of relationship between language proficiency and reading.
Morgan, J. (1996). Early phonological awareness training for at-risk children in junior kindergarten. Paper presented at the National Reading Conference. Charleston, SC	Case study of effects of phonemic awareness program.
Nanez, J. E., & Padilla, R. V. (1995). Bilingualism and processing of elementary cognitive tasks by Chicano adolescents. *The Bilingual Research Journal, 19*(2), 249–260.	Study of student learning processes.
Padrón, Y. (1992). The effect of strategy instruction on bilingual students' cognitive strategy use in reading. *Bilingual Research Journal, 16*(3–4), 35–51.	Describes student learning processes.
Pease-Alvarez, L., Garcia, E. E., & Espinosa, P. (1991). Effective instruction for language-minority students: An early childhood case study. *Early Childhood Research Quarterly, 6,* 347–361.	Teacher beliefs, no observational data.
Prado-Olmos, P., Syzmanski, M., & Smith, M. E. F. (1993). Students "DO" process: Bilingual students' interactions in a small cooperative learning reading group. *Bilingual Research Journal, 17*(3–4), 41–69.	Describes student learning processes.
Ramirez, J. D., Yuen, S. D., Ramey, D. R., Pasta, D. J., & Billings, D. (1990). *Final report: Longitudinal study of immersion strategy, early-exit and late-exit transitional bilingual education programs for language-minority children.* San Mateo, CA: Aguirre International.	Longitudinal study of models of instruction.
Rueda, R., & Garcia, E. (1996). Teachers' perspectives on literacy assessment and instruction with language-minority students: A comparative study. *Elementary School Journal, 96*(3), 311–332.	Descriptive study of teacher beliefs, no observational data.
Ruiz, N. T. (1995). The social construction of ability and disability: I. Profile types of Latino children identified as language learning disabled. *Journal of Learning Disabilities, 28,* 476–490.	Describes students and student learning processes.
Ruiz, N. T., Rueda, R., Figueroa, R. A., & Boothroyd, M. (1995). Bilingual special education teachers' shifting paradigms: Complex responses to educational reform. *Journal of Learning Disabilities, 28*(10), 622–635.	Descriptive study; focuses on teacher beliefs, no observational data.
Ruiz, N. T. (1989). An optimal learning environment for Rosemary. *Exceptional Children, 56*(2), 130–144.	Case study of misdiagnosed student.
Saunders, W., & Goldenberg, C. (1996). Four primary teachers work to define constructivism and teacher-directed learning: implications for teacher assessment. *Elementary School Journal, 97*(2), 139.	Descriptive study of teacher beliefs, no observational data
Slavin, R. E., & Madden, N. A. (1995, April). Effects of success for all in the achievement of English language learners. Paper presented at the American Educational Research Association, San Francisco.	Study of Korean-American students in Success for All.

REFERENCES

Arreaga-Mayer, C., & Perdomo-Rivera, C. (1996). Ecobehavioral analysis of instruction for at-risk language-minority students. *Elementary School Journal, 96,* 245–258.

August, D., & Hakuta, K. (1997). *Improving schooling for language-minority children.* Washington, DC: National Academy Press.

Beck, I. L., & McKeown, M. G. (1985). Teaching vocabulary: Making the instruction fit the goal. *Educational Perspectives, 23*(1), 11–15.

Blaunstein, P. (1995, November). *The best-kept secrets don't change education: Social marketing presentation.* Paper presented at the OSEP Cross-Project Meeting: Technology Educational Media and Materials for Individuals with Disabilities, Washington, DC.

Brophy, J., & Good, T. L. (1986). Teacher behavior and student achievement. In M. Witrock (Ed.), *The third handbook of research on teaching* (pp. 328–375). New York: Macmillan.

*Cardelle-Elawar, M. (1990). Effects of feedback tailored to bilingual students' mathematics needs on verbal problem solving. *Elementary School Journal, 91*(2), 165–175.

Chamot, A. U., Dale, M. O., Malley, J. M., & Spanos, G. A. (1993). Learning and problem solving strategies of ESL students. *Bilingual Research Journal, 16*(3 & 4), 1–34.

Chamot, A. U., & O'Malley, J. M. (1989). The cognitive academic language learning approach. In P. Rigg & V. Allen (Eds.), *When they don't all speak English* (pp. 108–125). Urbana, IL: National Council of Teachers of English.

Cohen, J. (1988). *Statistical power analysis for the behavioral sciences* (2nd ed.). Hillsdale, NJ: Lawrence Erlbaum Associates.

Cooper, H., & Hedges, L. V. (Eds.). (1994). *The handbook of research synthesis.* New York: Russell Sage Foundation.

Cummins, J. (1980). The cross-lingual dimensions of language proficiency: Implications for bilingual education and the optimal age issue. *TESOL Quarterly, 14*(2), 175–187.

Cummins, J. (1984). *Bilingualism and special education: Issues in assessment and pedagogy.* San Diego: College-Hill Press.

Delquadri, J., Greenwood, C. R., Whorton, D., Carta, J. J., & Hall, R. V. (1986). Classwide peer tutoring. *Exceptional Children, 52,* 535–542.

Delpit, L. (1994). *Other people's children.* New York: Basic Books.

**Echevarria, J. (1995). Interactive reading instruction: A comparison of proximal and distal effects of Instructional Conversations. *Exceptional Children, 61,* 536–552.

Echevarria, J. (1998). Preparing text and classroom materials for English-language learners: Curriculum adaptations in secondary school settings. In R. Gersten & R. Jiménez (Eds.), *Promoting learning for culturally and linguistically diverse students: Classroom applications from contemporary research* (pp. 210–229). Pacific Grove, CA: Brooks/Cole.

Echevarria, J., & Graves, A. (1998). *Sheltered content instruction: Teaching English-language learners with diverse abilities.* Des Moines, IA: Allyn & Bacon.

Echevarria, J., & McDonough, R. (1993). *Instructional conversations in special education settings: Issues and accommodations.* Washington, DC: National Center for Research on Cultural Diversity and Second Language Learning.

Fashola, O. S., Drum, P. A., Mayer, R. E., & Kang, S. (1996). A cognitive theory of orthographic transitions: Predictable errors in how Spanish-speaking children spell English words. *American Educational Research Journal, 33*(4), 825–844.

Ferguson, P. M., Ferguson, D. L., & Taylor, S. J. (1992). *Interpreting disability: A qualitative reader.* New York: Teachers College Press.

Figueroa, R. A., Fradd, S. H., & Correa, V. I. (1989). Bilingual special education and this special issue. *Exceptional Children, 56*(2), 174–178.

Fitzgerald, J. (1995). English-as-a-second-language learner's cognitive reading: A review of research in the United States. *Review of Educational Research, 65*(2), 145–190.

Gersten, R. (1996a). The double demands of teaching English language learners. *Educational Leadership, 53*(5), 18–22.

Gersten, R. (1996b). Literacy instruction for language-minority students: The transition years. *Elementary School Journal, 96*(3), 227–244.

Gersten, R., & Jiménez, R. (1994). A delicate balance: Enhancing literacy instruction for students of English as a second language. *The Reading Teacher, 47*(6), 438–449.

Gersten, R., Morvant, M., & Brengelman, S. (1995). Close to the classroom is close to the bone: Coaching as a means to translate research into classroom practice. *Exceptional Children, 62*(1), 52–66.

Gersten, R., & Woodward, J. (1994, April). *Lost opportunities: Observations of the education of language minority students.* Paper presented at the annual conference of American Educational Research Association, New Orleans.

Gersten, R., & Woodward, J. (1995). A longitudinal study of transitional and immersion bilingual education programs in one district. *Elementary School Journal, 95,* 223–240.

Glass, G., McGaw, B., & Smith, M. L. (1981). *Meta-analysis in social research.* Beverly Hills, CA: Sage.

Goldenberg, C. (1996). The education of language-minority students: Where are we, and where do we need to go? *Elementary School Journal, 93,* 353–361.

Goldenberg, C., & Patthey-Chavez, G. (1995). Discourse processes in Instructional Conversations: Interactions between teacher and transition readers. *Discourse Processes, 19,* 57–73.

**Goldenberg, C., Reese, L., & Gallimore, R. (1992). Effects of literacy materials from school on Latino children's home experiences and early reading achievement. *American Journal of Education, 100*(4), 497–536.

Goldenberg, C., & Sullivan, A. (1995, April). *Making change happen in a language-minority school: A search for coherence.* Paper presented at the annual meeting of the American Educational Research Association, San Francisco.

Good, T. L., & Grouws, D. A. (1977). Teaching effects: A process product study in fourth grade mathematics classrooms. *Journal of Teacher Education, 28*(3), 49–54.

*Henderson, R. W., & Landesman, E. W. (1995). Effects of thematically integrated mathematics instruction on students of Mexican descent. *Journal of Educational Research, 88*(5), 290.

Hiebert, J., & Wearne, D. (1993). Instructional tasks, classroom discourse, and students' learning in second-grade arithmetic. *American Educational Research Journal, 30,* 393–425.

Jiménez, R. T. (1997). The strategic reading abilities and potential of five low-literacy Latina/o readers in middle school. *Reading Research Quarterly, 32*(3), 224–243.

Jiménez, R., & Gersten, R. (in press). Lessons and dilemmas derived from the literacy instruction of two Latina/o teachers.

Kelly, B., Gersten, R., & Carnine, D. (1990). Student error patterns as a function of curriculum design. *Journal of Learning Disabilities, 23*(1), 23–32.

*Klingner, J. K., & Vaughn, S. (1996). Reciprocal teaching of reading comprehension strategies for students with learning disabilities who use English as a second language. *Elementary School Journal, 96,* 275–293.

Lee, O., & Fradd, S. H. (1996a). Interactional patterns of linguistically diverse students and teachers: Insights for promoting science learning. *Linguistics and Education: An International Research Journal, 8,* 269–297.

Lee, O., & Fradd, S. H. (1996b). Literacy skills in science performance among culturally and linguistically diverse students. *Journal of Research in Science Teaching, 32,* 797–816.

Lopez-Reyna, N. A. (1996). The importance of meaningful contexts in bilingual special education: Moving to whole language. *Learning Disabilities Research & Practice, 11*(2), 120–131.

Lucas, T., Henze, R., & Donato, R. (1990). Promoting the success of Latino language-minority students: An exploratory study of six high schools. *Harvard Educational Review, 60,* 315–340.

Mastropieri, M. A., Scruggs, T. E., Bakken, J. P., & Whedon, C. (1996). Reading comprehension: A synthesis of research in learning disabilities. In T. E. Scruggs & M. A. Mastropieri (Eds.), *Advances in learning and behavioral disabilities* (pp. 277–303). Greenwich, CT: JAI.

Miles, M. B., & Huberman, A. M. (1994). *Qualitative data analysis: A sourcebook of new methods.* Beverly Hills, CA: Sage.

Miniccuci, C., Berman, P., McLaughlin, B., McLeod, B., Nelson, B., & Woodworth, K. (1995). School reform and student diversity. *Phi Delta Kappan, 77*(1), 77–80.

Moll, L. C. (1988). Some key issues in teaching Latino students. *Language Arts, 65*(5), 465–472.

**Muñiz-Swicegood, M. (1994). The effects of megacognitive reading strategy training on the reading performance and student reading analysis strategies of third grade bilingual students. *Bilingual Research Journal, 18*(1–2), 83–97.

Nagy, W. E. (1988). *Teaching vocabulary to improve reading comprehension.* Newark, DE: International Reading Association.

Natriello, G., McDill, E. L., & Pallas, A. M. (1990). *Schooling disadvantaged children: Racing against catastrophe.* New York: Teachers College Press.

Noblit, G. W., & Hare, R. D. (1988). *Meta-ethnography: Synthesizing qualitative studies. Qualitative research methods series 11.* Newbury Park, CA: Sage.

Ogawa, R. T., & Malen, B. (1991). Towards rigor in reviews of multivocal literatures: Applying the exploratory case study method. *Review of Educational Research, 61,* 265–286.

Padrón, Y. N. (1994). Comparing reading instruction in Hispanic/limited-English-proficient schools and other inner-city schools. *Bilingual Research Journal, 18*(1), 49–66.

Patton, M. Q. (1990). *Qualitative evaluation and research methods* (2nd ed.). London: Sage.

Perez, B. (1994). Spanish literacy development: A descriptive study of four bilingual whole-language classrooms. *Journal of Reading Behavior, 26*(1), 75–94.

Pressley, M. (1996, April). *Embracing complexity: How and what I have learned about outstanding literacy instruction in the elementary grades.* Paper presented at the American Educational Research Association annual meeting, New York.

Ramírez, J. D. (1992). Executive summary: Longitudinal study of structured English immersion strategy, early-exit and late-exit transitional bilingual education programs for language-minority children. *Bilingual Research Journal, 16*(1), 1–62.

Reyes, E., & Bos, C. (1998). Interactive semantic mapping and charting: enhancing content area learning for language minority students. In R. G. R. Jiménez (Ed.), *Promoting learning for culturally and linguistically diverse students: Classroom applications from contemporary research* (pp. 133–152). Belmont, CA: Wadsworth.

Reyes, M. (1992). Challenging verable assumptions: Literacy instruction for linguistically different students. *Harvard Educational Review, 62*(4), 427–446.

Rosenshine, B. (1986). Synthesis of research on explicit teaching. *Education Leadership, 12,* 85–92.

Rosenshine, B., & Meister, C. (1994). Reciprocal teaching: A review of the research. *Review of Educational Research, 64*(4), 479–530.

Rosenthal, R. (1994). Parametric measures of effect size. In H. Cooper & L. V. Hedges (Eds.), *The handbook for research analysis* (pp. 231–244). New York: Russell Sage Foundation.

Rousseau, M. K., Tam, B. K. Y., & Ramnarain, R. (1993). Increasing reading proficiency of language-minority students with speech and language impairments. *Education and Treatments of Children, 16,* 254–271.

Ruiz, N. T. (1995). The social construction of ability and disability: II. Optimal and at-risk lessons in a bilingual special education classroom. *Journal of Learning Disabilities, 28*(8), 491–502.

Saunders, W., & Goldenberg, C. (1996). Four primary teachers work to define constructivism and teacher-directed learning: Implications for teacher assessment. *Elementary School Journal, 97*(2), 139–161.

*Saunders, W., O'Brien, G., Lennon, D., & McLean, J. (1998). Making the transition to English literacy successful: Effective strategies for studying literature with transition students. In R. Gersten & R. Jiménez (Eds.), *Effective strategies for teaching language minority students* (pp. 99–132). Belmont, CA: Wadsworth.

Stallings, J. (1980). Allocated academic learning time revisited, or beyond time on task. *Educational Leadership, 9*(11), 11–16.

Strauss, A., & Corbin, J. (1994). Grounded theory methodology: An overview. In N. K. Denzin & Y. S. Lincoln (Eds.), *Handbook of qualitative research* (pp. 273–287). Thousand Oaks, CA: Sage.

Swanson, H. L. (in press). What instruction works for students with learning disabilities? Results from a meta-analysis of intervention studies. In R. Gersten, E. Schiller, S. Vaughn, & J. Schumm (Eds.), *Issues and research in special education.* Mahwah, NJ: Lawrence Erlbaum Associates.

Tharp, R. G., & Gallimore, R. (1988). *Rousing minds to life.* Cambridge, England: Cambridge University Press.

Tikunoff, W. J., Ward, B. A., von Broekhuizen, L. D., Romero, M., Castaneda, L. V., Lucas, T., & Katz, A. (1991). *Final report: A descriptive study of significant features of exemplary special alternative instructional programs.* Los Alamitos, CA: The Southwest Regional Educational Laboratory.

Tuyay, S., Jennings, L., & Dixon, C. (1995). Classroom discourse and opportunities to learn: An ethnographic study of knowledge construction in a bilingual third-grade classroom. *Discourse Processes, 19,* 75–110.

Vaughn, S., Schumm, J. S., & Sinagub, J. M. (1996). *The focus group interview: Use and application in educational and psychological research.* Newbury Park, CA: Sage.

*Waxman, H. C., de Felix, J. W., Martinez, A., Knight, S. L., & Padrón, Y. (1994). Effects of implementing classroom instructional models on English language learners' cognitive and affective outcomes. *Bilingual Research Journal, 18*(3–4), 1–22.

Wolcott, H. F. (1994). *Transforming qualitative data: Description, analysis, and interpretation.* Thousand Oaks, CA: Sage.

Wortman, P. M. (1994). Judging research quality. In H. Cooper & L. V. Hedges (Eds.), *The handbook of research synthesis* (pp. 97–110). New York: Russell Sage Foundation.

Wortman, P. M., & Bryant, F. B. (1985). School desegregation and Black achievement: An integrative review. *Sociological Methods and Research, 13,* 289–324.

Yzaguirre, R. (1998). What's wrong with bilingual education?: Is it "lingual" or is it "education"? *Education Week,* pp. 46–47, 72.

Chapter 3

Reading Differences Between Low-Achieving Students With and Without Learning Disabilities: A Meta-Analysis

Douglas Fuchs
Lynn S. Fuchs
Peabody College of Vanderbilt University

Patricia G. Mathes
University of Texas—Houston Medical School

Mark W. Lipsey
Peabody College of Vanderbilt University

In 1977, the term *learning disabilities* (LD) was included as a category of exceptionality in the Education for All Handicapped Children Act (P.L. 94-142). Since that time, the percentage of students with LD has increased steadily so that students with LD now comprise 7% of the school-age population and more than 50% of all children with disabilities (U.S. Department of Education, 1995).

Despite increasing use of the LD label, serious conceptual and procedural questions have plagued the LD classification system (e.g., Kavale, Forness, & Lorsbach, 1991; Mercer, King-Sears, & Mercer, 1990; Shinn, Tindal, Spira, & Marston, 1987). Questions arise because LDs are a "soft disability" (Reschly, 1996) for which no physical markers are known. This permits subjectivity to permeate the identification process.

Additionally, because LD is associated with unexpected failure to learn, most definitions have incorporated the notion of a discrepancy between achievement and ability. The measurement of such discrepancies, however, has proven problematic due to poor reliability of difference scores and because varying discrepancy formulas and test instruments produce inconsistent identifications (Shepard, Smith, & Vojir, 1983).

As a consequence of these conceptual and procedural problems, some have questioned the meaningfulness of current LD definitions. Of course, a continuum of perspectives exists on this issue. At one extreme, critics (e.g., Algozzine, 1985; Ysseldyke, Algozzine, Shinn, & McGue, 1982) assert that underachieving students with and without the LD label are identical. A more moderate view (e.g., Hallahan, 1992; Kavale, 1995; Keogh, 1987; McLeskey & Waldron, 1990) concedes that the school performance of the two groups overlaps. At the same time, defenders of the construct (e.g., Kavale, Fuchs, & Scruggs, 1994) maintain that, on average, underachieving students with and without the LD label not only are distinguishable but also demonstrate distinctive educational needs.

Unfortunately, research designed to inform this debate has produced inconsistent findings. Substantive and methodological variations among studies appear to contribute to this inconsistency. With respect to substance, research has explored different performance domains (e.g., reading achievement vs. classroom behavior), using dissimilar measures within a given domain (e.g., reading comprehension vs. phonemic awareness). In terms of methods, different studies have used contrasting definitions of LD and underachievement, have involved demographically different groups, and have relied on varying statistical methods.

In an attempt to understand the apparent inconsistency in the database exploring differences between underachieving students with and without the LD label, we undertook a meta-analysis to synthesize the extant literature in the domain of reading. The purpose of this analysis was to provide parents, advocates, researchers, policymakers, and teachers with a definitive statement about whether, and if so how and to what extent, students with the LD label differ from their low-achieving peers. In this chapter, we provide an overview of the methods and results of that meta-analysis. Then, we highlight implications.

METHOD AND RESULTS

In conducting this meta-analysis, we searched the literature; we coded each study that met our inclusion criteria; and we analyzed the resulting database. In the following subsections, we summarize these methods and results. Within this description, we provide detailed information on the development of our coding system. For a thorough description of the literature search and the data analysis, see D. Fuchs, L. S. Fuchs, Mathes, and Lipsey (1998).

Inclusion Criteria and Search Strategies

Our goal was to identify all published and unpublished studies in which the reading achievement of LD and low-achieving (LA) nondisabled students could be compared. A *study* was defined by its participants: If two or more studies were conducted on the same students, the studies were counted as one. In a similar way, a single article could report more than one study if it included different samples of students with LD.

For inclusion, a study had to meet five criteria:

1. It had to present reading data.
2. Those data had to be reported separately for LD and LA groups.
3. Whenever the LD group included a mixture of students with high-incidence disabilities, students with LD had to constitute at least 85% of the group.
4. Participants had to be school age (i.e., kindergarten through Grade 12).
5. The study had to report data necessary for calculating effect sizes (ESs).

To identify studies that met these criteria, we undertook a comprehensive search of journal articles, Educational Resources Information Center (ERIC) documents, and dissertations in Dissertations Abstracts International (DAI) produced between January 1975 and December 1996. This search comprised three phases: a manual search of journals, two computerized database searches (ERIC and DAI), and an ancestral search of titles in the references of identified investigations. Eighty-six studies met our inclusion criteria.

Coding the Studies

To systematically derive information from the studies, we developed a coding form in two phases.

Phase 1.   As we initially read the studies, it was unclear which study characteristics would eventually prove worthy of coding. Therefore, we described many study features, knowing some would later be discarded. We began by reading a considerable portion of the research and becoming familiar with the typical range of study features described. We then developed a first-draft coding form with which we independently coded a sample study, Shinn, Ysseldyke, Deno, and Tindal (1986). After debriefing, we developed a second draft and accompanying code book. Then, we independently coded four studies, including Shinn et al. (1986) for a second time. After coding each study, we again discussed each item on the coding form. Throughout this process, definitions of codes were refined and decision rules about handling ambiguous situations were determined.

At this point, we began coding studies. However, within a couple of weeks, unacceptably low levels of interrater agreement indicated a need for more precise definitions; so, the coding form was revised again. This necessitated recoding 30 articles that had already been coded with the second draft. A 16-page coding form emerged from Phase 1 (contact the first author for the final coding form). Using this iteration of the coding form, five studies were coded with agreement of 90% or better on each study.

Then, the remaining journal articles and ERIC documents were coded independently. The two coders independently completed an additional 13 studies; agreement on each study exceeded 85%.

Recognizing the temptation to make reasonable inferences about information not clearly presented in studies, we instituted a no-guessing rule: If uncertainty arose about how to code an item, it was left blank. Later, an author determined the code. If questions still remained, the codes were discussed until consensus was achieved.

Phase 2. Approaching data entry, it became apparent that the 16-page coding form was too detailed; it contained codes inappropriate or irrelevant for many studies. Therefore, the form was reduced to 45 codes that would be entered into the computer (see Table 3.1 for coding categories and definitions). During this scaling-down process, we added one code: "reading," which was redefined by various subdomains (e.g., phonological awareness, lexical retrieval, reading readiness; see Table 3.1).

The final coding form differed in appearance from the 16-page version because it was briefer and designed to match the computer spreadsheet. So, for example, both coding form and spreadsheet now displayed one line of data for every reading measure in a study.

Selected study codes then were transferred from the 16-page coding form to the briefer, final form, which paralleled the computer spreadsheet. Before beginning this process, two coders independently transferred the codes of five studies from one form to the other, immediately checking accuracy. One coder then transferred the codes of all previously coded studies to the final coding form. An independent coder then checked this transfer of codes for every study.

When the coding form was revised, the dissertations had not yet been obtained. When dissertations were secured, they were coded by using the final coding form, not the 16-page version.

Preparing the Database for Analysis

Codes for the 86 studies were entered into an electronic spreadsheet. To ensure accuracy, two checkers examined the spreadsheet item by item. As one person read the database entry, the second person checked the information on the coding form.

TABLE 3.1

Coding Scheme Categories and Definitions

Category	Code Options	Definition of Code
Study	Author names	Author names.
Study Identification Number	Study ID number	Study identification number assigned by project coordinator.
Measure	Name of measure	Name of measure.
Measure Identification Number	Measure ID number	Measure identification number assigned by project coordinator.
Domain of Measure	Reading Mathematics Language arts Social skills Cognitive processing	The construct underpinning the measure from which effect size will be calculated In this meta-analysis, only measures of reading were analyzed. However, measures of other constructs will be analyzed in the future.
Subdomain	• Phonological awareness • Lexical retrieval • Reading readiness • Decoding • Reading connected text • Reading comprehension • Overall reading achievement • Vocabulary	Category or type of reading skill.
Test Format	• Timed • Untimed	Condition for administering the measure.
Technical Adequacy of Measure	• Yes • No • Unknown	Does the test have adequate reliability and validity for its use in the study?

(Continued)

85

TABLE 3.1
(Continued)

Category	Code Options	Definition of Code
Research Design	• Descriptive, one point in time • Descriptive, change score • Intervention posttest • Intervention change score	Type of research design employed. Applied in terms of the individual measure. Change scores reflect gain or slope data. Pretest scores were considered descriptive. Descriptive and intervention designs were kept separately to allow for the examination of response to treatment.
Source	• Journal • ERIC document • Dissertation • Other unpublished study	Type of document. If multiple documents of the same study were found, then its published version was used.
Date	Citation publication date	Earliest date of publication. If unpublished, earliest date of dissertation report or ERIC document.
Locale	• Urban metropolitan • Suburban • Rural • Mixed	Type of location at which the study was conducted.
LD Definition Supplier	• District • Researcher	Who applied the LD definition and determined whether students meet this definition?
LD Definition	• Discrepancy between achievement and ability • Judgment of multidisciplinary team • Cutoff score • Other/not specified	Primary definition used to define LD subjects.

Discrepancy	• 1.0 Standard Deviation • 1.5 Standard Deviation • 2.0 Standard Deviation • Regression	How a discrepancy between achievement and ability was defined in terms of standard scores.
LA Definition Supplier	• District • Researcher	Who applied the definition for LA membership?
LA Definition	• Matched with LD subject scores • Cutoff test score • Referred for special education, but found ineligible • Eligibility for compensatory or remedial services • Ability grouping • Teacher nomination	Definition used to define LA membership.
Referred LA Population	Percentage of LA population	Percentage of the LA group that had been referred for special education, but was not deemed eligible.
Methodological Quality of Study	• High • Medium • Low	The study's overall methodological quality (internal and external validity) as it impacts on the individual effect size.
Number in LD Subjects	Number in LD sample	Number in LD sample.
Number of LA Subjects	Number in LA sample	Number in LA sample.
LD Gender	Percentage of males in LD sample	Percentage of males in LD sample.
LD Race	Percentage of White participants in LD sample	Percentage of White participants in LD sample.

(*Continued*)

87

TABLE 3.1
(Continued)

Category	Code Options	Definition of Code
LD Grade	• PreK–kindergarten (K) • Grade K–3 • Grade K–6 • Grade 4–6 • Grade 4–8 • Grade 7–8 • Grade 9–12 • Grade K–12	Grade(s) of LD sample.
LD Socioeconomic Status	• High • Medium • Low • Mixed	Socioeconomic status reported for LD sample.
Area of LD Identification	• Reading/language arts • Math • Not specified	Academic area providing basis for the application of the LD label.
Instructional Setting of LD Subjects	• General education • Resource (part time) • Both (mixed sample: some 100% general education, some receive resource) • Other	Location where LD students receive special education services.
LD and LA in Same Setting	• Yes • No	Do LD and LA subjects receive reading instruction in the same setting?
LD Full Scale IQ	Full scale IQ standard score	Full scale IQ standard score.

LD Verbal IQ	Verbal IQ Standard Score	Verbal IQ Standard Score.
LD Performance IQ	Performance IQ Standard Score	Performance IQ Standard Score.
LD and LA of Comparable Age/Grade	• Yes • No	Are LD subjects comparable to LA subjects in age and/or grade level?
LD and LA of Comparable Gender	• Yes • No	Are LD subjects comparable to LA subjects in gender?
LD and LA of Comparable Race	• Yes • No	Are LD subjects comparable to LA subjects in race?
LD and LA of Comparable Socioeconomic Status	• Yes • No	Are LD subjects comparable to LA subjects in socioeconomic status?
LD and LA of Comparable IQ	• Yes • No	Are LD subjects comparable to LA subjects in IQ?
LD and LA of Comparable Achievement	• Yes • No	Are LD subjects comparable to LA subjects in achievement?
LD and LA of Comparable Achievement in Effect Size Domain	• Yes • No	Are LD subjects comparable to LA subjects in achievement in effect size domain?
Matched Pairs	• Not matched • IQ • Reading • Other achievement • Nonachievement • In same classroom	How LD and LA samples were matched if a matched pairs scheme was employed.

(Continued)

TABLE 3.1
(Continued)

Category	Code Options	Definition of Code
Effect Size Analysis	• Descriptive • T test • ANOVA • Correlation • Multiple regression • Chi square • Multiple comparison (e.g., SNK, Scheffe) • ANCOVA • Other	Type of statistic used to compute effect size.
LD Mean	Mean score of the LD sample	Mean score on the relevant measure of the LD sample.
LD Standard Deviation	Standard deviation score of the LD sample	Standard deviation score on the relevant measure of the LD sample.
LA Mean	Mean score of the LA sample	Mean score on the relevant measure of the LA sample.
LA Standard Deviation	Standard deviation score of the LA sample	Standard deviation score on the relevant measure of the LA sample.
Effect Size	Standardized mean difference effect size or its estimate (d)	Standardized mean difference effect size or its estimate (d) for the relevant measure.

Computation of Individual ESs

Typically, ES was computed as the standardized mean difference (d index): the difference between the means of the comparison groups divided by the pooled standard deviation (Hedges & Olkin, 1985). This represents LD–LA differences scaled in the uniform metric of standard deviation units. A positive ES reflects higher performance by the LA group. As recommended by Hedges (1981), this ES formula was adapted to yield an unbiased estimate of the underlying population effect. Whereas a majority of studies presented the information necessary to compute ES using the basic formula, some studies presented other comparison statistics. In such cases, ES was estimated from those other statistics.

Aggregation of ES Within Studies

We aggregated two or more ESs in the same study, if those ESs were identical on eight variables: reading subdomain, research design, sample size for LD, sample size for LA, grade level, and IQ (Full Scale, Verbal, and Performance). Thus, any two ESs in the same study, which did not match exactly on these eight dimensions, were judged to be independent, with one important exception. In a few instances, subgroups of a sample differed in size, but were identical with respect to the remaining seven variables. In these cases, ESs associated with these subsamples were eliminated. Also eliminated at this point were seven studies in which LD and LA students were matched on reading achievement or reading achievement and IQ. ESs from the remaining 79 studies (see Appendix) were included in the meta-analysis.

Preliminary Analyses

We undertook four preliminary analyses to formulate decisions about which data, in what form, should be incorporated into the major analyses.

Effect of Study Design. We examined the effect of four types of study designs: (a) descriptive/one point in time, (b) descriptive/change over time, (c) intervention/posttest only, and (d) intervention/change over time. Because we determined that the mean ESs of these designs differed significantly and because there were relatively few eligible ESs for the second through fourth design types, we decided to conduct analyses on only one type of design, which had the vast majority of ESs: the descriptive/one-point-in-time studies ($n = 202$).

How to Consolidate Data Across Reading Subdomains. We examined whether and if so how to consolidate data across the reading subdomains.

The 202 ESs included multiple records on the same samples. This occurred when a study author contrasted groups in more than one reading subdomain. Because this is statistically problematic for meta-analysis (Hedges & Olkin, 1985), we conducted preliminary analyses to examine empirically how ESs for the various reading domains behaved. We found that five reading domains (decoding isolated words, reading connected text, reading comprehension, overall reading, and vocabulary) yielded ES values sufficiently similar, as indexed by their central tendencies, to be considered comparable. However, the remaining domains (phonological awareness, rapid automatized naming, and reading readiness) were comparable neither with the other five domains listed previously nor with each other. The mean covariate-adjusted ESs for these three domains, respectively, were .05, .26, and −.40. Thus, we did not combine these three domains with the remaining five domains or with each other. This left 172 ESs.

Aggregating ESs on Identical Samples. With this smaller database, we identified independent samples that contributed more than one ES. These records were aggregated by averaging all variables (except reading subdomain). Because all other variable values in the averaged records were identical, this produced a single record for each independent sample. This resulted in a data file of 112 records, each representing an independent sample with an ES in one of the five reading subdomains or a mean ES averaged over two or more of the five subdomains.

Handling Outliers. The distribution of the 112 ESs revealed outliers at both ends. To reduce the possibly distorting effect of these outliers, we windsorized them. Two ESs less than −1.00 were increased to −1.00; five ESs greater than 1.75 were reduced to 1.75. This had a minimal effect on the overall mean ES.

Major Analyses

Are the ESs Homogeneous? Our first major analysis indicated considerable disagreement among the studies with respect to the magnitude of the differences between LD and LA groups in reading performance: The Q statistic indicated substantially greater variability among ESs than would be expected from sampling error alone, $Q(111) = 535.75, p < .001$. This finding led us to explore which study characteristics might be associated with variation in ES.

How Might We Consolidate the Large Number of Study Features? Before examining the relation between study features and ESs, we consolidated some study features. First, based on analyses we conducted, we consolidated our *definitions of LD and LA samples* to five levels of LD/LA definitional pairings; this resulted in 109 ESs.

Second, we conducted several focused factor analyses on sets of variables that seemed to be related conceptually and were better represented as multivariate composites. A varimax-rotated solution seemed to fit these variables nicely. We thereby reduced the *LD–LA student comparability data* to three factors: achievement, which incorporated variables related to reading comparability; demographic characteristics, including age, race, and socioeconomic status (SES); and gender comparability, IQ, and SES comparability. We refer to these three factors as (a) achievement comparability, (b) demographic comparability, and (c) gender comparability, respectively.

Finally, we conducted another factor analysis to examine relations among variables describing the *research methods* used for constructing the LD–LA samples. This analysis produced a sensible two-factor solution. The first factor showed a co-occurrence of the following: (a) lower IQ scores, (b) higher grade levels for the LD sample, and (c) referral of LA samples for special education testing; we called this factor "other sample features." The second factor cleanly combined the two variables describing whether the samples were district or researcher identified; we called this factor "identification source."

How Do the Clustered Study Features Relate to ESs?   We used weighted least squares regression, weighting each ES by the inverse of its variance. Our pool of predictor variables included the LD/LA definitional pairings, the five factor scores (reading comparability, demographic comparability, gender comparability, other sample features, and identification source), the three locale variables, technical adequacy, test format, study quality, and date of study. Predictors were entered simultaneously; then, the weakest was dropped and the model was refit. We repeated this process until all remaining variables were significant.

The regression model accounted for a statistically significant 41% of the variance among the ESs. The following variables made significant, independent contributions to the prediction of ES.

First, measurement format contributed to the prediction of ES, with a beta of .34. ESs were greater for the timed than the untimed measurement formats. For example, on tests requiring students to work in a fixed time (such as the Stanford Achievement Test or curriculum-based measurement), the difference between students with and without LD was larger than when tests permitted students as much time as they needed (e.g., Woodcock Reading Mastery Tests). This was true across reading domains.

Second, other sample features contributed to the prediction of ES, with a beta of .16. ESs were greater for LD samples with lower IQ and with higher LD grade; ESs were greater when LAs had been referred, but had never qualified as appropriate, for special education.

Third, LD/LA definitional pairings contributed to the prediction of ES. ESs were greater when LD samples were defined by discrepancies and when LA samples were defined by teacher judgment; the associated beta was .51. ESs were smaller when LD samples were identified by multidisciplinary team judgment and when LA samples were defined by data-driven methods; the associated beta was −.27.

Fourth, the three comparability factors contributed to the prediction of ES. ESs were greater when achievement and demographics were not comparable for LD and LA samples; the associated beta was .13. ESs were greater when gender and, to a lesser extent, IQ and SES, were comparable; the corresponding beta was .08.

Finally, methodological study quality contributed to the prediction of ES, with somewhat greater ESs for lower quality studies. The associated beta was .12.

WHAT DOES THIS META-ANALYSIS TELL US?

Across the many substantive and methodological variables associated with studies in this meta-analysis, ESs demonstrated considerable heterogeneity. Analyses were, however, successful in identifying a large proportion of the variance among ESs. Ten variables operated independently to explain the variation. In particular, three variables maximized the degree of reading impairment associated with the LD label and, therefore, provide insight into the theoretical nature of the disability. They also may help practitioners and researchers develop more effective assessment and intervention procedures for students with LD, as well as more precise measures of treatment success.

On the basis of these meta-analytic findings, we offer three conclusions, which may guide future research and practice. First, across the many different ways in which students become identified as LD, results leave no doubt that these students' reading achievement differs dramatically from other low-achieving, nondisabled students. Averaged across all the methodological and substantive variations in the studies, the mean effect size was .61 standard deviations units. This effect is sizable; it means than 72% of the LA population performs better in reading than the mean of the LD population. Moreover, when looking at ESs for timed measurements, whereby students were required to perform (i.e., read aloud, read silently, answer questions, match words to meanings) within a fixed time, the ESs increased to well beyond one full standard deviation unit. And, in a similar way, when LD and LA samples had been identified using data-based methods, the overall ES of .61 rose to beyond a full standard deviation unit. Findings, therefore, suggest that researchers and school personnel in fact do identify as LD those children who have appreciably more severe reading problems compared to other low-performing students who go unidentified. As with any comparison of two populations, some overlap between these populations does occur; that overlap, however, is not sufficient to call the LD label into question. Consequently, in light of the more severe magnitude of LD students' reading problems, it seems reasonable and desirable that more intensive forms of reading instruction be directed at this group of students.

Second, the ESs associated with timed tests were larger than those associated with untimed tests. The beta associated with this effect was an impressive .34. This strong effect associated with timed measurement format suggests theoretical and practical implications. Failure at achieving automaticity may represent an important characteristic of students with LD, which may be associated with the low performance on rapid-naming tasks (Wolf, 1991) of many of these children. The possibility that difficulties in achieving automaticity may represent a key feature of students with LD warrants additional study. Methods of identifying LD children might incorporate timed reading assessments to focus on students' failure to achieve automatic word-reading performance. In addition, with respect to treatment, researchers should develop methods for helping students with LD transition from accurate to automatic word reading. Finally, results suggest that the effectiveness of interventions for students with learning disabilities should be evaluated at least in part by how they influence students' performance on timed reading measurements.

Finally, results underscore the importance of objective measurement of reading performance in the identification process. Larger differences between LD and LA students emerged when definitional and selection criteria for inclusion to studies relied on objective forms of reading measurement, that is, the administration of tests. By contrast, when individual or team judgment was involved, differences between LD and LA samples on reading measures grew smaller. On the one hand, this finding provides a basis for questioning human judgment in the identification process. On the other hand, it suggests that other considerations, such as a focus on social behavior, may play a viable role in the identification of children whose overall performance profiles warrant special treatment. Practitioners should be mindful of the advantages and disadvantages associated with reliance on nonobjective forms of input to the multidisciplinary team process. Future research should continue to identify which types of nonobjective data may be important in the identification process and should continue to examine the role of social behavior deficits and the possibility of comorbidity in children with LD.

ACKNOWLEDGMENTS

The research reported in this chapter was supported in part by Grant H023E50004 from the Office of Special Education Programs, U.S. Department of Education, to Vanderbilt University. This chapter does not necessarily reflect the position or policy of the funding agency, and no official endorsement should be inferred. We wish to thank Holley Roberts and Susan Eaton for their hard work on the project.

APPENDIX
Published and Unpublished Studies (*N* = 79) From Which Data
Were Collected on the Reading Performance of LD and LA Students

Study #	Citation of Article (or of Articles Based on Same Study)
1	Ackerman, P. T., Dykman, R. A., Oglesby, D. M., & Newton, J. E. O. (1994). EEG power spectra of children with dyslexia, slow learners, and normally reading children with ADD during verbal processing. *Journal of Learning Disabilities, 27,* 619–630.
2	Ackerman, P. T., Weir, N. L., Metzler, D. P., & Dykman, R. A. (1996). A study of adolescent poor readers. *Learning Disabilities Research & Practice, 11,* 68–77.
3	Algozzine, B., & Ysseldyke, J. (1982, March). *Learning disabilities as a subset of school failure: The oversophistication of a concept* (Research Report No. 69). Duluth: University of Minnesota Institute for Research on Learning Disabilities. (ERIC Document Reproduction Service No. ED 218 852)
	Algozzine, B., & Ysseldyke, J. (1983). Learning disabilities as a subset of school failure: The over-sophistication of a concept. *Exceptional Children, 50,* 242–246.
4	Alley, G. R., Deshler, D. D., Waner, M. M., & Schumaker, J. B. (1980, January). *An epidemiological study of learning disabled adolescents in secondary schools: Health and medical factors* (Research Report No. 15). Lawrence: University of Kansas Institute for Research in Learning Disabilities. (ERIC Document Reproduction Service No. ED 217 632)
	Alley, G. R., Warner, M. M., Schumaker, J. B., Deshler, D. D., & Clark, F. L. (1980, January). *An epidemiological study of learning disabled and low-achieving adolescents in secondary schools: Behavioral and emotional status from the perspective of parents and teachers* (Research Report No. 16). Lawrence: University of Kansas Institute for Research in Learning Disabilities. (ERIC Document Reproduction Service No. ED 217 633)
	Deshler, D. D., Alley, G. R., Warner, M. M., Schumaker, J. B., & Clark, F. L. (1980, January). *An epidemiological study of learning disabled adolescents in secondary schools: Support services* (Research Report No. 19). Lawrence: University of Kansas Institute for Research in Learning Disabilities. (ERIC Document Reproduction Service No. ED 217 635)
	Deshler, D. D., Schumaker, J. B., Alley, G. R., Warner, M. M., & Clark, F. L. (1980, January). *An epidemiological study of learning disabled adolescents in secondary schools: Academic self-image and attributions* (Research Report No. 14). Lawrence: University of Kansas Institute for Research in Learning Disabilities. (ERIC Document Reproduction Service No. ED 217 631)

(Continued)

Study #	Citation of Article (or of Articles Based on Same Study)

Deshler, D. D., Schumaker, J. B., Warner, M. M., Alley, G. R., & Clark, F. L. (1980, January). *An epidemiological study of learning disabled adolescents in secondary schools: Social status, peer relationships, activities in and out of school, and time use* (Research Report No. 18). Lawrence: University of Kansas Institute for Research in Learning Disabilities. (ERIC Document Reproduction Service No. ED 217 634)

Schumaker, J. B., Warner, M. M., Deshler, D. D., & Alley, G. R. (1980, January). *An epidemiological study of learning disabled adolescents in secondary schools: Details of the methodology* (Research Report No. 12). Lawrence: University of Kansas Institute for Research in Learning Disabilities. (ERIC Document Reproduction Service No. ED 217 629)

Warner, M. M., Alley, G. R., Schumaker, J. B., Deshler, D. D., & Clark, F. L. (1980, January). *An epidemiological study of learning disabled adolescents in secondary schools: Achievement and ability, socioeconomic status, and school experiences* (Research Report No. 13). Lawrence: University of Kansas Institute for Research in Learning Disabilities. (ERIC Document Reproduction Service No. ED 217 630)

Warner, M. M., Schumaker, J. B., Alley, G. R., & Deshler, D. D. (1989). The role of executive control: An epidemiological study of school-identified learning-disabled and low-achieving adolescents on a serial recall task. *Learning Disabilities Research, 4,* 107–118.

5 Badian, N. A. (1996). Dyslexia: A validation of the concept at two age levels. *Journal of Learning Disabilities, 29,* 102–112.

6 Barbetta, P. M., Miller, A. D., Peters, M. T., Heron, T. E., & Cochran, L. L. (1991). Tugmate: A cross-age tutoring program to teach sight vocabulary. *Education and Treatment of Children, 14,* 19–37.

7 Becht, D. J. (1987). Use of the WISC–R and the K–ABC with low achievers, learning disabled, and students classified emotionally impaired. *Dissertation Abstracts International, 48*(04), 870B. (University Microfilms No. AAC87-14298)

8 Bender, W. N. (1985). Differential diagnoses based on the task-related behavior of learning disabled and low-achieving adolescents. *Learning Disability Quarterly, 8,* 261–266.

9 Cattoi, R. M. (1987). The relationship between cross-modal integration ability and reading achievement in average readers, poor readers, and learning disabled children. *Dissertation Abstracts International, 48*(03), 627B. (University Microfilms No. AAC87-12412)

10 Clever, A. R. (1991). Factors moderating the effect of low scholastic competence on global self-worth. *Dissertation Abstracts International, 52*(10), 3559B. (University Microfilms No. AAC92-06340)

11 Cooley, S. A. (1990). A therapeutical and empirical investigation of formulas for determining a severe discrepancy between aptitude and achievement used as a criterion in identification of learning disabilities. *Dissertation Abstracts International, 51*(11), 3696B. (University Microfilms No. AAC91-10879)

12 Duffitt, D. S. (1983). Analysis of language development and reading comprehension of learning disabled and chapter 1 students. *Dissertation Abstracts International, 44*(09), 2722B. (University Microfilms No. AAC84-01295)

13 Englert, C. S., Raphael, T. E., Anderson, L. M., Gregg, S. L., & Anthony, H. M. (1989). Exposition: Reading, writing, and the metacognitive knowledge of learning-disabled students. *Learning Disabilities Research, 5,* 5–24.

(Continued)

APPENDIX
(Continued)

Study #	Citation of Article (or of Articles Based on Same Study)
14	Fayne, H. R. (1981). A comparison of learning disabled adolescents with normal learners on an anaphoric pronominal reference task. *Journal of Learning Disabilities, 14,* 597–599.
15	Feldman, J. A. (1990). Subtypes of reading-disabled children: A comparison with low-achieving and normally achieving children. *Dissertation Abstracts International, 51*(07), 3562B. (University Microfilms No. AAC90-31242)
16	Fletcher, J. M., Shaywitz, S. E., Shankweiler, D. P., Katz, L., Liberman, I. Y., Stuebing, K. K., Francis, D. J., Fowler, A. E., & Shaywitz, B. A. (1994). Cognitive profiles of reading disability: Comparisons of discrepancy and low achievement definitions. *Journal of Educational Psychology, 86,* 6–23.
17	Fuchs, D., Fuchs, L. S., Bishop, N., & Mathes, P. G. (1992). *Differences between students classified learning-disabled and low-achieving: Implications for inclusive schooling.* Unpublished manuscript.
18	Fuchs, D., Fuchs, L. S., Mathes, P. G., & Simmons, D. C. (1997). Peer-assisted learning strategies: Making classrooms more responsive to diversity. *American Educational Research Journal, 34,* 174–206.
19	Goetz, N. (1986). Semantic encoding of learning-disabled, low-achieving, and normally achieving children (language formulation, hesitations). *Dissertation Abstracts International, 47*(08), 2996B. (University Microfilms No. AAC86-26950)
20	Gottlieb, J., Kastner, S., Gottlieb, B. W., Kastner, J., & Parker, I. M. (n.d.). *Use of incentive structure in mainstream classes.* Unpublished manuscript.
21	Granetz, S. B. (1984). The effects of sequential order on the short-term memory of dyslexic readers. *Dissertation Abstracts International, 46*(02), 399B. (University Microfilms No. AAC85-07436)
22	Gresham, F. M., MacMillan, D. L., & Bocian, K. M. (1996). Learning disabilities, low achievement, and mild mental retardation: More alike than different? *Journal of Learning Disabilities, 29,* 570–581.
23	Haager, D., & Vaughn, S. (1995). Parent, teacher, peer, and self-reports of the social competence of students with learning disabilities. *Journal of Learning Disabilities, 28,* 205–215, 231.
24	Hess, R. J. (1984). The influence of selected psychometric and demographic variables on special education classification and placement (discriminant analysis). *Dissertation Abstracts International, 45*(12), 3584B. (University Microfilms No. AAC84-29091)
25	Horton, S. V., & Lovitt, T. C. (1989). Using study guides with three classifications of secondary students. *The Journal of Special Education, 22,* 447–462.
26	Horton, S. V., & Lovitt, T. C. (1994). A comparison of two methods of administering group reading inventories to diverse learners. *Remedial and Special Education, 15,* 378–390.
27	Horton, S. V., Lovitt, T. C., & Bergerud, D. (1990). The effectiveness of graphic organizers for three classifications of secondary students in content area classes. *Journal of Learning Disabilities, 23,* 12–22, 29.
28	Horton, S. V., Lovitt, T. C., & Givens, A. (1988). A computer-based vocabulary program for three categories of student. *British Journal of Educational Technology, 19*(2), 131–143.
29	Horton, S. V., Lovitt, T. C., Givens, A., & Nelson, R. (1989). Teaching social studies to high school students with academic handicaps in a mainstreamed setting: Effects of a computerized study guide. *Journal of Learning Disabilities, 22,* 102–107.

(Continued)

APPENDIX

(Continued)

Study #	Citation of Article (or of Articles Based on Same Study)
30	Horton, S. V., Lovitt, T. C., & Slocum, T. (1988). Teaching geography to high school students with academic deficits: Effects of a computerized map tutorial. *Learning Disability Quarterly, 11,* 371–379.
31	Hurford, D. P., Darrow, L. J., Edwards, T. L., Howerton, C. J., Mote, C. R., Schauf, J. D., & Coffey, P. (1993). An examination of phonemic processing abilities in children during their first-grade year. *Journal of Learning Disabilities, 26,* 167–177.
32	Hurford, D. P., Schauf, J. D., Bunce, L., Blaich, T., & Moore, K. (1994). Early identification of children at risk for reading disabilities. *Journal of Learning Disabilities, 27,* 371–382.
33	Idol, L. (1987). Group story mapping: A comprehension strategy for both skilled and unskilled readers. *Journal of Learning Disabilities, 20,* 196–205.
	Idol-Maestas, L. (1985, December). *Group story mapping: A comprehension strategy for both skilled and unskilled readers* (Tech. Rep. No. 363). Urbana-Champaign: University of Illinois Center for the Study of Reading. (ERIC Document Reproduction Service No. ED 265 525)
34	Jenkins, J. R., Jewell, M., Leicester, N., Jenkins, L., & Troutner, N. M. (1991). Development of a school building model for educating students with handicaps and at-risk students in general education classrooms. *Journal of Learning Disabilities, 24,* 311–320.
35	Jenkins, J. R., Jewell, M., Leicester, N., O'Connor, R. E., Jenkins, L. M., & Troutner, N. M. (1994). Accommodations for individual differences without classroom ability groups: An experiment in school restructuring. *Exceptional Children, 60,* 344–358.
36	Jorm, A. F., Share, D. L., Maclean, R., & Matthews, R. (1986). Cognitive factors at school entry predictive of specific reading retardation and general reading backwardness: A research note. *Journal of Child Psychology and Psychiatry, 27*(1), 45–54.
37	Kastner, J., & Gottlieb, J. (1981). *Classification of children in urban special education: Importance of pre-assessment information and intelligence test scores.* Unpublished manuscript.
	Kastner, J., & Gottlieb, J. (1991). Classification of children in special education: Importance of pre-assessment information. *Psychology in the Schools, 28,* 19–27.
38	Levi, G., & Piredda, M. L. (1986). Semantic and phonological strategies for anagram construction in dyslexic children. *Journal of Learning Disabilities, 19,* 17–22.
39	Lyons, C. A. (1987, April). *Reading Recovery: An effective intervention program for learning disabled first graders.* Paper presented at the annual meeting of the American Educational Research Association, Washington, DC. (ERIC Document Reproduction Service No. ED 284 170)
	Lyons, C. A. (1988, Nov.–Dec.). *Patterns of oral reading behavior in learning disabled students in reading recovery: Is a child's learning disability environmentally produced?* Paper presented at the annual meeting of the National Reading Conference, Tucson, AZ. (ERIC Document Reproduction Service No. ED 302 841)
	Lyons, C. A. (1988 April). *The effect of instruction on the oral reading behaviors of children classified as learning disabled.* Paper presented at the annual meeting of the American Educational Research Association, New Orleans. (ERIC Document Reproduction Service No. ED 295 131)
	Lyons, C. A. (1989). Reading recovery: A preventative for mislabeling young "at-risk" learners. *Urban Education, 24*(2), 125–139.

(Continued)

99

Study #	Citation of Article (or of Articles Based on Same Study)
40	McPhail, J. C. (1993). Adolescents with learning disabilities: A comparative life-stream interpretation. *Journal of Learning Disabilities, 26,* 617–629.
41	Merrell, K. W. (1990). Differentiating low achieving students and students with learning disabilities: An examination of performance on the Woodcock–Johnson Psycho-Educational Battery. *The Journal of Special Education, 24,* 296–305.
42	Merrell, K. W., & Shinn, M. R. (1990). Critical variables in the learning disabilities identification process. *School Psychology Review, 19,* 74–82.
43	Moore, C. (1990). *Increasing reading fluency for learning-disabled and remedial readers.* Ft. Lauderdale, FL: Nova University, Educational Specialist Practicum. (ERIC Document Reproduction Service No. ED 323 519)
44	Moore, L. O. (1987). A comparison of lexical and semantic access for learning-disabled students, low reading achievers, and normals. *Dissertation Abstracts International, 49*(03), 470B. (University Microfilms No. AAC88-05720)
45	Mosley, J. R. (1987). A comparison of social skills of learning-disabled students and non-disabled low achievers. *Dissertation Abstracts International, 48*(04), 880B. (University Microfilms No. AAC87-16455)
46	Oberman, M. S. (1981). Corrective reading, self-esteem, locus of control and parental perception of disabled readers and disabled learners. *Dissertation Abstracts International, 42*(02), 634B. (University Microfilms No. AAC81-16309)
47	O'Shea, L. J., & Valcante, G. (1986). A comparison over time of relative discrepancy scores of low achievers. *Exceptional Children, 53,* 253–259.
48	Pagel, S. E. (1985). Influences of labeling and parental reactions on boys' causal attributions for success and failure in reading. *Dissertation Abstracts International, 46*(11), 3296A. (University Microfilms No. AAC86-00518)
49	Parker, I., Gottlieb, J., Gottlieb, B. W., Davis, S., & Kunzweiller, C. (1989). Teacher behavior toward low achievers, average achievers, and mainstreamed minority group learning-disabled students. *Learning Disabilities Research, 4,* 101–106.
50	Pascarella, E. T., & Pflaum, S. W. (1981). The interaction of children's attribution and level of control over error correction in reading instruction. *Journal of Educational Psychology, 73,* 533–540.
51	Pierangelo, R. A. (1980). Adolescent learning styles, self-concept and social interaction. *Dissertation Abstracts International, 41*(02), 6281A. (University Microfilms No. AAC80-18436)
52	Poikkeus, A. M. (1993). Social competence and friendship experiences of children with learning disabilities: A group comparison and a subtype analysis. *Dissertation Abstracts International, 54*(06), 3363B. (University Microfilms No. AAC93-31934)
53	Prasse, D. P., Siewert, J. C., & Breen, M. J. (1983). An analysis of performance on reading subtests from the 1978 Wide Range Achievement Test and Woodcock Reading Mastery Test with the WISC–R for learning disabled and regular education students. *Journal of Learning Disabilities, 16,* 458–461.
54	Renuart, J. A. (1986). Underachieving children: An analysis of psychometric characteristics of emotionally handicapped, learning disabled, and non referred underachieving. *Dissertation Abstracts International, 47*(11), 4059B. (University Microfilms No. AAC87-04204)
55	Scarborough, H. S. (1989). Prediction of reading disability from familial and individual differences. *Journal of Educational Psychology, 81,* 101–108.

(Continued)

Study #	Citation of Article (or of Articles Based on Same Study)
56	Scott, M. J. (1987). Examining the reading and spelling skills of slow learners: Frith's model of developmental dyslexia. *Dissertation Abstracts International, 49*(07), 1743B. (University Microfilms No. AAC88-18970)
57	Shaywitz, S. E., Escobar, M. D., Shaywitz, B. A., Fletcher, J. M., & Makuch, R. (1992). Evidence that dyslexia may represent the lower tail of a normal distribution of reading ability. *New England Journal of Medicine, 326*, 145–150.
58	Shaywitz, B. A., Fletcher, J. M., Holahan, J. M., & Shaywitz, S. E. (1992). Discrepancy compared to low achievement definitions of reading disability: Results from the Connecticut Longitudinal Study. *Journal of Learning Disabilities, 25*, 639–648.
59	Shinn, M. R., Habedank, L., Rodden-Nord, K., & Knutson, N. (1993). Using curriculum-based measurement to identify potential candidates for reintegration into general education. *The Journal of Special Education, 27*, 202–221.
60	Shinn, M., & Marston, D. (1985). Differentiating mildly handicapped, low-achieving, and regular education students: A curriculum-based approach. *Remedial and Special Education, 6*(2), 31–38.
61	Shinn, M. R., Tindal, G. A., Spira, D., & Marston, D. (1987). Practice of learning disabilities as social policy. *Learning Disability Quarterly, 10*, 17–28.
62	Shinn, M. R., Ysseldyke, J., Deno, S., & Tindal, G. (1982). *A comparison of psychometric and functional differences between students labeled learning disabled and low achieving* (Research Report No. 71). Duluth: University of Minnesota Institute for Research on Learning Disabilities. (ERIC Document Reproduction Service No. ED 218 853)
	Shinn, M. R., Ysseldyke, J. E., Deno, S. L., & Tindal, G. A. (1986). A comparison of differences between students labeled learning disabled and low achieving on measures of classroom performance. *Journal of Learning Disabilities, 19*, 545–552.
63	Silver, B. D. (1984). Social skills deficits in learning disabled adolescents. *Dissertation Abstracts International, 45*(09), 3085B. (University Microfilms No. AAC84-26684)
64	Smith, D. K., & Lyon, M. A. (1987, April). *Children with learning difficulties: Similarities and differences in cognitive abilities and achievement.* Paper presented at the annual meeting of the American Educational Research Association. (ERIC Document Reproduction Service No. ED 285 317)
65	Sparks, R. L., Ganschow, L., Javorsky, J., Pohlman, J., & Patton, J. (1992). Test comparisons among students identified as high-risk, low-risk, and learning disabled in high school foreign language courses. *Modern Language Journal, 76*, 142–159.
	Sparks, R. L., Ganschow, L., & Javorsky, J. (1993). Perceptions of low and high risk students and students with learning disabilities about high school foreign language courses. *Foreign Language Annals, 26*, 491–510.
66	Spector, J. E. (1983). Contrastive patterns of performance in learning-disabled and non-learning disabled readers. *Dissertation Abstracts International, 45*(05), 1405B. (University Microfilms No. AAC83-20779)
67	Tarkin, B. J. (1987). Long-term prediction of learning disabilities with the McCarthy scales of children's abilities. *Dissertation Abstracts International, 48*(11), 2838B. (University Microfilms No. AAC87-28483)

(Continued)

Study #	Citation of Article (or of Articles Based on Same Study)
68	Tindal, G., & Nolet, V. (1996). Serving students in middle school content classes: A heuristic study of critical variables linking instruction and assessment. *The Journal of Special Education, 29,* 414–432.
69	Tindal, G., Rebar, M., Nolet, V., & McCollum, S. (1995). Understanding instructional outcome options for students with special needs in content classes. *Learning Disabilities Research & Practice, 10,* 72–84.
70	Trelikes, F. R. (1985). A comparison of low achieving and learning disabled secondary students on academic achievement, behavior, attendance, language, self-concept, and perceptual and memory skills. *Dissertation Abstracts International, 45*(12), 3614A. (University Microfilms No. AAC85-03367)
71	Tur-Kaspa, H., & Bryan, T. (1993). Social attributions of students with learning disabilities. *Exceptionality, 4,* 229–243. Tur-Kaspa, H., & Bryan, T. (1995). Teachers' ratings of the social competence and school adjustment of students with LD in elementary and junior high school. *Journal of Learning Disabilities, 28,* 44–52.
72	Tur-Kaspa, H., & Bryan, T. (1994). Social information-processing skills of students with learning disabilities. *Learning Disabilities Research & Practice, 9,* 12–23.
73	Vaughn, S., Haager, D., Hogan, A., & Kouzekanani, K. (1992). Self-concept and peer acceptance in students with learning disabilities: A four- to five-year prospective study. *Journal of Educational Psychology, 84,* 43–50. Vaughn, S., Zaragoza, N., Hogan, A., & Walker, J. (1993). A four-year longitudinal investigation of the social skills and behavior problems of students with learning disabilities. *Journal of Learning Disabilities, 26,* 404–412.
74	Vaughn, S., & Hogan, A. (1990). Social competence and learning disabilities: A prospective study. In H. L. Swanson & B. Keogh (Eds.), *Learning disabilities: Theoretical and research issues* (pp. 175–191). Hillsdale, NJ: Lawrence Erlbaum Associates. Vaughn, S., Hogan, A., Kouzekanani, K., & Shapiro, S. (1990). Peer acceptance, self-perceptions, and social skills of learning-disabled students prior to identification. *Journal of Educational Psychology, 82,* 101–106.
75	Vaughn, S., McIntosh, R., Schumm, J. S., Haager, D., & Callwood, D. (1993). Social status, peer acceptance, and reciprocal friendships revisited. *Learning Disabilities Research & Practice, 8,* 82–88.
76	White, D. F., Saudargas, R. A., & Zanolli, K. (1990). LD children's regular classroom behavior before and after identification and placement. *Learning Disability Quarterly, 13,* 196–204.
77	Wilson, K. P. (1982). Cognitive processing and reading disability. *Dissertation Abstracts International, 43*(06), 2026B. (University Microfilms No. AAC82-26046)
78	Ysseldyke, J. E., Algozzine, B., & Epps, S. (1982, October). *A logical and empirical analysis of current practices in classifying students as handicapped* (Report No. 92). Duluth: University of Minnesota Institute for Research on Learning Disabilities. (ERIC Document Reproduction Service No. ED 228 824) Ysseldyke, J., Algozzine, B., & Epps, S. (1983). A logical and empirical analysis of current practice in classifying students as handicapped. *Exceptional Children, 50,* 160–166.

(Continued)

APPENDIX
(Continued)

Study #	Citation of Article (or of Articles Based on Same Study)
79	Ysseldyke, J. E., Algozzine, B., Shinn, M., & McGue, M. (1979). *Similarities and differences between underachievers and students labeled learning disabled: Identical twins with different mothers* (Research Report No. 13). Duluth: University of Minnesota Institute for Research on Learning Disabilities. (ERIC Document Reproduction Service No. ED 185 757) Ysseldyke, J. E., Algozzine, B., Shinn, M. R., & McGue, M. (1982). Similarities and differences between low achievers and students classified learning disabled. *The Journal of Special Education, 16,* 73–85.

REFERENCES

Algozzine, B. (1985). Low achiever differentiation: Where's the beef? *Exceptional Children, 52,* 72–75.

Fuchs, D., Fuchs, L. S., Mathes, P., & Lipsey, M. (1998). *Is LD just a fancy name for under-achievement? A meta-analysis of reading performance differences between low-achieving students with and without the LD label.* Unpublished manuscript. (Available from D. Fuchs, Box 328 Peabody, Vanderbilt University, Nashville, TN 37203)

Hallahan, D. P. (1992). Some thoughts on why the prevalence of learning disabilities has increased. *Journal of Learning Disabilities, 25,* 523–528.

Hedges, L. V. (1981). Distribution theory for Glass's estimator of effect size and related estimators. *Journal of Educational Statistics, 6,* 490–499.

Hedges, L. V., & Olkin, I. (1985). *Methods of meta-analysis.* Newbury Park, CA: Sage.

Kavale, K. A. (1995). Setting the record straight on learning disability and low achievement: The tortuous path of ideology. *Learning Disabilities Research & Practice, 10,* 145–152.

Kavale, K., & Forness, S. (1985). *The science of learning disabilities.* San Diego: College-Hill Press.

Kavale, K. A., Forness, S. R., & Lorsbach, T. C. (1991). Definition for definitions of learning disabilities. *Learning Disability Quarterly, 14,* 257–268.

Kavale, K. A., Fuchs, D., & Scruggs, T. E. (1994). Setting the record straight on learning disability and low achievement: Implications for policymaking. *Learning Disabilities Research & Practice, 9,* 70–77.

Keogh, B. K. (1987). Learning disabilities: In defense of a construct. *Learning Disabilities Research, 3,* 4–9.

McLeskey, J., & Waldron, N. L. (1990). The identification and characteristics of students with learning disabilities in Indiana. *Learning Disabilities Research, 5,* 72–78.

Mercer, C. D., King-Sears, P., & Mercer, A. R. (1990). Learning disabilities definitions and criteria used by state education departments. *Learning Disability Quarterly, 13,* 141–152.

Reschly, D. R. (1996). *Disproportionate minority representation in general and special education programs: Patterns, issues, and alternatives.* Des Moines: Iowa Department of Education.

Shepard, L. A., Smith, M. L., & Vojir, C. P. (1983). Characteristics of pupils identified as learning disabled. *American Educational Research Journal, 20,* 309–332.

Shinn, M. R., Tindal, G. A., Spira, D., & Marston, D. (1987). Practice of learning disabilities as social policy. *Learning Disability Quarter, 10,* 17–28.

Shinn, M. R., Ysseldyke, J. E., Deno, S. L., & Tindal, G. A. (1986). A comparison of differences between students labeled learning disabled and low achieving on measures of classroom performance. *Journal of Learning Disabilities, 19,* 545–552.

U.S. Department of Education. (1995). *Seventeenth annual report to Congress on the implementation of the Individuals with Disabilities Act*. Washington, DC: U.S. Government Printing Office.

Wolf, M. (1991). Naming speed and reading: The contribution of the cognitive neurosciences. *Reading Research Quarterly, 26,* 123–141.

Ysseldyke, J. E., Algozzine, B., Richey, L., & Graden, J. (1982). Declaring students eligible for disability services: Why bother with the data? *Learning Disability Quarterly, 5*(1), 37–43.

Ysseldyke, J. E., Algozzine, B., Shinn, M. R., & McGue, M. (1982). Similarities and differences between low achievers and students classified learning disabled. *The Journal of Special Education, 16,* 73–85.

Chapter 4

How Reading Outcomes of Students With Disabilities Are Related to Instructional Grouping Formats: A Meta-Analytic Review

Batya Elbaum
University of Miami

Sharon Vaughn
University of Texas at Austin

Marie Tejero Hughes
Sally Watson Moody
Jeanne Shay Schumm
University of Miami

> *Given that there are more students who need to learn to read than there are teachers to teach them, what is the best way to organize students, teachers, and the curriculum to manage instruction for the effective teaching of reading?*
> (Otto, Wolf, & Eldridge, 1984, p. 800)

Both general and special education teachers in the United States are faced with complex classroom ecologies (Speece & Keogh, 1996). The broadening range of cultural, linguistic, and academic diversity among students coupled with increasing class sizes poses a challenge for teachers in their efforts to provide appropriate reading instruction for all students. This challenge is particularly acute as teachers plan and implement instruction for students with disabilities for whom learning to read is very difficult. A variety of grouping formats, such as peer tutoring, have been offered as having promise for meeting individual needs within large, diverse classroom settings. However, the impact of these grouping formats on the development of reading skills for students with disabilities has not been determined. A synthesis of the research on grouping formats for reading instruction for students with disabilities is warranted, particularly in light of recent reforms in special education and in grouping practices for reading instruction.

Reform in Special Education

For decades, students with disabilities in need of specialized reading instruction were assigned part- or full-time to a special education classroom. This "pull-out" model has been criticized because it is thought to contribute to the academic and social isolation of students with disabilities (e.g., Leinhardt & Pallay, 1982; Will, 1986). In hope of eliminating perceived barriers to the success of students with disabilities attributed to placement in special education settings (e.g., social isolation from general education peers; instruction that was disconnected from general education curriculum), Will launched the Regular Education Initiative (REI).

The REI is arguably the reform in special education that has had the greatest impact on the educational community. This initiative called for the reduction of pull-out programs for students with disabilities and the inclusion of these students in the general education classroom. Thus, increasing numbers of students with disabilities are being included in the general education classroom for all or part of the school day. This has given rise to new challenges regarding grouping students for instruction and has led to a reexamination of general and special education teachers' roles and responsibilities in the teaching of reading to individual students, subgroups of students, and whole classes.

Reform in Grouping Practices for Reading Instruction

Until relatively recently, elementary classroom teachers used small, homogeneous (same-ability) groups for reading instruction (Barr & Dreeben, 1991; Slavin, 1987). Criticisms of this prevailing practice were raised on the grounds that ability grouping lowers self-esteem and motivation among students with reading problems, restricts friendship choices, and often "widens the gap" between high and low achievers (Calfee & Brown, 1979; Hiebert, 1983; Rosenholtz & Wilson, 1980). Documentation of differential treatment of "low" and "high" ability groups is copious (Barr, 1989). There is evidence that students placed in lower ability groups receive instruction that is inferior to that of their higher ability counterparts in terms of instructional time (Hunter, 1978), time on task (Gambrell, 1984), meaning orientation to reading tasks (Allington, 1980), appropriateness of reading materials (Gambrell, Wilson, & Gantt, 1981; Juel, 1988), and amount of material read (Allington, 1984; Gambrell, 1984). In addition, Oakes, Gamoran, and Page (1992) argued that students of minority groups are overrepresented in low-ability groups.

These criticisms were raised concurrently with the advent of popular attention to alternative grouping practices such as cooperative learning groups (e.g., D. W. Johnson & R. T. Johnson, 1975; Slavin, 1983a) and cross-age tutoring (e.g., Come & Fredericks, 1995; Labo & Teale, 1990). These sorts of grouping practices were intended to help classroom teachers accommodate individual differences and to avoid the social stigmas associated with ability grouping. Indeed, some advocates of the REI propose that such grouping practices can reduce the need for pull-out services (Reynolds, Wang, & Walberg, 1987; W. Stainback, S. Stainback, Courtnage, & Jaben, 1985). Recommendations for such grouping practices continue to appear in the professional literature (e.g., J. Flood, Lapp, S. Flood, & Nagel, 1992; Radencich & McKay, 1995) as well as in current basal reading series (Moody, Schumm, Fischer, & Jean-Francois, 1999), where they are presented as viable ways to help all students learn to read.

An important matter to note is that reforms in grouping practices have had an impact not only on the general education classroom, but on the special education classroom as well. Traditionally, students identified for special education services who had difficulty in learning how to read were assigned to a special education resource room. Students were often administered diagnostic measures and instruction was tailored to meet the specific learning needs of students. Recent research in special education resource rooms indicates that these classrooms have in many cases undergone dramatic changes (Vaughn, Moody, & Schumm, 1998). Teachers report using whole-class instruction coupled with other grouping formats (e.g., cooperative learning groups, student pairing). Therefore, whether students with disabilities are placed in special or general education classrooms for reading, they are likely to be involved in grouping formats such as pairing or cooperative learning groups.

Research on Grouping Formats: Student Pairing

Student pairing (students working together in groups of two) is a grouping format that both general (Schumm, Vaughn, & Elbaum, 1996) and special education (Moody, Vaughn, & Schumm, 1997) teachers report using to provide students with reading problems the additional support they need. A number of research reviews and syntheses have examined student pairs and have generally provided support for the effectiveness of this grouping format. We note, however, that these reviews differed from the present synthesis in that they either did not specifically target students with disabilities (e.g., Cohen, J. A. Kulik, & C. C. Kulik, 1982; Devin-Sheehan, Feldman, & Allen, 1976), investigated outcomes for students in a single type of disability such as behavior disorders (Scruggs, Mastropieri,

& Richter, 1985) or learning disabilities (Scruggs & Richter, 1985), focused on one kind of student pairing such as cross-age tutoring (Gredler, 1985), or were not specific to reading (e.g., Lloyd, Crowley, Kohler, & Strain, 1988; Scruggs et al., 1985; Scruggs & Richter, 1985). Mathes and L. S. Fuchs (1994) conducted a best-evidence synthesis of 11 studies of peer tutoring in reading for students with disabilities. The findings from this meta-analysis indicated overall positive outcomes (mean unbiased effect size of .36) from peer tutoring interventions for students with disabilities.

The role that students play within pairs is also relevant to the efficacy of student pairing. Students with disabilities frequently assume the role of tutee; the tutors assisting them may be students who are older or are more proficient readers. However, students with disabilities may also assume the role of tutor; this practice is sometimes known as reverse-role tutoring (Eiserman, Shisler, & Osguthorpe, 1987). Another configuration involves having pairs of students engage in reciprocal tutoring, wherein each student serves alternately as tutor and tutee. Reciprocal tutoring is an important component of a peer tutoring program designed for general education classrooms (classwide peer tutoring; Delquadri, Greenwood, Whorton, Carta, & Hall, 1986; Mathes, L. S. Fuchs, D. Fuchs, Henley, & Sanders, 1994). Because of these variations, we examined the role of the student with disabilities (i.e., tutor, tutee, reciprocal tutor–tutee) within pairs.

Three previous reviews examining reverse-role tutoring concluded that students with disabilities could indeed perform effectively in the role of tutor (Cook, Scruggs, Mastropieri, & Casto, 1986; Eiserman et al., 1987; Osguthorpe & Scruggs, 1986). These reviews were, however, not exclusive to reading and included tutoring in subjects such as sign language. Mathes and L. S. Fuchs' (1994) meta-analysis indicated that students with disabilities made greater gains in reading when they served in the role of tutor (ES [effect size] = .42) than when they were tutees (ES = .30) or did reciprocal tutoring (ES = .34). Mathes and Fuchs noted, however, that the mean effect sizes for different student roles were not reflected consistently in all studies, and that the outcomes in particular studies may have been affected by the specific tutoring treatments.

Variations in outcomes of student pairing may also be associated with the relative age of the partners involved in the pair. In some cases, tutors and tutees are same-age peers. In other situations, older students with or without disabilities tutor younger students, with or without disabilities, referred to as cross-age tutoring (Gredler, 1985). Osguthorpe and Scruggs (1986) and Scruggs et al. (1985) reviewed more than 25 studies related to cross-age tutoring in which students with disabilities acted as tutors for younger students with disabilities. Results indicated positive outcomes in academic achievement for both tutors and tutees, though no meta-analysis was conducted.

Small-Group Instruction

Small-group instruction is another frequently used, though understudied, grouping format for students with disabilities. Lou et al. (1996) recently published a review of the literature on within-class grouping. They pointed out that previous meta-analyses have reported positive academic outcomes of small-group instruction when compared to whole-class instruction (Kulik & Kulik, 1987; Slavin, 1987). Citing the inconsistencies and limitations of previous meta-analyses, Lou et al. (1996) designed a more comprehensive meta-analysis that addressed such issues as homogenous versus heterogeneous grouping and attempted to identify the conditions under which different grouping formats were most effective. While the researchers found evidence favoring small group instruction and homogeneous grouping for reading, data pertaining to students with disabilities were not included.

Another important question left unanswered by Lou et. al.'s synthesis is whether students can make progress in reading when working together in small, student-led groups. If students can, indeed, make significant gains through participation in student-led groups, the amount of direct contact time teachers need to have with students can be reduced. Mathes and Fuchs (1994) attempted to address a similar question with regard to tutoring, that is, whether a treatment is more effective when delivered by peers or by teachers, when instructional activities and amount of instructional time are the same. They found one study (McCracken, 1979) that provided such a comparison, and in this instance, results for peer-tutored students were not significantly different from those of teacher-tutored students. However, we are aware of no research on small groups for students with disabilities that directly compares gains associated with teacher-led and non-teacher-led groups.

Multiple-Grouping Formats

Another grouping practice reported in the literature on reading instruction consists of the use of combinations of different grouping patterns, which we refer to as multiple grouping formats. We include multiple grouping formats in our review for two reasons. Classroom teachers are being encouraged to use a variety of grouping formats for reading instruction (Flood et al., 1992); moreover, both general education teachers (Schumm et al., 1996) and special education teachers (Vaughn et al., 1998) report using a variety of grouping formats for reading instruction.

The effects of multiple grouping formats for students with disabilities have not been the focus of prior reviews and syntheses.

Previous reviews addressing grouping practices have compared the effectiveness of homogeneous versus heterogeneous grouping for reading instruction (e.g., Barr & Dreeben, 1991; Slavin, 1987), whole-class versus small-group instruction (e.g., Lou et al., 1996), student pairing (Mathes & L. S. Fuchs, 1994), and general education versus special education settings for students with disabilities (e.g., Leinhardt & Pallay, 1982). However, to date there has been no attempt to synthesize and systematically compare outcomes across different formats. The purpose of this meta-analysis, therefore, was to determine the extent to which outcomes in reading for students with disabilities are related to the grouping format used during their reading instruction.

METHOD

Procedures defined by Cooper (1989) were employed to identify the sample of studies to be used in the meta-analysis. Operational definitions of the critical terms involved in our primary research questions (e.g., grouping format, students with disabilities, reading outcomes) are provided in Table 4.1.

Study Eligibility

Search criteria were adopted with an aim to locating studies that met the following requirements:

1. Students with disabilities, as defined in our operational definitions, comprised all or some of the participants.
2. Participants were not students in ESOL (English for Speakers of Other Languages) programs.
3. The majority of participants were in Grades 1 through 6.
4. The grouping format used for the intervention was specified and corresponded to a category in our operational definition.
5. The intervention occurred in the area of reading/language arts (reading and strategy interventions in content areas were not included).
6. The intervention took place in school.
7. The language of instruction was English.
8. The study was reported/published between 1975 and 1995.

In order to be included in the meta-analysis, studies had to meet the following additional criteria:

TABLE 4.1
Operational Definitions

Grouping format: An arrangement of students for instructional purposes. Grouping formats to be investigated included pairs, small groups, whole class, and multiple grouping formats (see below). Individual instruction (i.e., one adult teaching a single child) would not be considered a grouping format.

Pairing: Students work together in groups of two. Pairs may be characterized with respect to (a) the role of the students in the pair and (b) the relative ages of the two students. Students working in pairs may take on one of four roles: tutor, tutee, reciprocal tutor–tutee (students take turns being tutor and tutee), or cooperative partner (students work together cooperatively, mutually offering corrections and feedback). When students engage in unidirectional or reciprocal tutoring with same-grade peers (who are typically of similar age), this is referred to as *peer tutoring*. When a student tutors a student in a lower grade (who is typically younger), this is referred to as *cross-age tutoring*.

Small groups: Students are placed in groups that typically range from 3 to 10 students. Groups may be characterized with respect to (a) whether the teacher is leading the group or the students are working independently of the teacher and (b) whether the students in the group are of similar or different ability levels with respect to reading. When the teacher is teaching the small group or directly guiding their activity, the group is referred to as *teacher-led*. When students in a small group are working together toward a common goal, e.g., to improve reading skill—and are doing so without the direct supervision of the teacher—the group is referred to as *non-teacher-led*, or *cooperative*.

Whole class: Instruction takes place during whole-group, or total-class, sessions.

Multiple grouping formats: Instruction makes use of a specified combination of grouping formats, e.g., pairing and small groups. (Note that instruction that relies primarily on one format and makes only occasional, nonsystematic use of another format does not qualify under the present definition.)

Students with disabilities: Students identified in the primary research as students with learning disabilities, behavior disorder, neurologically impaired, dyslexic, or emotionally disturbed. Students described as at risk, reading disabled, and eligible for Title I assistance are not included.

Reading outcomes: Outcomes in reading and language arts in the following categories: general reading (including tests comprised of several subtests that yield a composite reading score), reading comprehension, oral reading of words, oral reading of passages, decoding, spelling, composition/writing, language mechanics, and listening comprehension.

---

1. Outcomes were reported for a group or groups of students; that is, the study did not employ a single subject design.
2. The study used a comparison or control group, and students in the comparison/control group were also students with disabilities.
3. The groups provided a contrast of grouping formats or other contrast relevant to our research questions (e.g., a contrast of students' roles during pairing).

4. Results were reported quantitatively.
5. The data reported were sufficient for computation of an effect size (e.g., a study that reported posttest means but no standard deviations could not be included).

Literature Search

The literature search using informal and formal channels was conducted following procedures recommended by Cooper and Hedges (1994). A list of descriptors was developed and used to guide a computer search of the following online databases: PsychLit, Educational Resources Information Center (ERIC), Dissertations Abstracts OnDisc, and the Government Documents database. A hand search of the following journals was conducted for months not included on databases up to December 1995: *Reading Teacher, Reading Research Quarterly, Journal of Reading Behavior, Exceptional Children, Exceptionality, Journal of Learning Disabilities,* and *Learning Disabilities Research and Practice.* These searches yielded approximately 7,500 abstracts, of which many were duplicates due to the use of multiple databases.

Additionally, letters were sent to those researchers who had made presentations on the topic of grouping at meetings of the American Educational Research Association, the Council for Exceptional Children, the International Reading Association, and the National Reading Conference held between 1991 and 1995, as well as other researchers who have conducted or are currently conducting research on grouping practices. We asked these researchers to send us copies of any manuscripts currently in press or under review that related to grouping practices.

A procedure known as "footnote chasing" (White, 1994), in which the bibliographies of previous reviews or articles are used as sources, was also implemented. Studies from previous reviews were selected and the Social Science Citation Index was used to identify articles that cited key studies and reviews on grouping. A strong effort was made to retrieve studies belonging to the so-called "fugitive" literature. The main method used in our fugitive search was to contact all 50 State Departments of Education and three randomly selected school districts (urban, suburban, rural) from each state requesting manuscripts and/or technical reports that related to our meta-analysis. Finally, a hand search of books that might contain relevant studies was conducted. This involved searching our university library's main catalog as well as those of nine of the largest publishers in the field of education, using broad descriptors related to grouping.

Coding of Studies

Code Sheet. A code sheet and code book were developed to record information about each study in the sample. The code sheet included the following sections: (a) publication and coder information, (b) description of participants included in the study, (c) design and methodology, (d) characteristics of treatment and comparison groups, and (e) results and statistical analyses.

Pretest and Pilot Test of the Coding Procedure. Two pretests of the code sheet and coding procedure were conducted. For the first pretest, six coders independently coded the same three articles. The coders then met to discuss the coding procedure as a whole as well as the coding of specific items. The coders recommended a number of modifications, primarily in the wording of particular items and the number of choices provided (e.g., a "not reported" choice was added to certain items for consistency across items). For the second pretest, the same six coders independently coded another set of three articles. Once again the coders came together as a group and discussed any coding difficulties, and modifications were made to the code sheet.

Following the pretests, a pilot test was conducted on a larger sample of studies. Nine studies that represented a range of research designs and sources (e.g., dissertations, published studies) were selected for this purpose. Each coder was randomly paired with another coder, forming three teams of coders. Each team was assigned three of the nine articles to code. Each study was coded independently by the two coders on each team; then, the partners met to compare their coding of the three studies assigned to them. When an item was not coded identically by the two partners, the partners discussed the item, arrived at a code by consensus, and filled out a negotiation form to assure that a record was kept both of the item accounting for the inconsistency in coding and the resolution agreed on by the coding partners. The six coders were paired with different partners for a second round of coding. Procedures identical to those used in the first round were employed, using different studies.

Upon completion of the pilot test, coding for interrater reliability was conducted using three articles that had not previously been coded during the pretests or pilot. Each researcher independently coded the same three articles. The code sheets submitted by the six coders were compared to a master code sheet developed by the pair of researchers that had developed the original code sheet. Reliability, defined as the percent agreement between codes assigned by a given coder and those established by the master code sheet ranged from .82 to .99 with a mean of .90.

Computation of Effect Sizes

The basic index of effect size used in this meta-analysis was Glass' Δ, the difference between the treatment and control group means divided by the control group standard deviation (Glass, McGaw, & Smith, 1981). For between-group studies, we subtracted the mean of the control group's unadjusted posttest score from the mean of the treatment group's unadjusted posttest score and divided by the control group's posttest standard deviation.

Where authors of studies reported effect sizes based on *adjusted* posttest scores or gain scores, the reported effect sizes may be different from those computed for this meta-analysis. For example, the standard deviation of gain scores is usually smaller than the standard deviation of posttest scores (Glass et al., 1981), resulting in relatively larger effect sizes.

In the small number of cases in which means and standard deviations were not available, effect sizes were estimated from ts, Fs, or ps. All effect size computations were calculated by one of the authors and a research associate. Each computation was cross-checked to assure that the values used for calculation of the effect size corresponded to those reported in the study and that no computational errors were made.

Unit of Analysis.   The basic unit of analysis used in our computations was the independent sample, defined as a set of individuals not included in any other sample. A problem that arises in meta-analyses addressing multiple research questions is that the unit of analysis may change, depending on the way effect sizes are aggregated (Cooper, Nye, Charlton, Lindsay, & Greathouse, 1996). We thus adopted Cooper's (1989) "shifting unit of analysis," whereby each independent sample can contribute only one data point within a given aggregation. Cooper et al. underscored that this approach retains as much data as possible while minimizing any violations of the assumption that the data points used in the analyses are independent.

Calculation of Average Effect Sizes.   For each aggregation of effect sizes, we calculated a mean weighted effect size across independent samples of students. Weighted means give greater weight to effect sizes based on larger numbers of students in the sample. Calculation of the mean weighted effect size is also useful in that it allows for estimation of an associated confidence interval (Cooper, 1989).

To calculate the mean weighted effect size, $\Delta+$, each effect size was first multiplied by its weight, computed as the inverse of the variance associated with the effect size estimate (Cooper, 1989). Then the sum of these products was divided by the sum of the weights. If the 95% confidence interval for $\Delta+$ did not include 0, we concluded that the mean weighted effect size was reliably different from 0.

Homogeneity Analyses.   Homogeneity analyses (Cooper, 1989; Hedges & Olkin, 1985) were conducted to determine whether the variation in effect sizes within a particular aggregation could be accounted for by sampling error alone, or, conversely, whether specific coded features of the effect sizes could account for a significant amount of this variation. The test statistic Q_T (where "T" stands for "total") was calculated using the following formula:

$$Q_t = \sum_{i=1}^{n} w_i d_i^2 - \frac{\left(\sum_{i=1}^{n} w_i d_i\right)^2}{\sum_{i-1}^{n} w_i} \quad (1)$$

In order to examine differences due to specific variables of interest (e.g., grouping format), we calculated the between-groups heterogeneity statistic, Q_B (Hedges, 1994), calculated as $Q_T - Q_W$, where Q_W represents the sum of the Q statistics calculated separately for the effect sizes within each level (or category) of the variable of interest. For our analyses, we applied a fixed effects model as described by Hedges. When Q_B exceeds a critical value, this indicates that the variable in question is significantly associated with the variance in effect sizes.

ANALYSIS AND FINDINGS

Data Analysis Plan

Given the possibility that grouping format would be confounded with, or moderated by, other substantive variables (Lipsey, 1994), such as the length of the intervention and the focus of instruction, a number of analyses were conducted prior to examining the variation associated with grouping format. These analyses are reported in detail elsewhere (Elbaum, Vaughn, Hughes, Moody, & Schumm, 1998).

Figure 4.1 illustrates the aggregations of effect sizes used in the meta-analysis and gives the weighted mean effect size for each aggregation. Our intent was to follow up the main analysis by grouping format with further analyses of critical aspects of the individual formats. For pairing formats, we investigated whether the variation in effect sizes for pairs was related to type of pairing (peer [same-age] tutoring, cross-age tutoring, cooperative partners) and, for tutoring interventions, to the role of the student (tutor, tutee, reciprocal tutor–tutee).

We had also intended to conduct further analyses of the effect sizes for small groups, in order to examine the variation associated with type of group (teacher-led vs. non-teacher-led) and the ability-match of students within a group (same-ability vs. mixed-ability). However, we were unable to conduct these analyses as only one small-group study meeting eligibility criteria could be located.

Methodological as well as substantive variables can account for variation in effect sizes across studies (Cooper, 1989; Wortman, 1994). Our final analy-

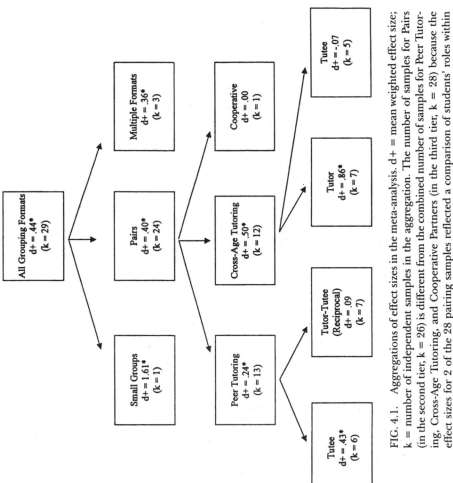

FIG. 4.1. Aggregations of effect sizes in the meta-analysis. d+ = mean weighted effect size; k = number of independent samples in the aggregation. The number of samples for Pairs (in the second tier, k = 26) is different from the combined number of samples for Peer Tutoring, Cross-Age Tutoring, and Cooperative Partners (in the third tier, k = 28) because the effect sizes for 2 of the 28 pairing samples reflected a comparison of students' roles within pairs and not a comparison of grouping formats.

ses address differences in effect sizes associated with key methodological variables. In the following sections, the reported mean weighted effect sizes are all reliably different from 0 (i.e., the calculated 95% confidence interval did not include 0) unless otherwise indicated by the abbreviation *n.s.*

The Effect Size Data Set

The data set for the meta-analysis of grouping formats consisted of 116 effect sizes (2 additional effect sizes were used in the analysis contrasting students' roles in tutoring interventions) based on 28 independent samples of students with disabilities. The 28 student samples came from 19 studies reported in 18 articles; 1 article (Scruggs & Osguthorpe, 1986) reported reading outcomes of two studies. The distribution of the 116 effect sizes that contrasted grouping formats was approximately normal with M (mean) = .37, SD (standard deviation) = .62, median = .30 and range from −1.08 to 2.19. The distribution of effect sizes averaged within independent samples (n = 28) was also relatively normal, with M = .41, SD = .51, median = .40 and range from −.36 to 1.61. Table 4.2 provides the study reference as well as pertinent information on each independent sample included in the analyses.

The majority of studies were conducted between 1986 and 1995. Two thirds of the studies had been supported by the U.S. Department of Education; the next most frequently identified funding agency was the National Institute of Health (10%).

Over two thirds of the studies included participants in Grades 4 and 5. Students in Grades 2 and 3 were included in half of the studies. Kindergarteners and first-graders were less frequently included. The socioeconomic status (SES) of the participants was reported in 8 of the 21 studies; across these studies, participants were equally divided between lower/lower-middle and middle/upper-middle class.

Analysis by Grouping Format

Our main research question concerned the association between reading outcomes and different instructional grouping formats. The three formats included in our analyses were pairs, small groups, and multiple formats. As indicated in Table 4.3, the mean weighted effect size for all types of grouping was Δ+ = .43. The mean weighted effect sizes for the three grouping formats analyzed separately were: Δ+ = 1.61 for small groups (k = 1); Δ+ = .40 for pairs (k = 24); and Δ+ = .36 for multiple grouping formats (k = 3). Because the single small-group effect size was very high and because this category contributed no variance to the sum of the within-group variances, the heterogeneity statistic was significant, $Q_w(2)$ = 7.36, $p < .05$. When the small-

TABLE 4.2

Descriptive Information on Studies and Independent Samples Included in the Meta-Analysis

Study #	Reference	Exceptionality	n of Students in Treatment Group[ii]	n of Students in Comparison Group[iii]	Grouping Format of Treatment Group[iv]	n of Effect Sizes[v]	Mean Effect Size
1	Cochran, Feng, Cartledge, & Hamilton (1993)	BD[a] BD[a]	4 4	4 4	pairing pairing	1 1	.59 .01
2	Englert & Mariage (1991)	LD[b]	11	17	small groups	3	1.61
3	Epstein (1978)	LD[b]	20	20	pairing	3	1.07
4	Friedman (1990)	LD[b] + OD[c]	9	9	pairing	6	.64
5	D. Fuchs, L. S. Fuchs, Mathes, & Simmons (1997)	LD[b]	20	20	pairing	3	.43
6	J. R. Jenkins, Jewell, Leicester, L. Jenkins, & Troutner (1991)	LD[b] + OD[c]	6	3	multiple formats	3	.03
7	J. R. Jenkins, Jewell, O'Connor, L. M. Jenkins, & Troutner (1994)	LD[b] + OD[c]	12	25	multiple formats	6	.38
8	Mathes & L. S. Fuchs (1993)	LD[b] LD[b]	22 23	22 22	pairing pairing	3 3	-.36 .08
9	Moore (1993)	LD[b] LD[b]	5 6	5 5	pairing pairing	9 9	.33 .10
10	Osguthorpe & Eiserman (1986)	LD[b] LD[b]	15 14	12 12	pairing pairing	1 1	-.21 -.09

	Study						
11	Scruggs & Osguthorpe (1986), Study #1	LD[b] + OD[c] LD[b] + OD[c]	12 9	17 14	pairing pairing	7 9	-.13 .42
12	Scruggs & Osguthorpe (1986), Study #2	LD[b] + OD[c]	14	13	pairing	7	-.12
13	Shishler, Top, & Osguthorpe (1986)	BD[a]	10	13	pairing	4	.76
14	Shoulders (1991)	LD[b] + OD[c] LD[b] + OD[c]	6 6	6 6	pairing pairing	1 1	.62 .99
15	Simmons, L. S. Fuchs, D. Fuchs, Mathes, & Hodge (1995)	LD[b]	18	21	pairing	7	.42
16	Sindelar (1982)	LD[b] + OD[c] LD[b] + OD[c] LD[b] + OD[c]	11 13 14	15 15 15	pairing pairing pairing	4 4 4	-.33 -.21 .18
17	Stevens, Madden, Slavin, & Farnish (1987), Study #2	LD[b]	6	14	multiple formats	4	.47
18	Top & Osguthorpe (1985)	LD[b] BD[a]	22 10	19 13	pairing pairing	4 4	1.21 1.13
19	Top & Osguthorpe (1987)	LD[b] + OD[c]	39	39	pairing	4	1.04
20	Trapani & Gettinger (1989)	LD[b] LD[b]	7 6	6 6	pairing pairing	1 1	.07 -.09

Note. The effect size comparisons from the study by Osguthorpe and Eiserman (1986) did not provide a contrast of grouping format. Thus, they were used only in the analysis of pairing.

[a]BD = Students with behavior disorders. [b]LD = Students with learning disabilities. [c]OD = Students with other disabilities. [i]Total number of studies = 20. [ii]Total number of students in treatment groups = 375. [iii]Total number of student in comparison groups = 412. [iv]Total number of independent samples = 30. [v]Total number of effect sizes = 118.

119

TABLE 4.3
Analysis by Grouping Format

Variable	Q_B	k	Mean Δ (Unweighted)	Mean Δ+ (Weighted)	95% C.I.	Q_W
Grouping Format	7.36*	28	.41	.43[a]	.29, .58	48.15*
Pairing		24	.37	.40[a]	.24, .56	40.51*
Small Groups		1	1.61	1.61[a]	.75, 2.48	0.00
Multiple Formats		3	.29	.36	−.17, .88	.28

[a]95% confidence interval does not include 0.
*$p < .05$.

group effect size was removed from the calculation, the heterogeneity statistic was not significant. This result indicates no reliable difference in the magnitude of outcomes associated with pairs versus multiple grouping formats.

Additional Analyses of Pairing Formats

Analysis by Type of Pair. The significant homogeneity statistic for pairing formats [$Q_W(23) = 40.51$, $p < .05$] indicated that there was more variance in effect sizes than could be explained by sampling error alone. We therefore examined whether the type of pairing—coded as either peer (i.e., same-age) tutoring, cross-age tutoring, or cooperative partners—accounted for a significant amount of this variance. As shown in Table 4.4, the nonsignificant heterogeneity test indicated no significant differences between mean weighted effect sizes for peer tutoring (Δ+ = .24), cross-age tutoring (Δ+ = .50), and cooperative partners (Δ+ = .00). The test of homogeneity was significant for cross-age tutoring [$Q_W(11) = 24.12$, $p < .05$], but not for peer tutoring [$Q_W(12) = 16.49$, n.s.].

Analysis by Role of Student Within Pair. The significant homogeneity test for cross-age tutoring was further investigated by aggregating the effect

TABLE 4.4
Analysis by Type of Pairing

Variable	Q_B	k	Mean Δ (Unweighted)	Mean Δ+ (Weighted)	95% C.I.	Q_W
Type of Pairing	3.57	26	.33	.35[a]	.20, .45	44.18*
Peer Tutoring		13	.30	.24[a]	.03, .45	16.49
Cross-Age Tutoring		12	.40	.50[a]	.28, .72	24.12*
Cooperative Partners		1	−.09	.00	−1.18, 1.00	0.00

[a]95% confidence interval does not include 0.
*$p < .05$.

sizes by role within this type of pair (see Table 4.5). Students who participated in cross-age tutoring were either tutors or tutees. Whereas the mean weighted effect size for cross-age tutors was quite high ($\Delta+ = .86$), the mean weighted effect size for cross-age tutees was near 0 ($\Delta+ = -.07$, n.s.). The significant heterogeneity statistic [$Q_B(1) = 15.69, p < .05$] indicates that role of student in cross-age tutoring accounts for a significant amount of variation in these effect sizes. (Table 4.5 includes the analogous analysis for peer tutoring interventions for descriptive purposes only.)

Analysis by Methodological Variables

Assessment of study quality is a complex issue from both a theoretical and practical standpoint (Wortman, 1994). For this meta-analytic review, we assigned studies a score in four areas: criteria for the identification of students with disabilities, sampling procedure, comparability of treatment and comparison/control groups, and check on fidelity of treatment (see Table 4.6). Scores on these four methodological variables were summed to yield a composite score indexing study quality. The composite scores ranged from 1 to 5. These scores were then used to create a dichotomous variable representing overall study quality. Scores between 1 and 3 were defined as *lower* quality; scores of 4 or 5 were defined as *higher* quality. Results of the analyses by methodological variables are presented in Table 4.6. As indicated in the table, higher quality studies were associated with significantly lower effect sizes than lower quality studies.

Clearly, the four variables we coded represent only a small subset of the design and implementation features that affect the internal and external validity of research studies. However, studies that were categorized as higher quality on the basis of our four coded methodological variables also exhibited other features (e.g., more complete descriptions of inter-

TABLE 4.5
Analysis by Role of Student in Peer Tutoring and Cross-Age Tutoring

Variable	Q_B	k	Mean Δ (Unweighted)	Mean $\Delta+$ (Weighted)	95% C.I.	Q_W
Peer Tutoring	2.44	13	.30	.24[a]	.03, .45	16.49
Tutee		6	.47	.43[a]	.11, .75	8.99
Reciprocal Tutor–Tutee		7	.16	.09	−.19, .37	5.06
Cross-Age Tutoring	15.69*	12	.40	−.50[a]	.28, .72	24.12*
Tutor		7	.66	.86[a]	.57, 1.15	6.57
Tutee		5	−.02	−.07	−.43, .29	1.86

[a]95% confidence interval does not include 0.
*$p < .05$.

TABLE 4.6
Analysis by Methodological Variables

Variable	Q_B	k	Mean Δ (Unweighted)	Mean Δ+ (Weighted)	95% C.I.	Q_W
30 independent samples from 20 included studies		30	.37	.39[a]	.24, .53	52.31*
Criteria for Identification of Students with Disabilities	2.13					
Reported		17	.27	.31[a]	.12, .49	29.73*
Not reported		13	.50	.53[a]	.29, .77	20.45
Sampling Procedure	7.86*					
Random or matching		15	.24	.36[a]	.14, .57	23.09
Other		14	.42	.35[a]	.15, .55	21.36
Not reported		1	1.61	1.61[a] .	.74, 2.48	0
Evidence of Comparability of Students in Different Groups	2.74					
Provided		22	.30	.30[a]	.13, .48	35.18*
Not provided		8	.55	.56[a]	.31, .81	14.39
Fidelity of Treatment Check	11.85*					
Implemented		14	.15	.13	-.08, .34	8.81
Not implemented		16	.56	.64[a]	.44, .84	31.65*
Overall quality rating	9.17*					
Higher		17	.15	.19*	.00, .39	22.40
Lower		13	.65	.65[a]	.43, .87	20.74

Note. The overall quality rating is the sum of scores on the four methodological features presented in the table.
[a]95% confidence interval does not include 0.
*$p < .05$.

ventions and comparison treatments, use of standardized measures, explanations of incomplete data, and/or subject attrition) that gave us greater confidence in their findings as compared to findings from other studies.

A final methodological variable relating to outcome variables was examined. Each outcome measure was categorized as either "standard" or "locally developed." Standard measures were defined as those with standard content and administration procedures, for example, the Wood-cock–Johnson Psycho-Educational Battery (Woodcock & M. B. Johnson, 1977), Comprehensive Reading Assessment Battery (L. S. Fuchs, D. Fuchs, & Maxwell, 1988), and so on. Locally developed measures were defined as measures whose content was determined by the researchers conducting the study (e.g., word recognition tests using words selected by the researchers) or measures that accompany a specific instructional program (e.g., the Von Harrison sight word test).

The majority of effect sizes (82 of 116 contrasting grouping formats) were based on standard measures, in particular, subtests of the Wood-cock–Johnson ($n = 28$) and the Comprehensive Reading Assessment Battery ($n = 27$). Fourteen of the 29 independent samples of students were assessed by means of standard measures only; 3 were assessed by means of locally developed measures only; and 11 samples were assessed with a combination of standard and locally developed measures.

To ascertain whether some of the variation in effect sizes might be associated with the standard versus local nature of the outcome measures employed, we aggregated the effect sizes by type of measure (standard vs. locally developed) within independent samples. Results of this analysis are presented in Table 4.7. The results of the heterogeneity test [Q_B (1) = .05, n.s.] indicated that the nature of the outcome measure (standard vs. locally developed) was not reliably associated with variation in effect sizes.

DISCUSSION

In her chapter on intervention research involving students with learning disabilities, Wong (1987) recognized the importance of one-to-one instruction in achieving academic progress for these students. At the same time, she acknowledged the fact that individual tutoring is simply not cost-efficient. As Wong put it, "The problem concerns the expense in providing one-to-one instruction, both in intervention research and in school practice" (p. 189). Wong, like many educators in general and special education, offered the possibility of exploring heterogeneous, small groups to meet the needs of students with learning disabilities. As classrooms in both general and special education settings grow in size and as the aca-

TABLE 4.7
Analysis by Outcome Measure: Standard Versus Locally Developed

Variable	Q_B	k	Mean Δ (Unweighted)	Mean Δ+ (Weighted)	95% C.I.	Q_W
Outcome Measure	0.05	39	.36	.37[a]	.24, .50	66.67*
Standard		25	.34	.36[a]	.21, .52	45.05*
Locally developed		14	.39	.40[a]	.15, .64	21.57

[a]95% confidence interval does not include 0.
*$p < .05$.

demic, cultural, and linguistic diversity of students increases, the importance of finding effective, economically feasible ways to manage instruction becomes more imperative.

The aim of this synthesis was to determine the extent to which the variation in effect sizes for reading outcomes of students with disabilities was associated with the grouping format (i.e., pairing, small groups, multiple grouping formats) used for reading instruction. In the majority of studies included in the meta-analysis, students with disabilities who received reading instruction in one of these grouping formats were compared to students with disabilities who received "traditional" reading instruction, that is, instruction that for the most part is delivered to the whole class. The average effect size for the grouping formats was .43, indicating that reading outcome measures for students taught in these grouping formats were, on average, nearly half a standard deviation higher than those of comparison students. Thus, the findings of this meta-analysis support the benefits of alternative instructional groupings for teaching reading to students with disabilities.

Small-Group Instruction

Perhaps the most important finding of the present review concerning small-group instruction is the paucity of studies that met criteria for inclusion in the meta-analysis. Only one study (Englert & Mariage, 1991) was located that used small-group instruction for teaching reading to students with disabilities and that provided data on a comparison group of students. Moreover, it is important to note that grouping format was not the primary research question addressed in this study (or, in fact, in most of the other studies in this review); that is, the intervention was not held constant across different grouping formats such as smaller and larger groups of students so that the effect of the grouping variable could be unequivocally interpreted. Hence, it is likely that the large effect size associated with the Englert and Mariage study is more directly attributable to the strength of the intervention— reciprocal teaching combined with semantic mapping—than to the use of small groups per se. Nonetheless, it is likely that the outcome of this intervention was potentiated by the use of relatively small instructional groups.

The large effect size associated with a reciprocal teaching intervention conducted in small groups is in line with previous research on small-group instruction carried out with regular education students (for a review, see Lou et al., 1996). It is important to note that the Lou et al. meta-analysis aggregated effect sizes for all academic areas and did not provide a separate analysis of reading outcomes. Lou et al.'s meta-analysis showed not only that small-group instruction was more effective than classroom instruction that did not involve within-class grouping, but also that instructional treatments significantly moderated the effects of small-group instruction. In particular, effect sizes were higher when instructional materials were varied for different groups of students. Thus, small groups may be especially effective when teachers differentiate materials and instruction according to the needs of students in different groups. This principle may be especially applicable to the teaching of reading to students with disabilities, insofar as these students may require different materials and more direct instruction than nondisabled peers in order to develop their reading skills.

Lou et al.'s (1996) meta-analysis also showed that effect sizes were significantly higher for smaller groups than for larger ones. The average effect size for three- to four-member groups was $\Delta+ = .22$, whereas that for five- to seven-member groups was $\Delta+ = -.02$. (In the small-group study we reviewed, students were in groups of five to six.) The finding that, for small groups, "smaller is better" naturally leads to the question of whether one-to-one instruction (i.e., one student instructed by an adult) is significantly more effective than small-group instruction. Polloway, Cronin, and Patton (1986) summarized the literature across academic areas on the efficacy of small-group instruction versus one-to-one instruction for students with mild to severe disabilities. Though they did not conduct an analysis of effect sizes, the authors reported that the most common finding in the studies reviewed was that the outcomes associated with small-group instruction and one-to-one instruction were comparable. They further identified several benefits of small-group instruction for students with disabilities: more efficient use of teacher and student time, lower cost, increased instructional time, increased peer interaction, and improved generalization of skills. Conway and Gow (1988) provided a review of the effectiveness of grouping for integrating students with disabilities in mainstreamed settings and emphasized the important role other members of the group provided in instructing students with disabilities.

Student Pairing

In our meta-analysis, the mean weighted effect size for student pairing ($\Delta+$ = .40) was quite similar to findings reported previously for students with disabilities (unbiased mean ES = .36; Mathes & L. S. Fuchs, 1994) and for general education students (mean ES = .40; Walberg, 1984, cited in Bloom, 1984). In the studies included in our analyses, the magnitude of peer tutoring effects did not differ significantly according to whether the students with disabilities acted as reciprocal tutor–tutees or only as tutees. One interpretation of this finding is that it is the instruction received from the tutor, and not the act of tutoring, that produces positive learning outcomes for students with disabilities. However, an alternate interpretation is that acting as a reciprocal tutor does not diminish the effect of peer tutoring, compared to tutoring interventions that do not include this component. The implication of this interpretation is that reciprocal tutoring interventions may allow students with disabilities to derive the benefit to self-esteem that comes from taking on the tutoring role (cf. Vaughn, McIntosh, & Spencer-Rowe, 1991) without losing the benefit to reading skills that comes from being tutored. From the point of view of classroom management, this arrangement may also present important advantages in that there are more pairing possibilities than if some students are only tutors and others only tutees. Also, there are potential benefits from reciprocal tutoring for the students without disabilities.

Though results across the cross-age tutoring studies vary, the effect sizes for cross-age tutors were, on average, significantly higher than those for cross-age tutees. Indeed, the mean effect size for tutees was not significantly different from zero. A possible explanation for this finding may be that the students who tutor younger students with disabilities are themselves students with disabilities and may lack either the content knowledge or teaching skill necessary to raise the level of reading of their tutees. Other research on students with mild disabilities may also provide some insights into the more positive outcomes of cross-age tutors compared to cross-age tutees. Many students with learning disabilities and behavior disorders exhibit high levels of attention problems (e.g., Lerner, Lowenthal, & Lerner, 1995). When these students serve in the role of the tutor, the need to direct another student's activity may require them to focus greater attention on the task and hence result in improving their own skills.

Outcomes for tutors and tutees who participate in cross-age tutoring interventions may also be related to the focus of the intervention as well as the outcome measures used. For example, in the studies included in the meta-analysis, only one independent sample of cross-age tutees showed a positive mean effect size for reading outcomes. This was also the only sample of cross-age tutees for whom the tutoring intervention focused on

reading comprehension. Moreover, of three outcome measures administered to students in this sample, only one—a measure of reading comprehension—was positive, whereas the individual effect sizes derived from
measures of oral reading of words and oral reading of passages were negative. Research by Lamport (1982) on cross-age tutors and tutees that
included students with learning disabilities showed a similar finding, in
that tutees who had been involved in a program that included word study,
oral reading, and skills activities outperformed controls on a measure of
reading comprehension but not on a measure of phonetic analysis (the
converse was true of the tutors). Thus, future research is needed to discern
which types of tutoring activities in reading are most likely to profit tutors,
which most likely to profit tutees, and which will profit both.

Multiple Grouping Formats

Multiple grouping formats yielded a mean effect size of $\Delta+ = .36$, similar in magnitude to the overall effect size for pairing. However, the very
large confidence interval associated with the calculated mean effect size
did encompass 0, indicating that we do not yet have unequivocal evidence
of the effectiveness of multiple grouping formats. Indeed, the three with-
in-sample effect sizes ranged from .03 to .47. This finding suggests that
further research is necessary to determine how and when the use of combinations of grouping formats for reading instruction is beneficial for students with disabilities in terms of measured reading outcomes. Such
research is important in that increasing numbers of teachers are reporting
that they use diverse grouping formats in their classrooms (Schumm et al.,
1996). To illustrate, teachers who worked with us over a 3-year period to
enhance reading outcomes for all students in their classrooms, but particularly for students with disabilities (Vaughn, Hughes, Schumm, & Klingner, 1998), reported that they preferred to use several instructional
practices and grouping formats during a 90-minute language arts block.
Some diversified their instructional format over a week-long series of lessons by using whole-class instruction for a part of each language arts period and having students work 2 days a week in pairs and another 2 days in
small groups. These practices correspond to the increasing emphasis on
flexible grouping formats (e.g., Radencich & McKay, 1995).

Implications for Practice

In this meta-analytic review, grouping formats representing three different alternatives to whole-group instruction for reading were found to be
quite effective, overall, for students with disabilities. The difference in
reading outcomes achieved through pairing and small-group instruction,

as well as some multiple grouping formats, is substantial enough to warrant careful attention to the interventions described in these studies.

In particular, we feel that the findings of the present meta-analysis with regard to peer and cross-age tutoring can have a positive influence on the ways in which teachers use student pairing for students with disabilities. Results of the meta-analysis showed that when students with disabilities work with *same-age* peers, the effect sizes are moderate whether students are tutees or reciprocal tutor–tutees. (No studies were found in which students with disabilities acted solely as tutors of their classmates.) When considering the use of peer tutoring approaches, several points warrant careful consideration. Peer tutoring approaches are designed primarily for practice and not as a substitute for teacher-led instruction (Maheady, Harper, & Sacca, 1988; Osguthorpe & Scruggs, 1986). Adequate preparation of tutors is an important consideration mentioned in almost every study of peer tutoring. Tutors need to be prepared in several ways. First, they need to be familiar with the *content* of what they are going to teach. Second, they need to be aware of procedures for *managing* the instructional situation including the behavior of the tutee. Third, tutors need to be provided with explicit procedures for providing *positive feedback* (Krause, Gerber, & Kauffman, 1981) and *correction* to the tutee. Also, we agree with the suggestion in Krause et al. that there are ethical principles that must be considered before implementing peer tutoring practices, not the least of which is to assure that both the tutor and the tutee benefit.

Despite these cautions, there are several reasons why the use of peer-mediated instructional practices should be taught to teachers and used as an alternative grouping procedure. We are aware that there are many instructional practices for teaching students with disabilities that are viewed as more "desirable" than "feasible" (Schumm & Vaughn, 1991). Peer-mediated instructional practices are an example of an instructional practice that can yield effective outcomes for students with disabilities in both special and general education classrooms and that teachers view as not just feasible to implement but also as enjoyable for students (D. Fuchs, L. S. Fuchs, Mathes, & Simmons, 1997; Vaughn et al., 1998). A second reason to promote the use of peer-mediated instructional practices is that they hold the potential to improve the social relationships of children. Many teachers and professionals have indicated that peer-mediated instruction results in positive social outcomes (Lamport, 1982; Maheady et al., 1988; Mathes & L. S. Fuchs, 1994).

With regard to cross-age tutoring, our findings showed that students with disabilities derive considerable benefit from tutoring younger students but do not appear to benefit from being tutored by an older student (with disabilities). Thus, whenever possible, students with disabilities should assume the role of tutor to students who are at least one grade level lower than they are. This may be easier to implement in special education classrooms than in general education classrooms. The positive effects of tutoring interventions for cross-age tutors may also hold for general education students. If this is the case, it may be worthwhile for schools to consider implementing cross-age tutoring programs particularly in classrooms where there are disproportionately high numbers of students with disabilities and/or students considered at risk for academic failure. It may also be fruitful for teachers to identify selected students (e.g., those with disabilities) to serve in the role of the tutor for lower grade students several times a week without involving all of the students in the class. If this approach is implemented it would be important to monitor carefully the outcomes of both tutors and tutees to ensure that all students profit from the tutoring activity.

The dearth of studies on small-group instruction in reading for students with disabilities was an unexpected finding of this review. Though the value of teacher-led small-group instruction in reading for students with disabilities may seem obvious to some, documentation of the effectiveness of particular interventions is needed. Moreover, it will be important to better understand the obstacles that may prevent teachers from making greater use of small-group instruction. For example, although some teachers report that they implement small-group instruction occasionally, observations in their classrooms over a year-long period indicate that this rarely occurs (Vaughn et al., 1998; see also Moody et al., 1997; Schumm et al., 1998). This may be due in part to the fact that organizing and implementing effective small-group instruction requires more planning and effort than is implied in the simple act of dividing students into groups. Small-group instruction requires the consideration of many student factors (Wilkinson, 1986), such as students' needs, characteristics, willingness to initiate in the group, and instructional level, to identify just a few. Lou et al. (1996) emphasized that for small-group instruction to be maximally effective, "within-class grouping practices require the adaptation of instruction, methods, and materials for small-group learning" (p. 423). This statement is likely to be particularly applicable to students with disabilities taught in small groups within regular classroom settings.

Implications for Future Research

Eagley and Wood (1994) stated that "a quantitative synthesis of research is typically not an endpoint or final step in the investigation of a research topic" (p. 486). This research synthesis is no exception. The most obvious need for future research is to conduct intervention studies that directly assess the effects of grouping on the performance of students with disabilities. We are aware that these studies are difficult to implement for several reasons. It is difficult to assign students to different grouping conditions and it is challenging to control the reading intervention implemented. Because teachers frequently use whole-class grouping arrangements for reading (Schumm et al., 1996; Vaughn et al., 1998) or use a variety of grouping formats (Moody et al., 1997), it is not easy to control the type of grouping arrangement implemented by teachers for a specified period of time. Also, students with severe learning or behavior problems often receive supportive instruction in reading by a special education teacher either within the general education classroom or in a special setting. This factor can influence both study design and study outcomes.

Nonetheless, studies that control for intervention while varying grouping format would be especially informative. Because intervention expense is largely related to group size, empirical evidence addressing this question is critical for determining policy. It also has direct bearing on the extent to which students with learning and behavior problems can be integrated successfully into general education classrooms for reading instruction.

Further research on the effects of teacher-led small-group instruction and student cooperative group work for students with disabilities is also sorely needed. Although cooperative learning groups are touted as being highly effective for both general and special education students (D. W. Johnson & R. T. Johnson, 1986; Sharan, 1980; Slavin, 1983b), there is little evidence documenting reading outcomes for students with disabilities. A recent critical review of cooperative learning for students with disabilities (Tateyama-Sniezek, 1990) suggests that equivocal results, lack of specific descriptions of what is meant by cooperative learning, and lack of comparison groups make it difficult to draw conclusions about the effectiveness of cooperative learning for students with disabilities, particularly in the area of reading.

Our findings also have implications for subsequent research syntheses. We believe that future syntheses should include content area reading interventions and should be extended to students with reading problems beyond students with learning disabilities. For this review, which was funded by the Office of Special Education Programs, we were particularly concerned to increase the knowledge base on youngsters with identified disabilities. However, we feel that this knowledge base can be enriched by integrating the results of studies that involve a broader range of students experiencing difficulty in reading. Also, in the process of conducting this review we observed that a large number of studies exist on the effectiveness of different grouping practices for mathematics instruction; we would recommend a similar review in that area.

Although the findings of the present synthesis do not resolve all of our questions concerning the most effective way of grouping students with disabilities for reading instruction, they provide important information that researchers and practitioners should consider in designing future studies and instructional interventions. We are optimistic that the findings will also have a positive influence on educational policy. As Lou and her colleagues (1996) remarked, "What a review can do is help inform policy by exploring the empirical basis of beliefs which underlie a particular philosophy and by suggesting directions for future research if the evidence is lacking" (p. 429).

ACKNOWLEDGMENT

The research reported in this chapter was funded under U.S. Department of Education Grant HO23E5005-96.

REFERENCES

Studies preceded by an asterisk were included in the meta-analysis.

Allington, R. (1980). Teacher interruption behaviors during primary-grade oral reading. *Journal of Educational Psychology, 72,* 371–377.

Allington, R. (1984). Content coverage and contextual reading in reading groups. *Journal of Reading Behavior, 16,* 85–96.

Barr, R. (1989). The social organization of literacy instruction. In S. McCormick & J. Zutell (Eds.), *Cognitive and social perspectives for literacy research and instruction,* Thirty-eighth Yearbook of the National Reading Conference (pp. 19–33). Chicago: National Reading Conference.

Barr, R., & Dreeben, R. (1991). Grouping students for reading instruction. In R. Barr, M. L. Kamil, P. B. Mosenthal, & P. D. Pearson (Eds.), *Handbook of reading research* (Vol. 2, pp. 885–910). New York: Longman.

Bloom, B. S. (1984). The 2 sigma problem: The search for methods of group instruction as effective as one-to-one tutoring. *Educational Researcher, 13,* 4–16.

Calfee, R., & Brown, R. (1979). Grouping students for instruction. In D. L. Duke (Ed.), *Classroom management,* Seventy-eighth Yearbook of the National Society for the Study of Education (pp. 144–182). Chicago: University of Chicago Press.

*Cochran, L., Feng, H., Cartledge, G., & Hamilton, S. (1993). The effects of cross-age tutoring on the academic achievement, social behaviors, and self-perceptions of low-achieving African-American males with behavioral disorders. *Behavioral Disorders, 18*(4), 292–302.

Cohen, P. A., Kulik, J. A., & Kulik, C. C. (1982). Educational outcomes of tutoring: A meta-analysis of findings. *American Educational Research Journal, 19,* 237–248.

Come, B., & Fredericks, A. D. (1995). Family literacy in urban school: Meeting the needs of at-risk children. *The Reading Teacher, 48*(7), 566–571.

Conway, R. N. F., & Gow, L. (1988). Mainstreaming special class students with mild handicaps through group instruction. *Remedial and Special Education, 9*(5), 34–41.

Cook, S. B., Scruggs, T. E., Mastropieri, M. A., & Casto, G. C. (1986). Handicapped students as tutors. *Journal of Special Education, 19*(4), 483–492.

Cooper, H. M. (1989). *Integrating research: A guide for literature reviews* (2nd ed.). Newbury Park, CA: Sage.

Cooper, H., & Hedges, L. V. (Eds.). (1994). *The handbook of research synthesis.* New York: Russell Sage Foundation.

Cooper, H., Nye, B., Charlton, K., Lindsay, J., & Greathouse, S. (1996). The effects of summer vacation on achievement test scores: A narrative and meta-analytic review. *Review of Educational Research, 66*(3), 227–268.

Delquadri, J., Greenwood, C. R., Whorton, D., Carta, J. J., & Hall, R. V. (1986). Classwide peer tutoring. *Exceptional Children, 52*(6), 535–542.

Devin-Sheehan, L., Feldman, R. S., & Allen, V. L. (1976). Research on children tutoring children: A critical review. *Review of Educational Research, 46*(3), 355–385.

Eagley, A. H., & Wood, W. (1994). Using research to plan future research. In H. Cooper & L. V. Hedges (Eds.), *The handbook of research synthesis* (pp. 485–500). New York: Russell Sage Foundation.

Eiserman, W. D., Shisler, L., & Osguthorpe, R. T. (1987). Handicapped students as tutors: A description and integration of three years of research findings. *B. C. Journal of Special Education, 11*(3), 215–231.

Elbaum, B., Vaughn, S., Hughes, M. T., Moody, S. W., Schumm, J. S. (1998). *The effect of instructional grouping format on the reading outcomes of students with disabilities: A meta-analytic review.* Document submitted to the Office of Special Education Programs, U.S. Department of Education, Washington, D.C.

*Englert, C. S., & Mariage, T. V. (1991). Making students partners in the comprehension process: Organizing the reading "posse." *Learning Disability Quarterly, 14,* 123–138.

*Epstein, L. (1978). The effects of intraclass peer tutoring on the vocabulary development of learning disabled children. *Journal of Learning Disabilities, 11,* 518–21.

Flood, J., Lapp, D., Flood, S., & Nagel, G. (1992). Am I allowed to group? Using flexible patterns for effective instruction. *The Reading Teacher, 45*(8), 608–616.

*Friedman, J. (1990). *An evaluation of the relative sensitivity to' student growth in reading and spelling of standardized achievement tests and curriculum-based measures.* Unpublished doctoral dissertation, Lehigh University, Bethlehem, PA.

*Fuchs, D., Fuchs, L. S., Mathes, P. G., & Simmons, D. C. (1997). Peer-assisted learning strategies: Making classrooms more responsive to diversity. *American Educational Research Journal, 34*(1), 174–206.

Fuchs, L. S., Fuchs, D., & Maxwell, L. (1988). The validity of informal reading comprehension measures. *Remedial and Special Education, 9*(2), 20–29.

Gambrell, L. (1984). How much time do children spend reading during teacher-directed reading instruction? In J. Niles & L. Harris (Eds.), *Changing perspectives on research in reading/language processing and instruction,* Thirty-third Yearbook of the National Reading Conference (pp. 193–198). Rochester, NY: National Reading Conference.

Gambrell, L., Wilson, R. M., & Gantt, W. N. (1981). Classroom observations of task-attending behaviors of good or poor readers. *Journal of Educational Research, 74,* 400–404.

Glass, G. V., McGaw, B., & Smith, M. L. (1981). *Meta-analysis in social research.* Beverly Hills, CA: Sage.

Gredler, G. R. (1985). An assessment of cross-age tutoring. *Techniques: A Journal for Remedial Education and Counseling, 1,* 226–232.

Hedges, L. V. (1994). Fixed effects models. In H. Cooper & L. V. Hedges (Eds.), *The handbook of research synthesis* (pp. 285–299). New York: Russell Sage Foundation.

Hedges, L., & Olkin, I. (1985). *Statistical methods for meta-analysis.* Orlando, FL: Academic Press.

Hiebert, E. H. (1983). An examination of ability grouping for reading instruction. *Reading Research Quarterly, 18,* 231–255.

Hunter, D. (1978). Student on-task behavior during second grade reading group meetings (Doctoral dissertation, University of Missouri–Columbia, 1978). *Dissertation Abstracts International, 39,* 4838A.

*Jenkins, J. R., Jewell, M., Leicester, N., Jenkins, L., & Troutner, N. M. (1991). Development of a school building model for educating students with handicaps and at-risk students in general education classrooms. *Journal of Learning Disabilities, 24,* 311–320.

*Jenkins, J. R., Jewell, M., O'Conner, R. E., Jenkins, L. M., & Troutner, N. M. (1994). Accommodations for individual differences without classroom ability groups: An experiment in school reconstructing. *Exceptional Children, 60,* 344–58.

Johnson, D. W., & Johnson, R. T. (1975). *Learning together and alone: Cooperation, competition, and indviduualization.* Englewood Cliffs, NJ: Prentice-Hall.

Johnson, D. W., & Johnson, R. T. (1986). Mainstreaming and cooperative learning strategies. *Exceptional Children, 52,* 553–561.

Juel, C. (1988). Learning to read and write: A longitudinal study of 54 children from first through fourth grades. *Journal of Educational Psychology, 80,* 437–477.

Krouse, J., Gerber, M. M., & Kauffman, J. M. (1981). Peer tutoring: Procedures, promises, and unresolved issues. *Exceptional Education Quarterly, 1*(1), 107–115.

Kulik, J. A., & Kulik, C. C. (1987). Effects of ability grouping on student achievement. *Equity & Excellence, 23,* 22–30.

Labo, L. D., & Teale, W. H. (1990). Cross-age reading: A strategy for helping poor readers. *The Reading Teacher, 43*(6), 362–369.

Lamport, K. C. (1982). The effect of inverse tutoring on reading disabled students in public school settings. *Dissertation Abstracts International, 44,* 729. (University Microfilms No. 83-15, 707)

Leinhardt, G., & Pallay, A. (1982). Restrictive educational settings: Exile or haven? *Review of Educational Research, 52*(4), 557–578.

Lerner, J. W., Lowenthal, B., & Lerner, S. R. (1995). *Attention deficit disorders: Assessment and teaching.* Pacific Grove, CA: Brooks/Cole Publishing.

Lipsey, M. W. (1994). Identifying potentially interesting variables and analysis opportunities. In H. Cooper & L. V. Hedges (Eds.), *The handbook of research synthesis* (pp. 111–123). New York: Russell Sage Foundation.

Lloyd, J. W., Crowley, E. P., Kohler, F. W., & Strain, P. S. (1988). Redefining the applied research agenda: Cooperative learning, prereferral, teacher consultation, and peer-mediated interventions. *Journal of Learning Disabilities, 21,* 43–52.

Lou, Y., Abrami, P. C., Spence, J. C., Poulsen, C., Chambers, B., & d'Apollonia, S. (1996). Within-class grouping: A meta-analysis. *Review of Educational Research, 66*(4), 423–458.

Maheady, L., Harper, G. F., & Sacca, M. K. (1988). Peer-mediated instruction: A promising approach to meeting the diverse needs of LD adolescents. *Learning Disability Quarterly, 11,* 108–113.

*Mathes, P. G., & Fuchs, L. S. (1993). Peer-mediated reading instruction in special education resource rooms. *Learning Disabilities Research and Practice, 8,* 233–243.

Mathes, P. G., & Fuchs, L. S. (1994). The efficacy of peer tutoring in reading for students with mild disabilities: A best-evidence synthesis. *School Psychology Review, 23*(1), 59–80.

Mathes, P. G., Fuchs, L. S., Fuchs, D., Henley, A. M., & Sanders, A. (1994). Increasing strategic reading practice with Peabody Classwide Peer Tutoring. *Learning Disabilities Research and Practice, 9,* 44–48.

McCracken, S. J. (1979). The effect of a peer tutoring program utilizing data-based instruction on the word recognition and reading comprehension skills of secondary age level handicapped students. *Dissertation Abstracts International, 40(08-A),* 4516. (University Microfilms No. 79-24, 399)

Moody, S. W., Schumm, J. S., Fischer, M., & Jean-Francois, B. (1999). Grouping suggestions for the classroom: What do our basal reading series tell us? *Reading Research and Instruction, 38*(4), 319–331.

Moody, S. W., Vaughn, S., & Schumm, J. S. (1997). Instructional grouping for reading. *Remedial and Special Education, 18*(6), 347–356.

*Moore, A. R. (1993). *Effects of strategy training and classwide peer tutoring on the reading comprehension of students with learning disabilities.* Unpublished doctoral dissertation, Indiana University, Bloomington.

Oakes, J., Gamoran, A., & Page, R. N. (1992). Curriculum differentiation: Opportunities, outcomes, and meanings. In P. Jackson (Ed.), *Handbook of research on curriculum* (pp. 570–608). New York: Macmillan.

*Osguthorpe, R. T., & Eiserman, W. D. (1986). The effects of three types of tutoring on the attitudes of learning disabled students and their regular class peers. In R. T. Osguthorpe, W. Eiserman, L. Shisler, & B. L. Top (Eds.), *Handicapped children as tutors. Final report (1985–86)* (pp. 65–96). Document submitted to the Office of Special Education and Rehabilitative Services, U.S. Department of Education, Washington, D.C. (ERIC Document Reproduction Service No. ED 280 248)

Osguthorpe, R. T., & Scruggs, T. E. (1986). Special education students as tutors: A review and analysis. *Remedial and Special Education, 7*(4), 15–26.

Otto, W. R., Wolf, A., & Eldridge, R. G. (1984). Managing instruction. In P. D. Pearson (Ed.), *Handbook of reading research* (pp. 799–828). New York: Longman.

Polloway, E. A., Cronin, M. E., & Patton, J. R. (1986). The efficacy of group versus one-to-one instruction: A review. *Remedial and Special Education, 7*(1), 22–30.

Radencich, M. C., & McKay, L. J. (1995). Flexible grouping for literacy in the elementary grades. Boston: Allyn & Bacon.

Reynolds, M. C., Wang, M. C., & Walberg, H. J. (1987). The necessary restructuring of special and regular education. *Exceptional Children, 53*, 391–398.

Rosenholtz, S. J., & Wilson, B. (1980). The effect of classroom structure on shared perceptions of ability. *American Education Research Journal, 17*, 75–82.

Schumm, J. S., Moody, S. W., & Vaughn, S. (1998). *Grouping for reading instruction: Does one size fit all?* Manuscript in preparation.

Schumm, J. S., & Vaughn, S. (1991). Making adaptations for mainstreamed students: General classroom teachers' perspectives. *Remedial and Special Education, 12*(4), 18–27.

Schumm, J. S., Vaughn, S., & Elbaum, B. E. (1996). Teachers' perceptions of grouping practices for reading instruction. *NRC Yearbook*, 543–551.

Scruggs, T. E., Mastropieri, M. A., & Richter, L. (1985). Peer tutoring with behaviorally disordered students: Social and academic benefits. *Behavioral Disorders, 10*, 283–294.

*Scruggs, T. E., & Osguthorpe, R. T. (1986). Tutoring interventions within special education settings: A comparison of cross-age and peer tutoring. *Psychology in the Schools, 23*, 187–193.

Scruggs, T. E., & Richter, L. (1985). Tutoring learning disabled students: A critical review. *Learning Disability Quarterly, 8*, 286–298.

Sharan, S. (1980). Cooperative learning in small groups: Recent methods and effects on achievement, attitudes, and ethnic relations. *Review of Educational Research, 50*, 241–271.

*Shisler, L., Top, B. L., & Osguthorpe, R. T. (1986). Behaviorally disordered students as reverse-role tutors: Increasing social acceptance and reading skills. *B. C. Journal of Special Education, 10*, 101–119.

*Shoulders, H. M. W. (1991). *The effects of rewards used on mildly handicapped students during peer teaching: Implications for instructional leadership.* Unpublished doctoral dissertation, University of Alabama, Huntsville.

*Simmons, D. C., Fuchs, L. S., Fuchs, D., Mathes, P., & Hodge, J. P. (1995). Effects of explicit teaching and peer tutoring on the reading achievement of learning-disabled and low-performing students in regular classrooms. *Elementary School Journal, 95*, 387–408.

*Sindelar, P. T. (1982). The effects of cross-age tutoring on the comprehension skills of remedial reading students. *The Journal of Special Education, 16*, 199–206.

Slavin, R. E. (1983a). *Cooperative learning.* New York: Longman.

Slavin, R. E. (1983b). When does cooperative learning increase student achievement? *Psychological Bulletin, 94*, 429–445.

Slavin, R. E. (1987). Ability grouping and student achievement in the elementary schools: A best-evidence synthesis. *Review of Educational Research, 57*, 293–336.

Speece, D. S., & Keogh, B. K. (Eds.). (1996). *Research on classroom ecologies: Implications for inclusion of children with learning disabilities.* Mahwah, NJ: Lawrence Erlbaum Associates.

Stainback, W., Stainback, S., Courtnage, L., & Jaben, T. (1985). Facilitating mainstreaming by modifying the mainstream. *Exceptional Children, 52,* 144–152.

*Stevens, R. J., Madden, N. A., Slavin, R. E., & Farnish, A. M. (1987). Cooperative integrated reading and composition: Two field experiments. *Reading Research Quarterly, 22,* 433–454.

Tateyama-Sniezck, K. M. (1990). Cooperative learning: Does it improve the academic achievement of students with handicaps? *Exceptional Children, 56*(5), 426–437.

*Top, B. L., & Osguthorpe, R. T. (1985). The effects of reverse-role tutoring on reading achievement and self-concept. In R. T. Osguthorpe, W. Eiserman, L. Shisler, & B. L. Top (Eds.), *Handicapped children as tutors. Final report* (1985–1986, pp. 65–96). Document submitted to the Office of Special Education and Rehabilitative Services, U.S. Department of Education, Washington, D.C. (ERIC Document Reproduction Service No. ED 267 545)

*Top, B. L., & Osguthorpe, R. T. (1987). Reverse-role tutoring: The effects of handicapped students tutoring regular class students. *Elementary School Journal, 87,* 413–423.

*Trapani, C., & Gettinger, M. (1989). Effects of social skills training and cross-age tutoring on academic achievement and social behaviors of boys with learning disabilities. *Journal of Research and Development in Education, 23,* 1–9.

Vaughn, S., Hughes, M. T., Schumm, J. S., & Klingner, J. (1998). A collaborative effort to enhance reading and writing instruction in inclusion classrooms. *Learning Disability Quarterly, 21*(1), 57–74.

Vaughn, S., McIntosh, R., & Spencer-Rowe, J. (1991). Peer rejection is a stubborn thing: Increasing peer acceptance of rejected students with learning disabilities. *Learning Disabilities Research and Practice, 6*(2), 83–88.

Vaughn, S., Moody, S. W., & Schumm, J. S. (1998). Broken promises: Reading instruction in the resource room. *Exceptional Children, 64*(2), 211–225.

Walberg, H. J. (1984). Improving the productivity of America's schools. *Educational Leadership, 41*(8), 19–27.

White, H. D. (1994). Scientific communication and literature retrieval. In H. Cooper & L. V. Hedges (Eds.), *The handbook of research synthesis* (pp. 41–55). New York: Russell Sage Foundation.

Wilkinson, L. C. (1986, June). *Grouping low-achieving students for instruction.* Paper presented at the Designs for Compensatory Education Conference, Washington, DC. (ERIC Document Reproduction Service No. ED 293 915)

Will, M. C. (1986). Educating children with learning problems: A shared responsibility. *Exceptional Children, 52,* 11–16.

Wong, B. Y. (1987). Conceptual and methodological issues in interventions with learning-disabled children and adolescents. In S. Vaughn & C. S. Bos (Eds.), *Research in learning disabilities: Issues and future directions* (pp. 185–196). Boston: Little, Brown.

Woodcock, R. W., & Johnson, M. B. (1977). Woodcock–Johnson Psycho-Educational Battery. MacAllen, TX: DLM Teaching Resources.

Wortman, P. M. (1994). Judging research quality. In H. Cooper & L. V. Hedges (Eds.), *The handbook of research synthesis* (pp. 97–109). New York: Russell Sage Foundation.

Chapter 5

A Meta-Analysis of Positive Behavior Support

Janet G. Marquis
University of Kansas

Robert H. Horner
University of Oregon

Edward G. Carr
State University of New York at Stony Brook

Ann P. Turnbull
University of Kansas

Marilyn Thompson
Arizona State University

Gene Ann Behrens
Elizabethtown College

Darlene Magito-McLaughlin, Michelle L. McAtee,
Christopher E. Smith, Kaarin Anderson Ryan, Ajit Doolabh
State University of New York at Stony Brook

The purposes of this meta-analysis are (a) to assess the effectiveness of positive behavioral support (PBS) using several different quantitative effect size measures calculated from single-case studies in the research database on PBS published between 1985 and 1996, (b) to explore the effect of specific participant and experimental characteristics on the measures of the effect size, and (c) to suggest directions for research and practice in conducting experiments and meta-analyses with single-case studies. The focus is on the application of PBS for people with developmental or cognitive disabilities and/or autism.

This meta-analysis using quantitative measures is based on an extensive descriptive research synthesis completed by Carr et al. (1999). The quantitative analysis presented here uses the same research database constructed for the descriptive research synthesis study. In this chapter we present only a brief description of the data collection procedures, definitions, and eligibility criteria used in constructing the database. Readers desiring more detail will find an extensive description in the Carr et al. monograph.

The reason for having a quantitative analysis that is separate from the descriptive synthesis is that combining the two would be quite cumbersome. Two factors contribute to the difficulty in combining both approaches. One factor is the lack of sufficient data for statistical analysis of many of the variables discussed in the descriptive synthesis. It was felt that many of these were important variables to include for a comprehensive understanding of positive behavior support, but that it would be confusing to include some variables in the quantitative analysis and not include others. A second, and more compelling, factor is the need for an extensive discussion of the statistical methods used in the meta-analysis. This is necessary because, unlike group designs, no general agreement exists on satisfactory meta-analytic techniques for single-case designs (Faith, Allison, & Gorman, 1996). Thus, it was necessary to describe the procedures and rationale for the analytic approach we adopted. To include this technical discussion in the descriptive synthesis would have been inappropriate.

We first present a brief definition of PBS, the rationale for the present meta-analysis of PBS, and a brief statement of the research questions posed. Following that we give the abbreviated description of the methods and procedures for building the database. The next section contains an extensive discussion of the statistical methods and issues. Following the results section we discuss the interpretation of the results and make recommendations for future research.

Positive Behavioral Support: Definition and Overview

PBS is the application of behavioral principles within the context of community norms to reduce problem behaviors and build appropriate behaviors that result in durable behavior change. A key concept in PBS is that deficient contexts must be remediated first in order to reduce problem behavior. Deficient contexts may be related to environmental conditions or to behavioral repertoires. Deficiencies in environmental conditions may involve lack of choice, inadequate teaching strategies, limited access to engaging materials and activities, or poorly chosen daily routines. Deficiencies in behavioral repertoires may be due to poorly developed skills in communication, self-management, or social interaction (Carr et al., 1999).

The problem behaviors included in this study are aggression, self-injury, tantrums, and property destruction. Reduction of these problem behaviors is important because the consequences of the behaviors may be physical danger to self and others as well as limited educational or employment opportunities, rejection by members of the community, and/or social isolation including separation from family (National Institutes of Health, 1991).

Rationale for a Review of Positive Behavior Support

Relatively few synthesis reviews have focused on PBS per se because this approach was not widely used until the mid- to late 1980s. Since that time a large number of research studies, conceptual papers, and intervention manuals related to PBS have been published (Carr, 1994; Donnellan, LaVigna, Negri-Shoultz, & Fassbender, 1988; Durand, 1990; Evans & Meyer, 1985; Horner et al., 1990; LaVigna & Donnellan, 1986; Meyer & Evans, 1989; M. D. Smith, 1990). Although many excellent reviews related to the issue of remediating problem behavior have been undertaken, these reviews usually have combined the analysis of PBS with the analysis of other approaches, or they have reviewed only a subset of PBS procedures (Didden, Duker, & Korzilius, 1997; Lancioni & Hoogeveen, 1990; Lennox, Miltenberger, Spengler, & Erfanian, 1988; Matson & Taras, 1989; O'Brien & Repp, 1990; Vollmer & Iwata, 1992). Combining the review of PBS with reviews of other approaches limited the possibility of analyzing PBS in depth.

In 1989, the National Institutes of Health commissioned a Consensus Development Conference to address the issue of destructive behavior. As a product of that conference, a synthesis review of PBS based on the literature that existed through 1989 was prepared (Carr, Robinson, Taylor, & Carlson, 1990). Shortly thereafter, a second analysis appeared reviewing the literature from 1976 to 1987 (Scotti, Evans, Meyer, & Walker, 1991). The latter review devoted attention to both PBS and non-PBS strategies. Finally, a recent review (Scotti, Ujcich, Weigle, Holland, & Kirk, 1996) extended the initial Scotti et al. review by analyzing both PBS and non-PBS intervention practices (but not outcomes) from 1988 to 1992. The lack of a recent synthesis that focuses exclusively on PBS provides an important justification for the descriptive research synthesis in the Carr et al. (1999) monograph and for this quantitative meta-analysis, which provides additional information to be used in conjunction with that report.

Research Questions

The meta-analysis presented in this chapter examines three broad substantive questions and one methodological question:

1. Overall, is PBS effective in reducing the incidence of problem behavior?
2. Do characteristics of the participant make a difference in the effectiveness of PBS? We examine whether the effectiveness is moderat-

ed by gender, age, diagnosis, level of retardation, or type of problem behavior.

3. Do characteristics of the intervention make a difference in the effectiveness of PBS? We compare stimulus-based interventions to reinforcement-based interventions, and we look at the effect of including a non-PBS strategy. Using the results of an assessment to design the intervention around the function of problem behavior also is examined.

4. Do certain characteristics of the experiment influence the estimate of the effectiveness of PBS? We investigate the influence of the number of data points in both the baseline and the treatment phases, the type of data collected (percent or frequency data), and the trends or slopes in the data.

METHODS

The following section contains the operational definitions of the variables included in the meta-analysis, information on the literature search and the eligibility criteria, and a description of the data collection methods.

Operational Definitions

From each article we extracted data with respect to four kinds of variables: participant characteristics, assessment practices, intervention strategies, and outcome measures.

Participant Characteristics

The following participant characteristics were recorded: (a) gender (male or female); (b) diagnosis (mental retardation, autism/pervasive developmental disability, mental retardation + autism/pervasive developmental disability; mental retardation and/or autism/pervasive developmental disability + other [e.g., anxiety disorder, motor skills disorder, tic disorder, etc.]); (c) age in years; (d) level of mental retardation (profound, severe, moderate, mild); and (e) type of problem behavior (aggression, self-injurious behavior, property destruction, tantrums).

Assessment Practices and Function of Behavior

Assessments are conducted to determine (a) classes of problem behavior, (b) antecedents that occasion and do not occasion problem behavior, and (c) variables that are related to the maintenance of problem behavior.

Although assessments may be classified into three different types (informal, formal, and functional analysis), for purposes of the meta-analysis we grouped all assessment types together. Because the goal of assessment is to provide information that can be used to develop an appropriate intervention strategy, we also determined whether the assessment had been used to design the intervention. The meta-analysis then compared cases in which an assessment was done and used to design an intervention to cases in which an assessment was either not done or not used in planning the intervention.

The variables that are related to maintaining the problem behavior are often referred to as the function of the problem behavior (Carr, 1993; Lee, 1988; Skinner, 1974). One product of an assessment is the determination of the function. Four functional categories were defined: attention, escape, tangibles/activities, and sensory reinforcement (Carr, 1977; Iwata, Dorsey, Slifer, Bauman, & Richman, 1982; Wiesler, Hanson, Chamberlain, & Thompson, 1985). Problem behavior sometimes functions to secure attention or comfort from others (Carr & McDowell, 1980; Lovaas, Freitag, Gold, & Kassorla, 1965; Martin & Foxx, 1973). Or, individuals may use problem behavior to escape or avoid difficult tasks or other aversive situations (Carr & Newsom, 1985; Carr, Newsom, & Binkoff, 1976, 1980; Patterson, 1982). Sometimes, problem behavior assists the individual with access to desirable tangible items and preferred activities (Derby et al., 1992; Durand & Crimmins, 1988). A fourth function for problem behavior is to generate sensory reinforcement, either visual, auditory, tactile, or even gustatory (Favell, McGimsey, & Schell, 1982; Rincover, Cook, Peoples, & Packard, 1979). More than one function may be served by a particular problem behavior (Day, Horner, & O'Neill, 1994; Haring & Kennedy, 1990; Iwata et al., 1982).

Intervention Strategies

Two categories of PBS intervention are investigated: stimulus-based interventions and reinforcement-based interventions. Next we briefly describe each type of intervention strategy. More detail on each type and variations for each are described in Carr et al. (1999).

Stimulus-Based Intervention.   Stimulus-based interventions are designed to make positive behavior more probable by remediating deficient environmental conditions, which provide too few stimuli that support positive behavior and too many that support problem behavior. Examples of environmental stimuli are activity patterns, choice options, and prompting. All variations of stimulus-based interventions attempt environmental remediation through manipulating stimuli.

Reinforcement-Based Intervention.   Reinforcement based interventions are designed to make positive behavior more probable by remediating deficient behavior repertoires, which make it difficult (or impossible)
to meet individual needs. The failure to have needs met often increases
the level of frustration, which leads to problem behavior. Thus, problem
behavior often becomes more probable when it is effective in achieving
the desired reinforcers, and the nonproblem behavior is not effective in
achieving the reinforcers. The alteration of behavior repertoires may be
achieved by modifying socially appropriate, functional behaviors that are
currently inadequately developed or absent (e.g., communication, job
skills, social skills, independent living skills, self-management behavior).
Reinforcement-based interventions focus on targeting specific behaviors
or classes of behaviors for consistent, systematic reinforcement.

Non-PBS Intervention.   Non-PBS interventions were defined as those
for which the primary goal was the reduction of problem behavior
through the direct application of reactive procedures contingent on the
display of problem behavior. An example of a non-PBS intervention is
time-out, which involves the withdrawal of all positive reinforcement for a
fixed time period after a problem behavior has occurred. Often these
interventions were combined with PBS interventions.

Behavior Change on the Part of Significant Others.   Both stimulus-
based interventions and reinforcement-based interventions potentially
result in changes in how other people respond to the person with disabilities. Another variable recorded in the database is whether a change in the
behavior of the person with the disability required a change of behavior
also for a person who was supporting the person with the disability.

Ecological Validity.   Ecological validity refers to the persons and places
(settings) involved in the intervention. Often the persons who carried out
the intervention (the intervention agents) were those who would normally
be expected to be the primary support people/caregivers in a particular
community setting; these were referred to as "typical" agents. "Atypical"
agents were those who would not normally be involved. "Typical" settings
were the living environments considered to be normative for an individual
of a given age (e.g., home, integrated school, group home/own home, job
site, neighborhood). Settings considered to be "atypical" were non-norma-
tive settings such as segregated schools, psychiatric wards/hospitals, medical
clinics, state institutions, and sheltered workshops.

Summary of Intervention Strategies.   To summarize, the following
aspects of an intervention were coded: (a) whether the intervention was

stimulus-based, reinforcement-based, and/or non-PBS based, (b) whether the intervention involved change on the part of significant others, (c) whether the intervention agent was a typical/atypical agent and whether the intervention setting was a typical/atypical setting.

Outcome Measures

Although we examined several outcome measures other than the occurrence of problem behavior, the small number of articles reporting outcomes other than the reduction of problem behavior made the analysis of these other outcomes not very useful.

Literature Search and Eligibility Criteria

The literature search was conducted using an initial set of selection criteria. Exclusion criteria were then applied to eliminate those articles that did not meet the specific methodological standards.

Initial Selection Criteria

The following six criteria were used in the initial selection of articles from the literature:

1. The article had to have been published between 1985 and 1996. All articles accessible to us by the cutoff date of December 31, 1996, were considered. Because some journals did not publish their final 1996 issue until 3 to 4 months past the cutoff date, we included a small number (eight) of in-press articles that we had obtained prior to the cutoff date. These were classified as 1996 articles. Including these articles allowed us to achieve a more up-to-date review.
2. To ensure high standards, only articles published in peer-reviewed journals were considered.
3. The article had to have been published in English.
4. All variations of *DSM–III* (*Diagnostic and Statistical Manual of Mental Disorders,* 3rd ed.), *DSM–III–R* (3rd ed., revised), *DSM–IV* (4th ed.), and AAMR (American Association on Mental Retardation) classifications related to mental retardation, autism, and pervasive developmental disorder, either as a primary or secondary diagnosis, were retained, including relevant dual diagnoses, for example, anxiety disorder of childhood with mental retardation.
5. Problem behavior had to be one of the following types: self-injury, aggression, property destruction, and/or tantrums.

6. The intervention had to be some variation of stimulus- and/or reinforcement-based intervention.

Literature Search

All relevant education, psychology, and medical journals listed in the four
previous reviews that had included a consideration of PBS (Carr et al., 1990;
Didden et al., 1997; Scotti et al., 1991, 1996) were searched. This initial
process produced additional references to other research articles, review
papers, books, book chapters, and newsletters, which were then pursued.
Abstract and index services were searched by crossing the disability diagnoses
with the problem behavior topographies. Included in this search were: Child
Development Abstracts and Bibliography, Current Contents/Social and
Behavioral Sciences, ERIC, MEDLINE, Psychological Abstracts, PsychINFO,
PsychLIT, PsychSCAN/MR, Social Science Citation Index. Information on
intervention for problem behavior was requested from organizations having
a stake in providing services for people with disabilities. The National Infor-
mation Center for Children and Youth with Handicaps provided a list of 33
stakeholder organizations that included The Association for Persons with
Severe Handicaps, The Arc (formerly the Association for Retarded Citizens),
Autism Society of America, Council for Exceptional Children, and The
National Down Syndrome Society.

Lastly, we asked leading researchers (14) to send us their published and
in-press papers dealing with the issue of problem behavior. A "leading
researcher" was defined as any individual who had at least three published
articles related to PBS.

From this search and using the initial selection criteria, we identified
216 articles from 36 journals.

Exclusion Criteria

The final sample of journal articles was selected from the 216 articles
on the basis of the following methodological criteria: (a) the article had to
report an adequate number of data points in the case of single-case
designs or adequate statistics for group designs, and (b) the study had to
employ an acceptable experimental design. We report first on the studies
using single-case designs and follow that with a discussion of the group
design studies.

For single-case designs, a criterion of adequate data was at least three
baseline data points and three intervention data points. This minimum
was necessary for calculating some of the quantitative effect sizes and their
standard errors. Twenty-three articles were excluded because no data were
reported; these articles were narrative case reports and extended anec-

dotes. An additional 31 articles were excluded because they reported fewer than three baseline points (often as few as one point) or fewer than three intervention data points.

A number of different single-case designs were considered acceptable. Among the acceptable designs we included were multiple baseline, reversal, and withdrawal designs, all of which meet the internal validity criteria explicated in standard methodology texts on single-case research designs (e.g., Hersen & Barlow, 1976). Articles based on such designs were retained for analysis. Empirical case reports that employed an AB design (i.e., a baseline, A, condition was followed by an intervention, B, condition) were excluded because this design does not meet the internal validity criterion. Twenty-eight articles employing single-case methodology were excluded because of inadequate design.

A small number of articles (12) used legitimate group designs, but only 1 of these articles is comparable to the studies used in this meta-analysis. Four studies were designed to increase adaptive behavior; decreases in problem behavior were considered incidental occurrences. Six studies did not report data adequate to calculate effect sizes; usually the standard deviation was missing. And one longitudinal study had no intervention component. An additional 33 articles were excluded because they did not use legitimate group designs but, rather, reported averaged pre/post measures for a group of participants with no control group. It was not possible to calculate an effect size from these articles.

The application of these criteria resulted in a final sample of 109 articles that were included, and 107 that were excluded. Some articles were excluded for more than one reason. The Carr et al. (1999) monograph contains a table showing the breakdown of the two sets of articles across the 36 journals.

Agreement on the Inclusion/Exclusion of Articles

To determine the agreement among the investigators on the selection of articles according to the criteria, 50 articles were randomly chosen from the 109 articles that were retained, and 50 articles were randomly chosen from the 107 that were initially included but later excluded due to the failure to meet the two methodological criteria. One of the coauthors who was not involved in the selection process evaluated the 100 articles according to the six initial inclusionary criteria (described earlier) and according to the two exclusionary criteria. The coauthor, who was not informed of the final decision for inclusion or exclusion of any article, was asked to judge each article as to whether it did or did not meet each set of criteria. The rater agreed with the original coder's decision that all 100 articles met the initial selection criteria (100% agreement), and that the 50 articles that had been excluded by the original exclusionary selection process should indeed have been excluded as specified by the methodological criteria used (100% agreement).

Data Collection Methods

In the following sections we discuss how the data were extracted and coded. We also discuss the agreement for the coding of the data.

How Data Were Extracted and Coded

In order to calculate effect sizes related to the occurrence of problem behavior, it was necessary to determine the data values from each article, thus re-creating the baseline and intervention data pertaining to the outcomes. Tabled data were used when published. Otherwise, values for the baseline points and the intervention-phase points were extracted and recorded from the published figures.

In many studies, the intervention condition alternated several times with the baseline condition (a reversal design). When this occurred, the final intervention conditions and data points were coded because the primary issue of interest was how well an individual was doing at the end of intervention.

Frequently, a single participant received more than one type of intervention. For example, a participant might have received one reinforcement-based intervention followed by two stimulus-based interventions, providing an opportunity to examine three outcomes. When this situation arose, we coded the data separately for each of the three outcomes. In contrast, if a participant had received the same stimulus-based intervention in each phase, we coded only the final outcome. For a given participant, therefore, an outcome was defined as each unique (nonrepetitive) variation of a reinforcement-based and/or stimulus-based intervention.

Agreement in Data Coding

Four coders scored the data from the 109 articles. To determine the agreement in the coding process, one of the coauthors who was not involved in the original scoring randomly selected 28 articles, 7 articles from each of the four original coders. The coauthor recoded all of the categorical and continuous data from this sample. For the problem behavior occurrence data, the Pearson product–moment correlation, based on point-by-point reliability, was $+0.99$ ($p = .000$). For the categorical variables (e.g., age, gender, problem behavior topography, etc.), Kappa values (Cohen, 1960) ranged from .82 to 1.00. Landis and Koch (1977) characterized Kappa values greater than .75 as representing excellent agreement beyond chance.

Data entry reliability (keystroke error rate) was also computed. Each of the four coders reentered data for seven randomly selected articles that they had previously scored. This involved a total of 81,921 keystrokes, of which 94 differed from the original entries, yielding an error rate of .11%.

STATISTICAL METHODS

The choice of an effect size measure to use in the quantitative meta-analysis of single-case research is not obvious. The question of the "effectiveness" of PBS seems to imply some kind of measure that addresses the change in the level of behavior between the baseline phase and the intervention phase. On the surface, this appears to be similar to a question about differences in means for group design studies. In those studies, a standardized mean difference (SMD) measure is often used to assess effects, but single-case designs pose special problems that make using a SMD measure problematic. Among those considerations are: (a) the small number of data points within each phase/condition, (b) the within-phase trends, and (c) the frequent presence of outliers. In order to deal with these problematic data conditions in single-case designs, a number of measures have been proposed in the literature (see Faith et al., 1996; Hershberger, Wallace, Green, & Marquis, 1999). We examined many of these different measures and found strengths and weaknesses in all of them.

In general, effect sizes for single-case designs may be classified by the analytic techniques employed. These techniques include descriptive nonparametric methods, time series analyses, SMDs, and regression approaches. We rejected one commonly used nonparametric descriptive technique, the percent nonoverlapping data (Scruggs, Mastropieri, & Casto, 1987), because it can be strongly influenced by an outlying data point in the baseline or, sometimes, by the number of data points in the various phases. Corrections for this problem often seemed arbitrary.

We also rejected using time series methods. These methods are often appropriate when data are collected repeatedly over time from the same person (time series data) because the data values may be correlated (serial correlation), and time series methods take into account the correlation. Ignoring the correlation leads to incorrect test statistics for making statistical inferences regarding the effect of an intervention in a specific time series. It is not clear, however, what the effect of serial correlation is in meta-analytic studies because the estimate of the intervention effect itself is not biased (Marquis, 1983). Ignoring the serial correlation may or may not influence either the estimate of the overall effect size in the meta-analysis or the statistical inferences drawn regarding the effect size. Because more research is needed to determine the effect of serial correlation in meta-analyses of single-case studies and because most single-case experiments do not have an adequate number of data points per phase (at least 50 points per phase; Glass, Willson, & Gottman, 1975) to determine the correct model for the serial correlation, we decided not to use this approach. Our results, however, do need to be interpreted with caution because the effect of serial correlation is an unresolved issue.

Selected Effect Size Measures

After considering several options and not finding one "best" measure that appeared to be satisfactory for estimating an effect size in single-case studies, we chose to measure effect size in multiple ways with a clear stipulation of the assumptions and limitations of each. Next we define two different SMD measures and one regression measure. Results across all measures were compared to determine the effectiveness of positive behavior support. In the following section, we first describe the measure used in the descriptive research synthesis. We then describe the effect size measures used in the meta-analysis, including the assumptions and limitations for each measure.

The Percentage Reduction Measure

The descriptive study by Carr et al. (1999) described the results in terms of a proportional change measure or a percentage reduction measure, sometimes referred to as a suppression index. In the following section, we define the measure and discuss its limitations and strengths.

Definition of the Percentage Reduction Measure. The percentage reduction measure is calculated as follows: The mean of the last three data points in the intervention phase is subtracted from the mean of the last three data points in the baseline phase; the difference is then divided by the mean of the last three baseline points, and the quotient is multiplied by 100. The multiplication by 100 allows one to refer to the measure as a "percent reduction." It may be expressed mathematically as:

$$\text{ES}_{\text{SUPPR}} = \frac{\bar{y}_{\text{base3}} - \bar{y}_{\text{intvn3}}}{\bar{y}_{\text{base3}}} * 100. \tag{1}$$

The suppression index has the advantage of being easily understood and of reflecting the way in which many single-case researchers and clinicians discuss the effect of a treatment. For that reason it was chosen to present the results of the descriptive research synthesis. An additional descriptor, success, was also used in the descriptive research synthesis. Success was defined as a suppression index value of at least 90 or a percent reduction of 90%.

Assumptions and Limitations of the Percentage Reduction Measure. From the point of view of conducting a quantitative meta-analysis, the suppression index is limited because its distribution is unknown, making it difficult to use in a statistical analysis. Another difficulty is the interpretation in a quantitative analysis because one assumption underlying the scale is that a decrease from two occurrences per time period to one occurrence per time period represents the same effect as a decrease from 100 occurrences to 50 (suppression index = 50 in both cases). The measure has large values when the intervention-phase behavior is extinguished, or nearly so, and this is true regardless of the level of behavior in the baseline phase.

Standardized Mean Differences

SMDs are often proposed to estimate effects in group designs that include an experimental and a control group (see Glass, McGaw, & M. L. Smith, 1981). In this section we define the two SMD effect sizes that parallel the commonly used effect size for group designs, and we discuss their limitations and strengths.

Definition of Standardized Mean Difference Measures.   For single-case designs a SMD effect size was discussed by Gingerich (1984) and Busk and Serlin (1992). SMD measures are calculated by taking the difference between the mean of the baseline points and the mean of the intervention points. To take into account the possible different metrics for the outcome variable in the various studies, the difference of the means is then "standardized" by dividing the difference by a measure of variance. The variance measure is usually either the standard deviation of the data across all phases or, if the variance across phases is not homogeneous, then the divisor is the standard deviation of the data in the control or baseline phase. The effect size is then a measure of the mean difference expressed in standard deviation units. The standardized mean differences used in this meta-analysis were computed as the ratio of the difference between the mean of the baseline data points and the mean of the treatment data points to the standard deviation of the data in the control or baseline phase. The decision to use the baseline variance in the denominator was based on a close examination of many journal articles used in the study and the strong perception derived from this examination that the variances across the phases were not homogeneous and, thus, pooling would not be appropriate. The order of subtraction in the numerator is arbitrary, but is usually chosen based on the expected direction of effects and the perception that positive scores are generally considered to be "better" than negative scores.

We calculated two different SMD measures. One measure was based on only the last three data points in each phase; we called this the SMD for three points, abbreviated as ES_{SMD3}. The other measure was based on all recorded data points in each phase, which was arbitrarily selected to be a maximum of 42, abbreviated as ES_{SMDALL}.

We chose the last-three-data-points measure primarily to be consistent and comparable with the proportional change measure (suppression) used in the descriptive analyses reported in Carr et al. (1999) and because three data points in either phase was the minimum number of data points for an experiment to be included in the study. It was also consistent with the single-case design assumption that the end-of-phase data are the best indicators of effect. We thought it possible that the last three data points might give a more accurate reflection of the level if trends exist and thus control for a misinterpretation of effect when there is a trend. Also, if the researcher had tried to achieve stability before intervening, using the last three points would give a more accurate reflection of the stable level. To calculate ES_{SMD3}, the mean of the last three data points within the treatment phase was subtracted from the mean of the last three data points within the baseline phase to form the numerator of the measure. The numerator was divided by the standard deviation of the last three points in the baseline phase. The SMD effect size (ES) based on three points in each phase is:

$$ES_{SMD3} = \frac{\bar{y}_{base3} - \bar{y}_{intvn3}}{SD_{base3}}. \tag{2}$$

The formula for ES_{SMDALL} is similar to that in Equation 2, except that the mean and standard deviation for all baseline points is substituted for $\bar{y}_{base3}$ and SD_{base3}, respectively, and the mean for all intervention points is substituted for $\bar{y}_{intvn3}$.

Limitations and Assumptions of Standardized Mean Differences. The SMD assumes either that no trends exist in the data or that the researcher is uninterested in the trends and concerned only with changes in level. The measure will yield large values to the extent that there are large mean differences between the phases and/or little variance in the baseline data. The primary limitation of the SMD is that because the measure does not consider any trends in the data, it can yield underestimates or overestimates of the effect, depending on the direction of the trends. For example, if the baseline trend is positive (upward), the SMD may underestimate the effect when the goal is to reduce the occurrence of the behavior. A special difficulty in using the last three data points of any phase to calculate a mean difference is that an aberrant data point among the three points may have a substantial effect on the estimate by either altering the mean and/or increasing the variance.

Regression-Based Measures

In an attempt to consider the trends in the data sets, we also examined several effect sizes based on regression procedures (Allison & Gorman, 1993; Center, Skiba, & Casey, 1985–1986; Faith et al., 1996; Gorsuch, 1983; White, Rusch, Kazdin, & Hartmann, 1989). A regression procedure uses the experimental outcome measure (in this study, the occurrences of problem behavior) as the dependent variable and the measurement occasion (sessions) as the independent variable. The regression measure discussed next is described in greater detail in Hershberger et al. (1999).

Definition of the Regression Effect Size. For the particular regression measure we used in this meta-analysis, we conducted two regression analyses: One used the baseline points to determine a best-fitting regression line for the baseline phase; the second used the intervention points to determine a best-fitting line for the intervention phase. The regression equation derived from the baseline points was used to predict an expected value of the behavior at the end of the intervention phase, which is equivalent to the assumption that the behavior would continue as is if no intervention were implemented. The expected value is, therefore, the value for the last time point of the intervention phase, but is predicted from the baseline regression. This is labeled $\hat{y}_{base}$. The regression analysis based only on the treatment-phase points also predicts a value at the end of the treatment phase, labeled $\hat{y}_{intvn}$. The numerator of the regression-based effect size is the difference between the two values that are predicted from the two different regression analyses. As in the SMD, the difference between the two predicted values is then divided by a variance measure in order to take into account the different metrics used in various studies. Because the numerator is estimated using linear regression estimates, the most appropriate denominator for the regression effect size is the standard deviation of the y residual scores. And because the variance did not appear to be homogeneous in the two phases around the regression lines, it was decided to use the residuals around the regression line for the baseline phase. This is:

$$S = \sqrt{\frac{\sum_{i=1}^{n_{base}} (y_i - \hat{y}_i)^2}{n_{base} - 2}}, \tag{3}$$

where y_i is the observed outcome (behavior measured in frequency or percent of intervals) at time i, and $\hat{y}_i$ is the predicted outcome (behavior in frequency or percent of intervals) at time i based on a linear regression equation for the baseline data of the individual, and n_{base} is the number of data points in the individual's baseline phase. The divisor assumes that the regression equation is linear and subtracts 2 from n_{base} because the equation includes two parameters, a slope and an intercept (Hershberger et al., 1999). The effect size measure itself is:

$$ES_{REG} = \frac{\hat{y}_{base} - \hat{y}_{intvn}}{S}, \tag{4}$$

where $\hat{y}_{base}$ is the predicted outcome at the end of the intervention phase based on a regression equation using only the baseline points, $\hat{y}_{intvn}$ is the predicted outcome at the end of the intervention phase based on a regression equation using only the intervention data points, and S is the standard deviation of the y residual scores in the baseline phase. This effect size measure has several advantages: It uses all the data, which means it generally is a more accurate reflection of the behavior and treatment; it takes into account the effect of existing trends; and it is less sensitive to outliers.

Assumptions and Limitations of the Regression Measure. The regression measure just described assumes that increases (or decreases) in behavior are linear. Although this may be true in the short term, it is probably not true in the long term. Generally, there is a limit to the frequency of behaviors, especially problem behaviors, and they tend to either reach a ceiling or floor and become more level after a period of time. The "leveling off" could be modeled with higher order polynomial terms or other nonlinear functions. The data in most single-case studies, however, are too sparse to allow more sophisticated mathematical modeling. For example, 20% of the studies involved in this meta-analysis have only three baseline data points, and 40% of the studies contain five or fewer data points in the baseline phase. The problem with the assumption of linearity in the regression effect size measure becomes quite apparent when the baseline phase has a moderately increasing slope and the intervention phase is very long with either a decreasing trend or stable values. In this situation, values for the regression effect size can become very large, and predicted values may actually fall outside the acceptable range of values, for example, negative frequencies and percents, or percents greater than 100. Because there is no logical maximum for a predicted frequency, and because it did not seem prudent to constrain some values and not others, we calculated the regression effect sizes using all predicted values, even if they were out of range. Often out-of-range predicted values resulted in reasonable effect sizes, and sometimes reasonable predicted values resulted in very large effect sizes. The lack of any pattern in the relationship between the effect sizes and the predicted values made the choice of ignoring the fact that the values were out of range seem more acceptable.

STATISTICAL ANALYSES

As noted previously, both of the SMD effect sizes and the regression measure have their strengths and weaknesses. The regression measure allows us to take into account trends, which the standardized mean differences do not. On the other hand, the regression measure is much more likely to give inflated (or deflated) values, which the SMD based on all data points tends not to do. The SMD based on the last three points of each phase is something of a compromise between the two (more inflated or deflated than the ES_{SMDALL} when there is a trend, but not as much so as the regression measure), but it is more vulnerable to misrepresentation of effect size when aberrant data points are present. We decided to conduct analyses using each of the three measures in the expectation that using all three would give us a broader view of the effects of positive behavior support and allow us to assess the effects of positive behavior support across a variety of data configurations.

The statistical analyses were conducted using a hierarchical linear modeling approach as described by Bryk and Raudenbush (1992). As they noted, this method allows an estimate of the average effect size across studies along with an estimate of the variance of the effect size parameters. In addition, it is also possible to test the effects of moderator variables that might explain the variance in the effect size parameters. If the effect sizes vary across outcomes, then the variation may be due to the "moderating" effect of certain variables. An example of a moderating variable might be the influence of an assessment on the effect size, for example, larger effect sizes for participants who received an assessment. Often, these moderating variables are the real focus of interest for the researcher. Using this approach, we estimate the average effect size across all studies. We also conduct analyses to determine if study characteristics, treatment methodology, or participant factors explain the variance in the effect size parameters. The statistical analyses were conducted using the Hierarchical Linear Modeling program (HLM), written by Bryk, Raudenbush, and Congdon (1996).

Readers interested in the technical details should consult Appendix A, which presents the mathematical model and information on the variance estimates used and the estimation procedures. Readers who are not technically inclined should note that the estimates of the means and of the effects for the moderator variables are generalized least squares (GLS) estimates rather than the more common ordinary least squares (OLS) estimates. An oversimplified explanation of what this means is that the effect size for each outcome in the analysis is inversely weighted by the variance of the effect size for that outcome. Factors that influence the variance of the effect size are the number of data points and the effect size itself. Studies with larger effect sizes and/or fewer data points will tend to have larger variances; consequently, these studies will have less influence in determining the overall estimate of the effect size. The reader will notice this effect especially in the results for the regression effect sizes, where the observed effect sizes are very large, but the GLS estimates are considerably smaller.

As mentioned previously, some participants in the experiments may have had more than one outcome reported in the database. In one set of analyses, the unit of analysis was the set of all outcomes for all of the participants, disregarding the fact that multiple outcomes may have come from a single individual. We refer to these as "outcome" results. The original database contained 366 outcomes; however, 12 outcomes were dropped because either it was impossible to calculate any effect size due to a lack of variance in the baseline or the metric by which the outcomes were measured was so unlike the others in the study that the effect sizes would have very different meanings (e.g., latency data). Thus, the basic outcomes database has 354 units for analysis.

In a second set of analyses, the effect sizes across all outcomes for an individual participant were combined. The unit of analysis in this case was the participant, and these are referred to as the participant results. Several methods have been suggested for combining multiple outcomes from the same subject (Allison & Gorman, 1993; Marascuilo & Busk, 1988; Shadish & Haddock, 1994). We chose to average the outcomes (when appropriate), and then conduct the same analyses as described earlier using the combined outcomes for the individual participant. An example of when it was not appropriate to average across outcomes for a participant occurred when the analysis was designed to determine if there were differences in effect sizes for stimulus-based interventions compared to reinforcement-based interventions. In this analysis, if the participant had some outcomes in which the intervention was reinforcement based and other outcomes in which the intervention was stimulus based, then the participant was removed from the participant analysis, but not removed from the outcomes analysis. Of the 220 participants included in the meta-analysis, 137 had only one outcome and 59 had only two. The other 24 persons had between three and eight outcomes. For these analyses, the variance for the individual participant effect size was calculated using the standard formula for the variance of a linear combination, assuming no correlation among the measures. (See Appendix A for the formula.) The assumption of no correlation among these effect sizes is problematic and currently both the existence of the correlation and its estimation are unresolved methodological issues. In the absence of any definitive solution, we make the no-correlation assumption with the caveat that one needs to be cautious in drawing conclusions. The most likely consequence is an overestimation of the participant effect size; the pattern of results is probably not affected.

No statistical analyses are reported when the numbers of units for the analysis (either outcomes or participants) in the relevant groups were too small. Although admittedly arbitrary, we considered 30 outcomes to be a reasonable number of outcomes for acceptably reliable results. However, the table of estimated means does contain the estimates for some of the smaller samples; these are intended to serve as baseline values for future studies and to suggest future areas of research.

RESULTS

In addition to the overall analysis to determine a general effect size, separate analyses were conducted for each condition or factor that the researchers thought might influence the effect size. Because three different effect sizes were calculated on two different units of analysis (participants and outcomes), altogether six analyses were conducted for each condition or factor. Careful examination of the results revealed that the pattern of results among the different effect sizes was very similar. Because of the similarity of results and the unwieldiness of reporting all results, we report in the text only the results for the SMD effect size calculated on all data points (ES_{SMDALL}). Also, we discuss in the text only the effect size when the unit of analysis was the outcome of the intervention. Because some participants had more than one outcome, the number of outcomes is larger than the number of participants (354 outcomes, 220 participants). We discuss outcomes for two reasons: Total outcomes is the method used for reporting results in the descriptive synthesis (Carr et al., 1999), and this is the most conservative result. The pattern of results was always the same for participants as for outcomes, but the effect sizes for participants were larger, probably because of smaller variances. Complete results for all effect sizes and all units of analysis are found in Appendix B. Also, because of the large number of analyses, we do not report formally statistical significance for each analysis. Instead, we draw conclusions of a strong effect or no differences between conditions/factors based on the corroborating evidence provided by a consistent pattern in the magnitude of effect sizes and of probability levels across all analyses for a specific variable. Because probability level is closely related to statistical significance, we do occasionally mention statistically significant results as a point of reference for the reader; we do not, however, draw conclusions based solely on the statistical significance of a single analysis.

We first present estimates of the overall mean of ES_{SMDALL} using several different statistical procedures. We then discuss results for three different kinds of moderator variables: study characteristic variables, participant factor variables, and intervention methodology variables. The study characteristic variables considered in these analyses include the slope, the number of points in the baseline and treatment phases, and the type of data (percent or frequency data). The participant characteristic variables included age, degree of retardation, diagnosis, type of problem behavior, and gender. Intervention characteristics included whether the intervention was stimulus based or reinforcement based, whether the intervention was based on an assessment, in what setting and by whom the intervention was carried out, and whether it included a nonpositive component. The function of the behavior is also reported with the intervention characteristics because different interventions may address different functions for a participant. Lastly, we report the results of a multiple variable analysis using several of the predictor variables simultaneously. These latter analyses were done to determine if the variables each independently predict the effect size or if they overlap in their predictive power.

Descriptive Statistics—Overall Effect Sizes

Three different estimates of ES_{SMDALL} are given in Table 5.1. These include the observed overall mean, the GLS estimate of the mean without any adjustments for study methodology, and the GLS estimate of the mean adjusted for study characteristics. The estimated means change dramatically when using the GLS estimates, which adjust for the effect size variance by weighting the effect size by the inverse of the variance. Under the conditions of only three baseline and intervention data points, zero slope and only one outcome, ES_{SMDALL} is 2.1 with additional negative adjustments of .035 needed for each additional baseline data point and −.3 needed for frequency data. The values for the GLS estimates are quite

TABLE 5.1
Overall Mean Estimated by Three Methods

	ES_{SMDALL} (n = 354)
Observed mean	2.8
Unadjusted GLS mean	1.6
Adjusted GLS mean[a]	2.1

[a]Mean is adjusted for study characteristics of slope, number of baseline points, number of treatment points, type of data (percent or frequency).

different from the observed mean values, indicating that the observed means can be quite misleading. For this reason, we do not report the observed means and concentrate in this report on the adjusted means obtained with the hierarchical modeling approach.

Analyses of Moderator Variables

As mentioned previously, we examined moderator variables concerned with study characteristics, participant characteristics, and intervention characteristics. In this section, we discuss the results for the specific moderator variables and for certain combinations of moderator variables. The primary focus in this section is on the participant and intervention characteristics because these are the variables of interest to the clinician or researcher. The study characteristic variables should be viewed primarily as control variables necessary for the interpretability of the results in the meta-analysis; their inclusion helps ensure that the results for the participant and intervention characteristics among all the studies are comparable and not due to the different characteristics of the studies themselves.

Study Characteristics

We first examine the influence on effect sizes of various design aspects of the experiment. In this analysis we look at the type of data (percent or frequency count), the number of data points in the baseline and in the treatment phases, and the slope. We examine the influence of these variables on the various effect sizes in order to determine the need for adjusting the estimate of the mean effect size.

Forty-three percent of the recorded data were frequency data. Usually the data type was not statistically significant for the various types of effect sizes and units of analysis; however, for ES_{SMDALL} in the outcome data, it had a very low probability value for about half of the variables, including both participant and treatment characteristics. The effect of collecting data as frequency counts was to decrease the effect size by about .3 to .5 units.

The number of baseline data points was significantly and negatively related to all of the effect sizes types; that is, as the number of baseline data points increased, the effect size decreased. The mean number of baseline points was 8.9. Forty percent of the studies had five or fewer baseline points. The mean number of treatment points was 19.8, and was rarely related to ES_{SMDALL}.

Because all of these experimental design variables were, either frequently or occasionally, related to the effect sizes, we decided to include all of them in the hierarchical linear modeling for the meta-analysis. Even when the design variables had no significant effects, they generally reduced the

random variance of the effect size parameter in the model. And, by including all of them as control variables, the results across all analyses of the participant and intervention variables were more comparable.

Results for Participant-Characteristic Variables

We now report the results for the analyses that examine participant
characteristics. As noted previously, we include the experimental design
effects in all analyses. To present these results in a meaningful manner, we
present an effect size for outcomes under the specific conditions of three
baseline data points, three intervention points, percent-type data, and
zero slope in the baseline data. Adjustments may need to be made to these
values for other conditions.

The participant-factor variables considered were age of the participant,
gender, degree of retardation, diagnosis, and type of problem behavior.
Reported next are the results of the hierarchical modeling using the effect
size as the dependent variable and the specific participant variable as an
independent variable that predicts the mean level of the effect size. All
analyses included the experimental design variables discussed earlier.
Results for the participant-characteristic variables are shown in Table 5.2,
which reports an overall effect size for a typical participant without the
characteristic and an overall effect size for a person with the characteristic. All means reported in the tables are different from zero as indicated
by a hypothesis test that is statistically significant.

Differences between means for different groups in a condition/factor are
not, however, necessarily statistically significant. Small mean differences
between the effect sizes of the groups indicate that group differences are not
likely. On the other hand, larger differences with small probabilities indicate
that PBS is likely more effective with one group in the factor/condition than
with the other group. As a point of reference, the reader may consider that
for the dichotomous variables, differences between the groups of .5 units or
greater were nearly always statistically significant at the .05 level, and sometimes smaller differences were also significant. Differences of less than .5
units need to be interpreted with caution.

Gender.   Seventy females and 142 males participated in these studies.
Gender was not reported for eight participants. There were no significant
differences between males and females, although the regression coefficients indicated that the mean effect size for males was somewhat lower
than that for females.

Age.   The ages of participants ranged from 2 years to 50 years old,
with a mean age of 14.5 years. Age was not a significant predictor. The

TABLE 5.2
Adjusted Mean Effect Size (ES$_{SMDALL}$) for Outcomes[a] Participant Characteristics

Variable	Mean	n
Gender		
Male	2.1	225
Female	2.3	115
Diagnosis		
Mental retardation (MR) only	1.9	200
Autism (Aut) only	2.0	32
MR & Aut only	2.1	38
(MR and/or Aut) and other	2.1	72
Level of retardation		
Mild	2.6	51
Moderate	2.2	52
Severe	1.9	91
Profound	1.5	109
Problem behavior types		
Aggression		
Yes	2.3	185
No	1.8	169
Self-injurious behavior		
Yes	1.9	187
No	2.2	167
Property destruction		
Yes	2.3	71
No	2.1	283
Tantrums		
Yes	2.4	79
No	2.0	275
Problem behavior configuration		
Single problem	1.9	242
Combination problems	2.4	112
Age—Mean at 14.5 years	2.1	314

[a]All means are adjusted for the slope, the number of baseline and treatment data points, and the type of data (percent or frequency).

coefficients for age indicated that PBS may be slightly more effective for the younger participants.

Degree of Retardation. Degree of retardation was reported for 183 out of the 220 participants in these analyses. The numbers of participants in each category are: mild, 32, moderate, 35; severe, 57; and profound, 59. Degree of retardation was a strong predictor for ES$_{SMDALL}$ with an estimated mean effect size of 1.5 for a person with profound retardation. As the degree of retardation becomes less, the effect size increases by .35 units. Thus, the estimated mean ES$_{SMDALL}$ for a person with mild retardation would be expected to be about 2.6.

Diagnosis. Participants were classified as having only mental retardation or developmental disability (MRDD; $n = 112$), autism/pervasive developmental disability only ($n = 23$), MRDD and autism/pervasive developmental disability, but no other disability ($n = 28$), and MRDD, autism/pervasive developmental disability and another disability ($n = 49$). None of the diagnostic categories was significantly related to any of the effect sizes.

Problem Behavior. The four types of problem behavior examined were aggression, self-injurious behavior, property destruction, and tantrums. Eighty participants had multiple problems; 140 had only a single problem. Because so few participants had only tantrums or only property destruction, we decided to examine the presence of each type of problem behavior, ignoring the possibility that the participant may also exhibit additional problem behaviors. For example, the analysis for aggression includes everyone who exhibited aggression even if they also had tantrums or some other problem behavior. We also compared the group of persons with only a single problem behavior to the group with multiple problem behaviors. ES_{SDMALL} showed statistically significant differences for the aggression group. The overall mean effect size for outcomes other than aggression was 1.8; for those with aggression, the effect size increased .5 units, indicating that PBS is generally effective with persons with problem behavior, but it is even more effective with persons who exhibit aggressive behavior. The pattern of PBS being more effective with persons with aggression was found for the other effect size measures also.

ES_{SMDALL} also showed strong differences when comparing outcomes with only one problem behavior to those with more than one. The estimated overall effect size was 1.9 for outcomes with a single problem behavior compared to an estimated overall effect size of 2.4 for those with more than one problem behavior.

Characteristics of the Intervention

In this section, we discuss the effect of conducting an assessment and the function of the behavior as addressed in the intervention. We also describe characteristics of the intervention including whether it is stimulus based or reinforcement based, whether it is carried out by a typical agent or an atypical agent, whether it is carried out in a typical setting or an atypical setting, and whether it included a nonpositive behavioral component. Data were also collected on some additional characteristics, but the number of cases is too small to use in a statistical analysis. The variables with limited data include environmental reorganization and the inclusion/exclusion of nonpositive behavior support for persons who received either or both stimulus- and reinforcement-based interventions. As with the participant variables, all categories of the intervention variables have effect sizes that are different from zero as indicated by a statistically significant hypothesis test. Only a few variables, however, have categories that are different from each other as assessed by a statistical test. Results for the intervention characteristics are reported in Table 5.3.

Assessment of Function. The analyses regarding assessment of function compared the effect sizes obtained when an assessment was done and the results used in planning the intervention to the effect sizes obtained when either an assessment was not done or the results of the assessment were not used. Two hundred nineteen outcomes involved an assessment that was used in planning an intervention, whereas 135 did not. A small probability for ES_{SMDALL} and the other effect sizes indicated strong differences between these two conditions. These results indicate that doing an assessment and using it to plan the PBS intervention probably results in a better outcome.

Function of Problem Behavior. As discussed previously, the four categories of behavioral function were attention, escape, tangibles, and sensory. Of the 354 outcomes, data on function of behavior are available for only 238 outcomes. No strong differences were found among the various functions.

Stimulus-Based and Reinforcement-Based Interventions. Interventions that included both a reinforcement-based component and a stimulus-based component had large increases for all effect sizes calculated on either unit of analysis. For ES_{SMDALL} the mean effect size for a single intervention type was 2.1; for combined interventions, it was 3.1. These results are based on 36 outcomes from 21 different participants and should be interpreted with caution because so few outcomes are involved; but the magnitude and consistency of the results across effect sizes indicates that further study is needed. Regarding single interventions, neither stimulus-only interventions nor reinforcement-only interventions showed strong differences.

PBS Interventions With a Nonpositive Component. Analyses were conducted to determine if there were significant differences between those outcomes with nonpositive support in addition to the positive behavior support and those outcomes with positive behavior support only. One hundred two outcomes involved additional nonpositive support and 252 involved only positive support. No statistically significant differences were

TABLE 5.3
Adjusted Mean Effect Size (ES_{SMDALL}) for Outcomes[a] Intervention Characteristics

Variable	Mean	n
Assessment		
Conducted & Used	2.3	219
Not conducted or Not used	1.9	135
Type of function		
Attention		
Yes	2.5	61
No	2.2	177
Escape		
Yes	2.3	160
No	2.1	78
Tangible		
Yes	2.3	43
No	2.3	195
Sensory		
Yes	2.1	26
No	2.3	212
Multiple		
Yes	2.6	47
No	2.2	191
Intervention type		
Stimulus-based (ST)		
Yes	2.2	190
No	2.0	164
Reinforcement-based (RF)		
Yes	2.2	200
No	2.0	154
Intervention configuration		
Single interventions	2.1	318
Combined interventions	3.1	36
Nonpositive behavioral support (non-PBS)		
Exclude non-PBS	2.1	252
Include non-PBS	1.9	102
Intervention agent		
Typical	2.6	147
Atypical	1.6	195
Intervention setting		
Typical	2.6	117
Atypical	1.7	237
Significant others change		
Yes	2.4	257
No	2.0	97

[a]All means are adjusted for the slope, the number of baseline and treatment data points, and the type of data (percent or frequency).

found between the two treatment conditions. The overall pattern was for the means to be lower in the group that received both positive and non-positive support. These results are generally consistent with the results reported for the suppression success rates, which showed little difference between the types of intervention strategy and the various combinations.

Interventions With Typical Agents.   The interventions for 147 outcomes involved typical agents; 195 outcomes involved interventions with atypical agents. The effect size was always much larger when typical agents were the primary implementers of the intervention compared to when they were not; the increase was from 1.6 for atypical agents to 2.6 for typical agents. These results indicate that, whereas PBS is effective with either a typical or an atypical agent, it appears to be more effective with a typical agent. This result needs to be interpreted with caution, however, because the interventions with typical settings and typical agents are closely related to each other. The discussion that follows addresses interventions in typical settings.

Interventions in Typical Settings.   Interventions in typical settings showed the same patterns of relationships as that of typical agents. One hundred seventeen outcomes occurred with the intervention in typical settings; 237 outcomes occurred in atypical settings. The effect size increased from 1.7 when the interventions were carried out in atypical settings to 2.6 in typical settings. As noted earlier, the results for typical agents and typical settings are not independent of each other. Altogether, nearly 88% of the outcomes involved receiving the intervention from an atypical agent in an atypical setting or receiving the intervention from a typical agent in a typical setting.

Significant Others Change Behavior.   The means generally are higher when a significant other changes behavior, but no significant differences were found for this variable.

Combinations of Factors—Multivariate Analyses

Multivariate analyses were conducted to examine the relationships among all the moderator variables that individually showed a very strong relationship with the effect size. These variables included aggression, degree of retardation, typical setting, typical agents, and assessment. In these analyses, the effect size was the dependent variable and the moderator variables were independent variables considered simultaneously in a regression analysis. The purpose was to determine if the statistically significant results for each of the individual variables would persist when controlling for the effects of the other variables. As noted previously, some of the conditions do not appear to occur independently of the occurrence of other conditions, and, thus, their effects may not be independent. Closer examination of the variables in the multivariate analysis revealed that the agent and setting variables, in addition to being related to each other, were also related to the degree of retardation. Persons with profound retardation tended to receive the intervention in atypical settings or with atypical agents. As the degree of retardation becomes less, the proportion of persons receiving interventions in typical settings and with typical agents increases. Moreover, examination of the data also revealed that the occurrence of aggressive behavior was related to the degree of retardation; most of the participants with aggressive behavior also had less severe levels of retardation. Thus, it appears that in these data there is a constellation of factors that tend to occur together: typical settings, typical agents, more moderate levels of retardation, and aggression. Clearly, there is a strong relationship between each of these four variables individually and the effect size, but there is also a relationship among the four variables themselves such that it is difficult to identify whether the significant effects are due to a specific one of these conditions or to some combination. Confirmation that the effects may be confounded is also found in the significance tests of the estimates of the individual parameters in the multivariate analysis, which indicate that the effects are not strictly additive because not all variables remain statistically significant in an analysis with all the variables in the model. Although the covariation among the factors is not unexpected, the effects do not always occur together and probably could be disentangled with more data in which the factors are not co-occurring. Therefore, caution must be used in interpreting the relationship between positive behavior support and the effect of any one of these variables (setting, agent, level of retardation, and aggression) because they are highly interrelated in this set of studies.

On the other hand, the effects of the assessment variable do not appear to be confounded with the other variables discussed previously. In the multivariate analyses, conducting an assessment and using it to design an intervention tends to remain significant, or at least have a very small probability level, even when the other moderator variables discussed earlier are in the model. This is an indication that the effects of assessment are relatively independent of the other statistically significant variables and that its effects are additive.

We also thought it possible that the types of intervention, stimulus based or reinforcement based, might be differentially effective with problem behaviors, functions of behavior, or some diagnostic groups. Analyses of variance to explore the possibility of these interactions revealed no differential effects of the intervention type.

DISCUSSION

In this section, we discuss the findings related to PBS and the interpretation of these results. As indicated earlier, many issues related to meta-analysis in single-case designs remain unresolved. Fundamental issues include the definition of an effect size and the interpretation of the magnitude of that effect size. Next we discuss these issues, considering factors such as publication bias and the nature of single-case studies. We then relate that discussion to the findings in this meta-analysis of PBS.

Definition and Interpretation of Effect Sizes

We first examine several ways to interpret the SMD effect sizes calculated in the meta-analysis. We discuss possible influences on the effect sizes and limitations of the interpretations.

Group Design Interpretations

As mentioned earlier, all three effect sizes calculated in this meta-analysis are primarily designed to assess a change in level by calculating an expected difference between a baseline level and an intervention level, using various methods to control for trends and to take into account differences in metric. This approach is analogous to the SMD approach often used for group design research. Thus, one possible way to interpret the obtained effect sizes is to compare them to the usual interpretations of SMDs found in group research. Cohen's (1988) suggestion for a "large" SMD effect size is .8; by this standard, the effect sizes found in this meta-analysis are very large. The smallest value of ES_{SMDALL} for outcomes was 1.5, which would be considered quite large in a group study context. One needs, however, to be somewhat cautious in interpreting these effect sizes as being comparable to group effect sizes. Two reasons for this caution are publication bias and the nature of single-case experiments.

Publication Bias. Publication bias refers to the tendency to publish studies based on the results, which is often manifest in publishing only studies with statistically significant results (usually group design studies) or large effects (single-case studies). In the case of single-case designs where statistical analyses are rarely used, the criterion for publication generally is that the experiment must have adequate controls so that the results are easily interpretable (elimination of confounding factors) and that the effects are large enough to be visually obvious using well-specified rules for visual presentation (Parsonson & Baer, 1978). If some participants do not respond, then the single-case design may not meet the criteria for establishing experimental control, and the study may be rejected for publication. By using only published studies in this meta-analysis, we limited our analysis to studies that met the peer-review criteria for acceptable experimental design. On the other hand, we probably also limited our access to other studies that may have met high standards of experimental design, but may not have been published, perhaps because of small effects. This difficulty is not unique to this meta-analysis or to meta-analyses of single-case studies, but, nevertheless, the possible effects of publication bias need to temper the interpretation of the results as publication bias may be a factor that contributes to the relatively large effect sizes.

Single-Case Methodology. A second consideration in the interpretation of the results was alluded to in the discussion earlier, namely, the nature of single-case experiments and their "effects." The purpose in many of these experiments is to demonstrate a functional relationship between the dependent variable, usually some behavior, and the introduction of an independent variable. The focus is on the functional relationship, and so the researcher has the flexibility to choose the particular behavior to be studied, to choose the intervention strategy the researcher considers most appropriate, and to choose the length of time over which the treatment occurs. This kind of flexibility and adaptability leads to experimental designs that are quite powerful and treatments that produce large effects. In contrast, the purpose of a group design does not allow these kinds of options in designing the experiment. Thus, it is not too surprising that the effect sizes in this meta-analysis (and probably in most single-case studies) are, by the standards of group designs, quite large.

Suppression Interpretation

One possible way to avoid the issue of using an inappropriate group design standard for interpretation is to adopt a standard more suitable for single-case designs in general or for the particular outcome of interest in the research. One approach might be to relate the calculated effect sizes to another criterion used in the research. In the case of PBS, such a criterion might be the suppression rate used in the descriptive synthesis. For example, the mean effect size for outcomes with a suppression rate of 80% or better was 2.4; this could perhaps be considered to be an indication of a very effective treatment. Suppression rates between 60% and 80% had a mean effect size value of 2.0, which could perhaps be considered an indication of a moderately effective treatment. Smaller effect sizes could be related to lower suppression rates and, thus, to less effective treatments. The standards would need to be worked out with single-case researchers and would need to consider both the types of outcomes and appropriate

criterion variables such as suppression. It is quite possible that an interpretation for mean-difference measures may vary across different outcome and criterion variables in single-case studies. For purposes of
interpreting the results of this meta-analysis, we consider both the related
suppression rates and group standards for the effect sizes. We realize that
these are not completely satisfactory approaches and that much more
research needs to be done.

Effectiveness of Positive Behavior Support

One of the questions posed for this meta-analysis was whether PBS was effective in reducing the incidence of problem behavior. The analysis used several standardized measures of effect and found a consistent pattern of results.
Considering only those outcomes in which the data were adequate to draw
reliable conclusions ($n \geq 30$), the GLS estimates of ES_{SMDALL} ranged from 1.5
standardized units to 3.1 units. Moreover, the effects are present across a
variety of subject characteristics including age, gender, problem behavior,
degree of retardation, diagnosis, and function of behavior. The effects also
are present for both stimulus-based and reinforcement-based interventions.
As mentioned earlier, in comparison to group design effect sizes these effects
are quite large. They are also associated with levels of suppression that usually exceed 80% and always exceed 40%.

We also examined differential effects for various categories of condi-
tions/factors and found few differences, indicating that PBS was generally
effective across a variety of situations. We also found that PBS was especially effective for some specific conditions or factors. One of these was
whether an assessment was completed and used in designing the treatment; PBS is more effective when the assessment is done. PBS was also
especially effective in a set of related factors/conditions that included a
typical agent, a typical setting, aggression, and more moderate degrees of
retardation. It was also noted that for these particular variables there was
some overlap in the participants who comprised each group and that,
because of this overlap, the estimates of the effects probably are not independent of each other.

Another set of findings indicated areas in which there are probable differences but the data were too sparse to draw reliable conclusions. Using
a single intervention (either reinforcement based or stimulus based)
appears to be less effective than using a combination of both. The differences appear to be large across all effect size measures, but only 21 participants received both interventions. Also, participants with multiple
functions for the behavior appeared to have larger effect sizes than other
participants, but, again, there were only 21 participants in each category.
More research is needed for these possible differences.

Methodological Issues in Single-Case Meta-Analysis

A number of methodological issues remain unresolved. These include the determination of a satisfactory measure of effect size and the effects of various design aspects such as the number of data points or the different types of data.

Experimental Design Questions

We examined a number of design factors that influenced at least some of the effect sizes. The one factor that was almost always statistically significant for all effect sizes and across both participant and outcomes data was the number of baseline data points. The coefficient was always negative, indicating that additional data points resulted in smaller effect sizes. This may be due to initial high levels of problem behavior and the researcher's reluctance, for ethical or realistic considerations, to extend the length of the baseline. Also for the usual kind of visual analysis, a large number of baseline data points is not always needed. On the other hand, the small number of baseline points may be misleading about the actual level of behavior and may result in an inflated effect size. Collecting more baseline data points would be desirable also because it might allow the fitting of a nonlinear (and more realistic) model to the data for use in calculating regression-based effect sizes to account for trends. Though more baseline data would be helpful, some research would need to be conducted to determine a standard for "adequate" baseline data and conditions under which the standard could be breached.

Another design variable that was often statistically significant for ES_{SMDALL} in the outcomes data was the data type—frequency or percent data. For all the variables relating to function and type of problem, and for several other variables, the effect of having frequency data compared to percent data was to lower the GLS estimates of the effect size by about .3–.5 units. This effect rarely occurred with the participant data.

Selection of an Effect Size Measure

In the beginning of this discussion section, we reviewed the problem of interpreting the SMD effect size in the context of single-case designs. A more fundamental issue for meta-analysis of single-case designs is the determination of an appropriate effect size measure.

If we assume that an appropriate effect size measure should detect changes in level between the baseline and the intervention phases while taking into account trends in either phase, then the selection of a measure remains problematic. Neither ES_{SMDALL} nor ES_{SMD3} considers trends. The regression measure holds promise if the issue of out-of-bounds values can be resolved satisfactorily. Several possibilities should be explored in future research. One possibility is to select a reasonable, although arbitrary, time point within the intervention phase at which to assess the treatment effect, for example, Session 5 or Session 10 or perhaps some number proportional to the number of baseline points. Then the predicted level based on the baseline regression would be the predicted value at that specified intervention session. This would reduce the problem of unreasonable estimates of treatment levels due to long intervention periods. Another possibility is to use some kind of robust estimation procedures that would trim the extreme values in the tails of the regression effect size distribution.

A larger issue, however, is the adequacy of "change-in-level" measures for single-case designs. In general, these effect sizes are adaptations of the kinds of measures used in group design studies, and their interpretations are usually closely tied to group design interpretations. These measures have at least two shortcomings:

1. They do not address replication of the effect, which is an important aspect of single-case design (see Hershberger et al., 1999).
2. They do not address the fundamental question of the functional relationship between the behavior and the introduction of an intervention, which is often the primary focus for single-case research.

The change in level of the behavior, although important, is often a secondary issue. Indeed, in a related study, we asked single-case researchers to evaluate the functional relationships in a small subset of the studies used in this meta-analysis. We then compared the values they assigned for the strength of the functional relationships to the values found for the change-of-level effect size measures. No relationship existed between the strength of the functional relationship and the magnitude of the effect size; it was quite clear that two different questions were being addressed by the two measures. Given that group and single-case designs are addressing somewhat different questions, perhaps more consideration needs to be given to developing other effect size measures that more adequately address the central issues in single-case studies. For example, one could develop a rigorous standard protocol that could be expressed numerically to assess the strength of a functional relationship.

CONCLUSIONS

The meta-analysis reported here examined the effectiveness of PBS as reported in the published research literature in the period 1985–1996. Using change-in-level effect size measures, the analysis indicated that PBS ıs effective acıoss all four problem behaviors examined and across a wide variety of participant characteristics and intervention strategies. There is some evidence from the analyses that PBS may be even more effective with typical agents, typical settings, milder levels of retardation, and aggression; however, these conditions tended to co-occur, making it difficult to draw any definite conclusions about the effect of any one of these variables. The analysis also indicated that PBS is more effective when an assessment has been completed and the results used to design the intervention. These results are consistent with the findings reported by Carr et al. (1999) in a research synthesis completed on the same database of PBS articles.

APPENDIX A
The Mathematical Model

The Level 1 model is

$$d_j = \delta_j + \varepsilon_j$$

where

δ_j represents the population effect size,
d_j represents the estimate of δ_j, and
ε_j represents the sampling error associated with d_j as an estimate of δ_j.
The assumed distribution of ε_j is N $(0,V_j)$.

The Level 2 model is

$$\delta_j = \gamma_0 + \gamma_1 W_{1j} + \gamma_2 W_{2j} + \ldots + \gamma_S W_{Sj} + u_j$$

where,

$W_{1j}, W_{2j}, \ldots, W_{Sj}$ are the moderator variables that predict the effect sizes, $\gamma_0, \ldots, \gamma_j$ are regression coefficients, and u_j is a Level 2 random error, which is assumed to be distributed as N $(0, \tau)$.

We now describe the estimation of the fixed Level 1 variances (V_j). Following our previous adaptation of Glass' SMD using the standard deviation of the control data as the standardizing variance, we calculate the variances for the SMD effect sizes based on using the baseline observations as control data and the treatment-phase observations as intervention data. Thus, the variances for ES_{SMD3} and ES_{SMDALL} use the following formula given by Rosenthal (in Cooper & Hedges, 1994).

$$V_j = \frac{n_{intvn} + n_{base}}{n_{intvn}\,n_{base}} + \frac{ES^2_{SMD}}{2(n_{base}-1)},$$

where n_{intvn} and n_{base} are the number of intervention and baseline observations, respectively, and V_j is the Level 1 variance, in this case calculated for the SMD effect size of interest (ES_{SMD3} and ES_{SMDALL}). For ES_{SMD3}, n_{intvn} and n_{base} would be equal to 3, whereas these values would vary by case for ES_{SMDALL}.

Variance estimates for the regression measure were calculated using the formula given in Hershberger et al. (1999). The estimate uses Kish's (1965) formula for the ratio of two variables:

$$\text{Var}\left(\frac{Y}{X}\right) = \frac{1}{X^2}\left[\text{Var}(Y) + \left(\frac{Y}{X}\right)^2 \text{Var}(X)\right].$$

In the estimation procedure, a maximum likelihood estimate of the variance τ is derived. Given this variance estimate, GLS estimates of the coefficients (γ_j) are obtained. As mentioned in the text, the weighting is done by the inverse of the variance, where the variance is ($\tau + V_j$).

APPENDIX B
Tables for All Effect Sizes

TABLE B5.1
Overall Mean Effect Sizes

	Participants			Outcomes		
	ES_{SMDALL} (n = 220)	ES_{REG} (n = 218)	ES_{SMD3} (n = 213)	ES_{SMDALL} (n = 354)	ES_{REG} (n = 348)	ES_{SMD3} (n = 343)
Observed means	3.0	10.2	4.3	2.8	9.2	4.1
Unadjusted GLS means	1.9	1.3	2.1	1.6	1.0	1.6
Adjusted GLS means[a]	2.4	1.9	2.4	2.1	1.7	2.0

[a]Means are adjusted for study characteristics of slope, number of baseline points, number of treatment points, and the type of data (percent or frequency). Participant means are also adjusted for the number of outcomes each participant had.

TABLE B5.2
Adjusted Mean Effect Sizes Across Outcomes

	ES_{SMDALL}		ES_{REG}		ES_{SMD3}	
Variable	M	n	M	n	M	n
Adjusted mean[a]	2.1	354	1.7	348	2.0	343
Gender						
Male	2.1	225	1.7	220	1.9	218
Female	2.3	115	1.8	114	1.9	111

(Continued)

Variable	ES_{SMDALL}		ES_{REG}		ES_{SMD3}	
	M	n	M	n	M	n
Diagnosis						
Mental retardation						
(MR) only	1.9	200	1.8	196	1.8	198
Autism (Aut) only	2.0	32	1.5	32	1.9	27
MR & Aut only	2.1	38	2.0	38	2.3	36
(MR and/or Aut) and other	2.1	72	1.3	72	1.8	70
Level of retardation						
Mild	2.6	51	1.8	48	2.3	51
Moderate	2.2	52	1.7	52	1.9	50
Severe	1.9	91	1.7	89	1.6	86
Profound	1.5	109	1.6	108	1.2	108
Problem behavior types						
Aggression						
Yes	2.3	185	1.8	181	2.0	179
No	1.8	169	1.6	167	1.8	164
Self-injurious behavior						
Yes	1.9	187	1.7	185	1.8	182
No	2.2	167	1.7	163	2.0	161
Property destruction						
Yes	2.3	71	1.6	70	2.0	67
No	2.1	283	1.8	278	1.9	276
Tantrums						
Yes	2.4	79	2.0	78	2.3	76
No	2.0	275	1.6	270	1.8	267
Problem behavior configuration						
Single problem	1.9	242	1.7	237	1.8	234
Combination problems	2.4	112	1.9	111	2.2	109
Assessment						
Conducted & used	2.3	219	1.9	214	2.2	213
Not conducted or Not used	1.9	135	1.6	134	1.7	130
Type of function						
Attention						
Yes	2.5	61	1.7	60	2.3	60
No	2.2	177	1.8	172	2.3	172
Escape						
Yes	2.3	160	2.1	156	2.4	157
No	2.1	78	1.5	76	1.9	75
Tangible						
Yes	2.3	43	2.2	41	2.1	40
No	2.3	195	1.8	191	2.3	192
Sensory						
Yes	2.1	26	1.4	26	2.0	26
No	2.3	212	1.9	206	2.3	206
Multiple						
Yes	2.6	47	2.3	46	2.5	46
No	2.2	191	1.7	186	2.2	186

(Continued)

Variable	ES$_{SMDALL}$		ES$_{REG}$		ES$_{SMD3}$	
	M	n	M	n	M	n
Intervention type						
Stimulus-based (ST)						
Yes	2.2	190	1.8	189	2.1	188
No	2.0	164	1.6	159	1.7	155
Reinforcement-based (RF)						
Yes	2.2	200	1.8	195	1.9	191
No	2.0	154	1.7	153	2.0	152
Intervention configuration						
Single interventions	2.1	318	1.7	312	1.9	307
Combined interventions	3.1	36	2.5	36	2.6	36
Nonpositive behavioral support						
Exclude non-PBS	2.1	252	1.8	247	2.0	242
Include non-PBS	1.9	102	1.6	101	2.0	101
Intervention agent						
Typical	2.6	147	1.8	146	2.3	141
Atypical	1.6	195	1.5	190	1.6	191
Intervention setting						
Typical	2.6	117	1.9	116	2.3	113
Atypical	1.7	237	1.6	232	1.7	230
Significant others change						
Yes	2.4	257	1.8	251	2.0	240
No	2.0	97	1.5	97	1.8	97
Age—mean at 14.5 years	2.1	314	1.8	308	1.7	304

[a]All means are adjusted for the slope, the number of baseline and treatment data points, and the type of data (percent or frequency).

TABLE B5.3
Adjusted Mean Effect Sizes Across Participants

Variable	ES$_{SMDALL}$		ES$_{REG}$		ES$_{SMD3}$	
	M	n	M	n	M	n
Adjusted mean[a]	2.4	220	1.9	218	2.4	213
Gender						
Male	2.3	142	2.0	140	2.3	138
Female	2.7	70	1.9	70	2.5	67
Diagnosis						
Mental retardation (MR) only	2.2	112	2.0	111	2.5	110
Autism (Aut) only	2.4	23	1.6	23	2.3	21
MR & Aut only	2.4	28	1.9	28	2.5	27
(MR and/or Aut) and other	2.4	49	1.5	48	2.1	47
Level of retardation						
Mild	2.8	32	2.0	31	2.8	32
Moderate	2.5	35	2.0	35	2.5	35

(Continued)

173

	ES_{SMDALL}		ES_{REG}		ES_{SMD3}	
Variable	M	n	M	n	M	n
Level of retardation *(Cont.)*						
Severe	2.2	57	2.0	57	2.3	53
Profound	1.9	59	1.9	58	2.0	58
Problem behavior type						
Aggression						
Yes	2.6	117	2.1	116	2.4	113
No	1.9	101	1.7	100	2.2	98
Self-injurious behavior						
Yes	2.1	113	1.9	112	2.3	111
No	2.5	106	1.9	105	2.4	101
Property destruction						
Yes	2.5	47	1.8	47	2.2	46
No	2.3	172	2.0	170	2.4	166
Tantrums						
Yes	2.7	60	2.1	60	2.6	59
No	2.1	160	1.8	158	2.1	154
Problem behavior configuration						
Single problem	2.1	142	1.8	140	2.2	136
Combination problems	2.6	78	2.0	78	2.5	77
Assessment						
Conducted & used	2.6	131	2.0	129	2.6	128
Not conducted or not used	2.1	88	1.8	88	2.0	84
Type of function						
Attention						
Yes	2.4	35	2.0	35	2.7	35
No	2.4	102	2.0	100	2.8	99
Escape						
Yes	2.5	92	2.3	91	3.0	90
No	2.2	47	1.8	47	2.5	46
Tangible						
Yes	3.0	19	3.9	18	2.8	18
No	2.4	119	2.2	118	2.8	117
Sensory						
Yes	2.1	14	1.7	14	2.5	14
No	2.4	126	2.2	124	2.8	123
Multiple						
Yes	3.1	21	3.3	21	3.0	21
No	2.3	119	2.0	117	2.8	116
Intervention type						
Stimulus-based (ST)						
Yes	2.4	123	1.9	123	2.6	121
No	2.4	89	1.8	87	2.2	84
Reinforcement-based (RF)						
Yes	2.5	115	2.0	113	2.3	110
No	2.3	100	1.9	100	2.5	98

(Continued)

TABLE B5.3
(Continued)

Variable	ES_{SMDALL}		ES_{REG}		ES_{SMD3}	
	M	n	M	n	M	n
Intervention configuration						
Single interventions	2.3	192	1.9	190	2.4	185
Combined interventions	3.3	21	3.0	21	2.9	21
Nonpositive behavioral support						
Exclude non-PBS	2.2	159	2.0	157	2.3	153
Include non-PBS	1.8	44	1.7	44	2.4	43
Intervention agent						
Typical	2.8	91	2.1	91	2.7	88
Atypical	1.8	115	1.5	114	2.1	112
Intervention setting						
Typical	2.8	73	2.1	73	2.6	70
Atypical	1.9	147	1.8	145	2.1	143
Significant others change						
Yes	2.4	151	2.1	149	2.5	144
No	2.2	68	1.6	68	2.1	68
Age—mean at 14.5 years	2.2	197	2.0	197	2.1	193

[a]All means are adjusted for the slope, the number of outcomes included for each participant, the number of treatment data points, and the type of data (percent or frequency).

REFERENCES

Allison, D. B., & Gorman, B. S. (1993). Calculating effect sizes for meta-analysis: The case of the single case. *Behavior, Research, and Therapy, 31,* 621–631.

Bryk, A. S., & Raudenbush, S. W. (1992). *Hierarchical linear models: Applications and data analysis methods.* Newbury Park, CA: Sage.

Bryk, A., Raudenbush, S., & Congdon, R. (1996). *HLM: Hierarchical linear and nonlinear modeling with the HLM/2L and HLM/3L programs.* Chicago: Scientific Software International.

Busk, P. L., & Serlin, R. C. (1992). Meta-analysis for single-case research. In T. R. Kratochwill & J. R. Levin (Eds.), *Single-case research design and analysis: New directions for psychology and education* (pp. 187–212). Hillsdale, NJ: Lawrence Erlbaum Associates.

Carr, E. G. (1977). The motivation of self-injurious behavior: A review of some hypotheses. *Psychological Bulletin, 84,* 800–816.

Carr, E. G. (1993). Behavior analysis is not ultimately about behavior. *The Behavior Analyst, 16,* 47–49.

Carr, E. G. (1994). Emerging themes in the functional analysis of problem behavior. *Journal of Applied Behavior Analysis, 27,* 393–399.

Carr, E. G., Horner, R. H., Turnbull, A. P., Marquis, J. G., Magito-McLaughlin, D., McAtee, M. L., Smith, C. E., Ryan, K. A., Ruef, M. B., & Doolabh, A. (1999). Positive behavior support as an approach for dealing with problem behavior in people with developmental disabilities: A research synthesis (AAMR Monograph). Washington, DC: American Association on Mental Retardation.

Carr, E. G., & McDowell, J. J. (1980). Social control of self-injurious behavior of organic etiology. *Behavior Therapy, 11,* 402–409.

Carr, E. G., & Newsom, C. (1985). Demand-related tantrums: Conceptualization and treatment. *Behavior Modification, 9,* 403–426.

Carr, E. G., Newsom, C. D., & Binkoff, J. A. (1976). Stimulus control of self-destructive behavior in a psychotic child. *Journal of Abnormal Child Psychology, 4,* 139–153.

Carr, E. G., Newsom, C. D., & Binkoff, J. A. (1980). Escape as a factor in the aggressive behavior of two retarded children. *Journal of Applied Behavior Analysis, 13,* 101–117.

Carr, E. G., Robinson, S., Taylor, J. C., & Carlson, J. I. (1990). Positive approaches to the treatment of severe behavior problems in persons with developmental disabilities: A review and analysis of reinforcement and stimulus-based procedures. *Monograph of The Association for Persons with Severe Handicaps, 4.*

Center, B. A., Skiba, R. J., & Casey, A. (1985–1986). A methodology for the quantitative synthesis of intra-subject design research. *Journal of Special Education, 19,* 387–400.

Cohen, J. (1960). A coefficient of agreement for nominal scales. *Educational and Psychological Measurement, 20,* 37–46.

Cohen, J. (1988). *Statistical power analysis for the behavioral sciences* (2nd ed.). Hillsdale, NJ: Lawrence Erlbaum Associates.

Cooper, H., & Hedges, L. V. (1994). The handbook of research synthesis. New York: Russell Sage Foundation.

Day, H. M., Horner, R. H., & O'Neill, R. E. (1994). Multiple functions of problem behaviors: Assessment and intervention. *Journal of Applied Behavior Analysis, 27,* 279–289.

Derby, K. M., Wacker, D. P., Sasso, G., Northup, J., Cigrand, K., & Asmus, J. (1992). Brief functional assessment techniques to evaluate aberrant behavior in an outpatient setting: A summary of 79 cases. *Journal of Applied Behavior Analysis, 25,* 713–721.

Didden, R., Duker, P. C., & Korzilius, H. (1997). Meta-analytic study on treatment effectiveness for problem behaviors with individuals who have mental retardation. *American Journal on Mental Retardation, 101,* 387–399.

Donnellan, A. M., LaVigna, G. W., Negri-Shoultz, N., & Fassbender, L. L. (1988). *Progress without punishment: Effective approaches for learners with severe behavior problems.* New York: Teachers College Press.

Durand, V. M. (1990). *Functional communication training: An intervention program for severe behavior problems.* New York: Guilford.

Durand, V. M., & Crimmins, D. B. (1988). Identifying the variables maintaining self-injurious behavior. *Journal of Autism and Developmental Disorders, 18,* 99–117.

Evans, I. M., & Meyer, L. H. (1985). *An educative approach to behavior problems: A practical decision model for interventions with severely handicapped learners.* Baltimore: Paul H. Brookes.

Faith, M. S., Allison, D. B., & Gorman, B. S. (1996). Meta-analysis of single-case research. In R. D. Franklin, D. B. Allison, & B. S. Gorman (Eds.), *Design and analysis of single-case research* (pp. 245–277). Mahwah, NJ: Lawrence Erlbaum Associates.

Favell, J. E., McGimsey, J. F., & Schell, R. M. (1982). Treatment of self-injury by providing alternate sensory activities. *Analysis and Intervention in Developmental Disabilities, 2,* 83–104.

Gingerich, W. J. (1984). Meta-analysis of applied time-series data. *Journal of Applied Behavioral Science, 20,* 71–79.

Glass, G. V., McGaw, B., & Smith, M. L. (1981). Meta-analysis in social research. Beverly Hills, CA: Sage.

Glass, G. V., Willson, V. L., & Gottman, J. (1975). Design and analysis of time-series experiments. Boulder: Colorado Associated University Press.

Gorsuch, R. L. (1983). Three methods for analyzing limited time-series (N of 1) data. *Behavioral Assessment, 5,* 141–154.

Haring, T. G., & Kennedy, C. H. (1990). Contextual control of problem behavior in students with severe disabilities. *Journal of Applied Behavior Analysis, 23,* 235–243.

Hersen, M., & Barlow, D. H. (1976). *Single case experimental designs.* New York: Pergamon.

Hershberger, S. L., Wallace, D. D., Green, S. B., & Marquis, J. G. (1999). Meta-analysis of single-case designs. In R. H. Hoyle (Ed.), *Statistical strategies for small sample research* (pp. 109–132). Newbury Park, CA: Sage.

Horner, R. H., Dunlap, G., Koegel, R. L., Carr, E. G., Sailor, W., Anderson, J., Albin, R. W., & O'Neill, R. E. (1990). Toward a technology of "nonaversive" behavioral support. *Journal of The Association for Persons with Severe Handicaps, 15,* 125–132.

Iwata, B. A., Dorsey, M. F., Slifer, K. J., Bauman, K. E., & Richman, G. S. (1982). Toward a functional analysis of self-injury. *Analysis and Intervention in Developmental Disabilities, 2,* 3–20.

Kish, L. (1965). *Survey sampling.* New York: Wiley.

Lancioni, G. E., & Hoogeveen, F. R. (1990). Non-aversive and mildly aversive procedures for reducing problem behaviors in people with developmental disorders. *Mental Handicaps Research, 3,* 137–160.

Landis, J. R., & Koch, G. G. (1977). The measurement of observer agreement for categorical data. *Biometrics, 33,* 159–174.

LaVigna, G. W., & Donnellan, A. M. (1986). *Alternatives to punishment: Solving behavior problems with non-aversive strategies.* New York: Irvington.

Lee, V. L. (1988). *Beyond behaviorism.* Hillsdale, NJ: Lawrence Erlbaum Associates.

Lennox, D. B., Miltenburger, R. G., Spengler, P., & Erfanian, N. (1988). Decelerative treatment practices with persons who have mental retardation: A review of five years of the literature. *American Journal on Mental Retardation, 92,* 492–501.

Lovaas, O. I., Freitag, G., Gold, V. J., & Kassorla, I. C. (1965). Experimental studies in childhood schizophrenia: Analysis of self-destructive behavior. *Journal of Experimental Child Psychology, 2,* 67–84.

Marascuilo, L., & Busk, P. L. (1988). Combining statistics for multiple-baseline AB and replicated ABAB designs across subjects. *Behavioral Assessment, 10,* 69–85.

Marquis, J. G. (1983). *Box–Jenkins–Tiao intervention analysis in short time series.* Unpublished doctoral dissertation, University of Kansas, Lawrence.

Martin, P. L., & Foxx, R. M. (1973). Victim control of the aggression of an institutionalized retardate. *Journal of Behavior Therapy and Experimental Psychiatry, 4,* 161–165.

Matson, J. L., & Taras, M. E. (1989). A 20-year review of punishment and alternative methods to treat problem behaviors in developmentally delayed persons. *Research in Developmental Disabilities, 10,* 85–104.

Meyer, L. H., & Evans, I. M. (1989). *Nonaversive intervention for behavior problems.* Baltimore: Paul H. Brookes.

National Institutes of Health. (1991). *Treatment of destructive behaviors in persons with developmental disabilities* (NIH Publication No. 91-2410). Washington, DC: Author.

O'Brien, S., & Repp, A. C. (1990). Reinforcement-based reductive procedures: A review of 20 years of their use with persons with severe or profound retardation. *Journal of The Association for Persons with Severe Handicaps, 15,* 148–159.

Parsonson, B. S., & Baer, D. M. (1978). The analysis and presentation of graphic data. In T. R. Kratchowill (Ed.), *Single subject research: Strategies for evaluating change* (pp. 15–40). New York: Academic Press.

Patterson, G. R. (1982). *Coercive family process.* Eugene, OR: Castalia.

Rincover, A., Cook, R., Peoples, A., & Packard, D. (1979). Sensory extinction and sensory reinforcement principles for programming multiple adaptive behavior change. *Journal of Applied Behavior Analysis, 12,* 221–233.

Rosenthal, R. (1994). Parametric measures of effect size. In H. Cooper & L. V. Hedges (Eds.), *The handbook of research synthesis* (pp. 231–244). New York: Russell Sage Foundation.

Scotti, J. R., Evans, I. M., Meyer, L. H., & Walker, P. (1991). A meta-analysis of intervention research with problem behavior: Treatment validity and standards of practice. *American Journal on Mental Retardation, 96,* 233–256.

Scotti, J. R., Ujcich, K. J., Weigle, K. L., Holland, C. M., & Kirk, K. S. (1996). Interventions with challenging behavior of persons with developmental disabilities: A review of current research practices. *Journal of The Association for Persons with Severe Handicaps, 21,* 123–134.

Scruggs, T. E., Mastropieri, M. A., & Casto, G. (1987). The quantitative synthesis of single-subject research: Methodology and validation. *Remedial and Special Education, 8,* 24–33.

Shadish, W. R., & Haddock, C. K. (1994). Combining estimates of effect size. In H. Cooper & L. V. Hedges (Eds.), *The handbook of research synthesis* (pp. 262–280). New York: Russell Sage Foundation.

Skinner, B. F. (1974). *About behaviorism.* New York: Vintage.

Smith, M. D. (1990). *Autism and life in the community.* Baltimore: Paul H. Brookes.

Vollmer, T. R., & Iwata, B. A. (1992). Differential reinforcement as treatment for behavior disorders: Procedural and functional variations. *Research in Developmental Disabilities, 13,* 393–417.

White, D. M., Rusch, F. R., Kazdin, A. E., & Hartmann, D. P. (1989). Applications of meta-analysis in individual subject research. *Behavioral Assessment, 11,* 281–296.

Wiesler, N. A., Hanson, R. H., Chamberlain, T. P., & Thompson, T. (1985). Functional taxonomy of stereotypic and self-injurious behavior. *Mental Retardation, 23,* 230–234.

Chapter 6

Technology, Literacy, and Disabilities: A Review of the Research

Cynthia M. Okolo
Albert R. Cavalier
Ralph P. Ferretti
Charles A. MacArthur
University of Delaware

Literacy instruction has always been a topic of great interest and, often, heated debate among educators. The past 15 years are no exception. During this time we have seen a number of important publications reviewing the research about literacy acquisition and instruction (e.g., Adams, 1990; Snow, Burns, & Griffin, 1998). Federal agencies, such as the U.S. Department of Education, have invested millions of dollars in basic and applied research about literacy instruction and reading disabilities. Policy papers (e.g., Learning First Alliance, 1998) have promulgated recommendations to guide literacy instruction, and federal education goals seek to guarantee literacy to all our nation's students.

Literacy-related difficulties are a major reason for students' referral to special education and a primary focus of special education instruction. It appears that technology is viewed as an important tool for assisting special educators in the provision of effective literacy instruction. For example, a recent survey of over 1,000 special educators showed that 85% use technology in literacy instruction, 97% believe that technology can help students acquire literacy skills, and 91% expect to increase their use of technology in the future (Burton-Radzely, 1998). In this chapter, we examine the research base underlying these high levels of optimism and implementation. Although a number of recent reviews have addressed the efficacy of technology for students with disabilities (e.g., Fitzgerald & Koury, 1996; Shiah, Mastropieri, & Scruggs, 1995; Woodward & Rieth, 1997), none has focused exclusively on literacy.

The chapter is divided into four major sections: (a) technology and word identification for students with mild disabilities, (b) technology and text comprehension for students with mild disabilities, (c) technology and writing for students with mild disabilities, and (d) technology and literacy for students with severe cognitive disabilities. Consistent with federal legislation, our definition of technology is broad and includes both instructional technology and compensatory technology devices and methods.

Because the research about literacy, technology, and disabilities is voluminous and diverse, we were compelled to limit the scope of this review. We have defined *literacy* as word identification and recognition, text comprehension, and text production. We recognize that this is a more narrow definition than that used by many contemporary educators (e.g., Lemke, 1998; D. R. Olson, 1994). Although there is a growing literature on other facets of literacy (e.g., pictographic augmentative and alternative communication), we address only reading and writing traditional orthography in this review. We also have excluded studies that focused on comprehension of pictures or video (e.g., Sharp, Bransford, Goldman, & Risko, 1995).

We also restricted the student populations examined in this review. We selected studies that included students with mild cognitive disabilities (learning disabilities, reading disabilities, mild mental disabilities); students considered at risk for reading disabilities; and students with severe cognitive disabilities. Although the impact of technology for the literacy acquisition of other populations (e.g., students with attention deficit disorders, physical disabilities, and sensory disabilities) is noteworthy, we excluded studies of these populations from our review. Furthermore, for students with mild disabilities, we limited our review to school-age learners. We acknowledge that literacy concerns and, in some cases, the nature of literacy interventions, are not qualitatively different for school-age students and adults with mild disabilities. However, delimiting the age range of students with mild disabilities provided us with a means of restricting an already lengthy review. Given that we could find so few studies about literacy and technology for individuals with severe cognitive disabilities, we did not restrict our review by age.

In addition, we narrowed our review by focusing on studies that were: (a) published in peer-reviewed journals or edited books, (b) published within 15 years of the date this chapter was written (1984 or later), and (c) experimental, or meeting rudimentary scientific requirements for selection, manipulation, and control of variables (Dillon & Gabbard, 1998). The process by which we identified eligible studies followed three steps. We first searched the Educational Resources Information Center (ERIC) and PsycINFO electronic databases using the keywords listed in the

Appendix. We then searched these two databases using author names from any relevant articles obtained in Step 1. Finally, we scanned the reference lists of each of the relevant articles obtained in Steps 1 and 2 for any additional articles.

We recognize that our criteria omit relevant studies about the use of technology for improving students' literacy. This is especially the case in the section about technology and severe cognitive disabilities, where few experimental studies, relative to more descriptive studies or implementation reports, were located. Furthermore, we acknowledge that case studies and other qualitative research approaches can offer equally valid information about the impact and use of technology. By focusing on only experimental studies, we do not intend to make implicit claims about the value or trustworthiness of any particular approach to research. Rather, our focus on experimental studies provided an additional constraint on the length of the review.

Meta-analysis is a commonly used strategy for analyzing the magnitude of the effects associated with treatments in a body of research (Cooper & Hedges, 1994), and has been employed as a preferred synthesis tool by other authors in this volume. After careful consideration, we decided to undertake a narrative review of the extant research findings. Many different aspects of technology and literacy are examined in this chapter, but, with a few noteworthy exceptions, there are no more than a handful of studies about any one topic. Given the absence of programmatic research and the fact that many studies were poorly designed or lacked the requisite information, we believed that a meta-analysis would be impractical or, worse, misleading. Nor could we consistently compute effect sizes for the intervention studies described herein.

More important, we chose not to undertake a meta-analysis or compute effect sizes when information was available on conceptual grounds. The computation of effect sizes would have oriented our review to the question: What is the effect of technology on literacy outcomes? In our judgment, this question directs attention to an insoluble problem. As we discuss further later, the effect of technology is not a function of technology itself, but also of the characteristics of the instruction it delivers or facilitates, the instruction that accompanies its use, the purpose for which it is used, and a host of additional factors. Therefore, the independent effect of technology can rarely be determined. Thus, our conclusions are based on a careful reading and analysis of the research rather than on numerical assessments of the strength or educational significance of results. Although some may claim that our conclusions are too subjective, we believe that a narrative review was the appropriate approach for this diverse body of studies in which technology is typically one component of an intervention.

TECHNOLOGY AND WORD IDENTIFICATION
SKILLS FOR STUDENTS WITH MILD DISABILITIES

Reading Difficulties of Students With Disabilities

During the last 20 years, a substantial body of evidence converges on the conclusion that students with learning disabilities and "slow learners" alike experience problems with reading because they have difficulty acquiring fluent and accurate word identification skills (Adams, 1990; Stanovich, 1988; J. K. Torgesen & Barker, 1995; Wagner, J. Torgesen, & Rashotte, 1994). Most students who experience reading problems are unable to use the alphabetic principle to capitalize on regularities in the phonological structure of words (Lundberg, 1995; Vellutino & Scanlon, 1991). As a result, these students are unable to efficiently decode orthography, that is, activate the phonetic representation underlying letter strings which allows the identification of words with minimal attentional demands (Roth & Beck, 1987).

Difficulties in processing the phonological features of language have been demonstrated in a variety of tasks that do not involve reading (J. K. Torgesen, 1993; J. K. Torgesen & Barker, 1995), including tasks that require students to represent phonological information in working memory, access phonological information in long-term memory, and demonstrate awareness of the phonological structure of language. The absence of phonological awareness is especially problematic for students with reading difficulties because reading (unlike speaking) requires an explicit awareness of the phonemic representation underlying the orthography (Lundberg, 1995; J. K. Torgesen & Barker, 1995). When confronted with unfamiliar text, students must be able to analyze the phonemic segments that correspond to the alphabet so that they can understand the relationship between written and spoken language. Without explicit instruction, students with reading difficulties will not develop phonological awareness (Lundberg, 1995). Consequently, much early reading instruction is incomprehensible to these students (Liberman, Shankweiler, & Liberman, 1989).

Students who experience problems with phonological processing often experience associated consequences that further exacerbate their reading difficulties (J. K. Torgesen & Barker, 1995). These students usually read less often and therefore receive less reading practice in school and at home compared to students without these difficulties. Further, much of the material they read is too difficult for them, frustrating their comprehension efforts and further reducing their motivation to practice (R. Olson, Foltz, & Wise, 1986; R. K. Olson & Wise, 1987). Finally, their reading lessons often focus on the correction of reading problems rather than the development of comprehension skills. As a consequence, reading becomes an activity devoid of meaning and interest for them.

There is general consensus in the scholarly community that reading practice is most effective when students read meaningful text with the goal of understanding its message (Adams, 1990; R. Anderson, Hiebert, Scott, & Wilkinson, 1985; Lundberg, 1995). To do this, students must access and coordinate a complicated set of component processes, some of which are very challenging for students with reading problems to use (Roth & Beck, 1987; J. K. Torgesen, 1986). In fact, inefficiencies in decoding and word recognition processes are highly predictive of comprehension difficulties (Lesgold & Curtis, 1981; Perfetti & Lesgold, 1977, 1979). This suggests that directed practice in deficient skills might facilitate efforts at constructing meaning from text. However, practice in these component skills does not substitute for reading meaningful text with the goal of understanding. When students practice decoding without also reading for understanding, motivational and transfer problems may ensue (Lundberg, 1995).

The Role of Computers in Teaching Students to Read Words

According to J. K. Torgesen (1986), students must learn four broad classes of skills to become fluent readers: (a) phonological word analysis, (b) rapid sight word recognition, (c) fluent word processing in extended text, and (d) comprehension of text. In this section, we focus on the first three of Torgesen's skill classes. We address comprehension skills and electronic text, as a tool to promote and support comprehension, in the next section of the chapter.

Practice in phonological word analysis enables students to recognize the sounds represented by letters and letter combinations, and to blend these sounds to produce an approximation to a word that is in their oral lexicon. Instruction in sight word recognition facilitates text processing by promoting the rapid and relatively effortless recognition of individual words. Training in fluent text processing enables students to accurately and fluently read words embedded in extended text. Finally, comprehension skills permit students to extract the meaning of written passages. Of course, skill in comprehension depends on the proficiency in many different component-processing skills (R. Anderson et al., 1985).

Computers have been used to promote the development of each of these classes of skill, although they have been used most extensively and effectively to promote proficiency in phonological analysis, word recognition, and text processing (J. K. Torgesen, 1986; J. K. Torgesen & Barker, 1995). This focus is not entirely surprising in light of the causal connection

between deficiencies in word identification skills and comprehension problems (Wagner et al., 1994), and the fact that improvement in word identification skills requires the kind of practice that computers are especially well
designed to deliver (J. K. Torgesen & Barker, 1995). Computers are able to
consistently provide a large amount of extended practice for students with
little teacher supervision, and they are able to monitor both the speed and
accuracy of students' responses (J. K. Torgesen, Waters, A. L. Cohen, & J. L.
Torgesen, 1988). The latter capability is especially important in promoting
the development of fluent word identification skills.

   Phonological Word Analysis. The aforementioned importance of
phonological awareness in the development of skilled reading has been
demonstrated in a number of instructional and noninstructional studies
that do not involve the use of computers (Lie, 1991; Lundberg, Frost, &
Peterson, 1988; Wagner et al., 1994). The success of these efforts has
encouraged the development of computer-based applications that promote the development of phonological *analysis* skills in students, that is,
the ability to isolate and segment individual phonemes within words.
Much less work has been done to develop computer applications that promote phonological *synthesis* skills, that is, the ability to combine a sequence
of phonemes to produce a recognizable word. This is because applications
that target synthesis skills require high-quality and relatively expensive
voice recognition technology (R. K. Olson & Wise, 1992; J. K. Torgesen &
Barker, 1995).

   Roth and Beck (1987) reported one of the earliest evaluations of computer software designed to promote students' orthographic knowledge
and decoding skill. Two commercially available programs, *Hint and Hunt*
(Beck & Roth, 1984b) and *Construct-a-Word* (Beck & Roth, 1984a), were
evaluated in this study. *The Hint and Hunt* program was designed to
improve the decoding of medial vowels and vowel combinations with two
tasks. First, students learned to associate a visual representation of these
subword units presented on a video monitor with the corresponding
phonemic representation presented via digitized speech. Second, students
played a computer game in which they selected words that contained
these vowel combinations as they were pronounced by the computer. The
Construct-a-Word program gave students practice matching initial consonants and consonant blends with common word endings as an aid to
decoding. Progress through these programs required students to meet
both speed and accuracy performance criteria.

   Roth and Beck (1987) tested the effects of these programs with fourth-
grade students from inner-city, low socioeconomic (SES) backgrounds,
many of whom were performing below grade level with respect to academic achievement. Students in the experimental group received 20

hours of practice with these programs over 20 weeks, whereas those in the control group received no practice of any sort. Students in each group were further subdivided into low and high subgroups on the basis of pretest performance on each of the outcome measures. These outcome measures were sensitive to the effects of practicing the target skills and to the possibility that comprehension would improve as a result of decoding practice. The pattern of results was remarkably consistent: Low-ability students in the experimental group improved more than those in any other condition on measures that assessed the speed and accuracy of decoding, word recognition, and on laboratory measures that assessed comprehension of words and sentences. In general, students in the experimental condition improved approximately 1 year more on most measures than those in the control condition. However, no group differences were obtained on standardized measures of literal, interpretative, and critical comprehension of lengthy passages. The latter finding was interpreted to be consistent with the view that comprehension of lengthy passages depends on complicated, attentionally demanding interactions among component information processes that are not simply accounted for by changes in word identification skills (see Perfetti & Lesgold, 1977, 1979; J. K. Torgesen, 1986).

Jones, Torgesen, and Sexton (1987) evaluated the effects of the *Hint and Hunt* program on the speed and accuracy of word analysis skills in 10-year-old students with learning disabilities. Students assigned to the experimental condition practiced different levels of the program for 15 minutes each day over the course of approximately 10 weeks. Students in the control condition, who were yoked to those in the experimental condition, spent the same amount of time practicing a spelling program. Practice with the *Hint and Hunt* program led to reliable improvements in the speed and accuracy of reading isolated target words and paragraphs containing them. These effects generalized to words that were not included in the practice set but contained the target subword units.

J. K. Torgesen, Greenstein, and Jones (1990) evaluated the efficacy of the *Hint and Hunt* and *Construct-a-Word* programs with 10-year-old students with learning disabilities. Those in the experimental group practiced with these programs for about 15 minutes per day for over 80 sessions, and a matched group of control students spent the same amount of time on computer-based mathematics practice. Experimental students improved more than controls on laboratory measures of rapid decoding of nonwords, but in contrast to the findings of Roth and Beck (1987), the groups did not differ on standardized measures of reading that should have been sensitive to practice in decoding. According to J. K. Torgesen and Barker (1995), these disparate findings might be attributable to the fact that control students in Torgesen et al.'s study received more intensive reading instruction in their resource room than experimental students in Roth and Beck's (1987) study. Perhaps, then, the provision of a relatively small amount of extra computer practice was not enough to boost the reading performance of students in Torgesen et al.'s experimental condition compared to those in the control condition. In any case, it seems as if the empirical evidence supports the efficacy of the *Hint and Hunt* (Beck & Roth, 1984b) and *Construct-a-Word* (Beck & Roth, 1984a) programs in improving the decoding skills of students with reading difficulties.

Phonological awareness is a complex process that involves skill in phonemic analysis and synthesis, as well as the ability to identify and segment phonemic information (J. K. Torgesen & Barker, 1995). Skill in phoneme identification is demonstrated by noticing the identities of phonemes across words; phoneme segmentation by pronouncing or counting the phonemes that comprise a word. Torgesen and his colleagues have developed two programs, *DaisyQuest* (G. C. Erickson, K. C. Foster, D. F. Foster, J. K. Torgesen, & Packer, 1992) and *Castle Quest* (G. C. Erickson, K. C. Foster, D. F. Foster, J. K. Torgesen, & Packer, 1993) to promote skill in phoneme identification and segmentation. These programs use an adventure game format to provide practice with a wide range of phonological awareness tasks including recognizing rhyming words, matching words on the basis of common first, middle, and last sounds, and counting the number of phonemes in a word.

Barker and J. K. Torgesen (1995) evaluated the effectiveness of these programs in improving the phonological awareness of students whose decoding skills were demonstrably inferior to those of their same-age peers. Students in this study, who averaged 7.4 years of age, were assigned to an experimental condition or one of two control conditions. Students in the experimental group received approximately 8 hours of instruction and practice in phonological awareness with the *DaisyQuest* and *Castle Quest* programs. Students in one control condition received comparable amounts of practice with the previously described *Hint and Hunt* (Beck & Roth, 1984b) program, and those in the other control condition practiced mathematics for comparable amounts of time. Students in the experimental condition showed dramatic improvements compared to the controls on the kinds of phonological awareness tasks that were used in training. In addition, the effects of training generalized to tasks that required students to delete or segment phonemes in words, as well as to those that tapped word analysis and identification. Practice with *DaisyQuest* and *Castle Quest* has also been shown to positively impact the phonological awareness of preschool and kindergarten students (K. C. Foster, G. C. Erickson, D. F. Foster, Brinkman, & J. K. Torgesen, 1994).

The previously described research supports the efficacy of computer programs that were designed to develop phonological word analysis in students with reading disabilities. In general, these programs embed learning activities in highly motivating, gamelike formats that are designed to promote students' phonological awareness and decoding skills. However, this is not how most students learn to read independently. When confronted with words that they cannot read, students generally ask another person to pronounce them (van Daal & Reitsma, 1990). Computers are especially well designed to provide this kind of speech feedback to readers on demand, either for words presented in isolation (van Daal & Reitsma, 1990) or in the context of coherent text (R. K. Olson & Wise, 1987, 1992). Moreover, computers equipped with speech synthesizers are uniquely equipped to segment the speech feedback at the level of the word, syllables, or subsyllables. Students with reading disabilities often fail to develop good word identification skills from normal reading experience, which usually entails whole-word feedback (R. K. Olson & Wise, 1992). Perhaps, then, these students would benefit more from feedback segmented into syllabic or subsyllabic units (R. K. Olson & Wise, 1992).

van Daal and Reitsma (1990) contrasted the effects of word- and subword-level synthetic speech feedback on the accuracy of reading easy and difficult words that were presented in isolation. Students with learning disabilities, who averaged nearly 10 years of age, were asked to read single words that appeared on a computer monitor. Students were assigned to one of three feedback conditions. In two of the conditions, students could request speech feedback at any time by using the mouse to click on a button that appeared on the monitor. Students in the whole-word feedback condition heard the word when they requested assistance while reading. Those in the subword feedback condition heard segmented speech feedback at the level of intrasyllabic units. Finally, students in the control condition read the words but were not permitted to request speech feedback. In each of these conditions, students practiced for approximately 10 minutes each day over the course of 3 to 4 weeks. Students in the whole-word feedback condition were much more likely to request feedback than those in the subword feedback condition, but the frequency of these requests was unrelated to their pretest reading level or the difficulty of the words. For words for which students requested feedback, both feedback conditions were associated with more accurate reading than the control condition. Students who received subword speech feedback were slightly but not statistically more accurate in reading words for which they did not request feedback. This led van Daal and Reitsma to speculate that the effects of segmented speech feedback generalized to unpracticed words.

van Daal and Reitsma (1993) reasoned that the failure of students to discriminate among difficult and easy words when requesting feedback in the van Daal and Reitsma (1990) study may have been an artifact of their experimental procedures and the characteristics of their sample. In the earlier study, difficult words were presented four times as often as easy words, which may have led students to infer that only difficult words were presented. Moreover, students with learning disabilities had been the sole recipients of training because of their well-documented difficulties with phonological processing. However, students with learning disabilities may be less selective in requesting feedback than those without disabilities because they may not know when to ask for help (van Daal & Reitsma, 1993). Finally, and related, the benefits of hearing speech feedback depend on the metacognitive sensitivity of the person requesting the feedback. If students do not carefully monitor their feeling-of-knowing (Nelson & Narens, 1990) with respect to these words, requests for speech feedback will not be optimally effective. Therefore, students with learning disabilities may benefit equally well from feedback whether or not they have the opportunity to request it.

To address these issues, van Daal and Reitsma (1993) replicated their earlier study with some important procedural modifications. First, they ensured that the frequency of difficult and easy words was balanced during practice. Second, they included a reading-level matched sample of students without disabilities to check if these students were more selective in their request for whole-word speech feedback than students with learning disabilities. Finally, students with learning disabilities, who were approximately 9 years old, were divided into two groups, one of which was given feedback on request and the other of which was given unsolicited feedback. With these changes, the authors found that students with disabilities were much more selective in their requests for feedback than they had been in the previous study (van Daal & Reitsma, 1990) and about as selective as their nondisabled peers. However, neither group was especially selective in their requests for feedback. Interestingly, all three groups of students showed comparable improvements in the accuracy of reading practiced words, although students with disabilities who received unsolicited speech feedback and those without disabilities showed greater gains in the speed of reading than students with disabilities who received solicited feedback. The latter finding suggests that students with learning disabilities, who were not highly selective in their requests for feedback, benefited from receiving whole-word speech feedback on every trial.

van Daal and Reitsma's (1990, 1993) work demonstrates that computer-generated speech feedback promotes the accurate and fluent reading of isolated words by students with learning disabilities. The availability of speech feedback may enable the reader to check on the accuracy of her phonological recoding of the word by listening to it, or alternatively, it may ease the burden on working memory during the process of phonological recoding (van Daal & Reitsma, 1990). In either case, the effectiveness of speech feedback is attributable to the support it provides for the use of the alphabetic principle during decoding. Interestingly, the alphabetic principle is first used in spelling, during which students convert phonemes into graphemes (Ehri & Wilce, 1987). In fact, empirical evidence suggests that spelling may bridge the relationship between implicit phonological awareness during the preschool years and later reading development (Cataldo & Ellis, 1988). This possibility led van Daal and van der Leij (1992) to predict that practice in spelling would enhance the effects of speech feedback on the reading and spelling of students with learning disabilities.

In this study (van Daal & van der Leij, 1992), students with learning disabilities, who were approximately 9.5 years old, were given practice in reading isolated words that appeared on a computer screen under one of three conditions. In the reading with speech feedback (RSF) condition, students could request whole-word speech feedback while practicing reading easy and difficult words. In the copy-from-screen (CFS) condition, students could request speech feedback as they read each word, but they were required to type the word at the keyboard while the word was on the screen. In the write-from-memory (WFM) condition, students could also request speech feedback, but they were required to type the word at the keyboard after the word disappeared from the screen. The latter two conditions were expected to promote higher levels of reading accuracy than the RSF condition because they were designed to intensify the connection between spelling and reading. In fact, all three conditions promoted comparable improvements in both the speed and accuracy of reading items from the practice set, although no improvement was seen for unpracticed items. In contrast, the CFS condition produced more accurate spelling that either of the two other conditions.

Both of these findings were somewhat surprising. In the first instance, the CFS and WFM conditions were expected to produce higher levels of reading accuracy than the RFS condition because both of the former conditions included spelling practice. However, it was noted that students consistently requested more speech feedback in the RFS condition. Perhaps the frequent use of speech feedback compensated for the absence of spelling practice in the RFS condition. In the second instance, the CFS and WFM conditions were expected to result in better spelling than the RFS condition because both of the former conditions included spelling practice. However, anecdotal observations suggested that the WFM condition was more demanding than the CFS condition, and the added burden of recalling the words from memory may have interfered with the process of establishing the grapheme–phoneme correspondences.

Wise and R. K. Olson (Wise, 1992; Wise, R. K. Olson, & Treiman, 1990) have studied the effect of different kinds of speech segmentation feedback on the identification of isolated words They have used DECtalk, a text-to-speech synthesizer, in most of their work because of its high degree of intelligibility for words generated outside of meaningful contexts. As we mentioned earlier, there is reason to believe that segmented feedback at the syllabic and subsyllabic levels may aid the word identification of students with reading disabilities because these students often fail to benefit from whole-word feedback (Wise & R. K. Olson, 1992). Many types of speech segmentation at the subsyllabic level are possible. Interestingly, there is little agreement among native speakers about where or how to best divide syllables even though most people agree about the number of syllables within each word (Wise, 1992). In onset–rime feedback, syllables are segmented into an *onset*, composed of a consonant or consonant cluster, and a *rime*, consisting of a vowel that could be followed by a string of consonants, for example, d/ish, c/lap. In vowel segmentation feedback, syllables are divided immediately following the vowel of the syllable, for example, di/sh, cla/p. Segmented speech feedback can also be provided on the basis of BOSS (Basic Orthographic Syllabic Structure) rules (Taft, 1979), which always preserve morphemic units in multimorphemic words, for example, dish/s, clap/s, read/er. Alternatively, in single grapheme–phoneme feedback, students hear the individual phonemes corresponding to graphemes, for example, b/a/th. Previous research (Treiman, 1985) has shown that adults and children find it much easier to divide syllables at the onset–rime boundary.

Wise et al. (1990) compared the effectiveness of onset–rime segmentation feedback with that of vowel segmentation feedback in promoting first-graders' word identification accuracy. During training, students saw an isolated word on the computer monitor and were told to touch it with a light pen to receive feedback. When a word was touched, the onset–rime segments (onset–rime condition) or the segments prior to and after the vowel (vowel segmentation condition) were sequentially highlighted on the computer screen and spoken concurrently by DECtalk. The child then tried to blend the segments without assistance while saying the word aloud during three training trials. Students' ability to identify the target words without segmented speech feedback was tested after the completion of training. First-graders' word identification accuracy was clearly superior after training with onset–rime segmentation.

Wise (1992) contrasted the effects of four kinds of speech segmentation feedback on the word identification accuracy of first- and second-grade students of high and low reading ability. Students were told to touch an isolated word that contained one, two, or three syllables with a light pen to receive speech feedback. In this study, students received either whole-word feedback, feedback based on BOSS rules, onset–rime feedback, or single grapheme–phoneme feedback. When they touched the word, the segments corresponding to the feedback condition were sequentially highlighted on the monitor and concurrently spoken by DECtalk. Six training trials were provided for each target word. Surprisingly, averaging across the three levels of syllabic complexity, whole-word feedback was at least as effective in promoting the word identification of low- and high-ability readers as BOSS feedback, and considerably better than either onset–rime feedback or grapheme–phoneme feedback. However, the effects of feedback depended on the syllabic complexity of the words. Phoneme–grapheme feedback was associated with much lower levels of word identification of one-syllable words than the other three feedback conditions, which did not differ from each other. Further, as the syllabic complexity of the words increased, the superiority of whole-word and BOSS feedback grew relative to onset–rime and grapheme–phoneme feedback. Wise (1992) attributed this outcome to the demands placed on the readers' working memory when a larger number of subsyllabic elements must be blended in words with a greater number of syllables.

In conclusion, the research evidence supports the efficacy of using the computer to promote the development of phonological word analysis skills of students with reading difficulties. At least four strategies for promoting these skills have been reviewed, and all have had success in promoting students' reading of isolated words. Roth and Beck's (1987) programs have targeted knowledge of medial vowels and vowel combinations to promote orthographic decoding. Torgesen and his colleagues (Barker & J. K. Torgesen, 1995; G. C. Erickson et al., 1992, 1993) have developed programs explicitly designed to promote students' phonological awareness skills. van Daal and his colleagues (van Daal & Reitsma, 1990, 1993; van Daal & van der Leij, 1992) have designed software that provides speech feedback to strengthen the grapheme–phoneme correspondences in students. Wise and R. K. Olson (Wise, 1992; Wise et al., 1990) have analyzed the effects of different kinds of speech feedback on students' word identification accuracy.

In general, the evidence suggests that instruction and practice in decoding and phonological awareness skills lead to more generalized improvements in reading than does the provision of whole-word speech feedback. Said differently, students who receive practice in decoding and phonological awareness skills are usually able to read unpracticed words. The same cannot be said for students who practice with whole-word speech feedback. We suspect that this occurs because the former two instructional strategies enable students to analyze and segment the subunits that comprise words. Students who learn phonological analysis and segmentation skills are better prepared to decode unfamiliar words than those who do not acquire these skills (Troia, 1999). In contrast, whole-word feedback may lead to more accurate word identification than phonological analysis training, but these improvements may not generalize to other words. Wise's (1992) analysis of the effect of different kinds of speech segmentation feedback shows that the process of blending a large number of subsyllabic units may place an undue burden on students' working memory, especially when the words contain a large number of syllables. This suggests that the provision of segmented speech feedback may actually impede the process of word identification unless students explicitly learn the rules for segmenting syllables and are taught to apply them in the contexts in which they are intended to be used. We return to this issue shortly.

Word Recognition Skills. It is generally agreed that fluent word recognition depends on the acquisition of associative links between graphemes and syllabic and subsyllabic phonemic units (Adams, 1990). Consequently, skill in word analysis and segmentation, as well as students' awareness of sounds, are important contributors to the development of students' lexicon of sight words (Adams, 1990; Ehri, 1998). Nevertheless, the development of word recognition is an important goal of reading instruction in its own right because it enables students with reading difficulties to acquire a repertoire of sight words even before they can use word analysis skills (J. K. Torgesen et al., 1988). Sight word recognition is relatively automatic because the visually encoded letter strings directly activate the corresponding semantic or phonological representations (Perfetti, 1985), thereby freeing resources for other attentionally demanding processes. A number of studies have used computer-based training to promote fluent word recognition in students with reading disabilities.

J. K. Torgesen et al. (1988) used a computer program called *WORDS* to provide extensive practice in word recognition to first-, second-, and third-graders with learning disabilities. Students saw a picture of an object on the computer screen or heard the word pronounced, and were then required to type in the word that corresponded to the picture or auditory stimulus from a set of two or three alternatives. All students performed this task under three different conditions. In the visual-only (VO) condition, students simply responded to a pictorial representation of the word. In the visual-auditory (VA) condition, students saw the picture and heard the word pronounced by a speech synthesizer. Finally, in the auditory-only (AO) condition, students heard the word pronounced without seeing the picture. Each of these three program variations produced dramatic and comparable gains in the accuracy and speed of word recognition compared to a no practice control condition. Despite the absence of performance differences among conditions, students expressed a preference for the VO and VA conditions over the AO condition. This was due to the availability of colorful graphics in the former two conditions.

According to A. L. Cohen, J. K. Torgesen, and J. L. Torgesen (1988), students who participated in J. K. Torgesen et al.'s (1988) study found it difficult to type their responses, frustrating their learning efforts, and slowing their progress through the program. Therefore, Cohen et al. eliminated the typing requirement from the *WORDS* program in one of their experimental conditions to see if it were easier for young children to use. Ten-year-old students with learning disabilities saw a picture of an object on the computer screen and were then required to select the word that corresponded to the picture from a set of two or three alternatives. All students made their selection by either pressing a number corresponding to the word of their choice (NT- No Typing) or typing (T) the word on the keyboard. As compared to a no practice control condition, sizable and equivalent posttest gains in word recognition accuracy and speed were obtained for both experimental conditions. However, the T condition produced much better spelling posttest accuracy than either the NT or no treatment control conditions, which did not differ from each other. Thus, both the T and NT versions of *WORDS* produced comparable improvements in word recognition accuracy, but practice in typing facilitated gains in students' spelling.

The findings from these studies suggest that computers can be used to support the development of a sight word vocabulary in students with learning difficulties. It seems as if the response modality, that is, whether the child directly selects or types the word, does not affect the accuracy of word recognition (A. L. Cohen et al., 1988) but may affect students' ability to spell these words. Therefore, if the goal of training to is to improve students' word recognition and spelling accuracy, they should be asked to type their responses during training.

There are, however, issues that raise concern about the value of word recognition training in improving students' reading. Students in these studies were never asked to read target words in the context of other meaningful units before, after, or during training. Consequently, we do not know if improvements in word recognition accuracy transferred to reading with extended texts for the purpose of understanding, or for that matter, what would be required to ensure that they would transfer (A. L. Cohen et al., 1988). Moreover, there is no evidence that word recognition training imparts generalizable reading skills to students. The best that can be said is that students learn to recognize individual words and that these words become part of their sight word vocabularies. Of course, this is especially helpful for words that do not conform to the conventional spelling system (Ehri, 1998). However, students who receive word recognition training in isolation do not learn strategies that enable them to recognize or understand untrained words that conform to the spelling system. Perhaps the greatest benefit of word recognition training is that it enables students who are unable to read with accuracy or fluency to have some independent reading experiences before they develop analytic decoding skills (A. L. Cohen et al., 1988). Thus, successful experiences during word recognition training may serve to foreshadow the acquisition of word identification skills.

Word Identification and Recognition in Meaningful Contexts. As we previously mentioned, there is general consensus in the literature that reading text in order to understand its meaning is the best reading practice (Adams, 1990; R. Anderson et al., 1985). When students read text for meaning, they must use a complex set of component information-processing skills, the fluent coordination of which requires extensive practice (J. K. Torgesen & Barker, 1995). Extended practice in reading words for meaning in context might elaborate the words' syntactic and semantic associations (Ehri, 1980) and enable students to strategically deploy word identification and recognition skills when their use is actually needed. Of course, the ultimate goal of instruction is to ensure that students can use all their knowledge, skills, and strategies to read meaningful text (Ehri, 1998).

R. K. Olson, Wise, and their colleagues (Olson & Wise, 1992; Olson et al., 1986; Wise, 1992; Wise et al., 1989; Wise, R. K. Olson, Ring, & M. Johnson, 1998) have systematically studied the effects of synthetic speech feedback on students' reading in meaningful contexts. Their work has sought to understand the degree to which different kinds of speech feedback enable students with reading disabilities to acquire generalizable phonological analysis and word recognition skills in context.

After establishing the intelligibility of the DECtalk speech synthesizer, R. Olson et al. (1986) sought to determine whether synthetic speech feedback that was requested by students with reading disabilities improved their word identification and comprehension of targeted words. Twenty-six students with reading disabilities between the ages of 8 and 18 years read stories of varying difficulty with the goal of comprehension. For some of the stories, which were displayed on a computer monitor, students received one of three types of speech feedback when they selected words that were too difficult for them to decode. In the whole-word condition, students saw the entire word highlighted on the monitor and simultaneously heard it spoken by DECtalk. In the syllable condition, they saw each syllable sequentially highlighted on monitor as DECtalk spoke them. In the subsyllable condition, they saw the onset and rime sequentially highlighted on the monitor as DECtalk spoke each subsyllabic unit.

Students were highly variable with respect to their accuracy in reading content words in the stories and relatively indiscriminate in selecting words for feedback. Many of the younger students had reading error rates that exceeded 50%, and a few of the older students had error rates of less than 3%. Moreover, many students selected fewer than 50% of the words for feedback that they initially read incorrectly. Therefore, R. Olson et al.

(1986) restricted their analyses to the performance of students who had reading error rates between 4% and 24% and also selected for feedback at least 47% of the words they initially read incorrectly. For these students, the provision of speech feedback was associated with dramatic gains in both later word recognition and comprehension accuracy. Similarly, words within stories for which speech feedback was provided were subsequently read more accurately and with better comprehension than those for which speech feedback was unavailable. Finally, the kind of speech segmentation feedback did not seem to differentially affect word recognition or comprehension accuracy, although the analyses lacked statistical power because of the small sample sizes. Although these findings are drawn from a highly selective and perhaps unrepresentative sample of students, they suggest that synthetic speech feedback in meaningful contexts can promote the word recognition and comprehension of students with reading disabilities.

The reader will recall from our discussion of Wise's (1992) study about the effects of speech segmentation feedback on the identification of isolated words that the provision of whole-word feedback, BOSS segmented feedback, and to a lesser extent, onset–rime feedback was associated with higher levels of word identification than single grapheme–phoneme feedback in students with high and low reading levels. R. K. Olson and Wise (1992) speculated that the difficulties associated with the blending of onset–rime units might be overcome by more extensive training than was provided by Wise (1992), especially if the training occurred in the context of reading meaningful stories.

This possibility was first pursued by Wise et al. (1989), who provided a semester of training to 62 third- and sixth-grade students with reading disabilities. Students were assigned to one of the following five conditions: whole-word feedback, syllable feedback, onset–rime feedback, a combination condition of first subsyllable and then syllable feedback, and no feedback. During training, stories were presented to students as they were in R. Olson et al. (1986), and they could select words for speech feedback that were difficult for them to decode. To check on the efficacy of long-term training, Wise et al. felt it necessary to exclude students from the analyses who had less than 4 hours of total reading time, leaving 36 students who averaged 6.7 hours of reading time during the semester.

Wise et al. (1989) found that students in the combination condition were less likely to target words for feedback than those in the other three feedback conditions, in part because it appeared these students were poorer readers before instruction. Analyses of gain scores in timed word identification accuracy showed that participants who received feedback generally showed larger gains than no feedback controls, although combination feedback did not yield larger gains than the control condition. In contrast, untimed word identification accuracy did not change in response to the provision of extensive training and the availability of feedback. However, when gain scores were summed across timed and untimed word identification tasks, students in the feedback conditions learned twice as many words as those in the no feedback control. Finally, tests of nonword decoding showed that students in feedback conditions improved more than those in the control condition, those who received segmented feedback gained more than those who received whole-word feedback, and those who received onset–rime feedback gained more than those who received whole-word feedback. According to the authors, the results obtained through the analyses of gain scores were mirrored by analyses that examined the time of testing as an independent variable. Thus, in this study, segmented and whole-word feedback appear to have comparable effects on students' timed word identification accuracy, but little improvement in the accuracy of untimed word identification was seen. Interestingly, most of the gains in timed word identification accuracy occurred for words that were not targeted for feedback. This suggests that students either learned these words from reading in meaningful contexts or they were able to generalize the use of the decoding skills they acquired in the feedback conditions to untargeted words.

R. K. Olson and Wise (1992) reported on a second phase of extended training with speech feedback for students with reading disabilities. The second phase used the same methodology as that reported by Wise et al. (1989), but provided a longer aggregate reading experience, included a larger sample, and provided less support to students for monitoring the targeting of words that were difficult to decode. In the second phase, 149 third- and sixth-grade students with reading disabilities averaged 8.1 hours of reading practice that included access to speech feedback for targeted words. Students were assigned to either a whole-word feedback, syllable feedback, onset–rime feedback, or a no feedback control condition. Eight of the students assigned to one of the three training conditions had fewer than 4 hours of total reading time and were excluded from subsequent analyses. The remaining students in the training conditions averaged 8.1 hours of total reading time, somewhat longer than students averaged in Wise et al. (1989).

R. K. Olson and Wise (1992) found that students in these three feedback conditions were equally good at monitoring target words for feedback, but that the overall level of targeting during Phase 2 was less accurate than in Phase 1 (Wise et al., 1989). This finding was attributed to the provision of less pretraining support and less experimenter monitoring of students' targeting accuracy during Phase 2. In general, students in the three feedback conditions showed substantial and comparable gains in word recognition accuracy, which was measured by aggregating across measures of timed and untimed word recognition, as compared to those in the no feedback control condition. Phase 2 students actually showed somewhat smaller gains in word recognition than those from Phase 1, but this was attributed to the relative severity of the sample's reading disabilities prior to the intervention. As in Wise et al., a small percentage of the words that students identified after training were actually targeted for feedback by them, suggesting that the students learned these words outside of the training context or that the training effects generalized to untargeted words. The accuracy of nonword decoding improved as a result of the provision of speech feedback, but students in the whole-word feedback condition improved most and those in the onset–rime condition improved least compared to those in the no feedback control condition.

Gains in nonword decoding were less dramatic in Phase 2 than in Phase 1 (Wise et al., 1989). Again, this difference between phases was attributed to the relatively lower level of support given to students during Phase 2 (R. K. Olson & Wise, 1992). Across both Phase 1 and 2 (R. K. Olson & Wise, 1992; Wise et al., 1989), the effects of feedback on students' nonword decoding depended on the severity of students' reading disability. Students with more severe reading disabilities were aided least by onset–rime feedback. In contrast, those with less severe reading disabilities benefited the most from onset–rime feedback. Across phases, the accuracy of word recognition did not seem to depend on the interaction of the severity of students' reading disability and the feedback condition. Finally, across phases, pretest measures of phonemic awareness were positively correlated with students' initial skill and later gains in nonword decoding and word recognition.

R. K. Olson and Wise's (1992) finding about the relationship between phonemic awareness and the effects of speech feedback on gains in word recognition and nonword decoding accuracy led Wise et al. (1998) to reevaluate the benefits of providing all of students' training in meaningful contexts. Perhaps students with reading disabilities, especially those with the most severe difficulties, need sequenced and structured phonological analysis training in isolation before practicing their decoding skills in meaningful contexts. To test this idea, Wise et al. contrasted the effects of two different supplemental strategies, phonological analysis (PA) and comprehension strategy (CS), on the nonword decoding and word recognition accuracy of students with reading disabilities. In total, 201 students from second to fifth grade participated in the study over a 2-year period. Both strategies used a guided discovery approach in which students learned by asking questions. Strategies were purported to increase students' error detection skills, were taught in the context of small-group instruction, and group training was interspersed with individualized computer practice in the context of reading stories. While reading these stories, students could target difficult to decode words for speech feedback. One-syllable words were segmented into onset-rimes, and multisyllable words were segmented according to BOSS (Taft, 1979) rules.

Despite commonalties, the PA and the CS conditions differed in important ways. Students in the PA condition spent about half of their time in exercises from the Auditory Discrimination in Depth program (Lindamood & Lindamood, 1975) and the Phonological Analysis with Letters program, which were meant to promote students' phonological analysis skills. After meeting performance criteria for these programs, students spent half their time reading stories on the computer and half their time practicing phonological analysis skills. Students who failed to target misread words for speech feedback were prompted to do so by an experimenter who monitored their targeting accuracy. In contrast, students in the CS condition were taught reading strategies modeled on reciprocal teaching (Palincsar & Brown, 1984). Students worked in small groups to learn these strategies, which were modeled by the teacher and then applied by the students to stories displayed on paper and the computer. As in the PA condition, students in the CS condition spent half their time in small-group instruction and the other half reading stories on the computer with speech feedback. However, students in the CS condition were not prompted by the experimenter to target misread words for speech feedback.

Wise et al. (1998) found that students in both the PA and CS conditions made substantial gains in word and nonword reading and in comprehension. The magnitude of these gains was greater than those observed in either Wise et al. (1989) or R. K. Olson and Wise (1992). Students in both the PA and CS conditions improved in nonword decoding accuracy, and perhaps not surprisingly, the PA students improved twice as much as those in the CS condition. Similarly, the phonemic awareness of both groups improved after training, and again, greater gains were seen for students in the PA condition. Students in both groups showed substantial gains in word recognition accuracy, but the difference between conditions was not as marked as it was for measures that tapped nonword reading, that is, phonological analysis and phonemic awareness. Nevertheless, students in the PA condition seemed to enjoy an advantage in word recognition accuracy over their CS peers, although the difference was not statistically significant on all measures of word recognition.

In general, students in the PA condition showed much greater gains than those in the CS condition on measures tailored to tap the skills taught during PA training. In contrast, students in both conditions showed comparable gains on standardized performance measures such as comprehension and word recognition. Wise et al. (1998) argued that many standardized reading tasks use words that require students to adapt skills learned during training. For example, many of the words seen on standardized reading tests are irregular with respect to pronunciation; that is, they require students to use nonstandard rules for segmenting syllables. Students in the PA condition were never taught to segment syllables because the computer automatically segmented words that were targeted during reading. Moreover, during training students saw words that conformed to standard phonics rules. Consequently, PA students were ill prepared to segment syllables, especially those that were irregular with respect to pronunciation. In general, this argument highlights the importance of systematically programming the generalization of trained skills to the contexts in which they will be used. Students with reading disabilities should not be expected to invent or spontaneously adapt skills for use in meaningful contexts (Wise et al., 1998).

The work of R. K. Olson and Wise shows that the provision of speech feedback in meaningful reading contexts can lead to improvements in the word recognition and comprehension accuracy of students with reading disabilities. However, simply exposing these students to speech feedback in meaningful contexts is not likely to overcome the effects of deficits in phonological analysis and phonemic awareness experienced by these students. In fact, their research (R. K. Olson & Wise, 1992; Wise et al., 1998) shows that the benefit students derive from the provision of speech feedback is directly related to their prior skill in phonological analysis and phonemic awareness. Further, students' ability to profit from segmented speech feedback depends on their ability to analyze and apply the segmentation rules in practice. Therefore, it seems necessary to teach students with reading disabilities the rules that can be used to analyze the relationship between orthography and phonology, and then to apply these rules in meaningful contexts.

TECHNOLOGY AND TEXT COMPREHENSION
FOR STUDENTS WITH MILD DISABILITIES

In this section, we review the research supporting two technology-based approaches to teaching or promoting students' comprehension: instruction in basic comprehension skills and electronic text.[1] The first set of studies examines the efficacy of programs designed to teach specific com-

---

[1]We have chosen the term *electronic text* to refer to text that is presented by a computer and is often enhanced through features (e.g., speech synthesis, supplementary information about words or concepts) that can promote comprehension. Electronic text has been referred to variously as: hypermedia stories, books, study guides, and basal readers; supported text; computer-mediated text; electronic books or storybooks; and CD-ROM books.

prehension skills. This body of research is slim, owing in part to the limitations of technology in providing the type of scaffolded and discourse-based cognitive strategy instruction that seems most conducive for promoting text comprehension (e.g., Palincsar & Brown, 1984; Rosenshine, Meister, & Chapman, 1996).

The second set of studies investigates a variety of issues related to students' use and comprehension of electronic text, or text presented by computer and often augmented with electronic enhancements such as definitions, speech feedback, and graphics. Educators have been optimistic that electronic enhancements to traditional text can promote students' text comprehension by compensating for poor component skills (such as word identification and vocabulary knowledge) and by prompting or modeling skills and behaviors that will promote comprehension in other contexts.

Passage Comprehension Skills and Vocabulary Instruction

Several studies have examined the computer's potential for providing skill-based instruction or practice in passage comprehension and vocabulary. Harper and Ewing (1986) used an alternating treatments design to compare the effectiveness of a commercial computer program and a comprehension skills workbook on the silent reading comprehension of nine junior high students with school-diagnosed learning disabilities or mild mental disabilities. Students' IQs ranged from 72 to 109. Students were assigned to levels within each treatment based on standardized test data and an informal reading inventory. The primary dependent measure was students' performance on comprehension questions asked within the instructional materials. When data were averaged across sessions, students scored 12 points higher, on a scale of 0 to 100, on computer sessions than workbook sessions. Only one student obtained a higher average score for the workbook sessions. Attention to task was observed in an unspecified manner, but no between-condition differences could be discerned. The majority of students (89%) reported they preferred working on the computer. However, the authors did not describe the nature of instruction provided by the computer and workbook, nor were attempts made to standardize the questions asked in the two treatments. Thus, differences in quality of instruction or difficulty of the dependent measure, rather than mode of presentation, might account for the observed differences.

In a study of computer-assisted vocabulary instruction, G. Johnson, Gersten, and Carnine (1987) focused on the impact of specific instructional design features. They contended that set size and schedules of review were important variables to consider in the delivery of vocabulary instruction to learners with disabilities. Their study compared two CAI (computer-assisted instruction) programs, which varied in these features, for their efficacy in teaching definitions of 50 words. Twenty-five high school students with learning disabilities, who scored at least 3 years below grade level on a standardized reading test and who could define fewer than 80% of the target words, participated in the study. Students were matched on pretest scores and then randomly assigned to either the large teaching set (LTS) or small teaching set (STS) condition. In the first, students used a commercial vocabulary software program that taught words in sets of 25, did not assign words based on students' prior knowledge, and included no cumulative review. The contrasting STS program introduced words in sets of no more than seven, provided instruction only on words students did not know, as determined by computer-presented assessments, specified mastery criteria before advancing to new words, and provided daily cumulative review.

The researchers terminated the study after 11 sessions because they found that some students were unable to reach their specified mastery criteria. At this point, more students in the STS condition had achieved mastery and had done so in significantly fewer sessions. Furthermore, their scores on target vocabulary words experienced only a slight drop (85% to 80% accuracy) over a 2-week period. There were no significant differences between conditions on transfer measures, which included an open-ended oral vocabulary test and a comprehension test of passages containing target vocabulary words. In fact, scores on these measures did not exceed 50%, suggesting that students needed more or different instruction to use their word knowledge flexibly when reading text. The authors concluded that the instructional design variables had greatest impact on the efficiency with which students learned to associate words with their definitions. However, the authors provided no information about how students used the LTS program, which contained several different activities, including an arcade game. Thus, design variables other than size of teaching set and review features might have influenced the results.

Hebert and Murdock (1994) investigated differences in students' acquisition of vocabulary knowledge when words and definitions were presented by a computer program that provided no speech, synthesized speech output, or digitized speech output. Three sixth-grade boys with language-learning disabilities participated in an alternating treatments design in which they were presented with 25 words in each 6-day treatment phase. All students obtained higher scores on multiple-choice tests of target words in the digitized speech treatment than in the no-speech treatment. Although, the digitized speech treatment was most effective for two of the three participants, by the final session scores obtained under the two speech conditions were within 5% of one another.

Xin, Glaser, and Rieth (1996) used the *Great Quake of 89* videodisc to teach 30 new vocabulary words to 10 fourth-grade students with learning disabilities. Over a 6-week span, students participated in enriched vocabulary lessons in which words, such as *earthquake* and *tremor*, were introduced with a video clip and then practiced through class discussion, used in context, practice activities, and repeated viewing of the relevant video sequence. Students attained 60% on a posttest of target vocabulary, which compared favorably with a 27% score attained by these students when they were taught in an unspecified "nonvideo format." Nearly all students reported that they enjoyed this type of instruction and high engagement rates, exceeding 85%, were observed during vocabulary lessons.

In summary, this set of studies cannot be used to argue that computers or videodisc-based programs provide more effective skill instruction in comprehension or vocabulary than other approaches. This research can support the conclusion that computers and videodiscs can be used effectively to teach students the definitions of vocabulary words. Speech feedback, whether synthetic or digitized, seems to enhance the efficacy of learning to associate words with their definitions, and instructional design variables such as set size and review schedules can increase learning efficiency. However, these results should be viewed as limited because, as G. Johnson et al. (1987) and others (Stahl & Fairbanks, 1986) have demonstrated, learning to associate a word with a definition may not have widespread impact on students' comprehension of text. Only the Xin et al. study (1996) addressed use of vocabulary in context.

Electronic Text

Early studies of electronic text, in part constrained by the expense of enhancements such as high-quality speech synthesis and lack of multimedia capabilities, focused on comparing differences in passage comprehension between students who read text on paper and those who read text presented by computer. As technology became more sophisticated, researchers added enhancements to electronic text that could promote better skills and strategies and compensate for reading disabilities. The first group of studies reviewed in this section compared students' comprehension when reading short passages of text presented by computer (online reading) to comprehension when reading text on paper (off-line reading). Some researchers also examined the manner in which students interacted with enhancements provided by the electronic texts. A second set of studies focused specifically on the impact of speech feedback on comprehension of passages and stories.

In a third group of studies, researchers examined the impact of electronic text when it was used as a vehicle for learning specific skills or information. Most often, students in these studies used electronic text as a supplement to more traditional classroom-based instruction. Here, too, researchers were concerned with students' patterns of interaction with the text and its impact on comprehension. However, the electronic texts used by students were specifically designed as a means to master skills or information (e.g., reading skills, state history) and typically contained more extensive enhancements than the texts used in the first group of studies.

Comparisons of Online and Off-Line Reading. We located six studies that focused on these comparisons. In the studies discussed here, passages ranged in length from 150 to 1,000 words, and, in several studies, the computer-presented passages were enhanced by textual features such as definitions of words used in the passage or additional background. Typically, comprehension was assessed through examiner-developed multiple-choice questions.

Keene and Davey (1987) examined differences in comprehension and strategy use among 51 high school students with learning disabilities who read two expository passages off- and online. Although students who read passages on the computer reported more frequent rereading and greater interest in the task, there were no group differences in immediate or delayed passage comprehension. Casteel (1988–1989) examined whether chunking text into segments of three to five words would enhance comprehension among 30 high school students with learning disabilities. He found higher comprehension in conditions in which text was chunked, but no differences attributable to on- or off-line reading.

Reinking and Schreiner (1985) and Reinking (1988) added four types of enhancements to electronic passages: (a) definitions of difficult vocabulary words, (b) passage paraphrases with lower readability levels, (c) supplemental background information in the form of additional text or illustrations, and (d) a statement of the main ideas of the passage. In the first study, students were randomly assigned to one of four conditions: (a) off-line reading, (b) reading passages online but without enhancements, (c) reading passages online with optional use of enhancements, and (d) reading passages online with required viewing of all enhancements. Reinking and Schreiner (1985) found that students' passage comprehension scores were highest when they were required to view all enhancements before responding to comprehension questions. In addition, mandatory viewing yielded the greatest advantage for the most difficult passages. When allowed to select enhancements, students made more selections on difficult passages and, across all passages, were most likely to select additional background information. Good readers obtained higher passage comprehension scores than poor readers. No other significant differences were found between the performance of good and poor readers in each condition.

In a later study, Reinking (1988) used the same conditions and textual enhancements in a within-subjects design. He replicated the finding that access to enhancements leads to higher comprehension than conditions in which students read printed text or unenhanced electronic text. However, in this sample, which contained students with more computer experience than students in the earlier study, mandatory use of enhancements did not produce better passage comprehension than optional use. Although optional or mandatory use of enhancements increased the amount of time students spent in these conditions, a statistical control for time demonstrated that comprehension scores remained significantly higher when students read enhanced text.

In contrast, Feldmann and Fish (1991) did not find that enhancements providing a description of the main idea and definitions improved the passage comprehension of high school students. Although the majority of the sample was judged to use the enhancements (with "use" undefined by the authors), there were no differences in passage comprehension among those who used them and those who read text online without enhancements. The authors found that students used enhancements more frequently when reading the more difficult of two passages. The authors did not use an offline reading condition for comparison with online conditions.

Similarly, Swanson and Trahan (1992) found no differences in the passage comprehension of students who read printed text, computer-presented text, or computer-presented text with an enhancement that forced them to reread before responding to questions. Interacting with the electronic passages required significantly more time, especially for students with learning disabilities. Swanson and Trahan reasoned that computer programs designed to improve reading comprehension might have an impact on students' metacognition, working memory, and attributions. They also measured these factors and found that students with learning disabilities who read the electronic text with enhancements performed more poorly on a working memory posttest. Given the observed working memory decrement, and the increased time spent processing computer text, without consequent gains in comprehension, the authors concluded that electronic text might be detrimental to students with learning disabilities. However, we wonder how participation in three 60–90 minute sessions of reading electronic text, as implemented in this study, could have been responsible for the observed decrement in general working memory performance, as measured by a posttest task unrelated to anything students read or may have learned during the study. Thus, it seems that the role of working memory in comprehending electronic text remains an open question.

In summary, these studies demonstrate that the medium by which text is presented, page or computer, has no appreciable impact on comprehension. Stated differently, viewing passages on a computer does not hamper the comprehension of poor readers or students with disabilities. The role of enhancements designed to promote passage comprehension is less clear. It is worth noting that only one and two enhancements, respectively, were used in the Swanson and Trahan (1992) and Feldmann and Fish (1991) studies, in contrast to the four used in the Reinking studies. Contradictory findings might also be accounted for by differences in sample characteristics, given that the Reinking studies employed poor readers and Swanson and Trahan's participants met stringent guidelines for learning disabilities. Finally, the Reinking studies suggest that, at least for less experienced computer users, required rather than optional use of enhancements leads to better comprehension.

Speech Feedback and Passage Comprehension. As discussed previously, poor word identification skills pose a formidable barrier to reading for many students with disabilities. When attentional resources must be devoted to decoding, comprehension suffers. Poor word-level skills make reading frustrating and laborious. Not surprisingly, students with poor skills read less than good readers, and, as a consequence, develop more limited general knowledge and vocabulary (Cunningham & Stanovich, 1998). Furthermore, frustrated rather than satisfied, poor readers are unlikely to develop the life-long love of reading that characterizes many highly successful learners.

Electronic text, in which words are read aloud via synthesized or digitized speech, may be highly advantageous for poor readers. When readers can obtain instantaneous aural presentation of written text, poor decoding skills are no longer an issue because readers are no longer restricted to text consistent with their word identification capabilities. Furthermore, as discussed earlier, computer-based pronunciation of unknown words can support the acquisition of phonological analysis and word identification skills. Several studies by Wise and Olson and their colleagues, reviewed earlier (R. Olson et al., 1986; Wise et al., 1998), supported the role of speech feedback in improving text comprehension. In this section, we describe nine additional studies that investigated the effect of speech feedback on students' comprehension of passages and stories.

Farmer, Klein, and Bryson (1992) examined the impact of a computer-based system that presented stories of 84 to 108 words in length to 14 students with learning disabilities attending a special school. Students, aged 13-10 to 18-10, all read at least 2 years below expected grade level. In a repeated-measures design, the researchers examined word recognition and comprehension when students read stories for which they could highlight and receive whole-word speech feedback for unknown words. In a comparison condition, students read comparable stories on the computer, with directions to highlight unfamiliar words, but with no speech feedback. Access to speech feedback made no difference in students' recognition of either words they had tagged as unfamiliar or untagged words. As measured by four questions at the conclusion of each story, there were no differences in students' story comprehension. The authors hypothesized that their comprehension measures may have been insensitive to differences among the conditions.

As the authors point out, students spent an average of only 2 hours with the computer system and tagged an average of 3.5 words per story when speech support was available. Thus, practice opportunities may have been insufficient for helping students master specific words, and the low rate of accessing speech feedback may have been insufficient to promote better story comprehension. Furthermore, the authors speculate that, although the DECtalk system used in this study has been shown to be only slightly less intelligible than human speech for poor readers (R. Olson et al., 1986), the difference may be sufficient to present an additional cognitive burden to participants in the study.

Olofsson (1992) modified a 200-word expository passage, used in the Swedish National Assessment program, for presentation by a computer program that provided whole-word synthesized speech feedback for user-targeted words. In a previous study, the author (Olofsson, 1990) documented the intelligibility of the synthetic speech used in the study, obtaining ceiling effects on words in context and an 88% recognition rate for words in isolation. In the present study, he compared the comprehension of 23 second-grade average readers and 10 students with disabilities, who read the passage via computer, to that of a 212-student sample from the national assessment. There were no differences in comprehension scores between average readers in the two groups. Comprehension data were not provided for the students with disabilities. Olofsson reported that, although students with disabilities targeted fewer words, about 80% conformed to the tendency exhibited by average readers to request pronunciations of morphemically complex words. However, the data on which these conclusions are based are not fully presented, nor is information provided about the nature and extent of students' disabilities.

In a follow-up study, Olofsson (1992) investigated the impact of a similar computer-based system on the word recognition and comprehension skills of 18 readers with disabilities in Grades 2 to 7. These students were attending special education classes in Sweden and had primary deficits in word-decoding skills. No other information was presented about their academic or demographic characteristics. Experimental students participated in 10 weeks of computer-aided reading in their special education classes, for an average of 25 computer sessions in which they read between 16 and 30 texts. Control students were selected from within the same classes. Assignment to conditions was nonrandom, however, and despite the author's attempt to match the two samples, control students had higher pretest scores on most dependent measures. The only information stated about the control condition is that the students "had the same amount of training and were taught by the same teachers as the experimental group."

Visual inspection of the rate of improvement in word-decoding skills shows virtually identical slopes for control and experimental groups, and for comprehension skills among the younger readers in both control and experimental groups. For the older readers, the slope of improvement in comprehension skills is much steeper in the experimental than control group. (These graphs are presented in Lundberg & Olofsson, 1993.) However, pretest differences, and the breakdown of results into age-sensitive cells containing 10 or fewer students per cell, make statistical analyses of the data, and conclusions based on them, tentative.

The authors also reported anecdotal information about students' use of speech feedback. Students needed initial teacher assistance to develop the habit of targeting unfamiliar words, with younger readers needing more instruction. Students were more likely to request help on longer words than shorter ones, even though misreading shorter words sometimes interfered with text comprehension. Teachers noted increased self-confidence among the experimental students, which was documented by their tendency to select increasingly more difficult books during free-reading time. Students did not report discomfort in using synthetic speech and teachers noted that minor intelligibility problems ceased after a few hours of experience.

The three studies just reviewed involved computer systems in which students decided when to access speech feedback by targeting specific words. Other studies have investigated the impact of simultaneous auditory and visual presentation of complete passages of text. Montali and Lewandowski (1996) examined the impact of bimodal presentation on the word identification skills and comprehension of Grade 8 and 9 students. Eighteen students, 16 with learning disabilities, scoring at the 25th percentile or below on a standardized achievement test, were designated as poor readers. Sixteen students from the same school with scores in the 45th to 60th percentile on the same test were selected as average readers. In a within-subjects design, students participated in three conditions: (a) visual: students read three passages on the computer screen, (b): auditory: students listened to three passages read by a recorded voice presented via a sound-edit program on the computer, and (c) bimodal: students viewed text on the computer screen that was highlighted as it was read. Text selections were taken from science and social studies books.

Although condition had no effect on students' ability to read words contained in the text, poor readers comprehended significantly better when passages were presented in the bimodal condition. In fact, poor readers' comprehension of text presented bimodally was similar to scores of the average readers in the visual condition. For poor readers, performance was comparable for visual and auditory presentations. For average readers, the bimodal presentation enhanced comprehension when contrasted with the auditory presentation, but visual and bimodal presentations yielded similar results. Both good and poor readers preferred the bimodal presentation.

Leong has conducted several studies investigating the use of the DECtalk system, also used by Wise and Olson, to provide speech feedback and other enhancements to promote comprehension. In an initial study (Leong, 1992), 67 students in Grades 6 through 8 were classified as above or below average by a median split on a basic reading skills assessment. During the pretest phase, students were asked to read along as the DECtalk system read 12 passages. Comprehension of each passage was assessed through short open-ended inference questions. Students were then assigned to one of two training conditions: (a) online reading only or (b) online reading with DECtalk speech (DECtalk condition). As in Montali and Lewandowski (1996), the complete passage was read in the DECtalk condition. In addition, preselected words, chosen for their potential difficulty, were highlighted on the screen and students were required to read and hear an explanation for each word. Students were then posttested with the same inference questions used in the pretest.

Leong (1992) analyzed data for each of the 12 passages and found that 10 passages showed a significant training effect when collapsed across conditions. However, students had significantly better comprehension for the DECtalk condition on only 2 of the 12 passages. Analysis of scores for average and below average readers suggested that the above-average readers benefited most from the DECtalk condition.

In two subsequent studies, Leong (1995) expanded on the DECtalk condition by adding enhancements in which students received explanations of difficult words and online prompts designed to promote metacognitive awareness of comprehension strategies. In the first study, 192 students in Grades 4 though 6 were categorized into average and below-average reader subgroups. Information about the inclusion of students with disabilities was not provided. Students viewed and listened to four expository passages, read by the DECtalk system, in one of four conditions: (a) online reading and no explanations of words, (b) online reading plus explanation of difficult words, (c) online reading, explanation of difficult words, and reading awareness prompts, and (d) online reading of simplified versions of the expository passages. Comprehension was assessed through inference questions and a summarization task. The author examined the impact of a variety of student characteristics on performance, but the main finding was one of no significant difference among conditions. Similarly, in a follow-up study with 12 teacher-nominated poor readers from sixth-grade classes, 12 reading-age-matched fourth-graders, and 12 chronological-age-matched sixth-graders, the author found no effects for condition.

Elkind, K. Cohen, and Murray (1993) examined the impact of the Bookwise system, which permits the user to scan printed pages of text into a computer program that subsequently displays and reads the text via synthesized speech. The system also includes a dictionary that defines and syllabicates selected words. Twenty-eight students, in Grades 5 through 7, who were attending a private day school for students with dyslexia, participated in the study. The authors compared performance on the Gray Oral Reading Tests–Revised (GORT–R) when students read passages unaided and when the Bookwise system read the passages to them. These data show that more than 70% of the sample scored at least one grade level higher when passages were read by Bookwise than when reading unaided. Comparison to scores obtained by a similar sample of students who read each GORT–R passage unaided on two occasions showed that most of the improvements could be attributed to the use of the Bookwise system, rather than to the opportunity to read passages twice. However, 14% of the sample showed no improvement and 14% had poorer comprehension when text was read to them.

To examine longer term impact of the Bookwise system, students used it to read literature from their English classes for a total of 20 to 25 hours over the course of a semester. No other details are provided about how the system was used. One class used the system each semester, permitting two opportunities for comparison between the school's typical instruction and instruction supplemented by Bookwise. Anecdotal evidence suggested that many students enjoyed using the system and that it promoted more extended and independent reading. Standardized reading tests, given at the beginning, midpoint, and conclusion of the study, showed that both classes made progress over the course of the year. However, neither class progressed more on any subtest in the semester they used the Bookwise system.

In summary, these studies do not provide clear evidence that speech feedback, either in the form of user-selected words or simultaneous aural and visual presentation of text, affects comprehension. When given the option to request speech feedback for unfamiliar words, students may not be able to monitor their errors (Nelson & Narens, 1990; van Daal & Reitsma, 1993) and thus do not request enough assistance to affect comprehension (e.g., Farmer et al., 1992; R. Olson et al., 1986; van Daal & Reitsma, 1990). Better results seemed to occur in studies in which students were trained and/or monitored in their use of speech feedback (R. K. Olson & Wise, 1992; Wise et al., 1989, 1998), and students' tendencies to request speech feedback may increase with experience and instruction (Olofsson, 1992). Thus, electronic text that provides speech feedback on demand may not promote better comprehension without accompanying instruction and monitoring.

Nor do these studies provide clear evidence that simultaneous auditory and visual presentation of text promotes comprehension, despite the seeming advantage of an enhancement that compensates for word identification difficulties. Although two studies (Elkind et al., 1993; Montali & Lewandowski, 1996) found advantages for bimodal presentation, Leong's studies (Leong, 1992, 1995) and the second Elkind et al. (1993) study failed to replicate this finding. We doubt that the quality of the speech feedback used in these studies can account for lack of effects, given that the DECtalk or other highly intelligible systems were used.

The parallel between the equivocal impact of specific types of speech feedback on word identification in the studies reviewed earlier and the mixed results obtained in these comprehension studies is instructive. Wise, R. K. Olson, and colleagues (e.g., R. K. Olson & Wise, 1992; Wise et al., 1998) demonstrated that the efficacy of speech feedback in improving word-level reading skills depended on the phonemic awareness and phonological analysis skills of the learner. Similarly, the impact of speech feedback on text comprehension may vary with user characteristics. Working with adults who have reading difficulties, Elkind and colleagues (Elkind, 1998b; Elkind, Black, & Murray, 1996) have investigated this possibility. Their research showed that simultaneous auditory and visual presentation of text was most advantageous for students who had poor reading rate, comprehension, or endurance when reading printed materials; good oral language capabilities as measured by a standardized vocabulary test; and strengths in integrating auditory and visual information. Comprehension scores from online reading did not improve, and sometimes decreased, for students who had difficulty integrating auditory and visual information, who read faster than the rate at which text was spoken, or who had relatively good comprehension when reading text off-line (Elkind, 1998a).

Elkind's work suggests that reader characteristics will mediate the impact of speech feedback. Except for comparisons between broadly defined good and poor readers, none of the studies reviewed previously examined the impact of student characteristics on outcomes. This seems a fruitful area for future research. Furthermore, with the exception of the Elkind et al. (1993) investigation of the Bookwise system in language arts classes, none of these studies examined how electronic text with speech feedback can support or enhance more typical classroom instruction. We turn next to studies in which the use of electronic text is tied to a clearer purpose—the mastery of skills or information that are part of a student's curriculum.

Electronic Texts and Classroom Instruction. Whereas the studies reviewed earlier investigated students' comprehension of electronic text passages, Boone and Higgins were among the first researchers to investigate the impact of electronically transformed books as a classroom-based instructional intervention. In a 3-year longitudinal study (Boone & Higgins, 1993; Higgins & Boone, 1991), these researchers converted sections of the Macmillan Basal Reader Series–R into an electronic format. Using HyperCard, they incrementally enhanced the computer-presented text with increasing levels of support in each of the 3 years. In initial years, electronic enhancements were designed to provide readers with additional information about the text through related pictures, animated graphic sequences, speech feedback, simple definitions, and synonyms. Later in the study, enhancements were added to guide the reader through strategies that promote comprehension, such as summarization, main idea matching, or rereading for specific detail (Higgins & Boone, 1990a).

The modified basal reading selections were designed to run on Apple Macintosh computers and were used independently by experimental group students, in general education classrooms, before or after teacher-directed reading activities. In Year 1, the experimental group obtained higher total test scores on a standardized reading achievement test in the kindergarten, second-, and third-grade samples. This finding was not replicated in subsequent years, however. Although the authors examined differences in subtest scores and between students of high and low ability, they conducted these tests as a series of pairwise comparisons, resulting in 12 to 24 separate tests per grade level. Because no adjustment was made for multiple comparisons, at least some of the significant results reported by the authors were likely to occur by chance alone.

Boone and Higgins (1993) also examined differences in achievement test scores for students who had participated in differing number of years of intervention. There appeared to be a benefit for longevity of the intervention. For example, students who participated in the experimental group for 3 years had higher scores than students: (a) who participated in the experimental group for 1 year or (b) who participated in the control group for 3 years. Students who participated in the intervention for only 1 year did not obtain higher scores than students who participated in the control group for 3 years.

One difficulty in interpreting these findings is the lack of information provided about instruction in the control group. Because hypermedia basal readers were used to supplement traditional reading instruction, it is possible that students in the experimental condition received additional reading instruction. Thus, disparities in the instructional time devoted to reading may account for some of the reported differences between experimental and control groups. Furthermore, the effects of additional instruction might be cumulative, accounting for the more robust effects obtained for students who participated in the intervention for 3 years.

MacArthur and Haynes (1995) designed an authoring system, SALT, that enabled teachers to develop electronic versions of textbooks and other reading material. They examined SALT's impact on a sample of 10 high school students with learning disabilities, aged 15 to 17. In a repeated-measures design, students read passages from a science textbook in two conditions. In a basic condition, computer-presented text contained the features found in paper textbooks (text, graphics, outlines, and questions) plus a word-processing feature for note taking. In the enhanced version, text and note-taking features were augmented with speech synthesis for any word, sentence, or chunk of text; an online glossary; links between questions and text; highlighted main ideas; and supplementary explanations. The two versions were counterbalanced across passage and order. Students were trained to use the program prior to data collection. They then were given 90 minutes to read and study a passage, take notes, and complete a multiple-choice posttest.

After reading and studying the enhanced version, students obtained significantly higher scores on the posttest, with 9 of 10 students earning better scores in this condition. All students reported they preferred the electronic text to the textbook, though two students thought they learned better from the teacher. In general, students rated highly the helpfulness and ease of use of all the features of the enhanced passage. Observations of students' interaction with the passage showed that all answered questions, expanded and looked at graphics, and read teacher explanations. All except one took notes and the majority used a copying feature to ease text entry. The glossary was used infrequently and use of the speech synthesis option varied widely. Two students used it to read almost all the text, whereas three students did not use it at all. It is important to note that several students found the synthetic speech difficult to understand.

Anderson-Inman and Horney (1998) reported results of several studies investigating the manner in which students used electronic text in classroom instruction and its impact on their achievement. In the Electro-Text Project (Anderson-Inman, Horney, Chen, & Lewin, 1994; Horney & Anderson-Inman, 1994), middle school students who were considered at risk for reading disabilities were provided with enhanced versions of the short stories used in their literature classes. An electronic data-collection tool, developed by the authors, operated transparently as students interacted with the text. As students read electronic versions of these stories, using enhancements at their discretion, the program recorded information about all their interactions with the text.

Horney and Anderson-Inman (1994) reported patterns and profiles of electronic text reading among a sample of 17 middle school students enrolled in a class designated for "lower-ability readers" and/or "underachievers." Students spent a portion of class time reading two electronic stories in a computer lab, monitored by their teacher. Students spent an average of 45 and 77 minutes reading the first and second stories, respectively. Based on an analysis of transcripts of real-time activity collected by the program, student responses to prompted writing activities and paper-and-pencil essay questions, observations, and student interviews, the authors documented six distinct patterns of electronic text interaction. These varied in their degree of interactivity and integratedness.

Skimming, or moving through the text rapidly without reading or studying, and *reading,* or moving through pages with minimal use of resources, were judged to be neither interactive nor integrative. In contrast, *responding,* in which students accessed one or more of the enhancements and wrote responses to prompts, and *checking,* in which students used resources systematically but without rereading or responding, were judged to be more interactive. *Reviewing,* or moving systematically through text that had been read previously to reread information and revisit enhancements, was considered integrative. *Studying,* in which students moved systematically through the text, reading pages and making use of their enhancements, was judged to be both interactive and integrative. Students tended to use more interactive and integrative patterns when reading the second story, although, as the authors acknowledged, improvements in the design of the second story, as well as the fact that story order was not counterbalanced, temper any conclusions about the role of experience. Overall, students spent about half of their time using the *studying* pattern.

In another study, Anderson-Inman and Horney (1993) provided 31 at-risk eighth-graders with improved versions of the electronic stories. This study included training in reading three electronic documents. Data were collected on students' independent reading of a fourth story. Analysis of story retells, student interviews, and paper-and-pencil questions, and computer monitor data revealed three types of electronic-text users:

- *Book lovers:* These students interacted at a superficial level with electronic enhancements, accessing them on the first few pages and then abandoning them in favor of a linear reading of the text. In postreading interviews, students indicated that they preferred to read a book and that accessing electronic resources slowed their reading. Verbal retells showed understanding of main ideas but lack of knowledge about many of the story's subtler details.

- *Studiers:* These students accessed many enhancements and had highly favorable opinions of electronic reading. Story retells were detailed and accurate.

- *Resource junkies:* These students seemed not to take the reading task seriously. They spent most of their time accessing preferred enhancements, but not in any systematic manner. Story retells were poor. Students enjoyed reading the electronic stories, emphasizing the novelty rather than the utility of the enhancements they chose to access.

In summary, the studies reviewed in this section show that the use of electronic text, when used to master skills or information in language arts and content-area classes, may offer modest benefits. The studies of electronically enhanced basal reading selections conducted by Boone and Higgins (1993) and Higgins and Boone (1991) showed stronger effects over time, although the significance of this results is difficult to determine in absence of information about the comparability of reading instruction in control and experimental classes. The MacArthur and Haynes (1995) study demonstrated that students understood content-area text passages better when they were enhanced with features designed to promote comprehension.

The studies of electronic text use by Anderson-Inman and her colleagues (Anderson-Inman & Horney, 1993; Horney & Anderson-Inman, 1994) are important because they show that students use electronic text in different ways. More interactive and integrative patterns of use tend to be associated with better comprehension. Different student characteristics and patterns of text use may account for some of the equivocal results reviewed in this section. Furthermore, instruction in the use of electronic text, teacher monitoring for effective integration of enhancements with content information, and experience may be important considerations.

Electronic Study Guides and Study Tools.   Electronic textbook selections, enhanced with electronic study guides, have been the focus of several investigations. Horton, Lovitt, Givens, and Nelson (1989) selected two passages of approximately 1,000 words from a world geography text. Participants were drawn from two remedial ninth-grade world geography classes. Ten remedial students, who scored below the 35th percentile on a standardized achievement test, and 9 students with learning disabilities participated in the experimental conditions. In addition, eight remedial students and four students with learning disabilities from the same classes participated in a procedure to assess the comparability of the two passages. The "neutral group" students served as a control condition and provided a means for assessing the comparability of the passages. They read each passage and responded to a 15-item multiple-choice test about its content. Scores on one passage were slightly lower (but not statistically significantly different from) the other passage. The authors assigned the passage on which students obtained lower scores to the computer-based study guide condition.

In a within-subjects design, experimental students participated in two conditions. In the computer-based study guide condition, a passage was presented by computer accompanied by a 15-item study guide consisting of short answer questions about main ideas. Students were required to complete the study guide twice. They then took a 15-item multiple-choice test on passage content via computer. In the second, a note-taking condition, a different passage was presented on paper. Students were directed to read and study by taking notes. They then took a 15-item quiz. Time allotted to each activity was controlled so that equal time was spent in each condition, and order of conditions was counterbalanced.

Both remedial students and students with learning disabilities performed similarly, scoring higher on a 15-item multiple-choice quiz in the study guide condition than in the note-taking condition. Both remedial students and those with learning disabilities in the study guide condition outperformed students in the control condition (who read the text on paper and took a 15-item multiple-choice test on its content). The requirement to take notes about the passage seemed to yield some benefit, as remedial students in the note-taking condition outperformed remedial students in the control condition. However, students with learning disabilities in the control condition performed similarly to their counterparts in the note-taking condition.

Given that students in the study guide condition were required to read and answer questions about material covered on a subsequent test, whereas students in the note-taking and control condition received no guidance about what or how to study, the findings of this study are not surprising. Furthermore, the centrality of the computer in this study is questionable. Essentially, the computer-based study guide could have been presented on paper. In subsequent studies, Higgins and colleagues developed electronic study guides to take fuller advantages of the capabilities of electronic text.

In two studies, Higgins and colleagues (Higgins & Boone, 1990b; Higgins, Boone, & Lovitt, 1996) adapted the first two chapters of a state history textbook to a hypermedia format. The text was broken down into 10 short (500–700 word) reading segments, and the following enhancements were added to each segment: additional explanatory passages, access to synonyms or other information for difficult words or phrases, and multiple-choice questions to which students were required to respond correctly before advancing. Students from participating social studies classes were randomly assigned to either: (a) lecture condition, in which students listened to and took notes from teacher lecture and read assigned text to complete a worksheet of multiple-choice questions, (b) lecture/hypermedia study guide condition, in which students listened to a teacher lecture and then worked through the hypermedia study guide for 15 minutes, or (c) hypermedia study guide condition, in which students worked with the hypermedia study guide for the full class session. All 10 sessions were 30 minutes in length, followed by a 10-minute quiz, and the experimenters scripted the teacher lectures to ensure that students in all conditions would be exposed to identical information.

In the first study reported in Higgins and Boone (1990b), the researchers found a trend toward higher daily test scores in the study guide condition. This trend was replicated in posttest and retention test data, however, there were no statistically significant effects for condition. Although the authors make comparisons among different educational groupings (remedial, learning disabled, average), the prolific use of statistical tests (e.g., separate analyses of variance [ANOVAs] for each day of the study), make it difficult to determine how many of these findings would have occurred by chance alone.

In a second study, Higgins and Boone (1990b) investigated the use of the same hypermedia study guides as a follow-up to teacher-presented instruction. Five students (two with learning disabilities) with the lowest posttest scores from Study 1 participated in a single-subject ABA design. Four of these students had previously participated in the lecture condition. Essentially, students interacted with the same 10 study guides they used in Study 1 for 10 full class sessions. All students showed modest increases over daily quiz scores earned during their participation in Study 1. Furthermore, only three of the five students' scores decreased when they returned to the baseline condition in which computer study guides were not used. However, different tasks were used to assess achievement during the intervention and return to baseline phases. Given limitations of the design and the fact that students were relearning information from Study 1 in Study 2, it is difficult to draw confident conclusions about the impact of the hypermedia study guides on students' achievement.

In what appears to be a reexamination of the data from Study 1 in Higgins and Boone (1990b), Higgins et al. (1996) analyzed data for only those students diagnosed as learning disabled or remedial readers (i.e., omitting average readers from the analyses). The authors found a significant effect for condition on posttest scores, with higher scores for students with learning disabilities who participated in the lecture/hypermedia study guide condition. This effect was not replicated when scores of remedial students were examined. A significant effect for condition occurred on daily quiz scores, on which students with learning disabilities in both hypermedia/lecture and hypermedia only conditions obtained similar scores. Remedial students obtained the highest daily quiz scores in the lecture/hypermedia condition. Unfortunately, the significance of these patterns could not be statistically verified through follow-up tests, possibly due to the small sample size and consequent lack of statistical power.

Although the authors described various patterns of responses to test questions, the only reliable finding was that students responded to factual questions more accurately than inferential questions. Furthermore, it appeared that students in the hypermedia conditions were accessing optional explanatory passages because they responded correctly to test questions on their content. Again, small sample size attenuated statistical power and thus limited the range of conclusions that could be drawn from patterns of student performance.

Taking a different approach, Anderson-Inman and colleagues (Anderson-Inman, Knox-Quinn, & Horney, 1996) used computers and software as tools for enhancing studying and learning across the curriculum. The primary software tool used in this work is *Inspiration* (Inspiration Software, Inc., 1994), which allows users to create electronic outlines and concept maps. In a 2-year implementation study, these researchers taught electronic study strategies that employed *Inspiration* and word-processing software to 30 middle and secondary school students from three different schools. Students were identified by their schools as having specific learning disabilities, but selection criteria for inclusion in the study varied slightly among the sites. The sample was diverse with respect to full-scale IQs (with a range of 77 to 119) and reading level, (with grade equivalent scores ranging from 1.3 to 10.0). Students participated in the intervention for either 1 or 2 years.

Students at each school were given a laptop computer and taught electronic study strategies tailored to the content-area courses in which they were enrolled. For example, students were taught to use the electronic outlining and concept mapping features of *Inspiration* to take notes during lecture classes, to study textbooks, and to record and synthesize information for written reports. Implementation procedures varied across the three schools on several features, including the degree to which electronic study strategy instruction was integrated into content-area courses.

The researchers collected a variety of information about project implementation and students' use of electronic study strategies through observations, interviews, students' products, and weekly contact reports. Based on these data, they classified students according to the extent and skill with which they used electronic study strategies. *Power Users* were observed to make made frequent, appropriate, and independent use of the strategies in as much of their schoolwork as possible. Some were observed to develop their own strategies to meet the demands of novel tasks. *Prompted Users* were observed to master a variety of strategies and to use word-processing tools for a variety of school assignments. However, they continued to need prompting and assistance to use computer-based outlining and concept-mapping tools on a regular basis. *Reluctant Users* were reported to develop limited knowledge of computer-based strategies and rarely used them without direct teacher supervision.

Anderson-Inman et al. (1996) analyzed the characteristics of learners within each of these three categories and found that IQ and reading level tended to be associated with extent of adoption. For example, Power Users had higher IQs and most read at or above the ninth-grade level.

The researchers also concluded that amount of instruction was correlated with levels of use, as half of the students in the Reluctant Users group had joined the study in its 2nd year. All three schools were represented in each category of users, so project implementation differences did not appear to affect observed use of the strategies. Because no data were provided about the amount of instruction each student received, it is difficult to make confident conclusions about the relative influence of instruction, IQ, and reading level on students' adoption of the strategies. Information about the relationship between levels of use of the instructed strategies and student outcomes, such as grades on content-area assignments, were not reported in this article.

In summary, the study by Horton et al. (1989) showed better mastery of content-area material with electronic text accompanied by online study guides, whereas perhaps the most confident conclusion we can draw from the Higgins studies (Higgins et al., 1996; Higgins & Boone, 1990b) is that students learned at least as well from electronic study guides as they did from more lectures on text content. Given that the electronic study guides required students to answer specific questions about the materials they were reading, it is perhaps not surprising that their use would be associated with higher scores on subsequent tests of that material. Problems with the data analytic strategies used in some of these studies also limit the conclusions we can draw from them. The Anderson-Inman et al. (1996) study demonstrates that individual differences, such as IQ and reading level, can have a significant impact on the mastery and adoption computer-based study tools for mastering content information.

TECHNOLOGY AND WRITING FOR STUDENTS WITH MILD DISABILITIES

Writing Difficulties of Students With Mild Disabilities

Current cognitive models of writing portray writing as a sophisticated problem-solving activity involving complex planning and evaluation processes, linguistic processes, and transcription processes (Berninger & Swanson, 1994; Flower & Hayes, 1981; Hayes, 1996). Students who find writing difficult, including those with learning disabilities and other mild disabilities, struggle with all these aspects of writing. They engage in relatively little planning, and their revisions are limited primarily to correction of mechanical errors (MacArthur, Graham, & Schwartz, 1991; MacArthur, Harris, & Graham, 1994). They experience difficulties with transcription processes, both spelling and handwriting, and these struggles affect the overall quality of their writing because cognitive resources devoted to transcription are not available for higher order processes (Graham, Berninger, Abbott, Abbott, & Whitaker, 1997). Students with writing difficulties are also less knowledgeable about criteria for good writing and about writing strategies (Graham, Schwartz, & MacArthur, 1993). Their written products, in comparison to those of their normally achieving peers, are typically shorter; contain more errors in spelling, punctuation, and capitalization; lack organization; are less cohesive; omit important genre components; and are lower in overall quality (for reviews see Englert, Raphael, L. M. Anderson, Gregg, & Anthony, 1989; Graham, Harris, MacArthur, & Schwartz, 1991).

Computers and Writing Instruction

Computers have been used in a variety of ways to support writing, to compensate for writing difficulties, and to provide instruction in component writing skills. This section begins with a review of research on the use of word processing with students with disabilities including studies that compared word processing to handwriting, studies that combined word processing with special instruction, and studies that focused on revising. We continue with discussions of studies of several types of software that supplement word processing, including spelling checkers, graphics and multimedia, and word prediction. We conclude with a summary of research on computer use in spelling instruction.

Word Processing

Word processors have several key features that may affect writing processes, particularly for individuals with writing problems (MacArthur, 1988, 1996). First, their editing power makes revision possible without tedious recopying, thus potentially encouraging more revision. Furthermore, students may be more likely to focus first on content and then revision. Second, editing power combined with desktop-publishing features make it possible to produce attractive published papers with minimal errors. Third, the visibility of the screen together with the use of typing rather than handwriting may facilitate collaboration among students. Two students can work together at a computer sharing the task of composing because both can see the work in progress and write sections without handwriting identifying their separate contributions. However, word processing is not as familiar to most students and may slow text production. One difficulty in conducting research on word processing is that the results are often confounded by students' limited typing skill.

One approach to studying the effects of word processing is to have students write compositions via word processing and handwriting, permitting carefully controlled studies that isolate the effects of word processing as a means of producing text. Vacc (1987) used this approach to study the impact of word processing on letter writing by eighth-grade students with mild mental disabilities. Four students wrote a series of letters following a single-subject, ABAB design with six letters in each phase and the order of condition counterbalanced. With word processing, students composed more slowly, wrote fewer words, and made more minor revisions. However, no consistent differences were found in overall quality of writing.

MacArthur and Graham (1987) compared composing by fifth- and sixth-grade students with learning disabilities under three conditions: handwriting, word processing, and dictation. Although students composed more slowly with word processing, the final drafts of papers written with a word processor did not differ from those written by hand on any of the measures used in the study including overall quality, length, story structure, vocabulary, syntactic complexity, or errors in spelling, capitalization, and punctuation. Furthermore, no differences were found in the number or type of revisions made although there was a difference in when revisions were made. With word processing, students made more revisions as they wrote the first draft, whereas nearly all revisions with handwriting were made on the second draft.

As part of an evaluation of a computer-based writing curriculum, MacArthur, Graham, Schwartz, and Shafer (1995) randomly assigned 113 students with learning disabilities in 12 classes, who had received writing instruction including regular use of word processing for a full year, to complete posttest writing samples via handwriting or word processing. No significant differences were found between word-processed and handwritten compositions in overall quality, length, or proportions of spelling, capitalization, and punctuation errors.

Thus, the available evidence indicates that word processing, in comparison to handwriting, results in a slower composing rate and increases the number of minor revisions made during composing but has little impact on the quality of writing. Although these studies were well designed, they raise questions of interpretation. First, it is not clear how much of the observed differences in rate were due to differences between typing and handwriting speed and how much to increased rereading and revision while composing with a word processor. It is interesting that the slower composing rates associated with word processing did not result in writing of lower quality. Other research has shown correlations between handwriting speed and writing quality for elementary school students and for students with learning disabilities at all ages (for a review see Graham et al., 1997). Perhaps, the negative effect of a slower composing rate was balanced by other factors favoring word processing, such as increased motivation and revision.

Word Processing and Typing Instruction. One study attempted to answer questions about typing proficiency by comparing students who received practice using word processing over 20 weeks with two other groups who received either typing instruction and word processing or an alternative keyboard with letters arranged alphabetically (Lewis, Graves, Ashton, & Kieley, 1998). Students wrote more slowly with word processing than with handwriting, and neither typing instruction nor the alternative keyboard increased composing speed. Unfortunately, the study did not collect data on how much time the students devoted to typing instruction, so it is impossible to tell whether the typing instruction was ineffective or the students simply did not practice enough. Furthermore, despite random assignment, groups differed significantly on pretest handwriting speed, and covariance was not used to correct for these differences. Thus, it is still unknown whether students who had received instruction that equalized typing and handwriting speed would write better with a word processor than by hand.

Word Processing and Writing Instruction. A second problem of interpretation in the word-processing studies is that they do not answer questions about the effect of using word processing in instruction. Perhaps, word processing has a positive effect only when combined with writing instruction that takes advantage of its power. A meta-analysis by Bangert-Drowns (1993) found that use of word processing in writing instruction programs produced a positive though relatively modest impact on students' writing. However, this analysis included no studies involving students with disabilities.

One study examined the effects of word processing in combination with writing instruction for students with learning disabilities (MacArthur et al., 1995). This study evaluated the effectiveness of a model of writing instruction that integrated word processing, strategy instruction, and a process approach. The experimental model was implemented in 12 elementary school classes for students with learning disabilities for a full school year. Students in the experimental classes made greater gains in the quality of their narrative and informative writing than students in 10 control classes who received a process approach to writing without computers or strategy instruction. Although this study established the effectiveness of the overall instructional model, it did not isolate the effects of word processing. Thus, it is not possible to know whether the effects were due to word processing, strategy instruction, or additional staff development on process writing.

Word Processing and Revising. Three studies have investigated the possibility that word processing in combination with instruction in revising can increase the amount and quality of revising and improve the overall quality of writing by students with learning disabilities (Graham & MacArthur, 1988; MacArthur, Schwartz, & Graham, 1991; Stoddard & MacArthur, 1992). Graham and MacArthur used a multiple-probe design across students to evaluate a strategy for revising opinion essays among elementary students. Instruction had a positive effect on the number of revisions made as well as on the length and quality of compositions and students' self-efficacy.

The other two studies investigated a peer-revising strategy (MacArthur et al., 1991; Stoddard & MacArthur, 1992). Students with learning disabilities wrote papers on a word processor and then met in pairs to discuss papers following a strategy that specified the roles of author and peer and included specific evaluation criteria. The first study (Stoddard & MacArthur, 1992) used a multiple-probe design with four pairs of seventh-grade students. Baseline and posttest probes required students to write and revise papers independently. For all students, instruction had positive effects on the number and quality of revisions and quality of the final draft. The second study (MacArthur et al., 1991) used a quasi-experimental design within a larger study of word processing and writing instruction. Three classes were randomly assigned to the treatment condition, and two were assigned to a control condition that included word processing and peer-revising groups but no strategy instruction. Compared to the control group, students who received strategy instruction made more and better revisions and improved the quality of their papers. However, these results did not generalize to revising without a partner.

Another study (Hine, Goldman, & Cosden, 1990) focused on the impact of collaborative writing on editing of errors in spelling and grammar. As part of a summer computer program, 11 students with mild educational disabilities, Grades 3 to 7, alternated writing independently and in pairs, using a word processor. Students were directed to revise their first drafts, but no instruction was provided. Students who were poor spellers corrected significantly more errors in the paired condition; better spellers did about the same in solo and paired conditions. As anticipated, error correction was limited by the skill of the better speller in the pair.

All of these studies focused on instruction in strategies for revising or the role of collaboration in revising rather than on the word processor itself. Although word processing removes a physical and motivational barrier to revising, it is possible that the revising strategies would work without a word processor. The studies did not address this question.

Spelling Checkers

Research on spelling checkers and students with writing disabilities has focused on demonstrating their potential utility and, more important, on understanding their limitations. MacArthur and his colleagues (MacArthur,

Graham, Haynes, & DeLaPaz, 1996) studied the use of a spelling checker with 27 middle school students with learning disabilities who had moderate to severe spelling problems. They misspelled 4% to 35% of their words in compositions. Unaided, they corrected 9% of their errors; with the spelling checker, they corrected 37% of their errors.

Although this study showed that spelling checkers improve spelling in students' written compositions, it also revealed they have important limitations. Of most concern, they fail to identify a word that is spelled correctly but is not the word a student intended to write, including homonyms and other real words (e.g., *back* for *bake*). In the MacArthur et al. (1996) study, 37% of students' misspellings were not identified for this reason, accounting for more than half of the uncorrected errors. A second serious limitation is that spelling checkers fail to suggest the correct spelling for many words, especially severe misspellings. In the MacArthur et al. study, the spelling checker failed to suggest the correct spelling for 42% of identified errors (or 26% of all errors). Different checkers vary widely in their ability to suggest the correct word. In a comparative study of 10 spelling checkers (MacArthur et al., 1996), performance on suggesting the correct spelling ranged from 46% to 66% of the identified errors; on severe misspellings, performance ranged from 16% to 41%.

McNaughton and colleagues (McNaughton, Hughes, & Ofiesh, 1997) designed an instructional strategy to overcome the limitations of spelling checkers. High school students with learning disabilities were taught strategies for generating additional suggestions when the intended word was not in the list of suggestions (e.g., type a phonetic spelling). They also learned to proofread a hard copy looking for errors the spelling checker missed because they were other real words. The strategy was studied using a multiple baseline design across three students; improvements in percentage of errors corrected and final error rate were found for all students.

Graphics and Multimedia

The capability to combine graphics, sound, and video with writing may enhance motivation, support generation of content, and compensate for limited writing ability. Using multimedia for writing has potential drawbacks as well. Creation of graphics and sounds may detract from attention to the written text and time spent writing and revising.

Only one experimental study was found that investigated the impact of multimedia on writing. Bahr, Nelson, and Van Meter (1996) investigated the effect of graphics-based computer writing software on the writing of fourth- through eighth-grade students with learning disabilities. The software allowed students to create graphic scenes and then type stories about them. The authors compared this software to text-based planning software that presented story grammar questions. No significant differences were found on measures of length or quality of written compositions. However, direct comparison of the quality of the text produced in the two conditions is problematic because judgments of the quality of multimedia should consider how text and graphics work together. It is difficult to imagine what measures of overall quality could be applied equally to text and multimedia documents. Furthermore, findings of no difference in this study should be interpreted with caution because the study used a repeated measures design with only nine students and, thus, had limited statistical power to detect differences.

Word Prediction

Although word prediction software was originally developed to reduce the number of keystrokes required to type words for individuals with physical disabilities, it may also have potential for students with serious spelling problems. Briefly, word prediction programs work as follows: As the user types the initial letters of a word, the program predicts the intended word and offers a list of possibilities. If the intended word is in the list, the user can select it rather than typing it, thus, reducing keystrokes and avoiding some spelling problems. The software often incorporates speech synthesis, which reads written text and predicted word choices. Programs vary in size of vocabulary, sophistication of prediction algorithms, and interface design.

The Lewis et al. study (1998), which looked at the effect of typing instruction and alternative keyboards on text entry speed, also included two word prediction conditions, one with speech synthesis and one without. Word prediction with speech was substantially slower than word processing, though word prediction without speech did not differ from word processing. Surprisingly, word prediction did not result in significantly fewer spelling errors. It is possible that students did not make much use of the word prediction features; no data were collected on extent of use.

MacArthur conducted three studies of word prediction using single-subject designs with 9- and 10-year-old students with learning disabilities and severe spelling problems. In the first study (MacArthur, 1998), five students wrote dialogue journals with their teachers over the course of a full year. In the baseline condition, students wrote with a standard word processor. During treatment phases, students used a word processor with speech synthesis and word prediction. The dictionary in the word prediction software began with 300 common words. Every word used by the teacher was automatically added to the dictionary for easy use by the student in responding. Likewise, words used by the student appeared in the dictionary with correct spelling. Thus, the dictionary was individually tailored to the writing of each student, and the small size of the dictionary made it relatively easy for students to identify the desired word from the list of predictions. The treatment had a strong effect on the readability and spelling of written dialogue journal entries for four of the five students in the study. During baseline, the writing of these four students ranged from 55% to 85% readable words and 42% to 75% correctly spelled words. All four increased their percentage of both readable and correctly spelled words into the 90% to 100% range.

The second study (MacArthur, 1999) used word prediction software with a dictionary of 10,000 words and a more sophisticated prediction algorithm. Three students wrote in daily journals in an alternating treatments design using three conditions—handwriting, word processing, and word prediction. The alternating treatments design revealed no impact of writing condition on the readability or spelling of students' writing, except for spelling by one student. Two explanations were offered for different effects in the two studies. First, the vocabulary list in the program used in Study 2 was larger and less specifically focused on the words used in the journal. The benefits of this larger vocabulary might not be evident given the rather limited vocabulary used by students in their journals. Second, the program was more sophisticated and powerful and required greater attention, effort, and motivation on the part of the students than the program used in Study 1.

To address the issues of vocabulary and motivation, MacArthur conducted a follow-up study using the same students and writing conditions but with a controlled writing task in a controlled environment. Students wrote from dictation using selections from graded reading passages at their instructional reading level. It was hypothesized that the benefits of the word prediction software with a large vocabulary would be evident when the writing task demanded that students spell more difficult words and classroom distractions were removed. Under these conditions, word prediction clearly improved legibility and spelling for two of the three students.

The importance of tailoring the vocabulary to the writing task is confirmed by another study of a special writing program that included a feature closely related to word prediction—word lists with speech synthesis that could be accessed by first letter (Zhang, Brooks, Frields, & Redelfs, 1995). The word lists contained 1,000 common words, words related to classroom themes, and words selected by individual students. Students with learning disabilities in Grades 2 to 5 were randomly assigned within grade to use handwriting, a word processor, or the special writing tool. Students using the special writing program produced papers rated higher in quality and with fewer spelling and grammatical errors than students in either of the other conditions.

Based on the few studies available, it appears that word prediction can make a difference for some students with severe writing problems, but that success depends on the design of the particular tool, the match between the tool and the writing task, and the motivation and skills of individual students in using complex tools.

Spelling Instruction

Studies have investigated a variety of questions about CAI in spelling. As discussed earlier, researchers from the Netherlands (van Daal & van der Leij, 1992) investigated one instructional design issue for spelling CAI, that is, whether it is better to practice words by copying them while they are displayed on the screen or by typing them from memory after display. In a study with elementary school students with writing disabilities, they found that copying words from the screen was superior to typing words from memory. The authors acknowledged that that a longer study might find that copying is best for initial acquisition whereas typing from memory is better for later practice, but this hypothesis awaits further investigation.

Constant time delay (CTD) procedures provide the opportunity for students to copy words until they are ready to write them from memory. CAI programs that use CTD initially pronounce a word with speech synthesis and display it on the screen for students to copy. Once students can copy the word correctly, its presentation on the screen is delayed for a set time period, giving students the opportunity to type the word from memory. If they cannot do so, they wait for the word to be displayed. Three studies of spelling CAI based on CTD procedures used multiple-probe designs across sets of words with a 12-year-old boy with a severe spelling problem (Kinney, Stevens, & Schuster, 1988), elementary students with mild disabilities (Stevens, Blackhurst, & Slaton, 1991), and high school students with learning disabilities or mild mental disabilities (Edwards, Blackhurst, & Koorland, 1995). All three studies found that all students learned the words to at least 90% accuracy. These studies demonstrate that students with spelling problems can learn spelling from CAI using CTD. However, the studies do not provide information about how this method compares to other methods; further research is needed to make this vital comparison.

MacArthur and his colleagues (MacArthur, Haynes, Malouf, Harris, & Owings, 1990) compared CAI to paper-and-pencil instruction (PPI) as means of delivering independent spelling practice for students with learning disabilities. The CAI and PPI programs differed in instructional design based on the capabilities of the two media (e.g., immediate feedback vs. delayed feedback, typing vs. handwriting). Significant achievement differences favoring the CAI group were found on weekly tests and a retention test. In addition, the CAI group had a higher engagement rate, and engagement accounted for about half of the group difference in achievement.

Other studies have attempted to isolate the effect of handwriting versus typing on a computer during spelling practice, with conflicting results. Cunningham and Stanovich (1990) hypothesized that the motor act of handwriting during spelling practice was important to learning. In an initial study and a replication, first-grade normally achieving students practiced different words under three conditions: handwriting, typing on a computer, and using letter tiles to form words. In both studies, students learned the words practiced by handwriting considerably better than those practiced in the other conditions.

Vaughn, Schumm, and Gordon (1992, 1993) attempted to replicate the Cunningham and Stanovich (1990) studies and extend them to students with learning disabilities. However, the first replication (Vaughn, Schumm, & Gordon, 1992) found no differences either for normally achieving students or students with learning disabilities. The second study (Vaughn, Schumm, & Gordon, 1993) replicated the Cunningham and Stanovich studies but with more intensive practice of the words. Again, no differences were found among conditions. Berninger and her colleagues (Berninger et al., 1998) also compared handwriting and word processing as means of practicing spelling within an instructional program that emphasized orthographic and phonological representations. No main effect of computer/handwriting condition was found, although handwriting was superior for learning easier words.

All of these studies comparing handwriting and typing were carefully designed, and no convincing explanation was offered for the disparate findings. One confound is that any differences obtained between handwriting and typing might be due to the need to search for letters on the keyboard rather than motor learning. Berninger and her colleagues (Berninger et al., 1998) attempted to address this possibility by having a research assistant point out the location of the keys to students, but this solution at best only partially resolved the problem. Results might be quite different for students who were familiar with the keyboard.

Although Berninger et al. (1998) found minimal difference between typing and handwriting, overall, students made gains both on the words taught and on a standardized test of spelling. The authors concluded that teaching orthographic and phonological representations made a larger difference than response mode. This finding points out an important limitation of all the preceding studies; that is, they treated spelling as rote learning instead of recognizing that students learn to spell, in part, by developing sound–symbol associations and knowledge of orthographic patterns (Treiman, 1993).

Wise and R. K. Olson (1992) directly addressed this instructional issue by developing CAI that used the speech synthesis capabilities of computers to allow students to explore orthographic and phonological representations as they attempted to spell words. They compared two versions of a spelling program, both of which presented words via speech synthesis and provided visual feedback on students' attempts to spell the words. One version pronounced only whole words. The other pronounced students' attempts to spell the word with the expectation that this feedback would focus attention on sound–symbol relationships. The results were inconclusive. In the first phase of the study, students receiving speech feedback performed better on spelling and on reading related nonwords. However, when the groups switched conditions for Phase 2, no differences were found. Further research is needed to pursue these potentially important findings. In general, research is needed on the design of CAI that teaches spelling as a process of learning orthographic and phonological representations rather than as a rote learning process.

LITERACY, TECHNOLOGY, AND SEVERE COGNITIVE DISABILITIES

In this section, we turn our attention to research that bears directly on issues related to the development of literacy skills in students and young adults with severe cognitive disabilities. Because of the complexity and diversity of needs that characterize this population, its members have long been considered to present the greatest challenge for educators seeking to foster literacy competence.

Many authorities in the field of literacy have asserted that for persons with severe disabilities to be successful in educational, vocational, and home environments in today's society, their access to written communication via reading and writing is essential (A. K. Smith, Thurston, Light, Parnes, & O'Keefe, 1989). Although communication systems that employ nonorthographic symbol systems are important alternatives, most speaking persons are not familiar with them. Learning to read and spell written language maximizes the potential for communication and participation in school and community life (Berninger & Gans, 1986).

Descriptive/observational studies of literacy and young students with severe disabilities suggest that their literacy-related experiences are quantitatively and qualitatively different than those of their nondisabled peers (Koppenhaver & Yoder, 1993; Light & McNaughton, 1993; Mike, 1995; M. M. Smith, 1992). It appears that the nature of their disabilities, the range of activities in which their caregivers engage them, and the environments that they inhabit often do not support the emergence of literacy (Koppenhaver, Coleman, Kalman, & Yoder, 1991). For example, students with speech impairments must learn to read without being able to orally communicate clearly with their parents or teachers, and students with physical impairments must learn to write despite difficulties in holding a pencil (Erickson, Koppenhaver, Yoder, & Nance, 1997).

Students with severe disabilities appear to receive less literacy instruction than do their nondisabled peers. When they do receive such instruction, their "participation" is primarily passive and interaction with their nondisabled peers during instruction is practically nonexistent. Literacy instruction for this population is marked by frequent and regular interruptions (Koppenhaver & Yoder, 1993). Due to a limited range of experiences, their knowledge of the world is probably severely limited and the process by which they learn language is probably markedly different (Foley, 1993). Furthermore, these students might possess a basic inefficiency in generating phonological codes. For students with severe disabilities, parents prioritize literacy much lower than their physical and other health needs; as a result, they have limited exposure to and opportunities to engage in various meaningful reading and writing activities (Light & McNaughton, 1993; Light & A. K. Smith, 1993; Rankin, Harwood, & Mirenda, 1994).

Given this very different developmental context, the instructional goals and objectives for students with severe disabilities are often more wide-ranging and typically more functional than those for students with mild disabilities. These goals and objectives are typically founded on the student's situational needs and prevailing task demands. As a result, researchers concerned with the literacy needs of students with severe disabilities have primarily—though not exclusively—directed their efforts toward research questions that are more pragmatic than those for other populations. In addressing this challenging area, a number of literacy investigators have begun to turn to assistive technologies as potential tools in accomplishing the clinical goals.

The Role of Assistive Technology

The availability of assistive technologies in and of themselves, of course, is not a panacea for these difficulties. The introduction of assistive technology into the reading and writing process adds its own complications. The use of augmentative communications systems, for example, typically imposes slow rates of communication, restricted vocabularies, the need for active participation by communication partners in constructing messages, and divided attention by teacher and student between the reading-and-writing activities and the need for continual repair of message breakdowns (Koppenhaver & Yoder, 1993). In sum, though technology can enhance opportunities for literacy and communication, it also can interfere with the central learner task of constructing meaning (Koppenhaver & Yoder, 1993). These challenges highlight the importance of developing effective literacy curricula and instructional methods for using technology to teach and augment the literacy skills of students with severe disabilities. There is ample evidence to support the contention that mere access to a computer does not guarantee improvements in an individual's ability to communicate (A. K. Smith et al., 1989).

Using the search techniques outlined previously, we located only seven experimental studies investigating issues related to literacy, technology, and severe cognitive disabilities. The primary research questions or hypotheses addressed in these seven studies fall largely into either of two categories: (a) evaluation of alternate access to text production tools (Osguthorpe & Chang, 1987, 1988) and (b) evaluation of different instructional methods for text comprehension and production skills (Dube, McDonald, McIlvane, & Mackay, 1991; McNaughton & Tawney, 1993; Stromer & Mackay, 1992, 1993; Wright & M. Anderson, 1987).

Evaluation of Alternate Access to Text Production Tools.   Osguthorpe and Chang (1987, 1988) trained participants to use a symbol processor, which consisted of a word processor that employed a graphics tablet with Rebus picture symbols, rather than keys, as its input mode and standard text as its output. The software was designed to permit the user to select picture symbols from the tablet, view the selection in both picture and word form on the monitor, and edit and print the communication (Osguthorpe & Chang, 1987). The first study (Osguthorpe & Chang, 1987) evaluated students' speed and accuracy in creating written communications with the symbol processor as accessed through either an Apple graphics tablet or a PowerPad. Twelve students with moderate to profound mental retardation, aged 7 to 16, participated in the study. During a 7-week treatment phase, half of the sample used the PowerPad for 20-minute sessions, three times per week. The other half used the graphics tablet. Midway through the study, students switched to the alternate communication board (graphics tablet or PowerPad). Working individually with a proctor, students received two to three training sessions in writing with the device and then were encouraged to write expressively about self-selected topics and audiences. Students' speed and accuracy in mastering Rebus symbols and using the board were assessed through tests in which students re-created on the computer sentences that were displayed on cards.

Osguthorpe and Chang (1987) reported that each group improved in speed and accuracy on each of the boards. Graphs of students' weekly speed and error rates in reproducing the test sentences showed steady improvements in both variables over time. The authors found that, when students switched communication boards, they experienced only slight, temporary decrements in speed and increases in error rates. They also reported that students were enthusiastic about using the systems and did not want to end their free expression sessions. Furthermore, teacher questionnaires and parent interviews showed that both types of respondents believed the system was motivating to students and improved their communication skills and attitudes. Although the authors stated that "most of them [students] produced understandable communications after a few sessions of practicing free expression," (p. 46), no systematic analyses of these data were reported.

In their second study (Osguthorpe & Chang, 1988), 43 students used the software with a PowerPad and Apple IIe computers. Participants were selected from two self-contained day schools for students with mental disabilities and a residential institution for individuals with severe and multiple disabilities. Students were randomly assigned, within school, to experimental or control groups. Following an unspecified period of instruction, the treatment group used the system approximately 15 to 20 minutes per day for 4 days per week over a span of 8 weeks. The control group participated in regular classroom instruction, which was not described. Nor do the authors explain whether participation in the experimental condition replaced or supplemented typical classroom instruction for these students. Pre- and posttest measures included the procedure used in Osguthorpe and Chang (1987) to assess speed and accuracy in mastering Rebus symbols, a standardized test of language comprehension, a Rebus symbol recognition test, and parent and teacher questionnaires and interviews.

Students who used the symbol processor made significantly more progress in language comprehension, although the magnitude of gains for experimental students varied among participating schools. Experimental students learned significantly more Rebus symbols than control students, which is not surprising given that control students did not receive instruction that would enable them to improve on this measure. The authors contended that speed and error rates in reproducing sentences underwent an "obvious improvement" for 86% of the experimental group and that some students made "substantial progress" in free expression. However, data to support these conclusions were not presented. Half of the teachers and 73% of the parents surveyed believed that the experimental students had made gains in language comprehension.

Although these studies offer convincing results about students' potential to learn to use an alternate text production system, the impact that such a system might have on the target behavior of written communication is less clear. Although improvement on language comprehension was impressive for some participants in the Osguthorpe and Chang (1987) study, the significance of these findings is limited by lack of information about the type of instruction provided to the control group, the type and frequency of response prompts that participants required in order to respond correctly, and the number of participants who were able to respond prompt-free by the end of the study. Furthermore, one of the main research questions that Osguthorpe and Chang (1988) investigated dealt with potential improvements in written communication, yet their only measures of writing were informal "comparisons" of writing samples at the beginning and end of the study by an "evaluator" who used some unspecified procedure. Unfortunately, both studies included only those participants "who might benefit from the symbol processor training" as recommended by their teachers. The use of such a vague criterion compromises the generalizability of the results.

Instructional Methods for Improving Text Comprehension and Production. The investigations of Dube et al. (1991) and Stromer and Mackay (1992, 1993) are part of a long-standing and systematic program of behavior analytic research initiated by Sidman and Stoddard at the Eunice Kennedy Shriver Center. The program focuses, in part, on a population of students who have proven to be typically very difficult to teach with conventional methods of instruction, that is, students with severe mental retardation. The general instructional procedure is one of matching-to-sample: A sample stimulus (e.g., a picture of a dog) is displayed along with two or more comparison stimuli (e.g., a picture of a dog and a picture of a cow) and the task is to choose the correct comparison. One of the comparison stimuli is always defined as correct. Successful "identity matching" consists of selecting the comparison stimulus that is identical to the sample (e.g., the picture of the dog). Matching printed words to their dictated names is considered by the investigators to be a rudimentary form of auditory receptive reading and matching printed words to their pictures is considered a rudimentary form of reading comprehension. The power in this paradigm lies not only in its demonstrated ability to teach students with severe retardation these relationships but also in the large number of new relationships that emerge in these participants without explicit teaching.

Dube et al. (1991) and Stromer and Mackay (1992, 1993) transferred an enhanced version of the traditional matching-to-sample procedure to a Macintosh computer with touch screen. In this "constructed-response" matching-to-sample procedure, the student's selection of a comparison stimulus (a word) is constructed by selecting in sequence its individual components (its letters). For example, a subject might be presented a picture of a bird as a sample and an array of comparison stimuli consisting of the letters D-S-R-O- L-I-N-B. The correct response would be to select the letters B-I-R-D in their proper order. In this way, the subject would learn not only to identify words but also to spell them.

In these three studies, investigators examined the following research questions: (a) would participants' acquisition of identity matching using a personal computer system and touch screen be comparable to the learning that had been achieved in numerous previous investigations with traditional (nonelectronic) instructional materials? (b) would the acquisition of identity matching to complex visual stimulus samples engender successful spelling performance and create equivalence classes? (c) would participants be able to spell correctly words that were dictated to them? and (d) would their spelling skills generalize to a more standard written spelling mode, to an oral spelling mode, and to reading printed words?

Dube et al. (1991), using a prompt-fading procedure, successfully taught generalized identity matching and constructed-response spelling to two young men with mental retardation who had mental age equivalent scores of approximately 4 years on the Peabody Picture Vocabulary Test (PPVT). Stromer and Mackay (1993) extended these findings in a study with two participants with mental retardation and PPVT mental age scores of less than 6 years. The authors taught "delayed" matching-to-sample (i.e., the sample disappeared before the comparisons were presented) in which some of the trials involved complex sample stimuli consisting of a picture and a printed word. After participants learned to spell the words via letter construction, spelling to dictated words emerged. One of the participant's data suggested that rudimentary written spelling, oral spelling, and oral naming might have also emerged.

Wright and M. Anderson (1987) compared the relative effectiveness of (a) CAI, (b) teacher instruction, and (c) seatwork on "numbers" (a control condition) on the acquisition of a sight word reading vocabulary. In the CAI condition, students used a specially designed software program that presented the target word in color and response choices in the form of words or pictures. After a correct response, the program "spoke" the target word via synthesized speech, displayed a picture of the target word, and played a short tune. In the teacher-directed condition, students learned sight vocabulary through a systematic procedure that entailed matching flashcards with pictures, pointing to flashcards with the target word, and then reading flashcards. Participants were from a special school, aged 4 to 18 years, had basic sight vocabularies of less than 20 words, and obtained an average age of 2–7 years on the British Picture Vocabulary Scale. Students were purportedly matched across the three conditions, but the authors reported no data to verify the comparability of the groups.

Using a pretest–posttest design, the researchers obtained no significant differences between CAI and teacher instruction of sight words, but the trend favored the teacher condition. Subanalyses revealed the interesting finding that participants with higher IQs performed better than participants with lower IQs with CAI, whereas participants with lower IQs per-formed better than those with higher IQs in the teacher instruction con-dition. One limitation of this study is group differences in the administration of dependent measures. A daily sight word vocabulary test was given to each of the two experimental groups. However, for some unspecified reason, the control group did not receive daily tests. Thus, the control group did not receive the benefit of any possible cueing or sensi-tivity that daily tests might have provided.

Using an alternating treatments design with replication across subjects, McNaughton and Tawney (1993) compared the relative effectiveness of teaching students to spell via (a) a student-directed cueing (SDC) method, (b) a copy-write-compare (CWC) method, and (c) a no-treatment control condition. They also compared these conditions on participants' retention of spelling skills. The participants were two young adults with cerebral palsy who used TouchTalker and LightTalker augmentative communica-tion aids to provide their responses. These participants had age equiva-lent scores of approximately 5 and 12 years on the PPVT.

The authors reported equivalent effectiveness between the SDC method and the CWC method in teaching spelling, whereas the SDC method was associated with better retention of the newly acquired words. However, the results were severely constrained by ceiling effects on both measures.

In summary, the number of published experimental studies about lit-eracy, technology, and severe cognitive disabilities is extremely small. Thus, it is not surprising that the questions that have commanded the interest of researchers barely "scratch the surface" of issues that are important to a fuller understanding of the potential benefit of assistive technology in the acquisition of literacy skills by students and adults with severe cognitive disabilities. The questions that have thus far been addressed only begin to map out fundamental issues related to access to literacy tools, acquisition of initial sight word "reading" vocabularies, and acquisition of initial "spelling" vocabularies. The studies reviewed herein are best viewed as provocative, albeit fragmented, glimpses of what might be possible if more systematic research efforts were devoted to the impor-tant issues in literacy with this population. They are the initial voyages through relatively uncharted waters in pursuit of empirical evidence that might be used to guide the design and implementation of effective pro-grammatic clinical interventions.

Although limited, the existing knowledge base derived from experi-mental and descriptive research has value not only in increasing aware-ness of the importance of literacy issues, but also in helping to define important questions and issues to be addressed in future research endeav-ors. A fundamental question, with important instructional and evaluative implications, involves the determination of assessment protocols that yield valid and reliable measurement of the reading fluency and comprehension skills and the written communication skills of students and adults with severe disabilities (A. K. Smith et al., 1989). Basic questions remain about the processes by which people with severe disabilities acquire literacy skills. For example, can phonological awareness be taught to students with severe speech or cognitive impairments and, if so, to what degree will direct and systematic training in phonological awareness in early childhood offset the significant reading and spelling problems that they typically exhibit (Blischak, 1994; Foley, 1993)? Can literacy instruction be improved by further research to determine the most effective direct intervention strategies for literacy learning by children and adults with severe disabilities (Koppenhaver & Yoder, 1993; A. K. Smith et al., 1989)? A related issue requiring attention is the degree to which activities designed to increase the automaticity of word recognition, such as computer-assisted drill and practice, can facilitate reading comprehension by students with severe disabilities (Foley, 1993). More generally, the field will benefit from additional programmatic research about the appropriate role of assistive technology in the development and instruction of literacy skills (Foley, 1993).

Similarly, a number of questions about adaptations to text and technology-based communication systems await investigation. These include studies that seek effective means for making print materials accessible to students with severe disabilities (Koppenhaver et al., 1991) and that examine ways that adaptations of print materials alter the nature of the learning process for students with severe disabilities (Koppenhaver et al., 1991). Few studies to date have investigated the process differences in reading (interpreting) graphic symbol communications and generating graphic symbol communications, and how they are associated with reading and writing traditional orthography (Rankin et al., 1994). And we still know little about the instructional design and human-factors considerations for optimal use of computers and other assistive technologies by students and adults with severe disabilities for literacy learning and performance. It will be especially important to determine how the sensory, physical, and cognitive demands of these assistive technologies interact with their specific disabilities (A. K. Smith et al., 1989).

SUMMARY AND CONCLUSIONS

In this chapter, we reviewed a body of experimental studies investigating the impact of technology-based applications on the literacy learning and literacy-related behaviors of students with disabilities. Before offering our conclusions, we wish to remind the reader that our definition of literacy was restricted to reading and writing text. Thus our focus has been on the ways in which technology can contribute to the development of students' print-based literacy. Furthermore, we circumscribed the studies reviewed by focusing on students with cognitive and learning disabilities and by examining only experimental studies published in peer-reviewed journals or edited books published in 1984 or later.

One criticism of the body of research on literacy, technology, and disabilities, as a whole, is the lack of systematic, programmatic research. With a few notable exceptions (e.g., Olson, Wise, and colleagues; MacArthur and colleagues; Torgesen and colleagues), there are few programmatic lines of research that can help us develop confident conclusions about how technology affects literacy learning and instruction. The quality of research in special education has come under scrutiny in recent years (Carnine, 1997; Gersten, Lloyd, & Baker, 1998). We agree that the field would benefit from improved research quality in the area of technology and literacy. Some common limitations in the research reviewed herein include sample sizes that limit the power of statistical tests and the validity of conclusions that researchers nevertheless chose to make, unsophisticated statistical analyses, and studies of limited duration. Furthermore, we often found insufficient information about the intervention or comparison conditions, characteristics of the sample, and the measures used to assess outcomes. Finally, individual differences that may have affected outcomes were rarely investigated in their own right.

As Clark (1983) cautioned us nearly two decades ago, it is not the technology itself that accounts for learning gains but rather the instructional design of the software and lessons accompanying them. Indeed, for the most part, we were pleased to note that the research reviewed herein has moved beyond media comparisons, in which poorly specified technology-based interventions are contrasted with traditional instruction. Most researchers either explicitly discussed specific instructional design features that were hypothesized to facilitate outcomes or compared different instructional features for their impact on student learning.

The body of research about technology and word identification is the methodologically strongest and most programmatic work reviewed in this chapter. It provides qualified support for the efficacy of technology-based interventions for the improvement of word identification skills. These interventions most frequently involve the provision of synthetic speech feedback to students upon request when reading isolated words (e.g., van Daal & Reitsma, 1990, 1993; Wise, 1992; Wise et al., 1990) or words in meaningful contexts (e.g., R. K. Olson & Wise, 1992; R. Olson et al., 1986; Wise et al., 1989). Practice in reading isolated words with speech feedback is often associated with improvements in students' phonological analysis skills (Beck & Roth, 1984a, 1984b; van Daal & Reitsma, 1990, 1993; van Daal & van der Leij, 1992; Wise, 1992; Wise et al., 1990). In general, these effects are most robust for outcome measures that require students to decode nonwords or words that are phonetically regular, that is, words that can be decoded by the application of the alphabetic principle. Training usually involves feedback for words that are phonetically regular, so assessing students' phonological analysis skills with irregular words or nonwords that do not conform to the alphabetic principle usually results in less favorable outcomes. Comprehension was rarely assessed in these studies because the interventions were clearly focused on improvements in word identification.

Roth and Beck (1987) reported that students' comprehension of words that were used in training improved as the result of practice reading with speech feedback. However, there is no evidence that practice in reading isolated words with speech feedback leads to general improvements in comprehension as gauged by standardized measures of reading comprehension.

The findings about the effects of reading words in meaningful contexts with speech feedback mirror those reported for practice in reading isolated words. In general, the provision of speech feedback for words read in meaningful contexts is associated with improvements in students' phonological word analysis skills (R. Olson et al., 1986; R. K. Olson & Wise, 1992; Wise et al., 1989, 1998). These effects are most pronounced for the decoding of nonwords or words that are phonetically regular.

It is generally believed that reading text for the purpose of understanding is the best way to promote skill and interest in reading (Adams, 1990; R. Anderson et al., 1985). Hence, we might expect that practicing reading in meaningful contexts with speech feedback to be more efficacious in promoting word identification than reading isolated words with speech feedback. Interestingly, we found no direct comparisons of these two approaches in promoting students' phonological word analysis skills.

As we noted earlier, students with reading disabilities often fail to develop good word identification skills from reading experiences that normally involve whole-word feedback. Therefore, it was thought that the provision of synthetic speech feedback at the level of the syllable or subsyllable would enable students with reading disabilities to establish the orthographic–phonemic correspondences for words practiced in isolation or in meaningful contexts (R. K. Olson & Wise, 1992). Contrary to intuitions, the provision of whole-word speech-synthetic feedback is often associated with improvements in word identification that are equal to or better than those obtained with segmented-speech feedback (R. Olson et al., 1986; R. K. Olson & Wise, 1992; van Daal & Reitsma, 1990; Wise, 1992). Moreover, the students with the most severe reading difficulties appear to benefit the least from segmented feedback (R. K. Olson & Wise, 1992). Segmented feedback, especially involving many single-grapheme units, places a great burden on working memory because it requires that students maintain the constituent sounds in memory while blending them in order to create a phonetic representation of the word (Wise, 1992).

We located only two studies that used technology-supported training to promote children's phonological awareness (Barker & J. K. Torgesen, 1995; K. C. Foster et al., 1994). Neither study determined whether improvements in phonological awareness were associated with changes in word identification or reading, or whether computer-supported training in phonological awareness and decoding led to improvements in skilled reading. This is surprising to us for two reasons. First, many studies have demonstrated that training in decoding and phonological awareness prior to reading instruction improves later reading (see Wise et. al., 1998). Second, preexisting individual differences in phonological awareness are highly predictive of students' responsiveness to reading interventions using synthetic speech feedback (R. K. Olson & Wise, 1992; Wise et al., 1998). The potential benefits of technology-supported phonological awareness training on students' skill in word identification and reading await investigation.

Studies examining the impact of technology-based interventions and applications on students' text comprehension yielded mixed findings. We first reviewed a small set of studies demonstrating that computer-based instruction can effectively assist students in learning to associate words with their definitions (e.g., Hebert & Murdock, 1994; G. Johnson et al., 1987; Xin et al., 1996).

We then analyzed a larger body of research investigating students' comprehension of and interaction with electronic text. These studies clearly showed that students' comprehension is similar for passages read on paper and those presented by computer. However, the advantage of electronic text lies not in the medium by which it is presented but in the enhancements to text that technology affords. Researchers examined a number of enhancements, ranging from relatively simple alterations or additions to single passages (e.g., Casteel, 1988–1989; Feldmann & Fish, 1991; Keene & Davey, 1987; Reinking & Schriener, 1985; Swanson & Trahan, 1992) to electronically enhanced stories or textbook passages with multiple levels of reader assistance (e.g., Anderson-Inman & Horney, 1998; Boone & Higgins, 1993; Higgins & Boone, 1991; MacArthur & Haynes, 1995).

This research defies simple conclusions because participants' characteristics, the type of enhancements added to the text, and the purposes for which students used the text differed across studies. Furthermore, the manner in which students used electronic text and electronic study tools appears to vary with learner characteristics and experience, with consequent implications for text comprehension (Anderson-Inman & Horney, 1993; Anderson-Inman et al., 1996; Horney & Anderson-Inman, 1994). In general, the methodologically stronger studies in this section that incorporated several different enhancements for promoting text comprehension offered tentative support for the potential benefits of electronic text (e.g., MacArthur & Haynes, 1995; Reinking, 1988; Reinking & Schreiner, 1985).

Based on our review of studies of speech synthesis as an enhancement to electronic text, we found little evidence that reading in meaningful contexts with speech feedback improves students' comprehension. This appears to be the case whether students select specific words for pronunciation (e.g., Farmer et al., 1992; Wise et al., 1989, 1998) or whether they simultaneously view and listen to computer-presented text (e.g., Elkind et al., 1993; Leong, 1992, 1995). Lack of support for speech feedback is somewhat surprising. If word-level skills are a major barrier to text comprehension, then providing access to those words through digitized or synthesized pronunciations should promote text comprehension. As discussed earlier, however, student characteristics undoubtedly mediate outcomes. For example, students' extant reading and vocabulary skills may partially account for conflicting findings (Elkind, 1998a, 1998b; Elkind et al., 1996). Furthermore, when given the choice to select words for pronunciation, students may not monitor their level of understanding (e.g., Nelson & Narens, 1990) and hence not request assistance when it is actually needed. Students' skill at requesting needed speech feedback may improve with experience (Olofsson, 1992). Direct teacher intervention to help students use enhancements appropriately and teacher-directed discussion of strategies and skills promoted in electronic text may be needed to optimize students' comprehension (e.g., Wise et al., 1998).

Research in the area of writing provides qualified support for the beneficial effects of assistive technology and offers some guidance on what works. Although not extensive, most research has focused on word processing and on tools to support transcription. The research on word processing indicates that simply providing students with word processors will have limited impact (MacArthur & Graham, 1987). However, instruction that takes advantage of the capabilities of technology can help students learn to revise more effectively and improve their writing overall (MacArthur et al., 1995; MacArthur, Schwartz, & Graham, 1991). Spelling checkers clearly help students with spelling problems, and their impact can be increased by instruction designed to compensate for their inherent limitations (MacArthur et al., 1996; McNaughton et al., 1997). Word prediction software can help students compensate for severe spelling problems so that their writing is readable by other people (MacArthur, 1998). We found no experimental studies about the impact of speech synthesis or speech recognition on elementary or secondary students' writing. As the capabilities of speech recognition software improve, it is likely that more research will be published.

One conclusion that emerges from the research on transcription support tools is that such tools create new burdens for users at the same time that they remove other burdens. For example, word processing removes the burden of handwriting, which can be quite significant for some writers, but unless students learn to type, word processing requires attention to typing, slows text production, and may interfere with higher order cognitive processes. Word prediction supports spelling but demands a fairly high level of attention to make use of the list of suggested words (MacArthur, 1999). The design of tools, selection of tools for individual students, and appropriate instruction can moderate these additional burdens.

Other than the work on revising and word processing, very little research has investigated the use of technology to support the problem-solving and social processes involved in writing. One study looked at the effects of graphics as a support for planning but found equivocal results (Bahr et al., 1996). Concept-mapping software has been examined as a support for studying (Anderson-Inman et al., 1996) but not as a tool for planning in writing. Other than the studies of peer revising, we found no experimental studies of collaborative writing. However, we did find a handful of carefully conducted case studies about collaborative writing (Cosden, Goldman, & Hine, 1990; Daiute & Dalton, 1993; Rueda, 1992). The Internet offers exciting possibilities for changing the social context of writing by connecting students with distant audiences and collaborators; but researchers have not explored its potential for students with disabilities.

In the area of technology and severe cognitive disabilities, we located only seven experimental studies. One set of studies (Osguthorpe & Chang, 1987, 1988) demonstrated that students can master communication boards, such as a graphics tablet or the PowerPad, and learn to use Rebus symbols as an alternative form of access to written communication. Although improvements in participants' language comprehension skills were documented, the impact of these communication systems on the primary target of the intervention, written communication, was assessed only through informal and subjective measures. A second set of studies examined a mix of instructional methods for promoting text comprehension and production. Three studies (Dube et al., 1991; Stromer & Mackay, 1992, 1993) provided support for the efficacy of a computer-presented match-to-sample procedure on students' spelling skills. A fourth study (McNaughton & Tawney, 1993) found differential outcomes for two different spelling instructional approaches, whereas a fifth (Wright & M. Anderson, 1987) found no differences between teacher-directed and computer-assisted instruction in sight words.

The lack of programmatic, experimental research is particularly acute in the area of technology for individuals with severe disabilities. In the face of over two decades of unprecedented advances in instructional and compensatory technologies and strategies for their effective use, it is disconcerting that so few experimental research reports have been published. The predominant research methodologies thus far have involved longitudinal case studies of a few participants, surveys, or other similar descriptive techniques. The majority of published papers about technology and literacy for people with severe disabilities are ones that reiterate the importance of literacy involving traditional orthography for this population, speculate about the causes of literacy problems, and describe clinical strategies for the remediation of these problems. Yet, as those speculations continued to be voiced in successive articles and chapters, they became framed as unassailable assertions rather than hypotheses that warranted direct experimental tests. Of course, this premature and unqualified embrace of relatively untested remediation strategies places clinicians and their students at some risk.

As a result of the efforts invested in descriptive/observational studies, however, we now have a rich trove of possible interventions to test and clinical research questions to answer. Furthermore, as technology becomes more sophisticated, new technology-based tools with unprecedented potential to facilitate communication are being developed. The next phase in the advancement of this area should focus on shifting the research balance toward direct experimental validations of these tools and strategies. We strongly encourage this shift.

In conclusion, technology continues to evolve in its power, speed, simplicity, and availability. It will continue to offer more sophisticated tools for facilitating literacy acquisition, enabling literate activities, and circumventing print-based barriers to information and understanding. Special educators seem committed to the use of technology in literacy instruction and believe that it offers many potential benefits for their students (Burton-Radzely, 1998). The research reviewed in this chapter suggests cautious optimism about technology's potential to improve the literacy skills and instruction of students with disabilities. The impact of technology on the literacy of students with disabilities will continue to defy a simple synthesis. Its effects will depend on the characteristics of its design, the instruction that accompanies it, the ways in which it is used, and the characteristics of the students who use it. Further attention to these factors in the design and conduct of future studies will enhance our understanding of technology's advantages and limitations. In addition, we know very little about how educators can integrate and make optimal use of technology as part of a classroom-based program of literacy instruction. Nor do we know much about the long-term effects of technology use. Most studies reviewed in this chapter were conducted over several weeks or months.

Most of the technology-based applications and interventions reviewed in this chapter were designed to circumvent disabilities or enhance existing capabilities. However, these studies remind us that technology introduces new challenges and demands of the user new skills, knowledge, and effort. We need further research that investigates the demands that technology tools place on different types of learners and how we might optimally prepare students to take advantage of their potential. Better designed studies investigating these and other issues are needed to assure that students receive optimal benefits from today's and tomorrow's technologies.

ACKNOWLEDGMENTS

Order of authorship of the second, third, and fourth author is alphabetical.

APPENDIX

In our searches of the electronic databases, we used various combinations and derivatives of the following keywords for the student/participant variable: DISAB*, LEARNING DISAB*, READING DISAB*, MILD DISAB*, MENTAL DISAB*, AT-RISK, SEVERE, PROFOUND, MENTAL, COGNITIVE, MULTIPLE, LANGUAGE, HANDICAP, IMPAIR*, and RETARDATION.

For the topic variable: LITERACY, READING, WRITING, SPELLING, ALPHABET, VOCABULARY, WORD-RECOGNITION, WORD-IDENTIFICATION, COMPREHENSION, PHONETIC, PHONOLOGIC*, and DECODING.

For the technology variable: TECHNOLOGY, VIDEODISC, COMPUTER, MICROCOMPUTER, DEVICE, ELECTRONIC-TEXT, ELECTRONIC-BOOK, COMPUTER-MEDIATED, HYPERTEXT, HYPERMEDIA, CD-ROM, AUGMENTATIVE-COMMUNICATION, WORD-PROCESSING, WORD-PREDICTION, SPELL-CHECKER, and SPELLING-CHECKER.

REFERENCES

Adams, M. J. (1990). *Beginning to read: Thinking and learning about print.* Cambridge, MA: MIT Press.
Anderson, R., Hiebert, E., Scott, J., & Wilkinson, I. (1985). *Becoming a nation of readers: The report of the Commission on Reading.* Washington, DC: The National Institute of Education.

Anderson-Inman, L., & Horney, M. A. (1993, April). *Profiles of hypertext readers: Results from the ElectroText project.* Paper presented at the annual meeting of the American Educational Research Association, Atlanta.

Anderson-Inman, L., & Horney, M. A. (1998). Transforming text for at-risk readers. In D. Reinking, M. C. McKenna, L. D. Labbo, & R. D. Kieffer (Eds.), *Handbook of literacy and technology: Transformations in a post-typographic world* (pp. 15–43). Mahwah, NJ: Lawrence Erlbaum Associates.

Anderson-Inman, L., Horney, M. A., Chen, D., & Lewin, L. (1994). Hypertext literacy: Observations from the ElectroText project. *Language Arts, 71*(4), 37–45.

Anderson-Inman, L., Knox-Quinn, C., & Horney, M. A. (1996). Computer-based study strategies for students with learning disabilities: Individual differences associated with adoption level. *Journal of Learning Disabilities, 29,* 461–484.

Bahr, C. M., Nelson, N. W., & Van Meter, A. (1996). The effects of text-based and graphics-based software tools on planning and organizing stories. *Journal of Learning Disabilities, 29,* 355–370.

Bangert-Drowns, R. L. (1993). The word processor as an instructional tool: A meta-analysis of word processing in writing instruction. *Review of Educational Research, 63,* 69–93.

Barker, T. A., & Torgesen, J. K. (1995). An evaluation of computer-assisted instruction in phonological awareness with below average readers. *Journal of Educational Computing Research, 13*(1), 89–103.

Beck, I. L., & Roth, S. F. (1984a). *Construct-a-Word teachers manual.* Allen, TX: Developmental Learning Materials.

Beck, I. L., & Roth, S. F. (1984b). *Hint and Hunt teachers manual.* Allen, TX: Developmental Learning Materials.

Berninger, V., Abbott, R., Rogan, L., Reed, E., Abbott, S., Brooks, A., Vaughan, K., & Graham, S. (1998). Teaching spelling to children with specific learning disabilities: The mind's ear and eye beat the computer and pencil. *Learning Disability Quarterly, 21,* 106–122.

Berninger, V. W., & Gans, B. M. (1986). Assessing word processing capability of the nonverbal, nonwriting. *Augmentative and Alternative Communication, 2,* 56–63.

Berninger, V. W., & Swanson, H. L. (1994). Modifying Hayes and Flower's model of skilled writing to explain beginning and developing writing. In E. C. Butterfield (Ed.), *Children's writing: Toward a process theory of the development of skilled writing* (pp. 57–82). Greenwich, CT: JAI.

Blischak, D. M. (1994). Phonologic awareness: Implications for individuals with little or no functional speech. *Augmentative and Alternative Communication, 10*(4), 245–254.

Boone, R., & Higgins, K. (1993). Hypermedia basal readers: Three years of school-based research. *Journal of Special Education Technology, 12*(2), 86–106.

Burton-Radzely, L. (Ed.). (1998). *A national perspective on special educators' use of technology to promote literacy: Technical report.* Washington, DC: MACRO International and the Council for Exceptional Children.

Carnine, D. (1997). Bridging the research-to-practice gap. *Exceptional Children, 63,* 513–522.

Carpenter, B., & Detheridge, T. (1994). Writing with symbols. *Support for Learning, 9*(1), 27–32.

Casteel, C. A. (1988–1989). Effects of chunked reading among learning disabled students: An experimental comparison of computer and traditional chunked passages. *Journal of Educational Technology Systems, 17*(2), 115–121.

Cataldo, S., & Ellis, N. C. (1988). Interactions in the development of spelling, reading and phonological skills. *Journal of Research in Reading, 11,* 86–109.

Clark, R. E. (1983). Reconsidering research on learning from media. *Review of Educational Research, 53*(4), 445–459.

Cohen, A. L., Torgesen, J. K., & Torgesen, J. L. (1988). Improving speed and accuracy of word recognition in reading disabled children: An evaluation of two computer programs. *Learning Disability Quarterly, 11,* 333–341.

Cooper, H., & Hedges, L. V. (1994). *The handbook of research synthesis.* New York: Russell Sage Foundation.

Cosden, M. A., Goldman, S. R., & Hine, M. S. (1990). Learning handicapped students' interactions during a microcomputer-based group writing activity. *Journal of Special Education Technology, 10,* 220–232.

Cunningham, A. E., & Stanovich, K. E. (1990). Early spelling acquisition: Writing beats the computer. *Journal of Educational Psychology, 82,* 159–162.

Cunningham, A. E., & Stanovich, K. E. (1998). What reading does for the mind. *American Educator, 22*(1&2), 8–15.

Daiute, C., & Dalton, B. (1993). Collaboration between children learning to write: Can novices be masters? *Cognition and Instruction, 10,* 281–330.

Dillon, A., & Gabbard, R. (1998). Hypermedia as an educational technology: A review of the quantitative research literature on learner comprehension, control, and style. *Review of Educational Research, 68*(3), 322–349.

Dube, W. V., McDonald, S. J., McIlvane, W. J., & Mackay, H. A. (1991). Constructed-response matching to sample and spelling instruction. *Journal of Applied Behavior Analysis, 24*(2), 305–317.

Edwards, B. J., Blackhurst, A. E., & Koorland, M. A. (1995). Computer-assisted constant time delay prompting to teach abbreviation spelling to adolescents with mild learning disabilities. *Journal of Special Education Technology, 12,* 301–311.

Ehri, L. C. (1980). The role of orthographic images in learning printed words. In J. Kavanaugh & R. Venezky (Eds.), *Orthography, reading, and dyslexia* (pp. 155–170). Baltimore: University Park Press.

Ehri, L. C. (1998). Grapheme-phoneme knowledge is essential for learning to read words in English. In J. L. Metsala & L. C. Ehri (Eds.), *Word recognition in beginning literacy* (pp. 3–40). Mahwah, NJ: Lawrence Erlbaum Associates.

Ehri, L. C., & Wilce, L. S. (1987). Does learning to spell help beginners learn to read words? *Reading Research Quarterly, 20,* 12–26.

Elkind, J. (1998a). Computer reading machines for poor readers. *Perspectives, 24*(2), 4–6.

Elkind, J. (1998b). *A study of the efficacy of the Kurzweil 3000 Reading Machine in enhancing poor reading performance.* Portola Valley, CA: Lexia Institute.

Elkind, J., Black, M., & Murray, C. (1996). Computer-based compensation of adult reading disabilities. *Annals of Dyslexia, 46,* 159–186.

Elkind, J., Cohen, K., & Murray, C. (1993). Using computer-based readers to improve reading comprehension of students with disabilities. *Annals of Dyslexia, 43,* 238–259.

Englert, C. S., Raphael, T. E., Anderson, L. M., Gregg, S. L., & Anthony, H. M. (1989). Exposition: Reading, writing, and the metacognitive knowledge of learning disabled students. *Learning Disabilities Research, 5,* 5–24.

Erickson, G. C., Foster, K. C., Foster, D. F., Torgesen, J. K., & Packer, S. (1992). *DaisyQuest* [Computer software]. Scotts Valley, CA: Great Wave Software.

Erickson, G. C., Foster, K. C., Foster, D. F., Torgesen, J. K., & Packer, S. (1993). *Castle Quest* [Computer software]. Scotts Valley, CA: Great Wave Software.

Erickson, K. A., Koppenhaver, D. A., Yoder, D. E., & Nance, J. (1997). Integrated communication and literacy instruction for a child with multiple disabilities. *Focus on Autism and Developmental Disabilities, 12*(3), 142–150.

Farmer, M. E., Klein, R., & Bryson, S. E. (1992). Computer-assisted reading: Effects of whole-word feedback on fluency and comprehension in readers with severe disabilities. *Remedial and Special Education, 13*(2), 50–60.

Feldmann, S. C., & Fish, M. C. (1991). The use of computer-mediated reading supports to enhance reading comprehension. *Journal of Educational Computing Research, 7*(1), 25–36.

Fitzgerald, G. E., & Koury, K. A. (1996). Empirical advances in technology-assisted instruction for students with mild and moderate disabilities. *Journal of Research on Computing in Education, 28*(4), 526–553.

Flower, L., & Hayes, J. R. (1981). A cognitive process theory of writing. *College Composition and Communication, 32*, 365–387.

Foley, B. E. (1993). The development of literacy in individuals with severe congenital speech and motor impairments. *Topics in Language Disorders, 13*(2), 16–32.

Foster, K. C., Erickson, G. C., Foster, D. F., Brinkman, D., & Torgesen, J. K. (1994). Computer administered instruction in phonological awareness: Evaluation of the DaisyQuest program. *Journal of Research and Development in Education, 27*, 126–137.

Gersten, R., Lloyd, J. W., & Baker, S. (1998). *Designing high quality research in special education: Group experimental design.* Washington, DC: ERIC/OSEP.

Graham, S., Berninger, V. W., Abbott, R. D., Abbott, S. P., & Whitaker, D. (1997). Role of mechanics in composing of elementary school students: A new methodological approach. *Journal of Educational Psychology, 89*, 170–182.

Graham, S., Harris, K., MacArthur, C. A., & Schwartz, S. S. (1991). Writing and writing instruction with students with learning disabilities: A review of a program of research. *Learning Disability Quarterly, 14*, 89–114.

Graham, S., & MacArthur, C. (1988). Improving learning disabled students' skills at revising essays produced on a word processor: Self-instructional strategy training. *The Journal of Special Education, 22*, 133–152.

Graham, S., Schwartz, S. S., & MacArthur, C. A. (1993). Knowledge of writing and the composing process, attitude towards writing, and self-efficacy, for students with and without learning disabilities. *Journal of Learning Disabilities, 26*, 237–249.

Harper, J. A., & Ewing, N. J. (1986). A comparison of the effectiveness of microcomputer and workbook instruction on reading comprehension performance of high incidence handicapped children. *Educational Technology, 26*(5), 40–45.

Hayes, J. R. (1996). A new framework for understanding cognition and affect in writing. In C. M. Levy & S. Ransdell (Eds.), *The science of writing* (pp. 1–27). Mahwah, NJ: Lawrence Erlbaum Associates.

Hebert, B. M., & Murdock, J. Y. (1994). Comparing three computer-aided instruction output modes to teach vocabulary words to students with learning disabilities. *Learning Disabilities Research and Practice, 9*(3), 136–141.

Higgins, K., & Boone, R. (1990a). Hypertext: A new vehicle for computer use in reading instruction. *Intervention in School and Clinic, 26*(1), 26–31.

Higgins, K., & Boone, R. (1990b). Hypertext study guides and the social studies achievement of students with learning disabilities, remedial students, and regular education students. *Journal of Learning Disabilities, 23*(9), 529–540.

Higgins, K., & Boone, R. (1991). Hypermedia CAI: A supplement to an elementary school basal reader program. *Journal of Special Education Technology, 11*(1), 1–15.

Higgins, K., Boone, R., & Lovitt, T. C. (1996). Hypertext support for remedial students and students with learning disabilities. *Journal of Learning Disabilities, 29*(4), 402–412.

Hine, M. S., Goldman, S. R., & Cosden, M. A. (1990). Error monitoring by learning handicapped students engaged in collaborative microcomputer-based writing. *Journal of Special Education, 23*, 407–422.

Horney, M. A., & Anderson Inman, L. (1994). The ElectroText project: Hypertext reading patterns of middle school students. *Journal of Educational Multimedia and Hypermedia, 3*(1), 71–91.

Horton, S. V., Lovitt, T. C., Givens, A., & Nelson, R. (1989). Teaching social studies to high school students with academic handicaps in a mainstream setting: Effects of a computerized study guide. *Journal of Learning Disabilities, 22*(2), 102–107.

Inspiration Software, Inc. (1994). *Inspiration 4.0* [Computer software]. Portland, OR: Author.

246   OKOLO ET AL.

Johnson, G., Gersten, R., & Carnine, D. (1987). Effects of instructional design variables on the vocabulary acquisition of LD students: A study of computer-assisted instruction. *Journal of Learning Disabilities, 20,* 206–213.

Jones, K. U., Torgesen, J. K., & Sexton, M. A. (1987). Using computer guided practice to increase decoding fluency in learning disabled children: A study using the Hint and Hunt I program. *Journal of Learning Disabilities, 20,* 122–128.

Keene, S., & Davey, B. (1987). Effects of computer-presented text on LD adolescents' reading behaviors. *Learning Disability Quarterly, 10,* 283–290.

Kinney, P. G., Stevens, K. B., & Schuster, J. W. (1988). The effects of CAI and time delay: A systematic program for teaching spelling. *Journal of Special Education Technology, 9,* 61–72.

Koppenhaver, D. A., Coleman, P. P., Kalman, S. L., & Yoder, D. E. (1991). The implications of emergent literacy research for children with developmental disabilities. *American Journal of Speech-Language Pathology, 1*(1), 38–44.

Koppenhaver, D. A., & Yoder, D. E. (1993). Classroom literacy instruction for children with severe speech and physical impairments (SSPI): What is and what might be. *Topics in Language Disorders, 13*(2), 1–15.

Learning First Alliance. (1998). *Every child reading: An action plan.* Washington, DC: Author. Available: http://www.learningfirst.org/readingaction.html#reading

Lemke, J. L. (1998). Metamedia literacy. In D. Reinking, M. C. McKenna, L. D. Labbo, & R. D. Keiffer (Eds.), *Handbook of literacy and technology* (pp. 283–301). Mahwah, NJ: Lawrence Erlbaum Associates.

Leong, C. K. (1992). Enhancing reading comprehension with text-to-speech (DECtalk) Computer system. *Reading and Writing: An Interdisciplinary Journal, 4*(2), 205–217.

Leong, C. K. (1995). Effects of on-line reading and simultaneous DECtalk auding in helping below-average and poor readers comprehend and summarize text. *Learning Disabilities Quarterly, 18,* 101–116.

Lesgold, A. M., & Curtis, M. E. (1981). Learning to read words efficiently. In A. M. Lesgold & C. A. Perfetti (Eds.), *Interactive processes in reading* (pp. 329–360). Hillsdale, NJ: Lawrence Erlbaum Associates.

Lewis, R. B., Graves, A. W., Ashton, T. M., & Kieley, C. L. (1998). Word processing tools for students with learning disabilities: A comparison of strategies to increase text entry speed. *Learning Disabilities Research and Practice, 13,* 95–108.

Liberman, I. Y., Shankweiler, D., & Liberman, A. M. (1989). The alphabetic principle and learning to read. In I. Y. Liberman & D. Shankweiler (Eds.), *Phonology and learning to read* (pp. 102–124). Ann Arbor: University of Michigan Press.

Lie, A. (1991). Effects of a training program for stimulating skills in word analysis in first-grade children. *Reading Research Quarterly, 26,* 234–250.

Light, J., & McNaughton, D. (1993). Literacy and augmentative and alternative communication (AAC): The expectations and priorities of parents and teachers. *Topics in Language Disorders, 13*(2), 33–46.

Light, J., & Smith, A. K. (1993). Home literacy experiences of preschoolers who use AAC systems and of their nondisabled peers. *Augmentative and Alternative Communication, 9*(1), 10–25.

Lindamood, C., & Lindamood, P. (1975). *Auditory discrimination in depth.* Columbus, OH: Science Research Associates Division, Macmillan/McGraw-Hill.

Lundberg, I. (1995). The computer as a tool of remediation in the education of students with reading disabilities: A theory-based approach. *Learning Disability Quarterly, 18,* 89–99.

Lundberg, I., Frost, J., & Peterson, O. (1988). Effects of an extensive program for stimulating phonological awareness in preschool children. *Scandinavian Journal of Psychology, 21,* 159–173.

Lundberg, I., & Olofsson, A. (1993). Can computer speech support reading comprehension. *Computers in Human Behavior, 9*(2–3), 283–293.

MacArthur, C. A. (1988). The impact of computers on the writing process. *Exceptional Children, 54,* 536–542.

MacArthur, C. A. (1996). Using technology to enhance the writing processes of students with learning disabilities. *Journal of Learning Disabilities, 29,* 344–354.

MacArthur, C. A. (1998). Word processing with speech synthesis and word prediction: Effects on the dialogue journal writing of students with learning disabilities. *Learning Disability Quarterly, 21,* 1–16.

MacArthur, C. A. (1999). Word prediction for students with severe spelling problems. *Learning Disability Quarterly, 22,* 158–172.

MacArthur, C., & Graham, S. (1987). Learning disabled students composing under three methods of text production: Handwriting, word processing, and dictation. *Journal of Special Education, 21,* 22–42.

MacArthur, C. A., Graham, S., Haynes, J. B., & DeLaPaz, S. (1996). Spelling checkers and students with learning disabilities: Performance comparisons and impact on spelling. *Journal of Special Education, 30,* 35–57.

MacArthur, C. A., Graham, S., & Schwartz, S. (1991). Knowledge of revision and revising behavior among learning disabled students. *Learning Disability Quarterly, 14,* 61–73.

MacArthur, C. A., Graham, S., Schwartz, S. S., & Shafer, W. (1995). Evaluation of a writing instruction model that integrated a process approach, strategy instruction, and word processing. *Learning Disabilities Quarterly, 18,* 278–291.

MacArthur, C. A., Harris, K. R., & Graham, S. (1994). Improving students' planning processes through cognitive strategy instruction. In E. C. Butterfield & J. S. Carlson (Eds.), *Advances in cognition and educational practice: Vol. 2. Children's writing: Toward a process theory of the development of skilled writing* (pp. 173–198). Greenwich, CT: JAI.

MacArthur, C. A., & Haynes, J. B. (1995). Student Assistant for Learning from Text (SALT): A hypermedia reading aid. *Journal of Learning Disabilities, 28*(3), 150–159.

MacArthur, C., Haynes, J., Malouf, D., Harris, K., & Owings, M. (1990). Computer assisted instruction with learning disabled students: Achievement, engagement, and other factors that influence achievement. *Journal of Educational Computing Research, 6,* 311–328.

MacArthur, C. A., Schwartz, S. S., & Graham, S. (1991). Effects of a reciprocal peer revision strategy in special education classrooms. *Learning Disabilities Research and Practice, 6,* 201–210.

McNaughton, D., Hughes, C., & Ofiesh, N. (1997). Proofreading for students with learning disabilities: Integrating computer use and strategy use. *Learning Disabilities Research and Practice, 12,* 16–28.

McNaughton, D., & Tawney, J., (1993). Comparison of two spelling instruction techniques for adults who use augmentative and alternative communication. *Augmentative and Alternative Communication, 9,* 72–82.

Mike, D. G. (1995). Literacy and cerebral palsy: Factors influencing literacy learning in a self-contained setting. *Journal of Reading Behavior, 27*(4), 627–642.

Montali, J., & Lewandowski, L. (1996). Bimodal reading: Benefits of a talking computer for average and less skilled readers. *Journal of Learning Disabilities, 29*(3), 271–279.

Nelson, T. O., & Narens, L. (1990). Metamemory: A theoretical framework and new findings. In G. Bower (Ed.), *The psychology of learning and motivation* (pp. 125–141). New York: Academic Press.

Olofsson, A. (1990). Beyond word processing: Computer speech in reading instruction. In F. Biglmaier (Ed.), *Reading at the crossroad: Proceedings from the 6th European Conference on Reading in Berlin 31.7–31.8 1989* (pp. 378–393). Berlin: Freie Universität.

Olofsson, A. (1992). Synthetic speech and computer aided reading for reading disabled children. *Reading and Writing, 4,* 165–178.

Olson, D. R. (1994). *The world on paper.* New York: Cambridge University Press.

Olson, R., Foltz, G., & Wise, B. (1986). Reading instruction and remediation with the aid of computer speech. *Behavior Research Methods, Instruments, and Computers, 18*(2), 93–99.

Olson, R. K., & Wise, B. W. (1987). Computer speech in reading instruction. In D. Reinking (Ed.), *Computers and reading: Issues for theory and practice* (pp. 156–177). New York: Teachers College Press.

Olson, R. K., & Wise, B. W. (1992). Reading on the computer with orthographic and speech feedback: An overview of the Colorado remediation project. *Reading and Writing, 4*(2), 107–144.

Osguthorpe, R. T., & Chang, L. L. (1987). Computerized symbol processors for individuals with severe communication disabilities. *Journal of Special Education Technology, 8*(3), 43–54.

Osguthorpe, R. T., & Chang, L. L. (1988). The effects of computerized symbol processor instruction on the communication skills of nonspeaking students. *Augmentative and Alternative Communication, 4*(1), 23–34.

Palincsar, A. S., & Brown, A. L. (1984). Reciprocal teaching of comprehension-fostering and comprehension-monitoring activities. *Cognition and Instruction, 2,* 117–175.

Perfetti, C. A. (1985). *Reading ability.* New York: Oxford University Press.

Perfetti, C. A., & Lesgold, A. M. (1977). Discourse comprehension and sources of individual differences. In M. A. Just & P. A. Carpenter (Eds.), *Cognitive processes in comprehension* (pp. 141–183). Hillsdale, NJ: Lawrence Erlbaum Associates.

Perfetti, C. A., & Lesgold, A. M. (1979). Coding and comprehension in skilled readers and implications for reading instruction. In L. B. Resnick & P. A. Weaver (Eds.), *Theory and practice of early reading* (Vol. 1, pp. 57–84). Hillsdale, NJ: Lawrence Erlbaum Associates.

Rankin, J. L., Harwood, K., & Mirenda, P. (1994). Influence of graphic symbol use on reading comprehension. *Augmentative and Alternative Communication, 10*(4), 269–281.

Reinking, D. (1988). Computer-mediated text and comprehension differences: The role of reading time, reader preference, and estimation of learning. *Reading Research Quarterly, 23,* 484–498.

Reinking, D., & Schreiner, R. (1985). The effects of computer-mediated text on measures of reading comprehension and reading behavior. *Reading Research Quarterly, 20,* 536–551.

Rosenshine, B., Meister, C., & Chapman, S. (1996). Teaching students to generate questions: A review of the intervention studies. *Review of Educational Research, 66,* 181–221.

Roth, S. F., & Beck, I. L. (1987). Theoretical and instructional implications of the assessment of two microcomputer word recognition programs. *Reading Research Quarterly, 22*(2), 197–218.

Rueda, R. S. (1992). Characteristics of teacher–student discourse in computer-based dialogue journals: A descriptive study. *Learning Disability Quarterly, 15,* 187–206.

Sharp, D. L. M., Bransford, J. D., Goldman, S. R., & Risko, V. (1995). Dynamic visual support for story comprehension and mental model building by young, at-risk children. *Educational Technology Research and Development, 43*(4), 25–42.

Shiah, R., Mastropieri, M. A., & Scruggs, T. E. (1995). Computer-assisted instruction and students with learning disabilities: Does research support the rhetoric? *Advances in Learning and Behavioral Disabilities, 9,* 162–192.

Smith, A. K., Thurston, S., Light, J., Parnes, P., & O'Keefe, B. (1989). The form and use of written communication produced by physically disabled individuals using microcomputers. *Augmentative and Alternative Communication, 5*(2), 115–124.

Smith, M. M. (1992). Reading abilities of nonspeaking students: Two case studies. *Augmentative and Alternative Communication, 8,* 57–66.

Snow, C. E., Burns, M. S, & Griffin, P. (Eds.). (1998). *Preventing reading difficulties in young children.* Washington, DC: National Academy Press.

Stahl, S. A., & Fairbanks, M. M. (1986). The effects of vocabulary instruction: A model-based meta-analysis. *Review of Educational Research, 56,* 72–110.

Stanovich, K. E. (1988). Explaining the differences between the dyslexic and garden-variety poor readers: The phonological-core variable-difference model. *Journal of Learning Disabilities, 21,* 590–612.

Stevens, K. B., Blackhurst, A. E., & Slaton, D. B. (1991). Teaching memorized spelling with a microcomputer: Time delay and computer-assisted instruction. *Journal of Applied Behavior Analysis, 24,* 153–160.

Stoddard, B., & MacArthur, C. A. (1992). A peer editor strategy: Guiding learning disabled students in response and revision. *Research in the Teaching of English, 27,* 76–103.

Stromer, R., & Mackay, H. A. (1992). Delayed constructed-response identity matching improves the spelling performance of students with mental retardation. *Journal of Behavioral Education, 2*(2), 139–157.

Stromer, R., & Mackay, H. A. (1993). Delayed identity matching to complex samples: Teaching students with mental retardation spelling and the prerequisites for equivalence classes. *Research in Developmental Disabilities, 14,* 19–38.

Swanson, H. L. & Trahan, M. F. (1992). Learning disabled readers' comprehension of computer-mediated text: The influence of working memory, metacognition, and attribution. *Learning Disabilities Research and Practice, 7,* 74–86.

Taft, M. (1979). Lexical access via an orthographic code: The Basic Orthographic Syllabic Structure (BOSS). *Journal of Verbal Learning and Verbal Behavior, 18,* 21–39.

Torgesen, J. K. (1986). Using computers to help learning disabled children practice reading: A research-based perspective. *Learning Disabilities Focus, 1*(2), 72–81.

Torgesen, J. K. (1993). Variations on theory in learning disabilities. In G. R. Lyon, D. B. Gray, J. F. Kavanagh, & N. A. Krasnegor (Eds.), *Better understanding learning disabilities: New views from research and their implications for education and public policies* (pp. 153–170). Baltimore: Brooks Publishing.

Torgesen, J. K., & Barker, T. A. (1995). Computers as aids in the prevention and remediation of reading difficulties. *Learning Disability Quarterly, 18,* 76–87.

Torgesen, J. K., Greenstein, J., & Jones, K. (1990). *Computer guided reading practice with learning disabled children: Effects on decoding and comprehension skills.* Paper presented at the National Reading Conference, St. Petersburg Beach, FL.

Torgesen, J. K., Waters, M. D., Cohen, A. L., & Torgesen, J. L. (1988). Improving sight word recognition skills in LD children: An evaluation of three computer programs. *Learning Disability Quarterly, 11*(2), 125–132.

Treiman, R. (1985). Phonemic analysis in spelling and reading. In T. H. Carr (Ed.), The development of reading skills. *New Directions for Child Development, No. 27* (pp. 5–18). San Francisco: Jossey-Bass.

Treiman, R. (1993). *Beginning to spell.* New York: Oxford University Press.

Troia, G. A. (1999). Phonological awareness intervention research: A critical review of the experimental methodology. *Reading Research Quarterly, 34*(1), 28–52.

Vacc, N. N. (1987). Word processor versus handwriting: A comparative study of writing samples produced by mildly mentally handicapped students. *Exceptional Children, 54,* 156–165.

van Daal, V. H. P., & Reitsma, P. (1990). Effects of independent word practice with segmented and whole-word sound feedback in disabled readers. *Journal of Research in Reading, 13,* 133–148.

van Daal, V. H. P., & Reitsma, P. (1993). The use of speech feedback by normal and disabled readers in computer-based reading practice. *Reading and Writing: An Interdisciplinary Journal, 5*(3), 243–259.

van Daal, V. H. P., & van der Leij, A. (1992). Computer-based reading and spelling practice for children with learning disabilities. *Journal of Learning Disabilities, 25*(3), 186–195.

Vaughn, S., Schumm, J. S., & Gordon, J. (1992). Early spelling acquisition: Does writing really beat the computer? *Learning Disability Quarterly, 15,* 223–228.

Vaughn, S., Schumm, J. S., & Gordon, J. (1993). Which motoric condition is most effective for teaching spelling to students with and without learning disabilities? *Journal of Learning Disabilities, 26,* 191–198.

Vellutino, F. R., & Scanlon, D. M. (1991). The preeminence of phonologically based skills in learning to read. In S. Brady & D. Shankweiler (Eds.), *Phonological processes in literacy: A tribute to Isabelle Liberman* (pp. 237–252). Hillsdale, NJ: Lawrence Erlbaum Associates.

Wagner, R., Torgesen, J., & Rashotte, C. (1994). The development of reading related phonological processing abilities: New evidence of bi-directional causality from a latent variable longitudinal study. *Developmental Psychology, 30,* 73–78.

Wise, B. (1992). Whole words and decoding for short-term learning: Comparisons on a "talking-computer" system. *Journal of Experimental Child Psychology, 54*(2), 147–167.

Wise, B. W., & Olson, R. K. (1992). How poor readers and spellers use interactive speech in a computerized spelling program. *Reading and Writing, 4,* 145–163.

Wise, B., Olson, R., Ansett, M., Andrews, L., Terjak, M., Schneider, V., Kostuch, J., & Kriho, L. (1989). Implementing a long-term computerized remedial program with synthetic speech feedback: Hardware, software, and real-world issues. *Behavior, Research Methods, Instruments, and Computers, 21,* 173–180.

Wise, B. W., Olson, R. K., Ring, J., & Johnson, M. (1998). Interactive computer support for improving phonological skills. In J. L. Metsala & L. C. Ehri (Eds.), *Word recognition in beginning literacy* (pp. 189–208). Mahwah, NJ: Lawrence Erlbaum Associates.

Wise, B. W., Olson, R. K., & Treiman, R. (1990). Subsyllabic units as aids in beginning readers' word learning: Onset–rime versus post-vowel segmentation. *Journal of Experimental Child Psychology, 49,* 1–19.

Woodward, J., & Rieth, H. (1997). A historical review of technology research in special education. *Review of Educational Research, 67,* 503–536.

Wright, A., & Anderson, M. (1987). Does a computer system help to teach a sight vocabulary to children with severe learning difficulties? *Western European Education, 19*(4), 78–90.

Xin, F., Glaser, C. W., & Rieth, H. (1996). Multimedia reading. Using anchored instruction and video technology in vocabulary lessons. *Teaching Exceptional Children, 29*(2), 45–49.

Zhang, Y., Brooks, D. W., Frields, T., & Redelfs, M. (1995). Quality of writing by elementary students with learning disabilities. *Journal of Research on Computing in Education, 27,* 483–499.

Chapter 7

Research Syntheses: Implications for Research and Practice

Ellen P. Schiller
Abt Associates Inc.

David B. Malouf
U.S. Department of Education

Until the start of the 20th century, all humanity had a disability. We were unable to fly. And people experimented with ways to overcome this disability. Leonardo DaVinci experimented with drawing designs for flying machines in the early 16th century. It was a dream to defy gravity, but even then the basic theory and research into aerodynamics had begun. For centuries it remained in the idea stage. But finally, in the 19th century, inventors began tinkering with DaVinci's basic designs and concepts, and conducting experiments that added to man's knowledge about the principles necessary for flight. Eventually this accumulation of knowledge gleaned from research—and paired with practical attempts to make it work—led to the invention of a machine in 1903 by the Wright brothers that actually could fly.

The research into the development of airplanes started with the insight and vision of one thinker, was developed further by a growing body of scientific research, was made real through experimentation, and finally turned into a workable product that continues to be refined and perfected.

Research in special education has followed a similar course. The Office of Special Education Programs (OSEP), U.S. Department of Education, has supported a research and dissemination agenda designed to promote the use of research knowledge in special education. This chapter discusses reasons why research knowledge tends to be underused in educational policy and practice, and suggests how research syntheses may contribute to improving the use of research knowledge. The chapter also discusses some "next steps" in the process of promoting research utilization, and it emphasizes that these syntheses represent a valuable and necessary component, but that they should be viewed as highly refined concepts for a design, rather than as end products of the process of research utilization.

THE PROBLEM OF LINKING RESEARCH AND PRACTICE

Other articles have set forth numerous reasons why educational research has been underused in practice (Fullan, 1992; Kennedy, 1997; Malouf & Schiller, 1995; Shavelson, 1988). For the purposes of our discussion, the reasons can be categorized into three broad areas suggested by Kennedy: (a) accessibility of research, (b) contextual factors associated with the education system, and (c) persuasiveness and relevance of research.

Accessibility of Research

Accessibility of research is perhaps the most obvious constraint on the use of research knowledge in education practice. Educational researchers have been accused of maintaining closed systems of communication—disseminating their findings primarily to other researchers. Often the research is written either in language that practitioners cannot understand, or in prose that does not engage them. Teachers cannot use research knowledge if it is not accessible and easily understood (Fleming, 1988; Fullan, 1992; Huberman, 1983).

Accessibility is a relatively easy factor to address in ways that are feasible and affordable, and that do not require systemic changes in our approaches to research or practice. Politicians and administrators can develop systems and products designed to make research accessible and understandable to practitioners and the public. They can tout these systems and products as tangible accomplishments, regardless of their ultimate value in promoting the use of research findings (Kennedy, 1997). Thus, efforts to make research accessible are politically viable, and are often the first resort when attempts are made to link research and practice.

However, if accessibility were the only barrier, the problem of connecting research to practice would have been solved by now. A series of research accessibility efforts have been undertaken over the past half century, with limited impact on practice. It has generally been conceded that improved accessibility will solve only part of the problem (McLaughlin, 1990; Miles, 1993).

Contextual Factors Associated With the Education System

Many aspects of the educational system in this country obstruct the use of research knowledge to improve practice. One important obstacle is the decentralized and fragmented nature of the educational system. This country has a historical investment in preventing overly centralized power over the educational system (Cohen & Spillane, 1992). Although the federal government is playing a greater role in education than in the past, there is still a deep-seated resistance to federal involvement in local schooling. Witness, for example, the outcry over recent moves to implement federal educational standards and national tests.

Similarly, states are often seen as the constitutional center of education, yet they are often given little control over implementing policy and effecting change. The Individuals with Disabilities Education Act (IDEA), for example, concentrates considerable authority and funding for special education services at the state level, but it is the exception; state control is seldom maintained across the full spectrum of regular and special education services.

School districts ultimately are the basic unit of educational governance, and they continue to have the greatest direct influence over curriculum, personnel, and resources (Cohen & Spillane, 1992). And even at the local level, such recent reforms as school-based management have given schools and teachers more autonomy over their budgets, curriculum, and governance, and therefore have widely dispersed the decision making process.

Thus, the system of educational policy and practice is comprised of a loosely connected array of federal, state, and local systems, individual schools and teachers, teacher-training programs, professional groups, and other entities. It is difficult in this context to discern effective points of entry for introducing research knowledge. For policymakers, research knowledge must compete for influence with a number of other political and social factors. The fact that information is produced by technically rigorous research methods is unlikely to be the most important consideration. Policymakers often give equal or greater importance to the compatibility of findings with current educational and social trends and ideologies, the broad acceptability of the findings in the context of increasing cultural diversity, and the degree to which findings support individual and organizational agendas (Huberman, 1983; Kennedy, 1997).

For teachers, research is a small and indistinct voice in a very crowded and noisy arena. They have limited flexibility or motivation to use research-based innovations because of demands arising from externally imposed curricula, heightened accountability, and increased student diversity; as well as such constraints as relative isolation, heavy work loads, inadequate preservice and inservice training, and insufficient resources (Cohen, 1988; Fleming, 1988; Fullan, 1992; Wasley, 1991). Though schools and teachers often change their practices, these changes are typically shaped by immediate constraints and needs and are rarely research driven (Cuban, 1988).

Persuasiveness and Relevance of Research

There are larger and more persistent questions beyond the issue of research accessibility and context. Is research even capable of contributing to practice? Is there even a logical link to be made?

The worlds of educational research and practice have been shaped by different forces and have evolved along different paths. Ultimately these two worlds incorporate different rules and standards for producing, accepting, and applying knowledge (Huberman, 1983, 1990). Research has often been shaped more by theory and a press for technical rigor than by real-world problems, or a press for practical usefulness. As a result, much educational research has become abstract and reductionistic, relying on methodologies that lack the capacity to produce persuasive findings that speak to the complex and unstable situations, and multiple ambiguous goals that educators face every day. In essence, educational research has been drawn to Schon's (1987) "high, hard ground overlooking a swamp" with "manageable problems" that can be solved using "research-based theory and technique" (p. 3). But for those who must work in the "swampy lowland," the messy and confusing problems—those of greatest human concern—"defy technical solution" (p. 3).

This mismatch between the methodologies and knowledge of research, and the realities and demands of practice, creates a "limits of science" problem (Malouf & Schiller, 1995). Propositions derived from systematic research can make only a minor contribution to practice, and must be combined with a much larger volume of "ordinary" knowledge (Lindblom & Cohen, 1979). The "limits of science" problem may in part account for the frequent overinterpretation or misinterpretation of research in practice (Fleming, 1988). It may also help explain why some research with the greatest influence on policy and practice has also come under the greatest methodological criticism (Kennedy, 1997). In essence, research must sometimes sacrifice rigor for relevance. Further, applying research knowledge to practice may require disregarding the rules of investigation and interpretation by which that knowledge is produced.

MAKING THE CONNECTION

Redefining the Relationship

To address these problems and establish a durable and valid connection between research and practice, we must rethink current notions and arrive at a clear, shared understanding of how research and practice can be meaningfully linked. This understanding should be based on certain recognized realities. For example, research will be used in the real-world context of the school, and multiple local factors will determine its use and outcomes. Also, research must compete with numerous political, organizational, social, and economic influences, so achieving a connection between research and practice will require strategic and coherent efforts. We must recognize that research knowledge will be mixed with other types of knowledge, such as "craft" knowledge and professional expertise. It is therefore unrealistic to base our efforts for promoting research utilization solely on a model involving the exact replication of research findings (Lindblom & Cohen, 1979; Schon, 1987; Shavelson, 1988).

Recent models for promoting the utilization of research knowledge have redefined the roles of researchers and practitioners, relaxed the distinctions between research and practice, and expanded the focus on the processes of research implementation (Malouf & Schiller, 1995; Schiller, Malouf, & Danielson, 1995).

Implementing and sustaining use is a complex undertaking. Gersten and Brengelman (1996) captured this complexity in a model of factors influencing sustained use of research-based practices: creating collegial support networks; linking changes in teaching to student learning; creating conceptual linkages from research to classrooms; offering technical support through coaching that includes feedback on a regular schedule with specific and focused comments on the actions of the teacher in order for them to practice the strategy and improve their instruction; recognizing the reality of classrooms by identifying instructional approaches that fit and are feasible with regular education teachers practices and link with something they do in the classroom with concrete ways of follow up in their classroom. These factors lead to conceptual changes in teaching to promote student learning (Englert & Tarrant, 1995; Fuchs, Fuchs, Hamlett, & Bentz, 1994; Gersten, Morvant, & Brengelman, 1995; Gersten & Woodward, 1990; Greenwood, Delquadri, & Hall, 1989; Joint Committee on Teacher Planning for Students with Disabilities, 1005; Vaughn & Schumm, 1995). It remains to be seen to what extent these practices and approaches will take root in the educational system and become common practice, but they demonstrate that research and practice can be effectively linked in nontraditional ways.

The Roles of Research Syntheses

Research syntheses such as those presented in this book can play several useful roles in promoting the use of research. First, collecting and synthesizing the findings of multiple research studies increase the accessibility of the research and facilitate its interpretation. Second, in cases where practitioners have been involved in the synthesis process, the accessibility and usability of research may be further enhanced (see chaps. 2 & 5, this volume). Third, by sorting out contradictions and testing boundary conditions of effects, these syntheses can provide additional guidance for linking research and practice, particularly when the effects of strong and persistent intervention are observed across studies. And finally, by strengthening the voice of research, these syntheses increase its visibility and persuasiveness in professional discourse.

The roles of research syntheses can be categorized and further discussed according to certain general functions that research can perform in relation to practice. The following functions have been derived from several sources: (a) testing for replication, (b) enlightenment and conceptualization, (c) reporting, and (d) "short-run empiricism" (Cronbach, 1975; Lindblom & Cohen, 1979). These functions, described in detail as follows, are not proposed as a comprehensive or rigid classification scheme:

1. *Testing for replication:* This is a linear approach whereby innovations are developed and tested in research, then disseminated and replicated in practice. Operant conditioning and differential reinforcement techniques are examples from behavioral psychology where interventions derived from research can be directly replicated in classrooms. Turnbull et al., in chapter 5 of this volume, report how positive behavioral supports for students with cognitive disabilities benefited from research on behavioral interventions and moved from laboratory studies to replication in small community-based settings.

Chapter 1, by Swanson, also exemplifies a replication function, predominantly because of the time period in which the studies were conducted. Interventions, such as direct instruction and strategy instruction, were designed in controlled settings and found to be effective in classrooms with particular populations of children with learning disabilities.

2. *Enlightenment and conceptualization:* Lindblom and Cohen (1979) asserted that most contributions of scientific inquiry to social problem solving have been accomplished through fundamental enlightenment of thought, not through "engineering" solutions. Chapter 3, by Fuchs and colleagues, exemplifies this function by exploring the fundamental distinctions between learning disabilities and other forms of low achievement. The

authors identify timed/untimed performance, high/low grade levels, and decision rules/judgment as factors upon which to differentiate these populations. Conceptual distinctions are made between learning disabilities and other low achievers both in the degree and kind of the problem, suggesting that there are quantitative and qualitative differences between the populations. In contrast to a "testing for replication" function, Fuchs and colleagues provide a way of conceptualizing the differences between the two populations, with multiple implications for policy and practice.

Gersten and Baker, in chapter 2, help us to think about teaching special education children who are second-language learners by working through the differences in language between researchers and practitioners. Their multivocal methodology identifies the issues and clarifies the use of words used by different audiences to ultimately recommend an emerging set of instructional components for teaching these students.

3. *Reporting:* Lindblom and Cohen (1979) described "reporting" as research that provides descriptive information to inform on the prevalence and severity of a problem, where it tends to occur, and how it tends to manifest itself. None of the chapters in the current volume is devoted primarily to the reporting function, although several provide this type of information as introductory material. A good example of the reporting function can be found in the National Longitudinal Transition Study, which provided extensive descriptive information on the transition and postschool experiences of students with disabilities (Wagner, 1989).

4. *Short-run empiricism:* Cronbach (1975) framed a final function for research syntheses as "short-run empiricism," where research provides working hypotheses and ideas that can be tried and evaluated empirically in practice. This function assumes that research and practice can be connected, and it sets up a cyclical and dynamic relationship between them.

New Approaches to Research and Development

In fact, research and development agendas are beginning to incorporate these recent advances in knowledge production to bridge the gap between research and practice. The advances make research accessible and plausible, and put it within a context to address important problems faced by end users of research.

Research methods have expanded over the last two decades. Brown (1992), in a personal account, illustrated how her traditional training as an experimental psychologist has evolved from conducting laboratory studies on how children learn to concentrating on conceptual changes in teachers and students. Further, the elements in her research designs set up classrooms that support self-reflective learning for students and teachers, address technology and the curriculum, and create accountability systems. Advances in cognitive psychology and school improvement contributed to Brown's shift in her research approach.

Brown (1992) characterized her research as design experiments, building on Collins' (1993) approach in artificial intelligence. The features of design experiments include:

- Balancing lab work with classroom work, being careful not to separate the individual from social interactions, motivation, or processes.
- Moving from an experimenter-controlled situation to students' initiating the use of a strategy.
- Collecting different types of data on students, teachers, and their interactions.
- Actively engaging teachers in the research.
- Continuing to apply rigor to the research (e.g., using pre/post designs with experimental and control groups; studying three to four classrooms for a year with up to 100 students; engaging in-depth analysis of some students, as well as contrasting cases of a few students).

Ultimately, the outcomes from the studies demonstrate how to improve classroom teaching by understanding both teaching and learning simultaneously in the context of classrooms. This design approach applies to special education, and actually returns special education to its roots—understanding individual differences and the support students with disabilities need to accelerate their learning.

In its current research, OSEP supports a variety of approaches to bridging the gap between research and practice. These approaches include researcher teams who use multiple methodologies to understand complex phenomenon of classrooms; use multiple expertise in the design and interpretation of the studies; involve teachers, curriculum developers, and family members as co-collaborators; and compare across multiple interventions. This research specifically focuses on linking research with practice and on the sustained use of innovations by building upon an emerging era of "reciprocal empiricism."

Next Steps for an Emerging Research and Development Agenda

Research syntheses have an important role to play in linking research knowledge with practice (Stroufe, 1997). Specific synthesis efforts are underway at the American Educational Research Association, National Academy of Science, and Office of Educational Research and Improvement.

OSEP, too, is contributing to the effort to provide research syntheses. Where do researchers, practitioners, and a federal agency go from here?

Federal demonstrations provide an opportunity. In a traditional research and demonstration agenda, promising research findings are validated through model demonstration projects. After validation of these models, discretionary funds support states and localities in implementing the validated practices, and technical assistance and outreach activities provide further implementation support. IDEA has a history of supporting demonstrations in the education of young children, the transition of youth with disabilities from school to work, and the provision of services to children who are deaf and blind.

Demonstrations also have their roots in a second tradition of social action. This tradition has as its concern those individuals, families, and groups deemed by society to have few of the necessities and amenities that constitute an acceptable economic, physical, and social standard of living. Specifically, this tradition has championed the cause of the poor, the disadvantaged, and the disabled. In these instances, individuals with little scientific or technical training, including social workers, community-based service providers, teachers, and school administrators, have developed and directed the demonstrations. In the 1960s, demonstrations were a prominent feature of social action programs.

Yet, despite the varying traditions and widespread use, demonstrations are poorly understood and their effectiveness is questionable (Glennan, Hederman, Johnson, & Rettig, 1978). According to Glennan et al., one reason for these difficulties is the ambiguity over what the term *demonstration* means. They suggested that a demonstration can serve three purposes:

- To prove or test the innovation under consideration.
- To show others the advantages of the innovation for the purpose of persuading them to use it.
- To represent political actions and demonstrate national concern about a problem.

When the intent of the demonstration is unclear, the likelihood of developing general principles to implement an innovation in another setting is limited. Moreover, the subsequent methodologies of demonstrations yield questionable findings. According to Glennan et al. (1978), findings from demonstrations provide little generalized information because they are often characterized by poor research designs, if any exist. At their best, demonstration evaluations are tools for guiding and evaluating local practice and serve as a social policy instrument.

Yet, even with these limitations, demonstrations continue to serve a political purpose by directing resources toward addressing social issues.

Headstart programs, whose effect on families and children is mixed, continues to receive public support for offering early education services to at-risk children. These resources become an avenue for supporting the implementation of research findings and improving services. To maximize these resources and minimize the mistakes from previous demonstrations, developers may benefit from a closer collaboration with researchers. Researchers have been criticized for being out of touch. Teachers and developers have been criticized for not understanding the issues. It is time to change the conversation and use funding mechanisms such as demonstrations combined with improved research designs and methodologies so that the resources, the people, and the methods come together to explain how children with disabilities learn in classrooms.

Conclusion

Leonardo DaVinci never did fly, nor would many of his ideas work exactly as he drew them. The Wright brothers did fly, and as each new experimenter drew on the research and practical experience of his or her predecessor, the modest flight of the Wright brothers evolved into intercontinental, supersonic travel.

In the same way, many education researchers build on the work of previous researchers. Today, these researchers, working with practitioners, are testing and formulating their hypotheses in the real environment of the classroom to develop a more complete picture of how to educate children with disabilities. This has been the hallmark of special education research. The syntheses in this book represent the fruit of this pioneering research. In the next several years, our community can reflect on its contributions from these research syntheses and take them to the next step—creating a dynamic and cyclical relationship, with research and demonstration contributing to improved educational practice and better results for students with disabilities.

ACKNOWLEDGMENTS

Ellen P. Schiller, PhD, is currently a Senior Associate with Abt Associates Inc., Bethesda, MD, and previously, a special assistant in the Division of Research to Practice, Office of Special Education Programs, U.S. Department of Education.

David B. Malouf, PhD, is currently a senior program analyst with the Division of Research to Practice, Office of Special Education Programs, U.S. Department of Education.

The views expressed are the views of the authors and do not reflect the policy of the Office of Special Education Programs, U.S. Department of Education.

REFERENCES

Brown, A. (1992). Design experiments: Theoretical and methodological challenges in creating complex interventions in classroom settings. *The Journal of the Learning Sciences, 2*(2), 141–178.

Cohen, D. K. (1988). Teaching practice: Plus que ca change. In P. W. Jackson (Ed.), *Contributing to educational change: Perspectives on research and practice* (pp. 27–84). Berkeley, CA: McCutchan.

Cohen, D. K., & Spillane, J. P. (1992). Policy and practice: The relations between governance and instruction. In G. Grant (Ed.), *Review of research in education* (Vol. 18, pp. 3–49). Washington, DC: American Educational Research Association.

Collins, A. (1993). Toward a design science of education. In E. Scanlon & T. O'Shea (Eds.), *New directions in educational technology* (pp. 7–12). New York: Springer-Verlag.

Cronbach, L. J. (1975). Beyond the two disciplines of scientific psychology. *American Psychologist, 30,* 116–127.

Cuban, L. (1988). Constancy and change in schools (1880s to the present). In P. W. Jackson (Ed.), *Contributing to educational change: Perspectives on research and practice* (pp. 85–105). Berkeley, CA: McCutchan.

Englert, C. S., & Tarrant, K. (1995). Creating collaborative cultures for educational change. *Remedial and Special Education, 16,* 325–336.

Fleming, D. S. (1988, April). *The literature on teacher utilization of research: Implications for the school reform movement.* Paper presented at the annual meeting of the American Educational Research Association, New Orleans, LA.

Fuchs, L. S., Fuchs, D., Hamlett, C. L., & Bentz, J. (1994). Classwide curriculum based measurement: Helping general educators meet the challenge of student diversity. *Exceptional Children, 60,* 518–537.

Fullan, M. G. (1992). *Teachers as critical consumers of research.* Paper commissioned by OECD for Seminar on Producers and Consumers of Research, Washington, DC.

Gersten, R., & Brengelman, S. (1996). The quest to translate research into practice: The emerging knowledge base. *Remedial and Special Education, 17,* 67–74.

Gersten, R., Morvant, M., & Brengelman, S. (1995). Closer to the classroom is close to the bone: Coaching as a means to translate research into classroom practice. *Exceptional Children, 62*(1), 52–66.

Gersten, R., & Woodward, J. (1990). Rethinking the regular education initiative: Focus on the classroom teacher. *Remedial and Special Education, 11*(3), 7–16.

Glennan, T. K., Hederman, W. F., Johnson, L. L., & Rettig, R. A. (1978). *The role of demonstrations in federal R&D policy.* Washington, DC: The Rand Corporation.

Greenwood, C. R., Delquadri, J., & Hall, R. V. (1989). Longitudinal effects of classwide peer tutoring. *Journal of Educational Psychology, 81,* 371–383.

Huberman, M. (1983). Recipes for busy kitchens: A situational analysis of routine knowledge use in schools. *Knowledge: Creation, Diffusion, Utilization, 4*(4), 478–510.

Huberman, M. (1990). Linkage between researchers and practitioners: A qualitative study. *American Educational Research Journal, 27*(2), 363–391.

Joint Committee on Teacher Planning for Students with Disabilities. (1995). *Planning for academic diversity in America's classrooms: Windows on reality, research, change, and practice.* Lawrence: The University of Kansas Center for Research on Learning.

Kennedy, M. M. (1997). The connection between research and practice. *Educational Researcher, 26*(7), 4–12.

Lindblom, C. E., & Cohen, D. K. (1979). *Usable knowledge: Social science and social problem solving.* New Haven, CT: Yale University Press.

Malouf, D. B., & Schiller, E. P. (1995). Practice and research in special education. *Exceptional Children, 61*(5), 414–424.

McLaughlin, M. W. (1990). The Rand Change Agent Study revisited: Macro perspectives and micro realities. *Educational Researcher, 19*(9), 11–16.

Miles, M. B. (1993). 40 years of change in schools: Some personal reflections. *Education Administration Quarterly, 29*(2), 213–248.

Schiller, E. P., Malouf, D. B., & Danielson, L. (1995). Research utilization: A federal perspective. *Remedial and Special Education, 16*(6), 372–375.

Schon, D. A. (1987). *Educating the reflective practitioner.* San Francisco: Jossey-Bass.

Shavelson, R. J. (1988). Contributions of educational research to policy and practice: Constructing, challenging, changing cognition. *Educational Researcher, 17*(7), 4–11, 22.

Sroufe, G. (1997). Improving the awful reputation of education research. *Educational Researcher, 26,* 26–28.

Vaughn, S., & Schumm, J. (1995). Responsible inclusion of children with learning disabilities. *Journal of Learning Disabilities, 28,* 264–270.

Wagner, M. (1989). *Youth with disabilities during transition: An overview of descriptive findings from the National Longitudinal Transition Study.* Menlo Park, CA: SRI International.

Wasley, P. A. (1991). *Teachers who lead: The rhetoric of reform and the realities of practice.* New York: Teachers College Press.

Chapter 8

The Methodology
of Meta-Analysis

Harris Cooper
Jeffrey C. Valentine
Kelly Charlton
University of Missouri, Columbia

Few disciplines present as much challenge to the research synthesist as does special education. The challenge arises primarily from the wide variety of research designs, outcome measures, and diagnostic labels that characterize research in special education. For example, it is not unusual to find the same special educational intervention tested using one-group pretest–posttest designs, nonequivalent control group designs, experimental designs, single-subject designs, and case studies. Outcomes measured for this one intervention might include academic achievement, social and behavioral adjustment, attitudes, and self-concept.

As difficult as the synthesis task may be, there are important reasons for special education researchers to undertake the challenge. First, accumulation is a cornerstone of the scientific enterprise and without syntheses special education research will be severely limited in its use by policymakers. If researchers easily succumb to the conclusion that "these studies, ostensibly evaluating the same intervention, are too dissimilar to warrant aggregation," it is a short leap to the conclusion that "this study cannot be generalized to settings, people, and programs not contained in them." Obviously, adopting this stance can be overly cautious and can greatly undermine the value of research. With this in mind, those who undertake the task of gathering, summarizing, and integrating special education literatures deserve added acclaim.

Second, special education researchers need to keep in mind the fact that the process of aggregation, and the glossing over of differences in settings, people, and program realizations that invariably accompanies it, occurs in all forms of research. For example, primary researchers who make no provision for individual differences in their analytic models have ignored scores of potential moderating variables that, if tested, might reveal important variations in a program's effects. In other words, the primary researcher may have overaggregated the data.

Finally, properly conducted research syntheses not only aggregate studies but also disaggregate them into meaningful subsets, allowing for the test of moderating influences. Do nonequivalent group designs reveal different results from experimental designs? Do students labeled "learning disabled" react differently to this treatment than students labeled "underachieving"? Often, a research synthesist can ask about influences on treatment effects that have never been tested in primary research.

Because of the pitfalls that confront research synthesists, it is critical that the methods used to integrate the results of studies be rigorous and open to public inspection. Over the past three decades, methods for the retrieval and analysis of research literatures have undergone enormous change. In the 1960s, literature reviewing was a largely narrative and subjective process. Today, research synthesis has a body of statistical techniques and decision rules all its own. In this chapter, we describe some statistical techniques frequently used by research synthesists who choose to quantitatively combine the results of related studies. We also delineate the threats to validity that enter the synthesis process during the data analysis stage. First, however, we describe some of the critical events in the evolution of quantitative research synthesis procedures and make reference to places where readers can find fuller treatments of the issues touched on here.

IMPORTANT EVENTS IN THE DEVELOPMENT OF META-ANALYSIS

A century ago, Karl Pearson conducted what is believed to be the first statistical synthesis of results of independent research (Pearson, 1904). Pearson gathered data from 11 studies of the effect of a vaccine against typhoid and for each study he calculated a new statistic called the correlation coefficient. He averaged the correlations and concluded that other vaccines were more effective. In 1932, Ronald Fisher presented a technique for combining the p values that came from statistically independent tests of the same hypothesis.

Early work on procedures for statistically integrating results of independent studies was ignored for many years. However, in the mid-1970s Rosenthal and Rubin (1978) undertook a review of 345 studies looking at the effects of interpersonal expectations on behavior. Glass and Smith (1979) conducted a review of the relation between class size and academic achievement and found 725 estimates of the relation, based on data from nearly 900,000 students. J. E. Hunter, Schmidt, and R. Hunter (1979) uncovered 866 comparisons of the differential validity of employment tests for Black and White workers. Each of these scholarly efforts led the investigators to resurrect quantitative synthesis procedures.

Glass (1976) coined the term *meta-analysis* to stand for "the statistical analysis of a large collection of analysis results from individual studies for purposes of integrating the findings" (p. 3). Shortly thereafter, Cooper (1979) and Cooper and Rosenthal (1980) made the empirical case for meta-analysis by showing that narrative review procedures led to inaccurate or imprecise characterizations of the cumulative research results. Glass, McGaw, and Smith (1981) then proposed that meta-analysis be viewed as a new application of analysis of variance and multiple regression procedures, with the outcomes of studies, in the form of effect sizes, treated as the criterion variable and the features of studies as the predictor variables. J. E. Hunter, Schmidt, and Jackson (1982) introduced an alternative meta-analytic model that (a) compared the observed variation in study outcomes to that expected by sampling error and (b) corrected observed correlations and their variance for known sources of bias. Rosenthal (1984) presented a compendium of meta-analytic methods including combining significance levels, effect size estimation, and the search for moderators of study results. Rosenthal's procedures for testing moderators of effect sizes were not based on traditional inferential statistics, but on a new set of techniques involving assumptions tailored specifically for the analysis of study outcomes. Light and Pillemer (1984) offered a text that emphasized the use of research synthesis to inform social policy. Their approach highlighted the importance of meshing quantitative procedures and narrative descriptions in the interpretation and communication of synthesis results. Hedges and Olkin's (1985) text, titled *Statistical Procedures for Meta-Analysis*, covered a wide array of meta-analytic procedures and established the procedures' legitimacy by presenting rigorous statistical proofs.

Since the mid-1980s, several other full-text treatments have appeared on meta-analysis. Some of these treat the topic generally (e.g., Cooper, 1998; J. E. Hunter & Schmidt, 1990), some treat it from the perspective of particular research design conceptualizations (e.g., Eddy, Hasselblad, & Shachter, 1992; Mullen, 1989), some are tied to particular software packages (e.g., Johnson, 1989), and some look at potential future developments in research synthesis (e.g., Cook et al., 1992; Wachter & Straf, 1990). In 1994, the first edition of *Handbook of Research Synthesis* was published (Cooper & Hedges, 1994). This book included 32 chapters contributed by specialists in information science, computer software, and statistics, as well as experts in the use of research synthesis for psychology, medicine, education, and public policy.

THE ELEMENTS OF META-ANALYSIS

The statistical techniques used by research synthesists have undergone considerable modification and expansion since Glass and Smith (1979) used analysis of variance and Rosenthal and Rubin (1978) used combined p levels from t tests and analyses of variance. Some of these techniques have been developed to address the unique characteristics of study-level data and inquiry. Other techniques have been imported from methodologies that share similar data and inquiry characteristics. In this section, we briefly introduce some of these statistical procedures. Obviously, we cannot fully explore all the meta-analytic procedures nor give full treatment to the included ones. As is true of primary research, each research synthesis evokes a unique set of data analysis problems that require a unique set of solutions.

To make some of the discussed procedures more concrete, we use as an example some results from a recently completed meta-analysis conducted by the authors (Cooper, Charlton, Valentine, & Muhlenbruck, 2000). This research synthesis attempted to answer the question, "What is the impact of summer school on students in need of academic remediation?" In addition to this general question, we also asked "Does remedial summer school have a different impact on students in special education compared to other types of students?"

Calculation of Effect Sizes

The most critical number in the meta-analyst's data set is the effect size. Cohen (1988) defined an effect size as "the degree to which the phenomenon is present in the population, or the degree to which the null hypothesis is false" (pp. 9–10). In meta-analysis, effect sizes are (a) calculated for the outcomes of comparisons, (b) averaged across comparisons to estimate general magnitudes of effect, and (c) compared between comparisons to discover if variations in outcomes exist and, if so, what features of comparisons might account for them.

Two effect size metrics are used most frequently in the special education literature. The first, called the d index by Cohen (1988), is a scale-free measure of the separation between two group means. Calculating the d index for any comparison involves dividing the difference between the two group means by either their average standard deviation or the standard deviation of the control group. The basic formula is as follows:

$$d = \frac{X_1 - X_2}{(SD_1 + SD_2)/2}$$

where X_1 and X_2 = the two group means; and SD_1 and SD_2 = the standard deviations of the two groups. This results in a measure of the difference between the two group means expressed in terms of their common standard deviation. Thus, a d index of .25 indicates that one fourth standard deviation separates the two means.

The second effect size metric is the r index, or correlation coefficient. Because the reporting of effect sizes is not yet standard, a meta-analyst often must estimate or calculate the effect size from other statistics present in a research report (see Rosenthal, 1994, for many of these approaches) and/or must adjust an effect size estimate to remove certain sampling biases (see Hedges & Olkin, 1985).

Typically, the r index is used to express the relationship between two continuous variables, such as class size and achievement. The d index is used to relate one dichotomous variable to a continuous variable, such as comparing students who do or do not attend summer school on academic achievement. The choice is determined by which metric fits best with the characteristics of the variables under consideration. In the summer school meta-analysis, for example, the overall average d index for remedial programs was d = .32, meaning the average students who went to summer school scored about one third of a standard deviation higher on the outcome measure than did controls.

In many special education research areas, primary investigators use more than one type of research design. Therefore, the components of the d index differ depending on the type of comparison. For example, in the summer school meta-analysis, when the comparison involved a single sample of students tested before and after a summer program, the d index was calculated by subtracting the postprogram mean score from the preprogram mean score and dividing this difference by the average of the pre- and postprogram standard deviations. When the comparison involved two samples of students, a sample that attended a summer program and a sample that did not, the d index was calculated by subtracting the control group mean from the attendee group mean and dividing this difference by the average of the two groups' standard deviations. In both cases, a positive d index indicated a positive effect of summer school.

A statistical problem arises when a single study contains multiple effect size estimates taken on the same sample of participants. There are several approaches meta-analysts use to handle such dependent effect sizes. Some treat each effect size as independent, regardless of the number that comes from the same sample of people. They assume that the effect of violating the independence assumption is not substantial. Other meta-analysts use the study as the unit of analysis. They calculate the mean effect size or take the median result and use this value to represent the study. Sophisticated statistical models also have been suggested as a solution to the problem of dependent effect size estimates (Gleser & Olkin, 1994; Raudenbush, Becker, & Kalaian, 1988), but due to their complexity they are yet rarely found into practice.

In the summer school meta-analysis, we used a shifting unit of analysis (Cooper, 1998). In this procedure, each effect size is coded into the data set as if it were an independent estimate. For example, if a single sample of students permitted comparisons of preprogram and postprogram math and reading scores, two separate d indexes were calculated. However, for estimating the overall effect of summer school, these two d indexes were averaged prior to entry into the analysis, so that the sample only contributed one effect size. However, in an analysis that examined the effect of summer school on math and reading scores separately, this sample would contribute one effect size to each estimate of the overall mean effect size. This shifting unit of analysis approach retains as much data as possible from each study while holding to a minimum any violations of the assumption that data points are independent.

The meta-analysis of the effects of remedial summer programs was based on 99 independent samples of students that gave rise to 385 separate comparisons. The 99 samples were described in 41 different research reports. The number of independent samples in a research report ranged from 1 to 10. Of the 99 samples, 18 were described by the researchers as containing students in special education.

Inspecting the Effect Size Distribution

Recently, meta-analyses have contained detailed information on the characteristics of the distribution of effect sizes. This information often includes stem-and-leaf displays and/or funnel plots (Greenhouse & Iyengar, 1994) that help assess whether publication bias might exist in the sample of comparison outcomes. The distribution of effects is also examined to determine whether it contains statistical outliers (Barnett & Lewis, 1978). If outliers are present the meta-analyst then must decide how to treat them. Some synthesists remove them from the data set entirely whereas others will modify the outlying values so as to make them conform more to the general distribution of results. For either option, the meta-analyst wishes to both make the distribution of effects more normal and to mitigate the effect of a few extreme values on measures of central tendency and dispersion, and on moderator analyses.

In the summer school meta-analysis, we inspected the distribution of the 385 d indexes using a stem-and-leaf plot. We noted that about 3% of the comparisons had unusually high d values, above $d = 1.50$. We then applied Tukey's (1977) definition that identifies values more than three interquartile ranges beyond the 75th percentile as statistical outliers. Three positive d-index values qualified as statistical outliers and these came from two different evaluations. We then examined these studies more closely. The descriptions suggested these studies had several characteristics that were potentially desirable and of substantive interest but that appeared only infrequently in other programs (e.g., parent involvement, in-residence programs). In fact, these studies might provide examples of "best practice." Therefore, we chose not to remove them from our data set. Instead, we set the value of the 13 comparisons with the highest d indexes to just above the value of their next nearest neighbor, in this case to $d = 1.50$. The process of adjusting extreme values so that they more closely conform to the overall distribution was called "Winsorizing" the data points by Barnett and Lewis (1978).

Vote Counting

After examining the distribution of effect sizes, it is common for meta-analysts to count the number of positive and negative findings that occur in the data set. This procedure, called a "vote count" can take several forms. First, the meta-analyst could take each finding and place it into one of three categories: statistically significant findings in a positive direction, statistically significant findings in a negative direction, and nonsignificant findings. The meta-analyst then would declare that the category with the largest number of findings should represent the literature as a whole.

The vote count of significant findings is unacceptably conservative. The problem is that chance alone should produce only about 5% of all comparisons falsely indicating a treatment has a positive effect, whereas this strategy requires that more than 33% of findings be positive and statistically significant before a treatment is ruled effective. Thus, the vote count of significant findings could, and often does, lead to the suggested abandonment of treatments when, in fact, no such conclusion is warranted.

A different way to perform vote counts in research synthesis involves counting the number of positive and negative results, regardless of significance. This method has the advantage of using all findings, but it suffers because the impact of the treatment under evaluation in each comparison is not considered—a comparison showing a large positive change is given equal weight to one showing a small negative change.

Still, the vote count of directional findings can be an informative complement to other meta-analytic procedures. Hedges and Olkin (1985) provided a technique by which the underlying magnitude of a treatment's effect can be estimated from the proportions of studies showing positive and negative directional outcomes (see also Bushman, 1994). This approach requires that the vote counter know the direction of each test of the treatment and the sample size associated with each condition, treatment, and control. In addition, the procedure is dramatically simplified if the sample sizes of the treatment and control conditions are equal within studies and also across all tests of the treatment. The vote counter uses these values to enter a table, provided by Hedges and Olkin, to find the estimated effect size.

In the summer school meta-analysis, we performed Hedges and Olkin's (1985) procedure on findings for samples described in reports that did not give enough information for us to calculate an effect size. Specifically, in addition to the 41 reports we used to calculate our overall d-value, we found 30 documents including 121 independent samples that did not report both the means and standard deviations or the statistical tests needed to generate a d-index. Ninety-five of the independent samples produced results that showed positive effects of summer school on all comparisons and 8 more samples were predominantly positive. Six samples showed neither predominantly positive nor negative effects of summer school. Eight independent samples produced all negative effects and four samples showed predominantly negative effects.

First, we had to devise an estimate for the "equal" sample sizes in our treatment and control conditions. The average total sample size in each independent sample was about 640, so equal samples in treatment and control conditions might be set at about 320. However, because the data set contained a few evaluations with very large samples, the median total sample size was 35, or about 17 in each condition. Therefore, we decided to use both of these values to enter the Hedges and Olkin's (1985) table.

Next, we had to calculate the proportion of results that were positive. Again, we decided to do this in two ways. First, we used as our proportion of positive results the number of independent samples that revealed all or predominantly positive findings ($n = 103$) divided by all findings that were either positive or negative ($n = 115$). This proportion was .896. Then, we entered the table using both the mean and median "equal" sample sizes within conditions. Using the mean sample size, the estimated effect size was $d = .10$. Using the median sample size the estimated effect size was $d = .44$. Next, we used as our proportions of positive results the number of independent samples that had all positive findings ($n = 95$) divided by the number of findings that were either all positive or all negative findings ($n = 103$). This proportion was .922. Using the mean condition sample size, the estimated d-value was $d = .12$. Using the median sample size, the estimated d value was $d = .49$.

In this way, the vote-count procedure provided a very rough estimate of the effect of remedial summer programs, suggesting that participants scored between one tenth and one half of a standard deviation higher on the outcome measure than did controls. Not too surprisingly, the estimate we found based on the studies that did yield d indexes, $d = .32$, fell quite nearly equidistant between these two extremes.

Combining Probabilities Across Studies

The meta-analyst might next consider combining the precise probabilities associated with the results of each study. Becker (1994; also see Rosenthal, 1984) cataloged 16 methods for combining the results of inference tests so that an overall test of the null hypothesis could be obtained. All of the methods require that the statistical tests (a) relate to the same hypothesis, (b) are independent, and (c) meet the initial statistical assumptions made by the primary researchers.

The combining probabilities procedure overcomes the improper weighting problems of the vote count. However, it has severe limitations of its own. Most important for special education synthesists, the combined probability addresses the question of whether or not an effect exists while giving no information on whether that effect is large or small, important or trivial. Further, the information obtained by combining p levels, that is, whether the null hypothesis is rejected, can be inferred from the calculation of a confidence interval to accompany the average effect size. If the confidence interval does not contain zero, then the null hypothesis can be rejected. For these reasons, the use of combined probabilities in meta-analysis has largely disappeared.

Measuring the Central Tendency and Dispersion of Effect Sizes

The most pivotal outcomes of a meta-analysis are the average effect sizes and measures of dispersion that accompany them. Both unweighted and weighted procedures are typically used to calculate average effect sizes across comparisons. In the unweighted procedure, each effect size is given equal weight in calculating the average effect. In the weighted procedure, each independent effect size is first multiplied by the inverse of its variance and the sum of these products is then divided by the sum of the inverses. The weighting procedure is generally preferred because it gives greater weight to effect sizes based on larger samples. Also, as noted earlier, confidence intervals are calculated for weighted average d indexes. Both Hedges and Olkin (1985) and Shadish and Haddock (1994) provided procedures for calculating the appropriate weights and confidence intervals.

In our meta-analysis of summer school evaluations, after we adjusted the extreme values the average unweighted d index for the 99 independent samples, as mentioned previously, was $d = .32$ When effect sizes were weighted by the inverse of their variances the average d index was $d = .26$. The median effect size was $d = .19$. Thus, making no distinctions based on methodological, program, measurement, or student characteristics, the average student outcome score after summer school was just less between two tenths and one third of a standard deviation higher than the average student score before summer school or without summer school. The 95% confidence interval for the weighted d index was bounded by a lower value of $d = .24$ and an upper value of $d = .28$. Clearly then, the null hypothesis that remedial summer school had no effect could be rejected.

In addition to the confidence interval as a measure of dispersion, research synthesists usually carry out a "homogeneity analyses." A homogeneity analysis compares the amount of variance in an observed set of effect sizes with the amount of variance that would be expected by sampling error alone. If there is greater variation in effects than would be expected by chance, then the meta-analyst begins the process of examining moderators of comparison outcomes.

There are numerous statistical packages that can be used to carry out a homogeneity analysis. In the summer school meta-analysis, we conducted the homogeneity analyses using the general linear model program of the Statistical Analysis System (SAS; SAS Institute, 1992). We found a highly significant homogeneity statistic, suggesting we reject the hypothesis that the d indexes were all estimating the same underlying population value, or that sampling error alone was responsible for the variation in effects.

Examining Variance in Effect Sizes

The search for why the outcomes of comparisons differ is the most interesting and informative part of conducting a meta-analysis. The synthesist calculates average d indexes for subsets of studies, comparing the average effect sizes for different methods, types of programs, outcome measures, and students. In fact, the synthesist can ask questions about variables that moderate outcomes even if no individual study has included the moderator variable. For example, a meta-analyst can ask whether summer school has different effects on students in special education programs versus students in regular education by comparing the average d index for special education versus regular education students. The results of such a comparison of average d values can suggest whether this student characteristic would be important to look at in future research and/or as a guide to policy.

After calculating the average effect sizes for different subgroups of comparisons, the meta-analyst statistically tests whether the group factor is reliably associated with different magnitudes of effect. As noted earlier, three statistical procedures for examining variation in effect sizes have appeared in the literature. The first approach applies statistical procedures typically used on primary research data, like ANOVA (analysis of variance) or multiple regression. The effect sizes serve as the dependent variable and comparison features serve as independent or predictor variables. This approach has been criticized based on the questionable tenability of the underlying assumptions (see Hedges & Olkin, 1985). Most notably, traditional inferential statistics assume that the error in measurement is relatively homogeneous across data points. This assumption is often violated in meta-analytic data sets.

The second approach compares the variation in obtained effect sizes with the variation expected due to sampling error (Hunter & Schmidt, 1990). This approach involves calculating not only the observed variance in effects but also the expected variance, given that all observed effects are estimating the same population value. A formal statistical test of the difference between these two values is typically not carried out. Rather, the meta-analyst adopts a critical value for the ratio of observed-to-expected variance to use as a means for rejecting the null hypothesis. The meta-analyst might also adjust effect sizes to account for methodological artifacts such as sampling error, range restrictions, or unreliability of measurements.

The third approach involves the homogeneity statistic described earlier. Analogous to ANOVA, comparisons are grouped by features and the average effect sizes for these groups are tested to determine if the averages are drawn from the same population. If this hypothesis is rejected, the grouping variable remains a plausible potential moderator of effect.

It is relatively simple to carry out a homogeneity analysis using computer statistical packages. The formulas and techniques for homogeneity analysis are described in Cooper (1998), Cooper and Hedges (1994), Hedges and Olkin (1985), Rosenthal (1984), and Wolf (1986).

To illustrate how a search for moderators of treatment outcomes might proceed, we examine whether the achievement labels given to students in summer school programs were associated with the effectiveness of the program. The evaluation reports used four different labels to distinguish the achievement or learning capabilities of students in remedial summer programs. Primary researchers labeled students as (a) *at risk* if children were having difficulties in school or were identified as potentially experiencing difficulties, (b) *below grade level or underachieving* if student test scores were used to identify underachievers, (c) *failed or retained* if students became eligible for summer school because they either failed a particular course or were to be retained in grade if they did not participate in the summer program, and (d) *learning or otherwise disabled* if a specified learning disability or other physical or emotional challenge was used to identify participants eligible for the program.

We found the students' achievement label was associated with a statistically significant amount of variation in estimates of the impact of summer school. Students with learning disabilities or physical or emotional challenges, $d = .34$, revealed the largest effect of summer school, followed by students labeled *underachieving*, $d = .27$, students who were failing a course or grade level, $d = .23$, and students labeled *at risk*, $d = .19$. However, it is important to note that in all four cases, the 95% confidence intervals calculated for all four average effects revealed that all students showed significant gains associated with attending summer school.

In addition to the achievement labels, we also examined methodological, program, outcome, and other student variations that might have been associated with the effect sizes revealed by evaluations of summer school. In each case we used a homogeneity analysis to guide our conclusions. Without the aid of statistics, the narrative research synthesist would have simply grouped the comparisons by shared features, examined the statistical significance of outcomes across studies, and decided intuitively whether the feature was associated with variation in outcomes. At best, this method is imprecise. At worst, it leads to incorrect inferences, most often involving the mislabeling of reliable effects as nonexistent and the inability to detect significant moderating variables.

In contrast, the meta-analyst employs a formal means for testing whether different features of studies explain variation in their outcomes. This is an extension of the same rules of inference required of primary researchers. Because effect sizes are sample statistics, they will vary somewhat even if they all estimate the same underlying population value. Homogeneity analysis allows the synthesist to test whether sampling error alone accounted for this variation or whether features of studies, samples, treatment designs, or outcome measures also play a role. If reliable differences do exist, the average effect sizes corresponding to these differences will take on added meaning and will help the synthesist make policy recommendations.

Sensitivity Analysis

An additional step in meta-analysis gaining popularity is the performance of sensitivity analyses. A sensitivity analysis is used to determine if and how the conclusion of an analysis might differ if it was conducted using different statistical procedures or data assumptions. There are numerous points at which a meta-analyst might decide a sensitivity analysis is appropriate. For example, there might be a set of comparisons that fall at the edge of the conceptual definition of what constitutes summer school. The effects of summer school might be tested with and without the inclusion of these comparisons. Or, some evaluations of summer school might have missing data. These comparisons might be omitted from one analysis and included in another analysis that makes conservative assumptions about what those values might be. Lastly, the calculation of weighted, unweighted, and median effect sizes can be considered a form of sensitivity analysis. In each case, the meta-analyst is seeking to determine whether a particular finding is robust across different sets of assumptions. If the answer is "yes," then greater confidence can be placed in the conclusion.

The summer school meta-analysis provided an interesting example of sensitivity analysis that involved our finding concerning students in special education. As is true for any data set composed of cases not under the control of the researcher, we found significant correlations among some of our predictor variables. The confounding of methodological, program, outcome measure, and student characteristics highlighted the fact that plausible rival hypotheses existed whenever we wished to claim a reliable link between the effect of a summer program and one of the moderating variables.

The confounding of moderator variables led us to perform some sensitivity analyses by statistically adjusting effect sizes. To do this, we used multiple regression procedures to adjust each d index so that it was no longer correlated with seven methodological factors that were significant moderators of the evaluation outcomes. Then, we reran the homogeneity analyses involving the student achievement label, as well as numerous others. In this second set of homogeneity analyses, when we adjusted the d index values to removed variance associated with methodological factors, the d value for students with disabilities decreased to $d = .23$ whereas that for "underachievers" rose to $d = .36$, and those for the other two groups of students remained nearly the same.

In sum then, meta-analysts have a wide array of techniques at their disposal. Some of these techniques have been developed specifically for analysis of meta-analytic data sets and others have been adopted from other research methodologies. The specific techniques used in any meta-analysis will differ somewhat depending on the characteristics of the data set and the questions asked by the research synthesist.

SOME THREATS TO THE VALIDITY OF META-ANALYTIC OUTCOMES

The development and use of statistical techniques to combine results of studies has been paralleled by a growing recognition that all aspects of research synthesis would benefit from more rigorous and systematic procedures. Several early attempts that framed research synthesis in the terms of a scientific process occurred independent of the meta-analysis movement.

For example, Feldman (1971) contended that research synthesis "may be considered a type of research in its own right—one using a characteristic set of research techniques and methods" (p. 86). Three years later, Taveggia (1974) described six common problems in literature reviews: selecting research; retrieving, indexing, and coding studies; analyzing the comparability of findings; accumulating comparable findings; analyzing the resulting distributions; and reporting the results. Jackson (1980) proposed six reviewing tasks "analogous to those performed during primary research" (p. 441). He examined a sample of 36 review articles from prestigious social science periodicals and concluded that "relatively little thought has been given to the methods for doing integrative reviews" (p. 459).

Cooper (1982, 1998) also demonstrated the isomorphism between research synthesis and primary research. He presented a five-stage model of research synthesis. Similar to primary research, research synthesis was said to involve problem formulation, data collection (the literature search), data evaluation, data analysis and interpretation (the meta-analysis), and public presentation. For each stage, Cooper codified the research question, its primary function in the review, and the procedural differences that might cause variation in reviews' conclusions.

In addition, Cooper applied Campbell and Stanley's (1966; also see Cook & Campbell, 1979) notion of threats-to-inferential-validity to research synthesis. He pointed out that at each stage of a research synthesis certain biases might be introduced into the process that would undermine the trustworthiness of findings. For example, Cooper pointed out that during problem formulation threats to the validity of a synthesis could occur if the synthesist did not pay proper attention to conceptual distinctions in definitions and hypotheses that were viewed as important by others in the field. The validity of a literature search could be compromised by the use of a few selective sources of research reports or by publication bias. Data evaluation can be threatened if information from research reports is missing or if the individuals extracting information from documents are poorly trained.

Matt and Cook (1994) expanded on Cooper's list of threats to validity. Here, we examine five threats to validity that can be introduced during the analysis stage of research synthesis. Two of these threats, namely (a) nonindependent effect sizes being treated as though they were independent and (b) failure to weight effect sizes by their degree of precision before averaging, have already been discussed. Three other threats associated with the conduct of a meta-analysis deserve brief mention.

One obvious threat to the validity of meta-analytic conclusions involves the rules of inference employed by a synthesist. The possibility always exists that the meta-analyst has used an invalid rule for inferring a characteristic of the target population. This occurs because the target population does not conform to the assumptions underlying the analysis techniques. Of course, this is not a shortcoming unique to the use of quantitative integration techniques. In nonquantitative syntheses, rules of inference also must be used but it is difficult to gauge their appropriateness because they are not very often made explicit. For meta-analyses, the suppositions of statistical tests are generally known and some statistical biases in reviews can be removed.

Another threat to validity is that the meta-analyst might capitalize on or suffer because of the probabilitistic nature of statistical findings. First, as in primary research, the meta-analyst might conduct many statistical tests without adjusting for "synthesis-wise" error rates. Second, because of gaps in the literature, a meta-analyst might discover so few tests of a particular hypothesis that the statistical power of the meta-analysis is low. Unlike a primary researcher, the meta-analyst cannot run more subjects (or in this case, more studies) so as to increase the sensitivity of tests. It is possible to expand the search for relevant research.

Finally, a threat to validity that recently has received considerable attention from meta-analysts involves the decision about whether a fixed-effects or random-effects model underlies the generation of study outcomes. Effect sizes in a meta-analysis are said to be fixed when sampling error is the only random influence on estimates of variance. However, other features of studies sometimes can be viewed as random influences. For example, in studies of summer school and achievement, variation in students will clearly be a source of random error. If this is the only source of random error, then the effects can be treated as fixed. However, the effect of the same summer school program might also differ from school to school or class to class because of unsystematic variation introduced by different program, components, coordinators, or classroom teachers. If the meta-analyst believes these sources of variance exist and are random, then the statistical analysis must proceed in a fashion that takes this additional random error into account.

It is rarely clear cut which model, fixed or random, is most appropriate for a particular set of effect sizes. To date, most meta-analysts have opted for the fixed-effects assumption because it is analytically easier to manage. Some meta-analysts argue that fixed-effect models are often used when random-effects models are more appropriate (and conservative). Others counterargue that a fixed-effect statistical model can be applied if a thorough, appropriate search for influences on effect sizes is part of the analytic strategy. We suspect that the use of random-effects models will increase due to recent attempts to explicate the random-effects model and to make its application more accessible to meta-analysis practitioners (Hedges & Vevea, 1998).

In the summer school synthesis, we chose to conduct the homogeneity analyses using both fixed-effect and random-effect models. This permitted us to compare the results under both sets of assumptions, thus giving us yet another form of sensitivity information. The weighted overall average d value using a random-effects model was $d = .26$, identical to the value we found using a fixed-effect model. However, the 95% confidence interval using the random-effect model widened to a lower estimate of $d = .21$ and a higher estimate of $d = .31$, compared to $d = .24$ and $.28$, respectively, under fixed-effect assumptions.

CONCLUSION

Every discipline can claim great variety in its methods and treatments. And, as we learn about a problem area we become more aware of the important implications of the finest nuances in meaning implied by small variations in methods, contexts, and program design. Still, special education research synthesists seem to confront a degree of heterogeneity more pronounced then most. Asserting that a set of studies is appropriate for aggregation grows more tenuous in positive relation to the variety of populations, methods, and outcomes. More careful attention to methods of synthesis is also required. With this in mind, those who undertake the task of gathering, summarizing, and integrating special education literatures deserve added acclaim.

REFERENCES

Barnett, V., & Lewis, T. (1978). *Outliers in statistical data*. Chicester, England: Wiley.
Becker, B. J. (1994). Combining significance levels. In H. Cooper & L. V. Hedges (Eds.), *Handbook of research synthesis* (pp. 215–230). New York: Russell Sage Foundation.
Bushman, B. J. (1994). Vote-counting procedures in meta-analysis. In H. Cooper & L. V. Hedges (Eds.), *Handbook of research synthesis* (pp. 193–214). New York: Russell Sage Foundation.
Campbell, D. T., & Stanley, J. C. (1966). *Experimental and quasi-experimental designs for research*. Chicago: Rand McNally.
Cohen, J. (1988). *Statistical power analysis in the behavioral sciences*. Hillsdale, NJ: Lawrence Erlbaum Associates.
Cook, T. D., & Campbell, D. T. (1979). *Quasi-experimentation: Design and analysis issues for field setting*. Chicago: Rand McNally.
Cook, T. D., Cooper, H. M., Cordray, D. S., Hartmann, H., Hedges, L. V., Light, R. J., Louis, T., & Mosteller, F. (1992). *Meta-analysis for explanation: A casebook*. New York: Russell Sage Foundation.
Cooper, H. M. (1979). Statistically combining independent studies: A meta-analysis of sex differences in conformity research. *Journal of Personality and Social Psychology, 37*, 131–146.
Cooper, H. M. (1982). Scientific guidelines for conducting integrative research reviews. *Review of Educational Research, 52*, 291–302.
Cooper, H. M. (1998). *Synthesizing research: A guide for literature reviews* (3rd ed.). Thousand Oaks, CA: Sage.

Cooper, H., Charlton, K., Valentine, J. V., & Muhlenbruck, L. (2000). *Making the most of summer school: A meta-analytic and narrative review.* Monograph Series of the Society for Research in Child Development. Malden, MA: Blackwell.

Cooper, H., & Hedges, L. V. (1994). *Handbook of research synthesis.* New York: Russell Sage Foundation.

Cooper, H. M., & Rosenthal, R. (1980). Statistical versus traditional procedures for summarizing research findings. *Psychological Bulletin, 87,* 442–449.

Eddy, D. M., Hassleblad, V., & Schachter, R. (1992). *Meta-analysis by the confidence profile method.* Boston: Academic Press.

Feldman, K. A. (1971). Using the work of others: Some observations on reviewing and integrating. *Sociology of Education, 4,* 86–102.

Fisher, R. A. (1932). *Statistical methods for research workers.* London: Oliver & Boyd.

Glass, G. V. (1976). Primary, secondary, and meta-analysis of research. *Educational Researcher, 5,* 3–8.

Glass, G. V., McGaw, B., & Smith, M. L. (1981). *Meta-analysis in social research.* Beverly Hills, CA: Sage.

Glass, G. V., & Smith, M. L. (1979). Meta-analysis of research on class size and achievement. *Educational Evaluation and Policy Analysis, 1,* 2–16.

Gleser, L. J., & Olkin, I. (1994). Stochastically dependent effect sizes. In H. Cooper & L. V. Hedges (Eds.), *Handbook of research synthesis* (pp. 339–356). New York: Russell Sage Foundation.

Greenhouse, J. B., & Iyengar, S. (1994). Sensitivity analysis and diagnostics. In H. Cooper & L. V. Hedges (Eds.), *Handbook of research synthesis* (pp. 383–398). New York: Russell Sage Foundation.

Hedges, L. V., & Olkin, I. (1985). *Statistical methods for meta-analysis.* Orlando, FL: Academic Press.

Hedges, L. V., & Vevea, J. L. (1998). Fixed and random effects models in meta-analysis. *Psychological Methods, 3,* 486–504.

Hunter, J. E., & Schmidt, F. L. (1990). *Methods of meta-analysis: Correcting error and bias in research findings.* Beverly Hills, CA: Sage.

Hunter, J. E., Schmidt, F. L., & Hunter, R. (1979). Differential validity of employment tests by race: A comprehensive review and analysis. *Psychological Bulletin, 86,* 721–735.

Hunter, J. E., Schmidt, F. L., & Jackson, G. B. (1982). *Meta-analysis: Cumulating research findings across studies.* Beverly Hills, CA: Sage.

Jackson, G. B. (1980). Methods for integrative reviews. *Review of Educational Research, 50,* 438–460.

Johnson, B. T. (1989). *DSTAT: Software for the meta-analytic review of research literatures.* Hillsdale, NJ: Lawrence Erlbaum Associates.

Light, R. J., & Pillemer, D. B. (1984). *Summing up: The science of research reviewing.* Cambridge, MA: Harvard University Press.

Matt, G. E., & Cook, T. D. (1994). Threats to the validity of research syntheses. In H. Cooper & L. V. Hedges (Eds.), *Handbook of research synthesis* (pp. 503–520). New York: Russell Sage Foundation.

Mullen, B. (1989). *Advanced BASIC meta-analysis.* Hillsdale, NJ: Lawrence Erlbaum Associates.

Pearson, K. (1904). Report on certain enteric fever inoculation statistics. *British Medical Journal, 3,* 1243–1246.

Raudenbush, S. W., Becker, B. J., & Kalaian, H. (1988). Modeling multivariate effect sizes. *Psychological Bulletin, 103,* 111–120.

Rosenthal, R. (1984). *Meta-analytic procedures for social research.* Beverly Hills, CA: Sage.

Rosenthal, R. (1994). Parametric measures of effect size. In H. Cooper & L. V. Hedges (Eds.), *Handbook of research synthesis.* New York: Russell Sage Foundation.

Rosenthal, R., & Rubin, D. (1978). Interpersonal expectancy effects: The first 345 studies. *Behavioral and Brain Sciences, 3,* 377–415.

SAS Institute. (1992). *SAS user's guide: Statistics* (Version 6). Cary, NC: Author.

Shadish, W. R., & Haddock, C. K. (1994). Combining estimates of effect size. In H. Cooper & L. V. Hedges (Eds.), *Handbook of research synthesis* (pp. 261–282). New York: Russell Sage Foundation.

Taveggia, T. C. (1974). Resolving research controversy through empirical cumulation: Toward reliable sociological knowledge. *Sociological Methods & Research, 2,* 395–407.

Tukey, J. W. (1977). *Exploratory data analysis.* Reading, MA: Addison-Wesley.

Wachter, K. W., & Straf, M. L. (Eds.). (1990). *The future of meta-analysis.* New York: Russell Sage Foundation.

Wolf, F. W. (1986). Meta-analysis: Quantitative methods for research synthesis. Beverly Hills, CA: Sage.

Chapter 9

Policy Decisions in Special Education: The Role of Meta-Analysis

Kenneth A. Kavale
The University of Iowa

Steven R. Forness
University of California, Los Angeles

Let's turn the clock back some 25 years; suppose that you have to decide whether or not to include "psycholinguistic training" for students in the recently designated special education classification of learning disabilities (LD). The elements of psycholinguistic training were formulated by Samuel A. Kirk, a prominent name in special education, were based on the widely used Illinois Test of Psycholinguistic Abilities (ITPA), and were targeted at the process deficits assumed associated with LD. Although appearing to be a useful remedial technique, your decision would probably require a more rational justification. Such justification might be gleaned from the available evidence that could be scrutinized to show "what the research says." The literature would reveal that the ITPA has served as the clinical model for a variety of remedial and developmental language programs. These programs are based on the assumption that language is comprised of discrete components, and these components can be improved with training. Suppose you acquired a reasonable sample of research studies that investigated the effectiveness of psycholinguistic training. In all likelihood you would not be able to make an unequivocal decision, the research evidence would be mixed with some positive and some negative evaluations. Under such circumstances, the policy decision about whether or not to include psycholinguistic training in the remedial curriculum becomes complex and difficult.

Research Integration and Policy Decisions

A single study, no matter how well done, is unlikely to provide the definitive answer on a subject. Research design and analysis is not an exact science; consequently, different choices among methods may lead to sometimes significant, sometimes subtle variance among outcomes. With no precise standards to judge which is "better," any single study may often be the source of controversy. Yet, ample findings are available, and it makes sense to combine the findings from many studies. Because knowledge should be cumulative, combining individual research studies into one corpus of knowledge is the best means of determining "what the research says."

The question now shifts to the best means of combining individual research studies. A variety of methods exist for synthesizing research studies but have also been open to debate. In a general sense, methods for integrating research must be rigorous and systematic; standards of objectivity, verifiability, and replicability are essential. The size of the available research literature often determines the method of research synthesis. But as a literature domain becomes larger and, therefore, more unwieldy, methods of integration often become less systematic and rigorous, and hence fail to meet the necessary scientific standards.

Narrative Reviews

Perhaps the most common method of research integration is the narrative synthesis whose goal is to provide a verbal report describing individual research studies to reach an overall conclusion. What is ultimately represented is a "review of the literature" where it is reported that Smith (2000) found X and Jones (2001) found Y. Although often a comprehensive rendering of the available research, this sort of serial presentation only reports findings one at a time rather than in combination. What is lacking is a synthesis that extracts knowledge from the reported findings. Any single study, because research outcomes are probabitistic, may produce findings that have occurred by chance. Therefore:

> It also follows that, if a large enough number of researches have been done on a particular topic, chance alone dictates that studies will exist that report inconsistent and contradictory findings! Thus, what appears to be contradictory may simply be the positive and negative details of a distribution of findings. (Taveggia, 1974, p. 398)

The narrative review often fails to accumulate findings and keeps them independent and isolated. Consequently, knowledge tends to be neither corroborated nor refuted. There is a status quo established where inconsistencies are viewed simply as temporal, spatial, contextual, or method-ological anomalies with limited influence on outcomes. The resulting review may appear to be an adequate summary but is likely to result in premature explanation and faulty understanding (Yin, Bingham, & Heald, 1976).

Too often, the situation develops where "the integrater must navigate between the Scylla and Charydis of 'hypercriticalness' and 'hypocritical-ness' " (Feldman, 1971, p. 96). The basic dilemma: What to do in the case of disagreement among individual study findings? Long ago, Bacon (1620/1989) discussed the influence of Idols (illusions) that may adverse-ly effect reasoning and suggest the possible restrictions and limitations that impinge on the narrative review process to make it a less objective means of accumulating evidence.

Yet, it is necessary to deal with inconsistent findings because "the vari-ance in our findings is essential, largely irreducible. It should be viewed as something to be studied in its own right" (Glass, 1976, p. 6). Light and Pillemer (1984) further suggested that such outcome variation may con-tain valuable information. An incorrect solution to the problem of study variation would be to impose various stipulative parameters incorporating a priori judgments of research quality that only serve to discount some findings and reduce the literature base. The reduced literature base reveals a certain consistency, but this consonance is achieved for the wrong reasons. The rendering of the remaining studies has been likened to "exercises in forcing an intransigent literature into the Procrustean bed of foregone conclusions" (M. L. Smith, Glass, & Miller, 1980, p. 26).

Numerical Reviews

The inability of narrative descriptions to provide synthesized knowledge led to alternative methodology based on the classification of study out-comes. The most typical procedure is to classify individual studies in a contingency table based on the statistical significance or nonsignificance. Such a "box score" integration is thus based on a "voting method" where the number of studies falling into significant or nonsignificant category are tallied, and the one containing the plurality of studies declared the "winner" (Light & Pillemer, 1984). The winning category is then used to draw conclusions about the topic under study.

Although seemingly more rigorous than narrative methods, numerical reviews also possess difficulties. The primary difficulty surrounds the uncertainties about the assumptions, meaning, interpretation, and rele-vance of statistical probabilities in deciding to accept or to reject hypothe-ses; statistical inference is primarily useful for eliminating chance findings, not in deciding subject matter issues (Carver, 1978). Regardless of how sophisticated the statistical analysis, significant probabilities (i.e., p < .05) neither confirm or refute a research hypothesis but only the null hypothesis (Lykken, 1968). The finding may be "significant" but such significance should not be confused with importance; a null hypothesis does not test a research hypothesis because it represents only a calculated description of uncertainty (Grant, 1962). Taken literally, the null hypothesis is almost always false, and the probability of refuting it is almost exclusively a function of sample size: The larger the sample, the greater the probability of refuting the null hypothesis (see Morrison & Henkel, 1970).

Fisher (1967) developed procedures for statistical significance testing in agronomy that is radically different from a field like special education. In agronomy, there exists a much closer association between research and statistical (i.e., null) hypotheses. For example, if a research investigation is directed at knowing whether using fertilizer will increase soybean yields, then, because soybeans receive their nutrients from the soil, refutation of the null hypothesis is valid. The situation in special education is not at all equivalent and, even if the null hypothesis is rejected, a number of alternative hypotheses must be ruled out before the validity of the scientific hypothesis is confirmed (Bolles, 1962).

The probability of rejection of a given null hypothesis is given by the power of the particular test. With the power of research in special education found to be modest (e.g., Hopkins, 1973), the failure to reject the null hypothesis results in the acceptance of the null hypothesis even when the probability of making a Type II error may often be more than .50. Although research in special education is typically rigid and conservative with respect to level of significance, little attention is paid to the power of a test that means the choice of significance level is practically meaningless (Meehl, 1978). Nevertheless, as sample size increases, it becomes easier to reject the null hypothesis and easier to accept the alternative hypothesis. Additionally, when many statistical tests are performed on a single data set, the alpha rate changes considerably; with 10 tests and a significance level of .05, the probability of Type I error in 1 or more of the 10 decisions is near .40 (Ryan, 1959).

With large-sample studies producing more statistically significant findings, numerical methods of research integration are biased against small-sample studies. For example, suppose in a pool of 10 studies, 9 with small samples are in the expected direction but not statistically significant, whereas 1 study with a large sample is significant. The voting method produces a box-score tally of one for and nine against, but this represents a conclusion at variance with common sense.

If the goal of research integration is to accumulate information, then strict decisions based on probability levels, because they are static, does not permit decisions that allow for adjustments in the degree of belief about a hypothesis (Rozeboom, 1960). With simple accept or reject decisions, this dichoto-mizing is antithetical to the scientific process of knowledge accumulation. The difficulties are compounded when a large number of studies with sig-nificance tests are combined. Hedges and Olkin (1980) demonstrated that the probability of *not* deciding that there is a positive effect using the box-score strategy is .77, and concluded that, "This procedure is shown to have extremely low power for the combination of treatment-effect sizes and sam-ple sizes usually found in social science research. Surprisingly, the power of this procedure decreases as the number of studies reviewed increase" (p. 359). With voting methods shown not to include all available positive evi-dence, Ladas (1980) concluded that, "the process of box score reviewing skews recommendations towards unwarranted pessimism" (p. 620). Thus, both theoretical and pragmatic difficulties are inherent in box score integra-tions and detract from their objectivity. The tenets of scientific methods are often not found when the task is to synthesize findings from a number of studies rather than performing a single experimental investigation. Conse-quently, research integration becomes subject to the whims and fancies of individual reviewers and, "thus do reviews become idiosyncratic, authoritar-ian, subjective—all those things that cut against the scientific grain" (Glass, McGaw, & M. L. Smith, 1981, p. 20).

Meta Analysis and Research Integration

Research integration requires an attitude that resembles techniques for col-lecting and analyzing primary data. Toward this end, Glass (1976) proposed meta-analysis as a means for statistically integrating a body of literature. As a statistical process, meta-analysis possesses the following advantages:

1. It uses quantitative-statistical methods for organizing and extracting information from large databases.
2. It eliminates study selection bias—no prejudgments about research quality are made.
3. It makes use of all information—study findings are transformed to commensurable expressions of magnitude.
4. It detects interactions—study characteristics that mediate findings are defined, measured, and their covariation studied.
5. It seeks general conclusions—practical simplicity is sought that does not obscure important interactive findings.

This systematic and statistical summarization of study findings permits the discovery of knowledge that lies untapped in special education research and reverses the embarrassing position of knowing less than has been proven.

Meta-analysis represents an inductive method of research integration whose aim is to provide insights of understanding in the sense that Kuhn (1970) termed the "decoding of reality." The understanding provided by meta-analysis may be conceptualized as consisting of four components: (a) clarifying the parameters of the phenomenon under study by summarizing data, (b) making explicit what is only implicit, (c) eliminating unessential elements by providing a conceptual whole, and (d) placing a phenomenon into an appropriate context (see Toulmin, 1961). Such understanding of collective findings is necessary for policy decisions because single studies probably give rise to as many contentious policy disputes as they settle (see Lindblom & Cohen, 1979). Meta-analysis appears to offer such a methodology (Hunt, 1997).

Methods of Meta-Analysis

Meta-analysis generally follows the activities found in "primary" research efforts. These activities include the empirical act of gathering information, defining problems by asking relevant questions, analysis under controlled conditions, proposing hypotheses suggesting possible solutions to the questions posed, and theory formulation in the form of generalizations that summarize data, predict new observations, and guide further research. The actual techniques of meta-analysis have been comprehensively outlined (e.g., Glass et al., 1981) and, although not unequivocally accepted (e.g., Abrami, Cohen, & d'Apollonia, 1988; Slavin, 1984), have become an accepted means of summarizing statistically a research domain (e.g., Cook, 1994; Cooper & Hedges, 1993; Rosenthal, 1984) that have served to enhance objectivity, verifiability, and replicability (Wachter & Straf, 1990).

Meta-analysis attempts to capture the texture of an entire domain by posing questions that are broad in scope. In the example presented earlier, the question posed was, "Is psycholinguistic training effective?" By defining comprehensive questions, meta-analysis focuses on the strategic level of scientific method by avoiding "errors of the third kind" (Type III), that is, the probability of solving the "wrong" problem when one should have solved the "right" problem (see Mitroff & Featheringham, 1974).

The basic statistic in meta-analysis is the "effect size" (ES) that represents a phenomenon in standard deviation (SD) units. Although simple in appearance, the ES possesses the advantage of transforming individual study findings into a common metric. Because the ES represents a standardized mean difference, comparisons based on different outcome measures are rendered comparable even though their conceptual comparability is not as straightforward. Although it might be argued that there is little justification for combining data from different measures, the arguments falter in the question of just how different two measures must be before they cannot be aggregated. Any rendering of "what the research says," however, involves implicit generalization across studies that is probably far less systematic than the process found in meta-analysis.

The flexibility associated with ES interpretation represents a significant advantage for the meta-analysis procedure. The meaning of ES is conveyed through notions of overlapping distributions, and comparable percentiles if unobjectionable assumptions about a normal distribution of outcomes is made. For example, if an intervention produces an ES of 1.00, then there is a 1 *SD* advantage for the group receiving the intervention. The group distributions (experimental vs. control) would thus be separated by 1 *SD* at their means and would show the average of the experimental group to be located above 84% of the area under the control group distribution. This indicates that a student at the 50th percentile of the control group would gain 34 percentile ranks as a result of intervention and rise to the 84th percentile of the control group distribution. The relationships suggest that the student receiving the intervention would be better off than 84% of the control group, whereas only 16% of the control group would be better off than the student receiving the intervention.

In addition to interpretations about percentiles and percentages along a distribution, the ES offers other possible interpretations. Cohen (1988), based on concepts about statistical power, suggested that ESs may be classified as small (.20), medium (.50), or large (.80). Although useful in a general sense, an ES possesses no inherent value and requires a context to provide meaning. Depending on the circumstances, an ES of 2.00 may be "poor," whereas an ES of .2 may be "good." It is not an a priori judgment but rather one based on the total number of the ES, which is likely to vary from setting to setting.

In some instances, ESs are themselves meaningful; zero and negative ES fall into this category. Additionally, comparison might be done within a single meta-analysis. Suppose two special education interventions (A and B) are compared with traditional instruction: The ES for comparisons of Intervention A and traditional instruction was .50 favoring Intervention A whereas Intervention B produced an ES of .25 when compared to traditional instruction. Thus, Intervention A was half again more beneficial than Intervention B. Finally, it is possible to add meaning to ES by reference to known interventions. It is the case, for example, that the average student will gain 12 months on achievement measures over the course of a school year; the average third-grader will score 3.0 in September and 4.0 in June. Thus, 1 year of instruction produces an ES of 1.00 equivalent to the 1.0 grade-equivalent standard deviation for most elementary-level standardized achievement tests. This level can be used as a basis for comparison. Suppose a new technique (Intervention X) is introduced, and the ES from a number of validation studies is .25. The obtained ES is one fourth as great as the effect of instruction itself (.25 vs 1.00); the new technique (Intervention X) benefits a treated subject by the equivalent of one-fourth year of schooling.

Kavale (1984) described the advantages of meta-analysis in terms of enhanced understanding and explanation; there is a clarity and explicitness in interpretation that permits firm conclusions about "what the research says." As Cooper and Rosenthal (1980) suggested, "conclusions based on meta-analysis will appear to be (and indeed they will be) more rigorous and objective" (p. 449). The synthesized research findings may then be combined with wisdom and experience to produce rational policy decisions.

META-ANALYSIS AND POLICY DECISIONS

The Case of Psycholinguistic Training

Let's return to the psycholinguistic training example cited earlier. The policy decision concerns whether or not to include psycholinguistic training in the remedial curriculum. Although you probably collected a number of primary research studies, a number of research summaries would also be available, but these would reveal very different interpretations that reflect basic philosophical differences about the nature of special education.

Hammill and Larsen (1974), using a vote-counting box-score methodology, constructed a table with either a "+" (significant) or "0" (nonsignificant) for total ITPA score, ITPA subtests, or both that summarized the findings from 39 studies. The findings led Hammill and Larsen to conclude that "researchers have been unsuccessful in developing those skills which would enable their subjects to do well on the ITPA . . . [and] . . . the idea that psycholinguistic constructs, as measured by ITPA, can be trained by existing techniques remains nonvalidated" (pp. 10–11).

Minskoff (1975) offered a more positive evaluation of psycholinguistic training and critiqued the Hammill and Larsen (1974) review. The focus became less on "what the research says" and rather on the shortcomings of research design and analysis among reviewed studies, on the inconsistency and confusion about interpretation, and on the need for new research employing more rigorous methodology. Minskoff wrote:

> Because of Hammill and Larsen's oversimplified approach, 39 studies with noncomparable subjects and treatments were grouped together. Moreover, for the most part, they reviewed methodologically inadequate studies in

which there was short-term training using general approaches to treatment primarily with mentally retarded or disadvantaged subjects having no diagnosed learning disabilities. (p. 137)

Minskoff then affirmed the assumption that psycholinguistic deficits can be remediated and doubt about psycholinguistic training "can be dangerous if it leads to the abolition of training methods that may be beneficial to some children with psycholinguistic disabilities" (p. 143). Newcomer, Larsen, and Hammill (1975) immediately contested the major points made by Minskoff and concluded that, "the reported literature raises doubts regarding the efficacy of presently available Kirk–Osgood psycholinguistic training programs" (p. 147). Thus, instead of an unencumbered conclusion, there was significant equivocation about "what the research says" with the rhetoric only serving to increase the skepticism and cynicism surrounding the question.

The policy question about psycholinguistic training did not achieve closure. In an effort to resolve the issue, Lund, Foster, and McCall-Perez (1978) offered a reevaluation of the 39 studies analyzed earlier by Hammill and Larsen (1974) to determine the validity of the negative conclusions they drew regarding the effectiveness of psycholinguistic training. Some studies were viewed as showing positive findings and "contraindicate the conclusions that such training is nonvalidated" (p. 317). Of studies showing negative findings, only two were found to be reported accurately; the remainder were found to be either equivocal or actually showed positive findings. Lund et al. concluded that:

> Our analysis indicates that some studies show significant positive results as measured by the ITPA, some studies show positive results in the areas remediated, and some do not show results from which any conclusions can be drawn. It is, therefore, not logical to conclude either that all studies in psycholinguistic training are effective or that all studies in psycholinguistic training are not effective. (p. 319)

Soon after, Hammill and Larsen (1978) contested the Lund et al. (1978) analysis and reaffirmed their original position with the statement that:

> The cumulative results of the pertinent research have failed to demonstrate that psycholinguistic training has value, at least with the ITPA as the criterion for successful training. It is important to note that, regardless of the reevaluation by propsycholinguistic educators, the current state of the research strongly questions the efficacy of psycholinguistic training and suggests that programs designed to improve psycholinguistic functioning need to be viewed cautiously and monitored with great care. (p. 413)

It seems apparent that, while polemics abounded, a primary question remained unanswered: What is really known about the efficacy of psycholinguistic training? Much of the equivocation and failure to achieve closure stemmed from the methods used to integrate research findings. The inherent difficulties with traditional methods resulted in research syntheses that lacked objectivity, verifiability, and replicability. In an effort to bring more rigor to the review process, Kavale (1981) used the methods of meta-analysis to investigate the efficacy of psycholinguistic training.

Meta-Analytic Findings About Psycholinguistic Training

The Kavale (1981) meta-analysis included 34 studies that yielded 240 individual ES measurements and an average ES ($\overline{ES}$) of .39. As a result of psycholinguistic training, the average subject stands at approximately the 65th percentile of subjects receiving no psycholinguistic training; the latter remain at the 50th percentile. An effect of this magnitude makes for a difficult policy decision. There is a modest positive effect, but it is not clear that the time and effort necessary to deliver psycholinguistic training is warranted.

To gain further insight, the ES data were aggregated by ITPA subtest, and the findings are shown in Table 9.1. The findings aggregated by ITPA subtest clarify the situation. Five of the nine ITPA subtests reveal small, albeit positive, effects; it is questionable, however, whether these psycholinguistic abilities respond to training and whether they should be subjected to training. The case is different for four subtests: Auditory and Visual Association, Verbal and Manual Expression. For these psycholin-

TABLE 9.1
Average Effect Size for Psycholinguistic Training by ITPA Subtest

ITPA Subtest	Number of Effect Sizes	Mean Effect Size	Percentile Equivalent
Auditory reception	20	.21	58
Visual reception	20	.21	58
Auditory association	24	.44	67
Visual association	21	.39	65
Verbal expression	24	.63	74
Manual expression	23	.54	71
Grammatic closure	21	.30	62
Visual closure	5	.48	68
Auditory sequential memory	21	.32	63
Visual sequential memory	21	.27	61
Auditory closure	3	−.05	48
Sound blending	3	.38	65

guistic abilities, training improves functioning from 15 to 23 percentile ranks and makes the average trained subject better off than approximately 65% to 73% of untrained subjects.

The findings for Verbal and Manual Expression are especially noteworthy. They produced the two largest ESs and suggest that these areas are particularly responsive to intervention. This finding was affirmed when the ITPA subtest data were aggregated by theoretical psycholinguistic dimension and construct; the Expressive Processes revealed the largest effects (ES = .59). These findings indicate the benefits of intervention for the Expressive Processes, particularly Verbal Expression, and are encouraging because they embody the "linguistic" aspects of the ITPA and the tangible area of productive language behavior. For a basic area like language, the average elementary school student gains about 1 *SD* (ES = 1.00) over the school year and exceeds about 84% of the students' scores made in a language achievement measure at the beginning of the school year. The approximate 60% success rate for training Verbal Expression is thus substantial. In fact, roughly 50 hours of psycholinguistic training (the average across 34 studies) produced benefits in the ITPA Verbal Expression subtest (ES = .63) exceeding that which would be expected from one half-year of instruction in language (ES = .50).

Although appearing to support a policy of including psycholinguistic training especially when the primary deficit area is related to verbal ability, the Kavale (1981) meta-analytic findings precipitated more debate. For example, Larsen, Parker, and Hammill (1982) suggested that Kavale reviewed a body of literature that was more favorable to psycholinguistic training and was thus different from that used earlier by Hammill and Larsen (1974). The difference in the literature base amounted to four studies that produced 28 additional ES measurements. When added to the 240 ESs previously calculated, the ES declined by .04 (.39 to .35) which means that instead of 65% of students receiving psycholinguistic training being better off, 64% would now be better off; this is an inconsequential decline that does not alter the picture.

In another critique, Sternberg and Taylor (1982) questioned the Kavale (1981) meta-analytic findings on a cost–benefit basis because the gains found for psycholinguistic training represented only about 15–20 more correct items across ITPA subtests. A distinction was made between statistical and practical significance with the question, "Does the increase of only two or three items per subtest within this instrument really make a *clinically significant* difference?" (p. 255).

The answer is affirmative, and the example provided by the Verbal Expression subtest demonstrates why. In concrete terms, the ES of .63 for Verbal Expression translates into about six more correct responses on the ITPA, but if these six items are viewed as proxies for perhaps hundreds of language skills, then the improvement shown on these seemingly few items is significant. An analogous scenario is provided by the old WISC–R (Wechsler Intelligence Scale for Children–Revised): a student with IQ 130 answers perhaps nine more Vocabulary or Information questions than a student with IQ 100. Does this mean that the difference between IQ 100 and 130 is solely these nine bits of knowledge? It seems safe to conclude that the underlying dynamics involve more than nine bits of information or nine words. Similarly, the demonstrated improvement on the Verbal Expression subtest of the ITPA represents more than six test items. Thus, for a student deficient in the areas amenable to psycholinguistic training, the advantages for the student probably surpass the particular subtests themselves and comprise a more complex amalgam of language abilities.

Although the policy decision about psycholinguistic training may be affirmative, a decision about which of the available methods is to be preferred also requires consideration. Among the most often used methods of psycholinguistic training, the Peabody Language Development Kits (PLDK) (L. M. Dunn & J. O. Smith, 1967) demonstrated the largest ES (.49) when compared to either ITPA-related activities (ES = .30) or a variety of other linguistic, perceptual, or motor training activities (ES = .35). Although the superiority of the PLDK appears contrary of expectation because ITPA-based activities should be more closely related to the criterion measure (i.e., ITPA), the findings are not surprising if viewed from the perspective of program structure. The PLDK represents a highly structured sequence of lessons designed to enhance general verbal ability. Although ITPA training activities are based on the Osgood–Kirk model (e.g., Bush & Giles, 1977; S. A. Kirk & W. D. Kirk, 1971; Lombardi & Lombardi, 1977), they, for the most part, are only rough guidelines that do not provide the same level of sequential and structured program found in the PLDK. Consequently, they do not represent a comprehensive training package but rather examples for psycholinguistic training activities that must be planned and structured by individual teachers (Kavale, 1982b).

The vexing policy decision about psycholinguistic training appears to be resolved with an affirmative but cautious response. Although an unequivocal endorsement of psycholinguistic training is not warranted, in particular instances (e.g., Verbal Expression) positive outcomes were demonstrated, and belies a conclusion like, "the overwhelming consensus of research evidence concerning the effectiveness of psycholinguistic training is that it remains essentially nonvalidated" (Hammill & Larsen, 1978, p. 412). The selected benefits of psycholinguistic training must be considered in policy judgments, and clearly Hammill and Larsen (1974) overstated their case when they concluded that, "neither the ITPA subtests not their theoretical constructs are particularly ameliorative" (p. 12).

Clearly, the findings regarding the benefits of psycholinguistic training for the Expressive Constructs, particularly Verbal Expression, and, to a lesser extent, the Representational Level subtests are encouraging. The decision about psycholinguistic training is thus not an all-or-none proposition and caution must be exercised lest "the baby gets thrown out with the bath water" because situations exist where the intervention is effective. Consequently, policy should dictate that psycholinguistic training be included when deemed an appropriate part of a remedial program.

Process Training and Policy

The question about the efficacy of process training has a long history in special education. The methods possess strong intuitive appeal and a clinical tradition attesting to their effectiveness. Psycholinguistic training is also a form of process training but holds a special place in the history of special education because of the confluence of forces during the late 1960s and early 1970s. Two other forms of process training have a longer history and present equally vexing policy decisions. Each is discussed to demonstrate the complexity surrounding policy decisions in special education and the advantages of meta-analysis in resolving the issues.

Perceptual-Motor Training

The most popular form of process training has been perceptual-motor programs designed to train the mind and its processes (abilities, capacities, powers, faculties) and represent "what Socrates and Plato said and what Itard, Sequin, Montessori, and Binet reiterated. It is what the Frostigs, Kirks, and Kepharts seem to have been saying more recently" (Mann, 1979, p. 537). The efficacy of perceptual-motor training was affirmed in clinical reports (e.g., Arena, 1969; Barsch, 1967; Van Witsen, 1967) but less sanguine conclusions were found in selective research reviews (e.g., Balow, 1971; Footlik, 1971; Hammill, Goodman, & Weiderholt, 1974). Although not favorable, caution was urged because the research reviewed was marked by faulty reporting and questionable methodological practices. Additionally, besides debate about the research evidence, philosophical disputes about perceptual-motor training appeared (e.g., Kephart, 1972; Mann, 1971) that served to make policy decisions even more complex.

Kavale and Mattson (1983) found 180 investigations assessing the efficacy of perceptual-motor training that produced 637 ES measurements and an ES of .08. This limited improvement indicates that a student no better off than average (i.e., at the 50th percentile) rises to the 53rd percentile and, at the end of treatment, is better off than 53% of control subjects, a gain only slightly better than no intervention at all (50%). Additionally, of 637 measurements, 48% were negative suggesting that the probability of obtaining a positive response to perceptual-motor training is only slightly better than chance (50%).

The effects of perceptual-motor training is thus negligible, but to gain perspective, ES data were aggregated into more discrete outcome classes: perceptual-motor (ES = .17), achievement (ES = .01), and cognitive (ES = .03). The aggregation process continued with ever more discrete renderings, but the accumulated findings speak for themselves: Regardless of how global or discrete the aggregation, the effects of perceptual-motor training present an unbroken vista of disappointing outcomes. There were no significant positive effects and nothing to indicate an effective intervention. Additionally, ES data were aggregated by special education category and grade level. Again, interpretation is unclouded: essentially zero effects for all groups and at all grades. Across all aggregated data, there were no instances suggestive of any selected benefits for perceptual-motor training.

Perceptual-motor training programs have taken a variety of forms, and the names associated with these programs reads like the roster from the Special Education Hall of Fame. The findings are shown in Table 9.2. The findings again offer a bleak picture with no programs suggesting the presence of positive effects for perceptual-motor training. For policy decisions, the meta-analytic findings also reveal the importance of including all relevant studies in the database. The studies investigating the efficacy of individual programs included studies performed by both program advocates and independent evaluators. For example, the Delacato program (see Delacato, 1959) based on the questionable concept of neurological patterning, was assessed by both Delacato disciples (see Delacato, 1966) and more critical investigators (e.g., Glass & Robbins, 1967). The Delacato sources produced an ES of .72 whereas the non-Delacato sources revealed an ES of −.24. An uncritical and selective rendering of this research would result in quite different policy decisions about the Delacato program.

TABLE 9.2
Average Effect Size for Perceptual-Motor Training Programs

Training Program	Number of Effect Sizes	Mean Effect Size	Percentile Equivalent
Barsch	18	.16	56
Cratty	27	.11	54
Delacato	79	.16	56
Frostig	173	.10	54
Getman	48	.12	55
Kephart	132	.06	52

The meta-analytic findings would support the policy statement offered by the Council for Learning Disabilities (1986) who suggested, "There is little or no empirical support for claims that the training of perceptual and perceptual-motor functions improves either academic performance or perceptual or perceptual-motor functions" (p. 247). Nevertheless, there remains the suggestion that the available evidence does not permit either a positive or negative evaluation of perceptual-motor training (e.g., Hallahan & Cruickshank, 1973). The meta-analytic findings found no such equivocation and provided unequivocal negative evidence regarding the value of perceptual-motor training. Yet, there is an overarching challenge to the research evidence presented by the deep historical roots and positive clinical tradition—these factors serve to cloud the decision process. Policy about perceptual-motor training thus remains contentious, although it should not.

Modality-Matched Instruction

The practice of assessing individual learning factors and devising subsequent instruction in accord with assessed ability patterns possesses a long history and intuitive appeal (e.g., R. S. Dunn, 1979). Within the context of aptitude × treatment interaction (see Cronbach & Snow, 1977), the special education interpretation of assessing modality preferences (usually auditory, visual, or kinesthetic) and matching those preferences to instructional methods (usually for reading) has not received support (e.g., Arter & Jenkins, 1979; Larrivee, 1981; Tarver & Dawson, 1978). Whether the model is termed learning styles, differential programming, or diagnostic-prescriptive teaching, the benefits are widely believed (e.g., R. S. Dunn & K. J. Dunn, 1978) and, with deep historical roots and strong clinical support, has prevented the modality model from being questioned as a validated special education practice (see Carbo, 1983).

Kavale and Forness (1987) synthesized data from 39 studies evaluating the modality model (i.e., assessing modality preferences and matching instruction to those preferences). The model includes two components, testing and teaching, and the 318 ES measurements calculated were used to assess each component.

On the assessment side, the ES indicates the level of differentiation between subjects chosen because of assessed modal preferences and those demonstrating no such preferences. Because the tests used to assess modality preferences have been shown to possess poor reliabilities (Ysseldyke & Salvia, 1980), the ES measurements were corrected for the influence of measurement errors in order to indicate a "true" level of group differentiation (see Hunter, Schmidt, & Jackson, 1982).

Across 113 ES measurements, the ES, after correction, declined from .93 to .51; on average, 70% of subjects demonstrating a modality preference could be differentiated clearly, whereas 30% could not be distinguished unequivocally. With the original ES (.93), the 1 *SD* difference typically used as a criterion to establish modality group membership was approached but, when corrected for measurement error, the better than 9 out of 10 correct decisions drops to 7 out of 10. Thus, there was, in actuality, considerable overlap between preference and nonpreference groups because of measurement error that reduced the distinction among modality groups to a level no better than, on average, two out of three correct placement decisions.

The effect of matching instruction to preferred modalities was measured in 205 ES that produced an ES of .14. This represents a six percentile rank improvement and indicates that 56% of subjects were better off after modality instruction, but this is only slightly above chance (50%) and indicates conversely that 44% of experimental subjects did not reveal any gain from modality-matched instruction. Furthermore, 72 ES measurements (35%) were negative indicating that over one third of students showing a preferred learning modality actually scored less well than comparison subjects receiving no special modality-matched instruction. Reading was the primary area where modality-based instruction was evaluated, and the levels of improvement were small. Modality-matched instruction produced gains from two (comprehension) to seven (vocabulary and spelling) percentile ranks. Across reading skills, 50% (6 out of 12) of the comparisons revealed modality teaching effects that were actually not different from zero (as shown by a 95% confidence interval).

The conventional wisdom about modality-matched instruction is found in statements such as:

> All children do not learn the same way. They rely on different sensory modes to help them. Some depend heavily on their sense of sight, others on their sense of hearing, and still others on their sense of touch. The mode they use influences their classroom behavior and achievement. (Barbe & Milone, 1980, p. 45)

The meta-analytic findings showing little (or no) gain in achievement when instructional methods were matched to preferred learning modality appears to contravene the conventional wisdom.

The negative evaluation of the modality model by Kavale and Forness (1987) was challenged by R. S. Dunn (1990), who suggested that the conclusions were biased and based on inappropriate choices. Kavale and Forness (1990) responded to Dunn's critique, and the specifics are not important. What is important is the fact that meta-analysis produces summary statements that are more precise, more dispassionate, and more detached. It is, therefore, more difficult to assail them in methodological grounds. The real reason for the disagreement surrounds advocacy and the less-than-disinterested view held by Dunn who had a vested interest in modality-based instruction through involvement in assessment devices (R. S. Dunn, K. J. Dunn, & Price, 1979) and intervention techniques (R. S. Dunn & K. J. Dunn, 1978). Although appropriate to defend one's interest, it is not appropriate to do so through misinterpretation and misunderstanding. The simple fact remains: Modality-based instruction is not effective. When, however, such conclusions encounter strong advocacy and intuitive appeal, it is difficult to dislodge the practice through evidence and reason.

The policy dispute about modality-matched instruction continued when R. S. Dunn, Griggs, Olson, Beasley, and Gorman (1995) offered a meta-analysis that reported an ES of .76, and led to the conclusion that, "individualizing instruction to match learning-style preferences improved students' academic achievement and attitude toward learning" (p. 359). The real differences in the meta-analyses surrounded the literature base, the most fragile part of the meta-analysis process. Any research synthesis is affected by the population of primary studies available, and the manner in which studies are selected for inclusion. Jackson (1980) demonstrated how the process of locating and selecting studies was often taken rather uncertainly by reviewers. The available literature is often widely dispersed and there is no reliable technique for determining whether the selected set of studies is representative. Consequently, locating as many studies possible is the best strategy for ensuring representativeness.

The R. S. Dunn et al. (1995) meta-analysis appears to possess a restricted literature base. A comprehensive search should seek to include all published *and* unpublished literature, but the Dunn et al. meta-analysis included 35 unpublished dissertations out of 36 studies in the literature base. Why was not more published literature included? Additionally, concern may be expressed when the included dissertations were all conducted under the direction of an individual who is an advocate for a particular position (see Curry, 1990). Of the 35 dissertations, 21 (58%) were completed at St. John's University where Dunn heads the Center for the Study of Learning and Teaching Styles. With such a heavy influence of dissertations from your "home court," the potential for bias is obvious, and unreliable findings may result. Besides questions about the literature base, the Dunn et al. meta-analysis raised other concerns about analysis and interpretation—particularly with respect to the variability associated with findings, the presence of outliers that may skew findings, and the lack of context in interpreting ES. The many inherent difficulties led Kavale, Hirshoren, and Forness (1998) to conclude:

> The Dunn et al. (1995) meta-analysis has all the hallmarks of a desperate attempt to rescue a failed model of learning style. The weak rationale, curious procedures, significant missions, and circumscribed interpretation

298   KAVALE AND FORNESS

should all serve as cautions to the educational community before accepting the findings as truth when, in reality, they remain far removed from the truth. (p. 79)

The Dunn et al. meta-analysis does little to alter the finding the modality-matched instruction is ineffective. The unbridled advocacy pursued by Dunn appears to be an obstacle to rational policy decisions and should be abandoned, because when all is said and done, learning is really a mater of substance over style.

Policy for Process Training

The question of process training presents a vexing policy decision for special education. A limited number of selected benefits were found (e.g., psycholinguistic training) but generally most methods revealed no benefits and judgments about them are rightly negative (e.g., perceptual-motor training, modality-matched instruction). Yet, they reveal a stubborn resistance because of seductive clinical reports, intuitive appeal, and deep historical roots that maintain them as established practice.

Although the attacks on process training have been vigorous (e.g., Mann & W. A. Phillips, 1967), they apparently have not been convincing enough to alter policy. A partial explanation may be found in the long-standing belief that processes possess a reality that must be considered in remedial efforts. For a fundamental process like language, this assumption is probably true and accounts for the selected benefits of psycholinguistic training. The same is not the case for perceptual-motor training and modality-matched instruction where their elements (e.g., perception, learning style) are neither well understood nor obvious, and may contribute to the negative findings for these interventions. Although decidedly negative, fundamental belief and policy is not altered. Instead, questions about the negative research findings are raised, and the debate becomes centered on philosophical issues that are not so easily resolved. Consequently, the philosophical, clinical, and historical foundation overshadow research evidence, and policy about process training has not appreciably changed.

Policy Decisions for Special Education

Special education faces a number of policy decisions, and meta-analytic findings can assist the process. Although policy formulation is based on a number of factors, research evidence should be primary and then modified by wisdom and experience to meet real-world contingencies. It is therefore imperative to possess a clear and unencumbered rendering of "what the research says." Meta-analysis can provide such a rendering that is illustrated in the following examples.

Treatment for ADHD

Among the more controversial and emotionally loaded issues faced by special education is the practice of treating ADHD (attention deficit hyperactivity disorder) with stimulant medication. For some time, the medical community considered stimulant medication to the treatment of choice (e.g., Barkley, 1990), and it continues to be used with about 1 million students with ADHD being treated with stimulant medication (DuPaul & Stoner, 1994). This conclusion, however, was challenged for some time: first in critical reviews suggesting the available research shows limited positive effects (e.g., Sroufe, 1975), and, second, in the form of ideological, ethical, and moral attacks on stimulant medication (e.g., Schrag & Divoky, 1975).

Kavale (1982a) found 135 studies assessing the effectiveness of stimulant medication for the treatment of ADHD. The ES across 984 ES measurements was .58, which indicates that the average treated subject moves from the 50th to the 72nd percentile as a result of drug intervention. This gain suggests that the average treated subject would be better off than 72% of untreated subjects.

The most impressive gains (ES = .80) were found for behavioral outcomes with substantial benefits found on ratings of behavioral functioning, lowered activity levels, and improved attending skills. Cognitive functioning also exhibited positive improvement and are in accord with laboratory studies showing the salutary effects of stimulant medication on tasks that tap aspects of attention and memory (e.g., Gittelman & Kanner, 1986). Unlike past evaluations (e.g., Barkley & Cunningham, 1978), the meta-analytic findings showed stimulant medication to have a positive effect on academic performance. Students treated with stimulant medication would be expected to gain about 15 percentile ranks on standardized achievement tests when compared to nontreated students. With the exception of arithmetic, the gains in academic achievement represent a level of improvement equal to approximately a half-year's worth of schooling (ES = .50); the effects of drug treatment exhibited a similar gain in only 10 weeks. Pelham (1986) discussed the resistance to acknowledging positive effects for medication in academic achievement (e.g., Gadow, 1983). Any enhanced academic performance is usually attributed to improved attention and reduced impulsivity. When, however, the effects of attention were held constant in the meta-analysis (through partial correlation), the positive effects for achievement was reduced by only 20% suggesting that factors other than solely attention were operating to enhance academic performance.

From both a perspective of efficacy and efficiency, stimulant medication appears to be an advantageous intervention for ADHD. No empirical analysis, however, can hope to unravel the complex ideological and moral issues associated with medication policy. Consequently, the controversy over the use of stimulant medication has not abated (e.g., Wilens & Biederman, 1992), and there is increased concern that stimulant medication may be viewed as a cure for ADHD (e.g., Cowart, 1988). Nevertheless, stimulant medication remains the most prevalent treatment modality for ADHD. Over time, there has been a change in focus from the symptom of hyperactivity to inattentiveness suggesting the possibility of a shift in the nature of the population studied along with the availability of improved assessment instruments suggesting the possibility of better data being collected. These factors, along with the fact that the Kavale (1982a) meta-analysis was some 15 years old, suggests that an updated meta-analytic review is warranted.

Crenshaw, Kavale, Forness, and Reeve (1999) performed a meta-analysis on the drug research published between 1981 and 1995, and generally used the same procedures and criteria employed by Kavale (1982a) to permit comparison and continuation. Across 115 studies, the ES was .64, which was slightly larger but comparable to the ES of .58 found by Kavale. The ES of .64 obtained by Crenshaw et al. means that the average subject treated with stimulant medication moves from the 50th to 74th percentile; this is also comparable to Kavale's findings (24 vs. 22 percentile rank increase).

On behavioral outcome measures, Crenshaw et al. (1999) obtained an ES of .74 that is again comparable to the behavior ES of .80 found by Kavale (1982a). Improved behavior would thus be demonstrated by 74% and 80% of drug-treated subjects in the Crenshaw et al. and Kavale studies respectively when compared to untreated control subjects. With respect to academic outcomes, greater differences between the meta-analyses were found. The Crenshaw et al. study obtained an ES of .46 compared to the ES of .38 found by Kavale. The positive improvement, however, was similar and amounted to only a three percentile rank difference (68 vs. 65) meaning that the average subject receiving stimulant medication demonstrates, on average, a 17 percentile rank academic outcome gain. The differences between meta-analyses is accounted for primarily by findings for standardized achievement tests (e.g., Wide Range Achievement Test). The Kavale study included almost entirely standardized achievement measures, whereas the Crenshaw et al. investigation included more classroom-type assessments (e.g., percentage of work completed). In the Crenshaw et al. meta-analysis, the ES for achievement tests was .25 compared to an ES of .52 for classroom-type measures. With classroom measures, students on stimulant medication demonstrated academic skills more than .5 SD above the average student in the comparison group.

Thus, in an extension of a meta-analysis published in 1982, Crenshaw et al. (1999) also found positive effects that were quite comparable to the Kavale (1982a) findings. With studies published between 1980 and 1995, similar findings emerged with behavioral outcomes again showing a stronger drug response than academic outcomes. Since 1980, with revised diagnostic criteria, more reliable assessment instruments, and more emphasis on behavioral observation, the conclusion attesting to the efficacy of stimulant medication on behavioral and academic outcomes was affirmed.

Diet Treatment and ADHD

The enduring controversy over the use of stimulant medication led to efforts to find alternative treatments. One such alternative was exemplified in the "Feingold diet," a treatment approach popularized during the mid-1970s as a more natural intervention than stimulant medication. Although the proliferation of "Feingold Associations" (see *Pediatric News,* 1980) promoting the use of the diet to treat hyperactivity has abated, the Feingold diet had significant impact on policy. Dr. Benjamin Feingold (1975) offered the hypothesis that the ingestion of artificial (synthetic) food additives (colors and flavors) contributes to hyperactivity. The suggested treatment was based on the tenets of the Feingold Kaiser-Permanente (K-P) diet designed to eliminate all foods containing any artificial food additives from the diet (B. F. Feingold & H. S. Feingold, 1979).

B. F. Feingold (1976) reported that between 40% and 70% of subjects demonstrated a marked reduction in hyperactive behavior as a result of diet modification. Kavale and Forness (1983) investigated the validity of this report by examining 23 experimental studies assessing the efficacy of the Feingold K-P diet. The 23 studies produced 125 *ES* measurements, and yielded an ES of .12 but a median *ES* of .05 suggesting a skewed distribution with the obtained ES probably overestimating the treatment effect. In relative terms, the ES of .12 indicates that a subject no better off than average (i.e., at the 50th percentile), would rise to the 55th percentile as a result of the Feingold K-P diet. When compared to the 22nd percentile rank gain for treatment with stimulant medication, the 5 percentile rank improvement for diet modification is less than one fourth as large. Although the average ages and IQ levels were similar for drug-treated and diet-treated subjects, the average treatment duration differed: 39 weeks for a diet study and 10 weeks for a drug study. In relation to ES (.12 vs. .58), these comparisons suggest that when compared to Feingold K-P diet treatment, treatment with stimulant medication is approximately five times as effective in about one fourth the time. Thus, the Feingold K-P diet is cast in an unfavorable light because it produces a substantially lower treatment effect than stimulant medication while approximating the negligible effects of, for example, perceptual-motor training (ES = .08).

The meta-analytic findings offered little support for the Feingold hypothesis; the modest and limited gains found suggest a more temperate view of the efficacy of the Feingold K-P diet than that asserted by the diet's proponents. The negative evaluation of the Feingold diet has found support in previous evaluations (e.g., Mattes, 1983; National Advisory Committee on Hyperkinesis and Food Additives, 1980; Stare, Whelan, & Sheridan, 1980), but these evaluations appeared to have little effect on the steadfastness of belief about the efficacy of the Feingold diet. Instead, attention was directed at a number of possible defects in the available research studies (e.g., Rimland, 1983). The empirical evidence appears sound, however, and suggests that artificial additives serve merely a cosmetic function with no negative effects on behavior and learning (see Mattes, 1983). The use of the Feingold diet appears to be predicated, not on research evidence that is decidedly negative, but rather sociological factors like the desire for a natural treatment and a distrust of food manufacturers. These are not sufficient grounds for dismissing more critical empirical evaluations of the Feingold K-P diet because more appropriate medical, psychological, or educational intervention may be postponed (Conners, 1980).

The treatment of ADHD presents an interesting policy question for special education. The major contributor to policy formulation in the form of synthesized research findings reveals stimulant medication to be an effective treatment, but the research evidence is undermined by significant ideological, ethical, and moral attacks decrying its use. One attempted solution was a more natural alternative treatment like the Feingold diet, but its effects were quite modest in relation to the improvement found for stimulant medication. This is the point where wisdom and experience become critical for policy formulation. By assuming that stimulant medication is effective, attention must then be directed at ensuring drug treatment is used appropriately. Problems related to overprescription or the failure to use combined treatments to enhance efficacy, for example, have been discussed, and it is imperative that these issues be resolved for effective policy. Although resolution is necessary, it must take place in a context acknowledging the effectiveness of stimulant medication. The research base indicates this to be the most efficacious intervention, and optimal policy can only be achieved when this fact is acknowledged.

The Integration of Special Education Students

Since the mid-1960s, the major policy question in special education has surrounded the question of integration of students in special education. Up until that time, special education was defined by the special class that meant a separate and segregated system. Beginning with L. M. Dunn's (1968) analysis and formalized in the *Education for All Handicapped Children Act* in 1975, mainstreaming became the norm. The press for integration continued with the Regular Education Initiative and more recently Full Inclusion. It is evident that integration became the norm, but the nature of the debate became centered on the question *where* special education students should be educated.

Kauffman (1993) suggested the necessity for "keeping place in perspective" (p. 7) primarily because of limited knowledge about how placement determines what is possible and what is probable with respect to instruction and educational outcomes. From neither historical analysis (e.g., MacMillan & Hendrick, 1993) nor evaluations of placement effects (e.g., Hallahan, Keller, McKinney, Lloyd, & Bryan, 1988) is it possible to conclude that location is the primary factor in producing special education outcomes. Of greater importance, however, is what actually happens instructionally and the types of interactions that transpire in the particular setting (Gottlieb, Alter, & Gottlieb, 1991). The *what* is thus of greater import than the *where*. Missing from the debate, however, is critical discussion about what happens, instructionally and socially, in special education settings that leads to Type III error (Mitroff & Featheringham, 1974). Too much emphasis has been placed on the merits of different settings when they have relatively little effect per se on whether or not special education is effective.

Although there is a long history of research investigating these questions, the findings have proved difficult to interpret and conclusions have been equivocal (e.g., Guskin & Spicker, 1968; S. A. Kirk, 1964; Meyers, MacMillan, & Yoshida, 1980). Nevertheless, legislation and litigation emphasized the "least restrictive environment" concept, and there has been a decided trend toward integration and primary placement in the general education class (Kavale, 1979). It is also important to note that advocacy for the mainstreaming movement was built primarily on ideological and philosophical arguments (e.g., Christopolos & Renz, 1969; L. M. Dunn, 1968) rather than empirical foundations, which suggests that the commitment to integration was probably more steadfast than warranted by the research evidence (MacMillan, 1971).

Carlberg and Kavale (1980) performed a meta-analysis on 50 studies examining the benefits of special class versus regular class placement. The 50 studies produced 322 *ES* measurements and yielded an ES of −.12. (The *ES* statistic was arranged so that a positive *ES* favored the special class whereas a negative *ES* favored the regular or mainstreamed class.) Approximately 58% of the *ES*s were negative: In more than half the cases, special classes were less effective than regular classes. Because the average subject in the comparison regular class would be at the 50th percentile, the effects of approximately 2 years of special class placement was to reduce the relative standing of the average subject in the special class by five percentile ranks; students in a special class were slightly worse off than if they had remained in the regular class.

Special education placement studies generally measured two outcomes. In the Carlberg and Kavale (1980) meta-analysis, achievement and social/personality variables revealed ESs of −.15 and −.11 respectively. Thus, special class placement was inferior to regular class placement for the two major outcomes measured; students in the special class declined by six and four percentile ranks on achievement and social/personality measures respectively. These findings lent support for a negative, albeit small, effect for special class placement suggesting that special class placement produced no tangible benefits. In practical terms, however, the transformation of this negative ES suggests that the average loss due to special class placement over approximately 2 years was only about 1 or 2 *months* of academic achievement, a relatively negligible outcome. Thus, special class placement was only slightly less efficacious than regular class placement.

By the late 1970s, integration and the concept of mainstreaming came to be defined primarily by the resource model of service delivery (e.g, Deno, 1973; Hammill & Weiderholt, 1972; Reger, 1973). A resource program represents a structure where a teacher has responsibility for providing supportive educationally related service to special education students during specified time periods. An integral component is also a place, the resource room, where students receive specific instruction on a regularly scheduled basis, though receiving the majority of their education in a general education program.

By the mid-1980s, the resource model became the most frequently used special education service provision particularly for students with high-incidence mild disabilities (Friend & McNutt, 1984). Although the resource model continued to develop (e.g., McLoughlin & Kelly, 1982; Speece & Mandell, 1980), evaluations revealed considerable variability in outcomes and equivocal conclusions about efficacy (Sindelar & Deno, 1978; Wiederholt & Chamberlain, 1989).

Wang and Baker (1985–1986) performed a meta-analysis on 52 studies investigating the efficacy of mainstreaming defined as placements in settings other than the special class. The 52 studies produced 455 *ES* measurements and yielded an ES of .11 with about 40% negative *ES*. The ES of .11 indicates that 54% of students in the mainstream would be better off than those in comparison groups. For comparisons involving mainstreamed versus nonmainstreamed special education students, the ES was .43 indicating that 67% of students in the mainstream were better off by about 17 percentile ranks as a result of a more integrated placement.

When, however, the comparison group was nonhandicapped peers, the mainstreaming ES was −.31 meaning that students in the mainstream lost 12 percentile ranks. There was a positive, albeit small, effect favoring mainstreamed settings; special education students in integrated programs outperformed those in self-contained settings but still performed lower than their nonhandicapped peers.

The findings from meta-analyses investigating special education placements suggested only a modest effect on outcomes for different settings. The emphasis on setting brought about by the implementation of the Cascade Model (see Deno, 1970) with its continuum of placement options has made "place" the focus of attention (e.g., Leinhardt & Pallay, 1982); yet, little advantage was found for any placement as evidenced by the small ES associated with evaluations of different settings.

Although studies of special education placement generally focus on particular categories of special education, they in reality investigate heterogeneous groups of students who have been classified according to diverse and often ambiguous criteria that may vary significantly across settings. Students classified into one category in one setting are likely to be different from those similarly identified in another setting (Hallahan & Kauffman, 1977). The reliance on categorical labels may thus limit the kinds of conclusions that may be drawn from research about placement (Heller, Holtzman, & Messick, 1982).

Although difficult to draw conclusions related to categories of special education, some general conclusions may be possible as evidenced from the Carlberg and Kavale (1980) meta-analysis. It was possible to aggregate *ES* measurements into three special education classifications: mental retardation (MR) (IQ 50–75), slow learner (SL) (IQ 75–90), and learning disabled (LD) and emotional or behavior disorder (E/BD), and the findings are shown in Table 9.3. Special class placement was most disadvantageous for special education students whose problem was lower IQ levels (MR and SL). In comparison to general education peers, SL students lost 13 percentile ranks whereas students with MR declined by 6 percentile ranks. For students with LD and E/BD in special classes, however, an

TABLE 9.3
Average Effect Size by Special Education Classification
for Special Versus Regular Class Placement

Diagnosis	Average Effect of Special vs. Regular Placement	Number of Effect Sizes
MR (IQ 50–75)	−.14	249
SL (IQ 75–90)	−.34	38
LD and E/BD	.29	35

improvement of 11 percentile ranks was associated with their placement. The average student with LD or E/BD in a special class was thus better off than 61% of those who remained in a general education class.

The ESs for special education classification exceeded those found overall for outcomes and thus deserve attention. The most fundamental question is why some students (e.g., MR and SL) placed in special classes were slightly worse off than they would have been had they remained in a general education classroom. The significant variable may be intelligence and how it relates to teacher expectation: If a student is placed in a special class because of a low IQ, it may lower teacher expectations about performance that results in less effort on the teacher's part and less learning on the student's (see Rosenthal & Jacobson, 1968). The lower expectancy, be it conscious or unconscious, may divert instructional efforts away from academic pursuits. Additionally, differences, for example, in the structure of the curriculum and the nature of the outcome assessments may make the special class a place whose goal is maintenance. Consequently, the special class may function as an instrument for preserving existing educational and social order, and not necessarily an arrangement for providing enhanced educational opportunities.

On the other hand, the average intelligence of students with LD and E/BD (at least, by definition) may not dampen teacher expectation. Teachers in special classes may take a more optimistic view of the students they serve and strive to provide significant efforts aimed at improving academic functioning. Perhaps these efforts represent the "real" special education, not a system seeking the status quo but a system focusing on individual learning needs and abilities in order to design the most effective program of *academic* remediation necessary to overcome *academic* deficits.

In summary, policy about the best placement for students in special education are complex and not easily answered. It seems evident that statements like, "There is no compelling body of evidence that segregated special education programs have significant benefit for students" (Gartner & Lipsky, 1987, p. 131) are not entirely warranted, and statements about particular placements cannot be so definitive. The studies of special education placement included a number of service delivery options and, because no service arrangement proved more effective, it appears that outcome differences were related to indeterminate and imperceptible variables not easily assessed or controlled. As MacMillan (1971) noted some 25 years ago, "The real issue is not whether special classes or regular classes are better but rather where the best interests of the students might be" (p. 9), and this statement remains just as valid today. The debate has focused on placement to such an extent that setting has come to be equated with treatment itself (Epps & Tindal, 1988). Clearly, setting is not the salient variable that determines academic success; as an independent variable, setting provides little insight into what may constitute effective instruction (Kaufman, Agard, & Semmel, 1985). The findings related to special education placement may, in fact, indicate the lack of differences between special and general education at the level of instruction. Features of instruction are probably the major influence on outcomes, but these are not unique to setting. Setting is thus a macrovariable; the real question becomes one of examining what happens in that setting.

SPECIAL Education and Special EDUCATION

With the finding that the setting where special education students are placed has almost no influence, the question shifts to what happens in that setting. What is the nature of the instructional program being delivered?

The interventions discussed earlier (i.e., psycholinguistic training, perceptual-motor training) represent the historic tradition of special education. From its inception, special education developed unique procedures designed to enhance student performance. The procedures would not be routinely used in a general education setting and came to define what special education is. Because of their special nature, questions soon arose about their efficacy. Special education was thus held accountable for the use of these practices and the resulting outcomes.

Policy for SPECIAL Education

Table 9.4 presents a meta-analytic summary of methods and techniques that represents a number of special interventions and define special education practice. The findings from the quantitative syntheses do not paint an optimistic picture about their efficacy. Recall that an ES of 1.00 repre-

TABLE 9.4
Summary of Meta-Analyses for SPECIAL Education Interventions

Intervention	Number of Studies	Mean Effect Size	Standard Deviation of Effect Size
Perceptual-motor training	180	.08	.27
Diet modification	23	.12	.42
Modality instruction	39	.14	.28
Social skills training—E/BD	41	.20	.54
Social skills training—LD	52	.21	.68
Psychotropic medication	70	.30	.75
Psycholinguistic training	34	.39	.54
Stimulant medication	135	.58	.61

sents the average achievement gain of the average student at the end of 1 year's worth of instruction. With ES of 1.00 as a yardstick, the special education interventions evaluated do not appear impressive because, on average, the special education student would gain only about 2 months credit on an achievement measure. With most special interventions revealing ES below .50, they thus represent less advantage than one half-year's worth of schooling. It would not be unreasonable to demand that special interventions accelerate the rate of academic gain expected from general education if students in special education are to eliminate the discrepancies in their educational performance.

The special interventions demonstrated effects that primarily ranged from negligible to small by any standard. None approached the magnitude that would be necessary to enhance performance at a rate that would propel a special education student toward grade-level performance. For special interventions, the obtained ES are not eloquent testimony to the efficacy of practices that have almost come to define special education. To provide perspective, consider that something as simple (setting aside financial considerations) as reducing class size in general education (e.g., from 35 to 25) can enhance achievement (ES = .31) (see Glass & M. L. Smith, 1979). Six of the eight interventions did not produce the same effect magnitude, and suggests that the efficacy of special practices defining special education must be called into question.

In evaluating the effectiveness of special education, another complication arises besides the modest ES magnitude, and is illustrated by examining the data in Table 9.4. Besides the ES shown in the second column, the associated standard deviation is displayed in the third column; the standard deviation is a measure of dispersion around the mean and represents an index of variability. When compared to the ES, the standard deviation reveals magnitudes sometimes two to three times greater; in every case, the intervention exhibited greater variability than effectiveness. If the two statistics are combined (ES $\pm$ SD), they form a theoretical expectation about the magnitude of intervention efficacy (see Kaplan, 1964). Simple arithmetic using this theoretical representation reveals that special education practice may vary from negative to zero to positive over a wide range. Although these are merely theoretically possible values, it does demonstrate that special interventions are more variable than beneficial in their effects. This variability makes policy decisions difficult and complex; the variability makes special education essentially indeterminate.

The findings from the meta-analyses for special education interventions reviewed suggest that they do not conform to the parameters of "perfect" knowledge that would dictate a policy represented by a lawful set of input–output associations (i.e., do A in circumstance X and Y and do B in circumstance Z) (see Brodbeck, 1962). Instead, the interventions examined indicate that special education is best viewed as imperfect (i.e., unlawful) knowledge, and should not operate on the basis of prescriptive action, a single course of action over a variety of situations. Imperfect knowledge is also confounded by the fact that generalizations in the behavioral sciences tend to change over time (see Gergen, 1973) because of modifications in the values underlying perceptions about what is important and desirable (Eisner, 1979). Special education, at least in the form of the special practices reviewed, needs to be understood as an enterprise that is variable, indeterminate, unlawful, and value-laden. Under such circumstances, it is little wonder that special education has not demonstrated unequivocal efficacy.

In order to define its uniqueness, special education developed *special* interventions, but their very uniqueness cast them in the role of instant and simple solutions for the educational needs of special education students. The difficulty, however, was that the special practices never fulfilled the promise of being either *the* solution or *the* answer. The meta-analytic findings demonstrated clearly that no claim could be made for any special education intervention having provided either *the* solution or *the* answer. Special education has also failed to resolve a number of conceptual problems that mediate intervention effectiveness.

The first conceptual problem relates to what is believed about certain interventions. The strong clinical tradition and historical roots of many special education interventions (e.g., perceptual-motor training, modality-matched instruction) influence strongly perceptions about their efficacy. Any negative research evidence is dismissed as inconclusive; questions about efficacy never achieve closure and basic beliefs are not altered. A good example is the modality concept where better than 9 out of 10 teachers surveyed believed that modality strengths and weaknesses should be considered, and that students learned best when instruction was modified to match individual modality patterns (Arter & Jenkins, 1977; Kavale & Reese, 1991).

A second conceptual problem surrounds the nonproductive ways issues have come to be perceived. A prime example here is the concept of individualized instruction, the cornerstone of most special education models. In its classic sense as embodied in diagnostic-prescriptive teaching (see Peter, 1965), nothing is more fundamental to special education intervention than the idea that a student is assessed to determine strengths and weaknesses, and then instruction is designed to capitalize on strengths and remediate weaknesses. Although seemingly uncontentious, the basic idea of diagnostic-prescriptive teaching has become contorted and polarized into diametrically opposed theoretical models (Quay, 1973). For example, Ysseldyke and Salvia (1974) discussed the Process (ability) Model where the goal is to identify processes that are strong or weak in order to prescribe remediation for the process deficits themselves with interventions (e.g., perceptual-motor training) versus the Skill (behavioral) Model where the goal of task analysis is to assess academic skill development and design instruction to foster skill acquisition. The emphasis is on component skills and their integration rather than the training of processes that presumably underlie skill development. In reality, neither model is satisfactory by itself (see Smead, 1977), and the primary effect of such philosophical debate is to deflect attention away from actual instructional practice.

Lloyd (1984) emphasized a similar point in an analysis of individualized instruction and its embodiment in aptitude-treatment interactions (ATI). Characteristics or aptitudes of certain students will interact with certain kinds of instructional programs or treatments in such a way that the students will learn better than if they had all been given one or the other treatment. The concept of ATI is central for individualized instruction in special education and is embodied in three models: (a) Remedial—a particular treatment is provided to remedy impediments to student learning, (b) Compensatory—a particular treatment will compensate for gaps in student knowledge or skill, and (c) Preferential—particular treatments will match with a student's preferred style of learning like modality-matched instruction discussed earlier (see Salomon, 1972). Lloyd analyzed the three models and concluded that there was little empirical support for any of these ATI hypotheses. It was concluded that the assumption that some kinds of instruction are better for some students whereas other kinds are better for other students may not be valid; instruction instead should be based on "skills students need to be taught" (p. 14) which represents the fundamental premise of diagnostic-prescriptive teaching.

Policy for Special EDUCATION

The methods and techniques reviewed earlier emphasized the *special* aspect of special education; they were interventions that would be found only in special education and not usually used in general education. The meta-analytic findings, however, suggested only modest effectiveness for a majority of practices that were developed to define the nature of special education. In addition to these unique and singular interventions, special education has also developed interventions that emphasize the *education* part of special education. Over time, there has been less stress in special education on developing techniques aimed at enhancing the more hypothetical constructs associated with learning and more emphasis on methods that feature more substantive aspects of learning by adapting general education techniques for the purposes of special education.

Hagin (1973) reviewed intervention methods in special education and noted a shift in policy. Early efforts, prior to 1965, viewed the problems of special education students from a pathology perspective; academic disability was regarded as a disease entity and interventions (e.g., perceptual-motor training) were aimed at removing the pathology. After 1965, emphasis shifted to what was termed an "educational mismatch model" where school failure was viewed as the result of a mismatch between educational methods and a student's developmental level. The educational mismatch model was gradually replaced (by about 1980) with a "learning process model" that was concerned with substantive aspects of learning particularly as they related to cognitive, linguistic, and social factors. Special education thus slowly shifted its emphasis from *special* to *education*. A number of quantitative research syntheses have assessed the effectiveness of interventions emphasizing *education*, and a review of these meta-analyses is useful for comparisons with *special* interventions.

Improving Reading Comprehension

For special education students with high-incidence disabilities like LD, reading difficulties often represent the primary academic problem area. The reading problems often include a failure to recognize words and associate them with concepts, or a failure to recognize and interpret sentences that prevents the creation of a representation of the text and, ultimately, a failure to comprehend text (Perfetti, 1985). Although special education students were more likely to receive interventions aimed at enhancing decoding skills (e.g., Gillingham & Stillman, 1968), there has been increasing recognition that reading comprehension skills also need to be taught (Ysseldyke, Thurlow, O'Sullivan, & Christenson, 1989).

In response to the need of special education students for reading comprehension instruction, a number of techniques were developed. The array of interventions might include cognitive interventions (e.g., specific problem-solving skills, advanced organizers, approaching text with specific schema or rules, teaching students to remember specific facts), cognitive-behavioral interventions (e.g., self-monitoring behavior during reading, self-questioning about text), vocabulary interventions (e.g., correcting oral reading errors, pronunciation and meaning of words in isolation and context), pre- and midreading interventions (e.g., story previews, questions about the story), and direct instruction interventions (e.g., programmed materials, rapid oral responding, continuous evaluation and correction of inaccurate responding, teacher praise for attending and responding).

To determine the effectiveness of reading comprehension interventions for students with LD, Talbott, Lloyd, and Tankersley (1994) performed a meta-analysis on the findings from 48 studies and, across 255 *ES* measurements, the ES was 1.13 indicating that the average student with LD receiving a reading comprehension intervention scored at the 87th percentile on an outcome measure. Thus, a student receiving one of these interventions was better off than 87% of students not receiving a special reading comprehension intervention.

In a similar meta-analysis, Mastropieri, Scruggs, Bakken, and Whedon (1996) reviewed 68 studies investigating reading comprehension interventions for students with LD. The ES across 205 *ES* measurements was .98 that, in relative terms, translates into raising the performance of the average special education student from the 50th percentile to the 84th percentile on an outcome measure. As a result of reading comprehension instruction, the average trained subject was better off than 84% of subjects not receiving this special instruction.

The similar findings furnished by two independent investigations of attempts to enhance reading comprehension provides the verification for concluding that the real effect is about 1 *SD* (ES = 1.00). The ES of 1.06 for teaching reading comprehension (across both meta-analyses) represents what would be expected from an average student after 1 year of reading comprehension instruction. The special methods designed to enhance reading comprehension produced the same effect (ES = 1.00) in approximately 10 hours; students with LD can thus enhance the rate at which they improve their ability to better comprehend what they read.

Mnemonic Instruction

With the recognition that many students in special education possess memory deficits as a primary characteristic (e.g., Torgesen & Kail, 1980), efforts were directed at improving memory through the use of elaborative learning strategies. Because many memory deficits are language based (e.g., Kail & Leonard, 1986; Torgesen & Goldman, 1977; Vellutino & Scanlon, 1982), the goal is to enhance the representation of words in memory through training in more purposive information-processing strategies. One such strategy is mnemonic training that attempts to transform difficult-to-remember facts into a more memorable form. A common method is the keyword approach that reconstructs unfamiliar verbal stimuli into acoustically similar representations, and elaborates the reconstructed stimuli with response information (Atkinson, 1975). For example, in the domain of science, to teach the fact that the mineral *apatite* is No. 5 on Moh's hardness scale, is *brown* in color, and is used for making *fertilizer*, students are first taught a "key word" for apatite, a familiar concrete word that is orthographically or phonetically similar. In this case, *ape* is the key word. Then, students are taught a rhyming "peg words" for recalling the numbers 1 through 10 (e.g., 1 is *bun*, 2 is *shoe*, 3 is *tree*); in the case of apatite, 5 is *hive*. Finally, students are shown an interactive illustration of a *brown ape* pouring a bag of *fertilizer* on a *beehive*. Students are thus provided with a direct retrieval route for all factual information associated with the mineral apatite.

The method capitalizes on the three "mnemonic R's" (Levin, 1983) that include (a) *recoding*, where the unfamiliar stimulus term is recoded into a more familiar, concrete proxy (e.g., apatite = ape), (b) *relating*, where the recoded stimulus is related to the to-be-learned information via an interactive episode (e.g., a picture of a brown ape pouring fertilizer over a hive), and (c) *retrieving*, where the learner is provided with a direct retrieval route from the stimulus (apatite) to all associated information (brown, 5, fertilizer). Mnemonic instruction has proved effective for teaching vocabulary (e.g., Mastropieri, Scruggs, & Fulk, 1990; Mastropieri, Scruggs, Levin, Gaffney, & McLoone, 1985; Scruggs, Mastropieri & Levin, 1985) and science facts (e.g., Scruggs, Mastropieri, Levin, & Gaffney, 1985; Scruggs, Mastropieri, McLoone, Levin, & Morrison, 1987). Additionally, mnemonic instruction has been successfully incorporated into existing curricular materials through a model of "reconstructive elaborations" where to-be-learned content is reconstructed along the dimensions of meaningfulness and concreteness, and linked with stimulus and response information for the student (Mastropieri & Scruggs, 1991). Through the use of acoustic, symbolic, and mimetic reconstructions, content area information has been successfully adapted for classroom use (e.g., Mastropieri, Scruggs, Whittaker, & Bakken, 1994; Scruggs & Laufenberg, 1986; Scruggs & Mastropieri, 1989, 1992).

Mastropieri and Scruggs (1989) synthesized the experimental literature investigating the effectiveness of mnemonic instruction for students in special education. Across 19 studies, the ES was 1.62 indicating that the average student in special education receiving mnemonic instruction would be better off than 95% of students not receiving such instruction. The expected 45 percentile rank gain on an outcome assessment means that students in special education may almost double their original scores when instructed mnemonically. The associated standard deviation (.79) is also noteworthy because it indicates the presence of no negative effects (i.e., a situation where control subjects outperform experimental subjects). The uniformly positive effects (range = .68 to 3.42) for mnemonic instruction suggests that it represents an effective means for enhancing the academic performance of students in special education.

Direct Instruction

Direct instruction is usually represented through a set of behaviorally oriented teaching procedures. The term began as a general description of effective teaching behaviors (e.g., Rosenshine, 1976) and moved to a more comprehensive view that included not only effective instruction but also curriculum design, classroom management, and teacher preparation (Gersten, Woodward, & Darch, 1986). The term became formalized as *direct instruction* (DI) (Engelmann & Carnine, 1982; Gersten & Keating, 1987), a prescriptive set of instructional materials that are scripted for teachers so as to ensure that effective teaching behaviors are incorporated into individual lessons. DI is the basis for programs like *Reading Mastery: DISTAR Reading* (Engelmann & Bruner, 1988) and *Corrective Reading Program* (Engelmann, Becker, Hanner, & Johnson, 1988). Each program is structured around six critical features (see Gersten, Carnine, & Woodward, 1987) that include:

1. An explicit step-by-step strategy.
2. Development of mastery at each step in the process.
3. Strategy (or process) corrections for student errors.
4. Gradual fading from teacher-directed activities toward independent work.
5. Use of adequate systematic practice with a range of examples.
6. Cumulative review of newly learned concepts.

White (1988), using the methods of meta-analysis, synthesized 25 studies investigating the effectiveness of DI and found an ES of .84. Students in special education taught with DI procedures would be better off than 80% of students taught with comparison instructional methods and would be expected to gain about 30 percentile ranks on an outcome measure as a result of DI. Reading and math outcome assessments revealed ES of .85 and .50, respectively. The use of DI appears to be a useful teaching technique for enhancing the academic performance of students in special education.

The examples of reading comprehension instruction, mnemonic instruction, and DI represent effective practices whose common element is an emphasis on the *education* part of special education. A number of other practices falling into this category have been developed, and the findings are summarized in Table 9.5. When compared to the unique procedures that traditionally define special education (see Table 9.4), the interventions emphasizing instruction paint a different picture of efficacy. The students in special education receiving these interventions would be better off than 70% to 95% of students not receiving these interventions and would gain from 20 to 45 percentile ranks on an outcome assessment. On a standardized achievement test with a population mean of 100 and a standard deviation of 15, the use of the interventions listed in Table 9.5 would raise the average achievement score from 100 to anywhere from about 108 to 124. For about half of the interventions reviewed, the effects

TABLE 9.5
Summary of Meta-Analyses for Special EDUCATION

Intervention	Number of Studies	Mean Effect Size	Standard Deviation of Effect Size
Computer-Assisted Instruction	22	.52	.33
Peer Tutoring	19	.56	.69
Early Intervention	74	.67	.73
Formative Evaluation	21	.70	.53
Direct Instruction	25	.84	.76
Behavior Modification	41	.93	.48
Reading Comprehension	82	.98	1.05
	48	1.13	1.79
Mnemonic Strategies	19	1.62	.79

parallel or exceed the benefits that accrue from 1 year's worth of instruction in general education (ES = 1.00). In all cases, the benefits represent more advantage than one half-year of school, and suggest these interventions can successfully accelerate the rate of academic gain for students in special education.

When considered in relation to the associated standard deviation, the interventions summarized in Table 9.5 also demonstrate less variability. When compared to the special interventions presented earlier where the standard deviation revealed magnitudes two to three times greater than ES (see Table 9.4), for a majority of the interventions presented here, the standard deviation was smaller than the ES, and in no instance was it more than about 20% greater than ES. Thus, the interventions shown in Table 9.5 reveal them to be more effective than variable, which means that instances of negative effects (i.e., comparison [control] students outperform special education students receiving these same interventions) are unlikely. The limited variability makes these interventions far more determinate and, with the substantial ES magnitude, permits a positive response to questions about their effectiveness.

SPECIAL Education Versus Special EDUCATION

Although judgments about the efficacy of special education remain equivocal for some interventions, the findings shown in both Tables 9.4 and 9.5 also indicate instances with far less equivocal findings and suggest the possibility of terming some interventions effective (e.g., mnemonic training) and others ineffective (e.g., perceptual-motor training). In examining the interventions, it seems that the variations in efficacy may be related, at a very fundamental level, to differences in the way the nature of special education is conceptualized.

The differences in conceptualization appear to be related to whether *special* or *education* is emphasized in special education. The interventions displayed in Table 9.4 appear to emphasize *special* by being unique and different methods that would not be routinely used in general education. For the most part, these interventions were designed solely for the purposes of special education and had the goal of enhancing hypothetical and unobservable constructs that were presumably the cause of learning deficits. Education, in the form of the acquisition of new knowledge, was secondary to improving skills and abilities that underlie academic learning and presumably needed to be intact before more academic learning could occur. In contrast, the interventions displayed in Table 9.5 appear to emphasize *education* by adapting and modifying instructional methodology. These are primarily interventions that had their origin in general education and were transformed by special education to accommodate the needs of students in special education. Academic achievement was a primary goal; the enhanced acquisition and assimilation of content area knowledge was a major goal for these interventions. Rather than focusing on hypothetical constructs presumably related to learning ability, the interventions emphasizing *education* attempt a more direct approach by adapting instruction to enhance the academic learning of students in special education.

The contrast between these two emphases is shown in Table 9.6, which compares methods of SPECIAL (i.e., unique and different) education and special EDUCATION (i.e., adapting and modifying instruction).

The seven SPECIAL education interventions produce an ES of .25 that translates into only about a 10% advantage for students receiving these interventions. For example, in the case of perceptual-motor training, the Feingold

TABLE 9.6
SPECIAL Education Versus Special EDUCATION

SPECIAL Education		Special EDUCATION	
Method	*Mean Effect Size*	*Method*	*Mean Effect Size*
Stimulant Medication	.58	Mnemonic Strategies	1.62
Psycholinguistic Training	.39	Reading Comprehension	1.13
Psychotropic Medication	.30		.98
Social Skills Training	.21	Behavior Modification	.93
	.20	Direct Instruction	.84
Modality Instruction	.14	Early Intervention	.67
Feingold Diet	.12	Peer Tutoring	.56
Perceptual-Motor Training	.08	Computer-Assisted Instruction	.52
	Mean = .25		Mean = .91

diet, modality-matched instruction, and social skills training, the average student in special education would gain only three to eight percentile ranks on an outcome measure. On average, the upper 50% of the group receiving these special interventions exceeds only about 56% of the group not receiving such interventions; this modest level of improvement is only slightly above chance (50%). In addition, on average, about 25% of *ES* for SPECIAL education intervention were negative indicating that in about one in four instances the student not receiving the SPECIAL intervention does better on an outcome measure. Given the limited benefits, the wisdom of including SPECIAL education interventions in a program is open to serious question.

In sharp contrast are interventions that can be termed special EDUCATION and emphasize effective and validated instructional techniques. The seven interventions in this group produced an ES of .91. As a group, special EDUCATION is almost four times as effective as SPECIAL education, and is likely to move the average student in special education from the 50th to the 82nd percentile. The 32-percentile-rank gain is better than five times the gain demonstrated from SPECIAL education interventions, and means that the average student would be better off than 82% of those not receiving special EDUCATION. Even the smallest ES for special EDUCATION (.52) is twice as effective as the average SPECIAL education intervention (.25). Four special EDUCATION practices produced gains comparable to 1 year's worth of schooling (ES = 1.00), and two exceeded that level in a treatment period of about 20 days compared to the average 180-day school year. Even for interventions that employ a theoretical matching strategy (i.e., ATI), the more substantive mnemonic instruction (ES = 1.62) was 10 times more effective than modality-based instruction (ES = .15). Students in special education, for example, receiving mnemonic instruction would be better off than 98% of students not receiving such instruction, and would gain over 1½ years of credit on an achievement measure compared to about 1 month for modality-matched instruction. The policy implications appear unencumbered: Special education interventions that emphasize EDUCATION over SPECIAL are far more effective. When grounded in sound instructional methodology, special EDUCATION can sometimes be up to 20 times more effective than SPECIAL education practices that attempt to "cure" special education students by overcoming the negative effects on learning caused by a variety of hypothetical and unobservable constructs.

Policy Decisions for Special Education

Policy formulation in special education is a fragile process. The inherent variability and indeterminateness of special education makes prescriptive policy difficult to achieve. Special education, thus, needs to be treated as an enterprise that is unlawful and unknowable in the complete and closed sense in which scientists speak. Although special education involves a degree of "uncertainty" (Glass, 1979) and "risk" (Kaplan, 1964), rational decision making is not precluded but requires the situation be approached with options rather than truths. Meta-analysis provides a means for extracting these options. For example, meta-analysis provided insight into which form of process training or which treatment of ADHD is to be preferred. Additionally, meta-analysis showed that where special education students are placed has little bearing on outcomes. Finally, meta-analysis provided insights into the very nature of special education and demonstrated that a focus on *education* (i.e., adapting and modifying instruction) produces superior outcomes than those emphasizing *special* (i.e., unique and different) methods.

The primary advantage of meta-analysis is in providing policymakers with an explicit and objective rendering about "what the research says." This rendering moves the policy process beyond the false assumption that decisions (or complicated and interconnected systems of decisions termed policies) ought to be based on a "critical" or "perfect" study (e.g., Cronbach, 1982). By providing a pattern of research findings across a landscape of different circumstances, meta-analysis provides policymakers with images that can be rationally extrapolated to new circumstances. The use of research findings is primarily a problem of extrapolation (e.g., from category A to category B, from school X to school Y) and a single study, no matter how well done, is a poorer basis from which to make such an extrapolation.

In terms of real-world policy, findings from the theoretical world of research do not automatically apply. D. C. Phillips (1980) termed this distinction between the theoretical and real world the "is/ought dichotomy": Research findings take an *is* form (i.e., X is Y) whereas policy implications cannot be so steadfast and take an *ought* form (i.e., because of A, B and C ought to be done). Simon (1969) made a similar description between state and process descriptions; the former characterizes knowledge whereas the latter characterizes knowledge acted upon. There is, however, no necessary process description from a state description, or, no *ought* from an *is*. Simon further suggested that policy should be based on information that reduces the distinction between an existing and desired state through means–ends analysis, but also necessary are judgments. Meta-analysis may be conceptualized as a form of means–ends analysis. Within their context, decisions are necessary about the best criterion for decision making within means–ends analysis. A common form is the "minimax" criterion where policy is decided so as to minimize the maximum loss that might be incurred. Scriven (1958) suggested this criterion is too pessimistic and should be replaced by a "minimim" criterion that seeks to minimize the minimum risk. Although this criterion may be appropriate for the more tightly structured natural sciences, it may not be optimal for special education with its inherent variability and indeterminateness. Consequently, instead of methods that seek optimal solutions, special education should seek "satisficing" decision methods whose goal is to provide satisfactory (i.e., good) solutions (see Simon, 1969). As a satisficing method, meta-analysis represents a powerful tool for decision making by providing sufficient but not necessary conditions for special education policymaking.

REFERENCES

Abrami, P. C., Cohen, P. A., & d'Apollonia, S. (1988). Implementation problems in meta-analysis. *Review of Educational Research, 58,* 151–179.

Arena, J. I. (Ed.). (1969). *Teaching through sensory-motor experiences.* San Rafael, CA: Academic Therapy Publications.

Arter, J. A., & Jenkins, J. R. (1977). Examining the benefits and prevalence of modality considerations in special education. *The Journal of Special Education, 11,* 281–298.

Arter, J. A., & Jenkins, J. R. (1979). Differential diagnosis-prescriptive teaching: A critical appraisal. *Reveiw of Educational Research, 49,* 517–555.

Atkinson, R. C. (1975). Mnemotechnics in second-language learning. *American Psychologist, 30,* 821–828.

Bacon, F. (1989). *Novum organum* [The new organon] (T. Fowler, Trans.). Oxford, England: Oxford University Press. (Original work published 1620)

Balow, B. (1971). Percepual-motor activities in the treatment of severe reading disability. *Reading Teacher, 25,* 513–525.

Barbe, W. B., & Milone, M. N. (1980). Modality. *Instructor, 89,* 44–47.

Barkley, R. A. (1990). *Attention deficit hyperactivity disorder: A handbook for diagnosis and treatment.* New York: Guilford.

Barkley, R. A., & Cunningham, C. E. (1978). Do stimulant drugs improve the academic performance of hyperactive children? *Clinical Pediatrics, 17,* 85–92.

Barsch, R. H. (1967). *Achieving perceptual-motor efficiency* (Vol. 1). Seattle: Special Child Publications.

Bolles, R. C. (1962). The difference between statistical hypotheses and scientific hypotheses. *Psychological Reports, 11,* 639–645.

Brodbeck, M. (1962). Explanation, prediction, and "imperfect" knowledge. In H. Feigl & G. Maxwell (Eds.), *Minnesota studies in the philosophy of science* (Vol. III, pp. 93–131). Minneapolis: University of Minnesota Press.

Bush, W. J., & Giles, M. T. (1977). *Aids to psycholinguistic teaching* (2nd ed.). Columbus, OH: Merrill.

Carbo, M. (1983). Research in reading and learning style: Implications for exceptional children. *Exceptional Children, 49,* 486–494.

Carlberg, C., & Kavale, K. (1980). The efficacy of special versus regular class placement for exceptional children: A meta-analysis. *The Journal of Special Education, 14,* 295–309.

Carver, R. P. (1978). The case against statistical significance testing. *Harvard Educational Review, 48,* 378–399.

Christopolos, F., & Renz, P. (1969). A critical examination of special education programs. *The Journal of Special Education, 3,* 371–379.

Cohen, J. (1988). *Statistical power analysis for the behavioral sciences* (2nd ed.). Hillsdale, NJ: Lawrence Erlbaum Associates.

Conners, C. K. (1980). *Food additives and hyperactive children.* New York: Plenum.

Cook, T. D. (1994). *Meta-analysis for explanation: A casebook.* New York: Russell Sage Foundation.

Cooper, H., & Hedges, L. V. (Eds.). (1993). *The handbook of research synthesis.* New York: Russell Sage Foundation.

Cooper, H., & Rosenthal, R. (1980). Statistical versus traditional procedures for summarizing research findings. *Psychological Bulletin, 87,* 442–449.

Council for Learning Disabilities. (1986). Measurement and training of perceptual and perceptual-motor functions: A position statement. *Learning Disability Quarterly, 9,* 247.

Cowart, V. S. (1988). The ritalin controversy: What's made this drug's opponents hyperactive? *Journal of the American Medical Association, 259,* 2521–2523.

Crenshaw, T. M., Kavale, K. A., Forness, S. R., & Reeve, R. E. (1999). Attention deficit hyperactivity disorder and the efficacy of stimulant medication: A meta-analysis. In T. E. Scruggs & M. A. Mastropieri (Eds.), *Advances in learning and behavioral disabilities* (Vol. 13, pp. 135–165). Stamford, CT: JAI.

Cronbach, L. J. (1982). *Designing evaluations of educational and social programs.* San Francisco: Jossey-Bass.

Cronbach, L. J., & Snow, R. E. (1977). *Aptitudes and instructional methods: A handbook for research on interactions.* New York: Irvington.

Curry, L. (1990). A critique of the research on learning styles. *Educational Leadership, 49,* 50–52, 54–56.

Delacato, C. H. (1959). *The treatment and prevention of reading problems: The neurological approach.* Springfield, IL: Thomas.

Delacato, C. H. (1966). *Neurological organization and reading.* Springfield, IL: Thomas.

Deno, E. (1970). Special education as developmental capital. *Exceptional Children, 37,* 229–237.

Deno, E. (1973). *Instructional alternatives for exceptional children.* Reston, VA: Council for Exceptional Children.

Dunn, L. M. (1968). Special education for the mildly retarded—Is much of it justifiable? *Exceptional Children, 35,* 5–22.

Dunn, L. M., & Smith, J. O. (1967). *Peabody Language Development Kits.* Circle Pines, MN: American Guidance Service.

Dunn, R. S. (1979). Learning—A matter of style. *Educational Leadership, 36,* 430–432.

Dunn, R. S. (1990). Bias over substance: A critical analysis of Kavale and Forness' report on modality-based instruction. *Exceptional Children, 56,* 352–356.

Dunn, R. S., & Dunn, K. J. (1978). *Teaching students through their individual learning styles.* Englewood Cliffs, NJ: Prentice-Hall.

Dunn, R. S., Dunn, K. J., & Price, G. E. (1979). *Learning style inventory.* Lawrence, KS: Price Systems.

Dunn, R. S., Griggs, S. A., Olson, J., Beasley, M., & Gorman, B. S. (1995). A meta-analytic validation of the Dunn and Dunn model of learning style preferences. *The Journal of Educational Research, 88,* 353–362.

DuPaul, G. J., & Stoner, G. (1994). *ADHD in the schools: Assessment and intervention strategies.* New York: Guilford.

Eisner, E. (1979). *The educational imagination.* New York: Macmillan.

Engelmann, S., Becker, W. C., Hanner, S., & Johnson, G. (1988). *Corrective reading program: Series guide* (rev. ed.). Chicago: Science Research Associates.

Engelmann, S., & Bruner, E. C. (1988). *Reading mastery: DISTAR reading.* Chicago: Science Research Associates.

Engelmann, S., & Carnine, D. W. (1982). *Theory of instruction: Principles and applications.* New York: Irvington.

Epps, S., & Tindal, G. (1988). The effectiveness of differential programming in serving mildly handicapped students: Placement options and instructional programming. In M.

Wang, M. Reynolds, & H. Walberg (Eds.), *Handbook of special education: Research and practice* (Vol. 2, pp. 172–215). Oxford, England: Pergamon.

Feingold, B. F. (1975). *Why your child is hyperactive.* New York: Random House.

Feingold, B. F. (1976). Hyperkinesis and learning disabilities linked to the ingestion of artificial food colors and flavors. *Journal of Learning Disabilities, 9,* 551–559.

Feingold, B. F., & Feingold, H. S. (1979). *The Feingold cookbook for hyperactive children.* New York: Random House.

Feldman, K. A. (1971). Using the work of others: Some observations on reviewing and integrating. *Sociology of Education, 44,* 86–102.

Fisher, R. A. (1967). *Statistical methods for research workers* (13th ed.). Edinburgh: Oliver & Boyd.

Footlik, S. W. (1971). Perceptual-motor training and cognitive achievement: A survey of the literature. *Journal of Learning Disabilities, 3,* 40–49.

Friend, J., & McNutt, G. (1984). Resource room programs: Where are we now? *Exceptional Children, 51,* 150–155.

Gadow, K. D. (1983). Effects of stimulant drugs on academic performance in hyperactive and learning disabled children. *Journal of Learning Disabilities, 16,* 290–299.

Gartner, A., & Lipsky, D. K. (1987). Beyond special education: Toward a quality system for all students. *Harvard Educational Review, 57,* 367–395.

Gergen, K. J. (1973). Social psychology as history. *Journal of Personality and Social Psychology, 26,* 309–320.

Gersten, R., Carnine, D., & Woodward, J. (1987). Direct instruction research: The third decade. *Remedial and Special Education, 8,* 48–56.

Gersten, R., & Keating, T. (1987). Long-term benefits from direct instruction. *Educational Leadership, 44,* 28–31.

Gersten, R., Woodward, J., & Darch, C. (1986). Direct instruction: A research-based approach to curriculum design and teaching. *Exceptional Children, 53,* 17–31.

Gillingham, A., & Stillman, B. (1968). *Remedial teaching for children with specific disability in reading, spelling, and penmanship.* Cambridge, MA: Educator's Publishing Service.

Gittelman, R., & Kanner, A. (1986). Psychopharmacotherapy. In H. Quay & J. Werry (Eds.), *Psychopathological disorders of childhood* (3rd ed., pp. 455–494). New York: Wiley.

Glass, G. V. (1976). Primary, secondary, and meta-analysis of research. *Educational Researcher, 5,* 3–8.

Glass, G. V. (1979). Policy for the unpredictable (uncertainty research and policy). *Educational Researcher, 8,* 12–14.

Glass, G. V., McGaw, B., & Smith, M. L. (1981). *Meta-analysis in social research.* Beverly Hills, CA: Sage.

Glass, G. V., & Robbins, M. P. (1967). A critique of experiments on the role of neurological organization in reading performance. *Reading Research Quarterly, 3,* 5–51.

Glass, G. V., & Smith, M. L. (1979). Meta-analysis of research on class size and achievement. *Educational Evaluation and Policy Analysis, 1,* 2–16.

Gottlieb, J., Alter, M., & Gottlieb, B. W. (1991). Mainstreaming academically handicapped children in urban schools. In J. W. Lloyd, N. N. Singh, & A. C. Repp (Eds.), *The regular education initiative: Alternative perspectives on concepts, issues, and models* (pp. 95–112). Sycamore, IL: Sycamore.

Grant, D. A. (1962). Testing the null hypothesis and the strategy and tactics of investigating theoretical models. *Psychological Review, 69,* 54–61.

Guskin, S. L., & Spicker, H. H. (1968). Educational research in mental retardation. In N. R. Ellis (Ed.), *International review of research in mental retardation* (Vol. 3, pp. 217–278). New York: Academic Press.

Hagin, R. A. (1973). Models of intervention with learning disabilities: Ephemeral and otherwise. *School Psychology Monograph, 1,* 1–24.

Hallahan, D. P., & Cruickshank, W. M. (1973). *Psychoeducational foundations of learning disabilities*. Englewood Cliffs, NJ: Prentice-Hall.

Hallahan, D. P., & Kauffman, J. M. (1977). Labels, categories, behaviors: ED, LD, and EMR reconsidered. *The Journal of Special Education, 11,* 139–149.

Hallahan, D. P., Keller, C. E., McKinney, J. D., Lloyd, J. W., & Bryan, T. (1988). Examining the research base of the regular education initiative: Efficacy studies and the adaptive learning environments model. *Journal of Learning Disabilities, 21,* 29–35.

Hammill, D. D., Goodman, L., & Weiderholt, J. L. (1974). Visual-motor processes: Can we train them? *Reading Teacher, 27,* 469–478.

Hammill, D. D., & Larsen, S. C. (1974). The effectiveness of psycholinguistic training. *Exceptional Children, 41,* 5–14.

Hammill, D. D., & Larsen, S. C. (1978). The effectiveness of psycholinguistic training: A reaffirmation of position. *Exceptional Children, 44,* 402–414.

Hammill, D. D., & Wiederholt, J. L. (1972). *The resource room: Rationale and implementation*. Philadelphia: JSE Press.

Hedges, L. V., & Olkin, I. (1980). Vote-counting methods of research synthesis. *Psychological Bulletin, 88,* 359–369.

Heller, K. A., Holtzman, W. H., & Messick, S. (1982). *Placing children in special education: A strategy for equity*. Washington, DC: National Academy Press.

Hopkins, K. D. (1973). Preventing the number one misinterpretation in behavioral research, or how to increase statistical power. *Journal of Special Education, 7,* 103–107.

Hunt, M. (1997). *How science takes stock: The story of meta-analysis*. New York: Russell Sage Foundation.

Hunter, J. E., Schmidt, F. L., & Jackson, G. B. (1982). *Meta-analysis: Cumulating research findings across studies*. Beverly Hills, CA: Sage.

Jackson, G. B. (1980). Methods for integrative reviews. *Review of Educational Research, 50,* 438–460.

Kail, R. V., & Leonard, L. B. (1986). Sources of word-finding problems in language-impaired children. In S. J. Ceci (Ed.), *Handbook of cognitive, social, and neuropsychological aspects of learning disabilities* (Vol. 1, pp. 185–202). Hillsdale, NJ: Lawrence Erlbaum Associates.

Kaplan, A. (1964). *The conduct of inquiry*. San Francisco: Chandler.

Kaufman, M., Agard, T. A., & Semmel, M. I. (1985). *Mainstreaming: Learners and their environment*. Cambridge, MA: Brookline Books.

Kauffman, J. M. (1993). How we might achieve the radical reform of special education. *Exceptional Children, 60,* 6–16.

Kavale, K. A. (1979). Mainstreaming: The genesis of an idea. *The Exceptional Child, 26,* 3–21.

Kavale, K. A. (1981). Functions of the Illinois Test of Psycholinguistic Abilities (ITPA): Are they trainable? *Exceptional Children, 47,* 496–510.

Kavale, K. A. (1982a). The efficacy of stimulant drug treatment for hyperactivity: A meta-analysis. *Journal of Learning Disabilities, 15,* 280–289.

Kavale, K. A. (1982b). Psycholinguistic training programs: Are there differential treatment effects? *The Exceptional Child, 29,* 21–30.

Kavale, K. A. (1984). Potential advantages of the meta-analysis technique for research in special education. *The Journal of Special Education, 18,* 61–72.

Kavale, K. A., & Forness, S. R. (1983). Hyperactivity and diet treatment: A meta-analysis of the Feingold hypothesis. *Journal of Learning Disabilities, 16,* 324–330.

Kavale, K. A., & Forness, S. R. (1987). Substance over style: Assessing the efficacy of modality testing and teaching. *Exceptional Children, 54,* 228–234.

Kavale, K. A., & Forness, S. R. (1990). Substance over style: A rejoinder to Dunn's animadversions. *Exceptional Children, 56,* 357–361.

Kavale, K. A., Hirshoren, A., & Forness, S. R. (1998). Meta analytic validation of the Dunn and Dunn model of learning-style preferences: A critique of what was Dunn. *Learning Disabilities Research and Practice, 13,* 75–80.

Kavale, K. A., & Mattson, P. D. (1983). "One jumped off the balance beam": Meta-analysis of perceptual-motor training. *Journal of Learning Disabilities, 16,* 165–173.

Kavale, K. A., & Reese, J. H. (1991). Teacher beliefs and perceptions about learning disabilities: A survey of Iowa practitioners. *Learning Disability Quarterly, 14,* 141–160.

Kephart, N. C. (1972). On the value of empirical data in learning disability. *Journal of Learning Disabilities, 4,* 393–395.

Kirk, S. A. (1964). Research in education. In H. A. Stevens & R. Heber (Eds.), *Mental retardation: A review of research* (pp. 57–99). Chicago: University of Chicago Press.

Kirk, S. A., & Kirk, W. D. (1971). *Psycholinguistic learning disabilities: Diagnosis and remediation.* Urbana: University of Illinois Press.

Kuhn, T. S. (1970). *The structure of scientific revolutions* (2nd ed.). Chicago: University of Chicago Press.

Ladas, H. (1980). Summarizing research: A case study. *Review of Educational Research, 50,* 597–624.

Larrivee, B. (1981). Modality preference as a model for differentiating beginning reading instruction: A review of the issues. *Learning Disability Quarterly, 4,* 180–188.

Larsen, S. C., Parker, R. M., & Hammill, D. D. (1982). Effectiveness of psycholinguistic training: A response to Kavale. *Exceptional Children, 49,* 60–66.

Leinhardt, G., & Pallay, A. (1982). Restrictive educational settings: Exile or haven? *Review of Educational Research, 52,* 557–578.

Levin, J. R. (1983). Pictorial strategies for school learning: Practical illustrations. In M. Pressley & J. R. Levin (Eds.), *Cognitive strategy research: Educational applications* (pp. 213–237). New York: Springer-Verlag.

Light, R. J., & Pillemer, D. B. (1984). *Summing up: The science of reviewing research.* Cambridge, MA: Harvard University Press.

Lindblom, C. E., & Cohen, D. K. (1979). *Usable knowledge: Social science and social problem solving.* New Haven, CT: Yale University Press.

Lloyd, J. W. (1984). How shall we individualize instruction—Or should we? *Remedial and Special Education, 5,* 7–15.

Lombardi, T. P., & Lombardi, E. J. (1977). *ITPA: Clinical interpretation and remediation.* Seattle: Special Child Publications.

Lund, K. A., Foster, G. E., & McCall-Perez, G. C. (1978). The effectiveness of psycholinguistic training: A reevaluation. *Exceptional Children, 44,* 310–319.

Lykken, D. T. (1968). Statistical significance in psychological research. *Psychological Bulletin, 70,* 151–159.

MacMillan, D. L. (1971). Special education for the mildly retarded: Servant or savant? *Focus on Exceptional Children, 2,* 1–11.

MacMillan, D. L., & Hendrick, I. G. (1993). Evolution and legacies. In J. I. Goodlad & T. C. Lovitt (Eds.), *Integrating general and special education* (pp. 23–48). Columbus, OH: Merrill/Macmillan.

Mann, L. (1971). Psychometric phrenology and the new faculty psychology: The case against ability assessment and training. *The Journal of Special Education, 5,* 3–14.

Mann, L. (1979). *On the trail of process.* New York: Grune & Stratton

Mann, L., & Phillips, W. A. (1967). Fractional practices in special education: A critique. *Exceptional Children, 33,* 311–317.

Mastropieri, M. A., & Scruggs, T. E. (1989). Constructing more meaningful relationships: Mnemonic instruction for special populations. *Educational Psychology Review, 1,* 83–111.

Mastropieri, M. A., & Scruggs, T. E. (1991). *Teaching students ways to remember: Strategies for learning mnemonically.* Cambridge, MA: Brookline Books.

Mastropieri, M. A., Scruggs, T. E., Bakken, J. P., & Whedon, C. (1996). Reading comprehension: A synthesis of research in learning disabilities. In T. E. Scruggs & M. A. Mastropieri (Eds.), *Advances in learning and behavioral disabilities* (Vol. 10, pp. 277–303). Greenwich, CT: JAI.

Mastropieri, M. A., Scruggs, T. E., & Fulk, B. J. (1990). Teaching abstract vocabulary to LD students with the keyword method: Effects on comprehension and recall. *Journal of Learning Disabilities, 23,* 92–107.

Mastropieri, M. A., Scruggs, T. E., Levin, J. R., Gaffney, J. S., & McLoone, B. B. (1985). Mnemonic vocabulary instruction for learning disabled students. *Learning Disability Quarterly, 8,* 57–63.

Mastropieri, M. A., Scruggs, T. E., Whittaker, M. E. S., & Bakken, J. P. (1994). Applications of mnemonic strategies with students with mental disabilities. *Remedial and Special Education, 15,* 34–43.

Mattes, J. A. (1983). The Feingold diet: A current reappraisal. *Journal of Learning Disabilities, 16,* 319–323.

McLoughlin, J. A., & Kelly, D. (1982). Issues facing the resource teacher. *Learning Disability Quarterly, 5,* 58–64.

Meehl, P. E. (1978). Theoretical risks and tabular asterisks: Sir Karl, Sir Ronald, and the slow progress of soft psychology. *Journal of Consulting and Clinical Psychology, 46,* 806–834.

Meyers, C. E., MacMillan, D. L., & Yoshida, R. K. (1980). Regular class education of EMR students, from efficacy to mainstreaming: A review of issues and research. In J. Gottlieb (Ed.), *Educating mentally retarded persons in the mainstream* (pp. 176–206). Baltimore: University Park Press.

Minskoff, E. (1975). Research on psycholinguistic training: Critique and guidelines. *Exceptional Children, 42,* 136–144.

Mitroff, I. I., & Featheringham, T. R. (1974). On systematic problem solving and the error of the third kind. *Behavioral Science, 19,* 383–393.

Morrison, D. E., & Henkel, R. E. (Eds.). (1970). *The significance test controversy: A reader.* Chicago: Aldine.

National Advisory Committee on Hyperkinesis and Food Additives. (1980). *Final report to the Nutrition Foundation.* New York: The Nutrition Foundation.

Newcomer, P. L., Larsen, S. C., & Hammill, D. D. (1975). A response. *Exceptional Children, 42,* 144–148.

Pediatric News. (1980). Food color link to hyperactivity debated. *14,* 2.

Pelham, W. E. (1986). The effects of psychostimulant drugs on learning and academic achievement in children with attention-deficit disorders and learning disabilities. In J. Torgesen & B. Wong (Eds.), *Psychological and educational perspectives on learning disabilities* (pp. 160–168). New York: Academic Press.

Perfetti, C. A. (1985). *Reading ability.* New York: Oxford University Press.

Peter, L. J. (1965). *Prescriptive teaching.* New York: McGraw-Hill.

Phillips, D. C. (1980). What do the researcher and the practitioner have to offer each other? *Educational Researcher, 9,* 17–20, 24.

Quay, H. C. (1973). Special education: Assumptions, techniques, and evaluative criteria. *Exceptional Children, 40,* 165–170.

Reger, R. (1973). What is a resource room program? *Journal of Learning Disabilities, 6,* 607–614.

Rimland, B. (1983). The Feingold diet: An assessment of the reviews by Mattes, by Kavale and Forness and others. *Journal of Learning Disabilities, 16,* 331–333.

Rosenshine, B. (1976). Classroom instruction. In N. L. Gage (Ed.), *The psychology of teaching methods: The seventy-fifth yearbook of the National Society for the Study of Education* (pp. 109–143). Chicago: University of Chicago Press.

Rosenthal, R. (1984). *Meta-analytic procedures for social research.* Beverly Hills, CA: Sage.

Rosenthal, R., & Jacobson, L. (1968). *Pygmalion in the classroom.* New York: Holt, Rinehart & Winston.

Rozeboom, W. W. (1960). The fallacy of the null-hypothesis significance test. *Psychological Bulletin, 57,* 416–428.

Ryan, T. A. (1959). Multiple comparisons in psychological research. *Psychological Bulletin, 56,* 26–47.

Salomon, G. (1972). Heuristic models for the generation of aptitude-treatment interaction hypotheses. *Review of Educational Research, 42,* 327–343.

Schrag, P., & Divoky, D. (1975). *The myth of the hyperactive child.* New York: Pantheon.

Scriven, M. (1958). Definitions, explanations, and theories. In H. Feigl, M. Scriven, & G. Maxwell (Eds.), *Minnesota studies in the philosophy of science* (Vol. II, pp. 88–130). Minneapolis: University of Minnesota Press.

Scruggs, T. E., & Laufenberg, R. (1986). Transformational mnemonic strategies for retarded learners. *Education and Training of the Mentally Retarded, 21,* 165–173.

Scruggs, T. E., & Mastropieri, M. A. (1989). Reconstructive elaborations: A model for content area learning. *American Educational Research Journal, 26,* 311–327.

Scruggs, T. E., & Mastropieri, M. A. (1992). Classroom applications of mnemonic instruction: Acquisition, maintenance, and generalization. *Exceptional Children, 58,* 219–229.

Scruggs, T. E., Mastropieri, M. A., & Levin, J. R. (1985). Vocabulary acquisition of retarded students under direct and mnemonic instruction. *American Journal of Mental Deficiency, 89,* 546–551.

Scruggs, T. E., Mastropieri, M. A., Levin, J. R., & Gaffney, J. S. (1985). Facilitating the acquisition of science facts in learning disabled students. *American Educational Research Journal, 22,* 575–586.

Scruggs, T. E., Mastropieri, M. A., McLoone, B. B., Levin, J. R., & Morrison, C. (1987). Mnemonic facilitation of text-embedded science facts with LD students. *Journal of Educational Psychology, 79,* 27–34.

Simon, H. A. (1969). *The sciences of the artificial.* Cambridge, MA: MIT Press.

Sindelar, P. T., & Deno, S. L. (1978). The effectiveness of resource programming. *The Journal of Special Education, 12,* 17–28.

Slavin, R. (1984). Meta-analysis in education. How has it been used? *Educational Researcher, 13,* 6–15.

Smead, V. S. (1977). Ability training and task analysis in diagnostic-prescriptive teaching. *The Journal of Special Education, 11,* 113–125.

Smith, M. L., Glass, G. V., & Miller, T. I. (1980). *The benefits of psychotherapy.* Baltimore: Johns Hopkins University Press.

Speece, D. L., & Mandell, C. J. (1980). Resource room support services for regular teachers. *Learning Disability Quarterly, 3,* 49–53.

Sroufe, L. A. (1975). Drug treatment of children with behavior problems. In F. J. Horowitz (Ed.), *Review of child development research* (Vol. 4, pp. 137–162). Chicago: University of Chicago Press.

Stare, F. J., Whelan, E. M., & Sheridan, M. (1980). Diet and hyperactivity: Is there a relationship? *Pediatrics, 66,* 521–525.

Sternberg, L., & Taylor, R. L. (1982). The insignificance of psycholinguistic training: A reply to Kavale. *Exceptional Children, 49,* 254–256.

Talbott, E., Lloyd, J. W., & Tankersley, M. (1994). Effects of reading comprehension interventions for students with learning disabilities. *Learning Disability Quarterly, 17,* 223–232.

Tarver, S. G., & Dawson, M. M. (1978). Modality preference and the teaching of reading: A review. *Journal of Learning Disabilities, 11,* 5–17.

Taveggia, T. C. (1974). Resolving research controversy through empirical cumulation: Toward reliable sociological knowledge. *Sociological Methods and Research, 2,* 395–407.

Torgesen, J. K., & Goldman, T. (1977). Rehearsal and short-term memory in reading disabled children. *Child Development, 48,* 389–396.

Torgesen, J. K., & Kail, R. V. (1980). Memory processes in exceptional children. In B. K. Keogh (Ed.), *Advances in special education* (Vol. 1, pp. 55–99). Greenwich, CT: JAI.

Toulmin, S. (1961). *Foresight and understanding.* New York: Harper & Row.

Van Witsen, B. (1967). *Perceptual training activities handbook.* New York: Teachers College Press.

Vellutino, F. R., & Scanlon, D. M. (1982). Verbal processing in poor and normal readers. In C. J. Brainerd & M. Pressley (Eds.), *Verbal processes in children: Progress in cognitive development research* (pp. 189–254). New York: Springer-Verlag.

Wachter, K. W., & Straf, M. L. (Eds.). (1990). *The future of meta-analysis.* New York: Russell Sage Foundation.

Wang, M. C., & Baker, E. T. (1985–1986). Mainstreaming programs: Design features and effects. *The Journal of Special Education, 19,* 503–521.

White, W. A. T. (1988). A meta-analysis of effects of direct instruction in special education. *Education and Treatment of Children, 11,* 364–374.

Wiederholt, J. L., & Chamberlain, S. P. (1989). A critical analysis of resource programs. *Remedial and Special Education, 10,* 15–37.

Wilens, T. E., & Biederman, J. (1992). The stimulants. *Psychiatric Clinics of North America, 15,* 191–222.

Yin, R. K., Bingham, E., & Heald, K. A. (1976). The difference that quality makes: The case of literature reviews. *Sociological Methods and Research, 5,* 139–156.

Ysseldyke, J. E., & Salvia, J. (1974). Diagnostic-prescriptive teaching: Two models. *Exceptional Children, 41,* 181–185.

Ysseldyke, J. E., & Salvia, J. (1980). Methodological considerations in aptitude-treatment interaction research with intact groups. *Diagnositque, 6,* 3–9.

Ysseldyke, J. E., Thurlow, M. L., O'Sullivan, P., & Christenson, S. L. (1989). Teaching structures and tasks in reading instruction for students with mild handicaps. *Learning Disabilities Research, 4,* 78–86.

Author Index

Subject Index